International Norms *and* Cycles *of* Change

International Norms *and* Cycles *of* Change

Wayne Sandholtz &
Kendall Stiles

OXFORD
UNIVERSITY PRESS

OXFORD
UNIVERSITY PRESS

Oxford University Press, Inc., publishes works that further Oxford University's objective
of excellence in research, scholarship, and education.

Oxford   New York
Auckland   Cape Town   Dar es Salaam   Hong Kong   Karachi   Kuala Lumpur   Madrid   Melbourne
Mexico City   Nairobi   New Delhi   Shanghai   Taipei   Toronto

With offices in
Argentina   Austria   Brazil   Chile   Czech Republic   France   Greece   Guatemala   Hungary   Italy
Japan   Poland   Portugal   Singapore   South Korea   Switzerland   Thailand   Turkey   Ukraine
Vietnam

Library of Congress Cataloging-in-Publication Data

International norms and cycles of change/Wayne Sandholtz and Kendall Stiles.
    p. cm.
  Includes bibliographical references and index.
  ISBN 978-0-19-538008-8 ((hardback) : alk. paper) 1. Jus cogens
(International law) I. Sandholtz, Wayne. II. Stiles, Kendall W.
  KZ1261. I58 2009
  341'.1—dc22

                                                        2008038531

1 2 3 4 5 6 7 8 9

Printed in the United States of America on acid-free paper

Note to Readers
This publication is designed to provide accurate and authoritative information in regard to the subject
matter covered. It is based upon sources believed to be accurate and reliable and is intended to be current
as of the time it was written. It is sold with the understanding that the publisher is not engaged in rendering
legal, accounting, or other professional services. If legal advice or other expert assistance is required, the
services of a competent professional person should be sought. Also, to confirm that the information has
not been affected or changed by recent developments, traditional legal research techniques should be used,
including checking primary sources where appropriate.

(Based on the Declaration of Principles jointly adopted by a Committee of the
American Bar Association and a Committee of Publishers and Associations.)

You may order this or any other Oxford University Press publication by
visiting the Oxford University Press website at www.oup.com

We dedicate this book to our parents,
Willis Arthur and LaMyrl Boyack Sandholtz
and
Carrol James and Lois Evelyn Stiles

Contents

INTERNATIONAL NORMS AND CYCLES OF CHANGE

Acknowledgments

This project began with a wayward e-mail. Wayne Sandholtz sent an early version of what would become the introduction to this volume to a colleague of Ken Stiles's at Brigham Young University. The colleague printed out the paper, Stiles saw it sitting in the communal printer, made a copy for himself, and was soon in touch with Sandholtz. Four years later, this book is the result.

Sandholtz had realized that, for all the attention paid to international norms in recent years, scholars could offer only rudimentary explanations of how rules change over time. He developed a model centered on dispute-driven cycles of norm change and put it to work to explain the development of international rules against the wartime plundering of artistic and cultural treasures. The resulting book, *Prohibiting Plunder: How Norms Change*, assesses linked cycles of norm change stretching from the Napoleonic Wars to the looting of the Iraqi National Museum in Baghdad in April 2003. Sandholtz also claimed that the cycle model captured a fundamental and ubiquitous dynamic of norm change. Ken Stiles proposed collaborating to test that proposition in a variety of normative domains.

Realizing that such a project would require a team of researchers, both principal authors recruited excellent students—undergraduate and graduate—to work on the book. In fact, had it not been for a set of superb group papers by some of Stiles's students, the idea of applying the Sandholtz model to a wide variety of cases would not have emerged. In some cases, students contributed preliminary research work; they receive credit in various footnotes. In other instances, the students became the sole or lead authors of chapters. They are, from the University of California, Irvine,

Titus Chih-Chieh Chen, William Chiu, and Alix van Sickle; and from Brigham Young University, Brook Gotberg, Taylor Nuttall, and Heather Jacques Wood.

In short, the book was been collaborative from the beginning. Though the authors' names vary from chapter to chapter, this is emphatically not an edited volume. Sandholtz, Stiles, and the various student contributors began with a single theory and sought to test it systematically in diverse substantive areas. The cycle model thus informs every chapter, and each chapter addresses the same set of propositions and questions. The authors commented on each others' chapters, fine-tuned the theoretical framework together, and reworked their material in a process resembling the cycles we theorize in the book. Specifically, after writing first drafts of the chapters, we all met in Provo for a day-long workshop funded by the BYU Kennedy Center and the Center for Global Peace and Conflict Studies at UC Irvine. Members of the BYU Political Science Department joined us and commented on specific chapters in extremely useful ways. We are grateful to Daniel Nielson, Wade Jacoby, and Scott Cooper for their insights. After this initial process, we circulated and commented on second drafts, with Sandholtz and Stiles providing final editing and polishing.

The experience has been uniquely satisfying, having provided us with both an opportunity to create a piece of scholarship but also to hone our mentoring skills. It is worth noting that our student-authors have distinguished themselves in significant ways beyond this project. As the book goes to press, Titus Chen is completing his dissertation and preparing to begin a postdoctoral fellowship at the Center for International Studies at the University of Southern California. Two of the BYU students are completing law school at this writing—Taylor Nuttall at Pennsylvania State University and Heather Jacques Wood at BYU. Brook Gotberg finished her studies at Harvard Law School and is now an associate at Sullivan & Cromwell LLP in Los Angeles. We wish them the very best in their future careers.

This comment would not be complete without further thanks to our spouses and families. Judith Haymore Sandholtz and Rebecca Stiles have provided unflagging support. Likewise, we thank our respective institutions for their support, including the College of Family Home and Social Sciences of BYU, which funded the salaries of the BYU student-authors, and the Center for Global Peace and Conflict Studies at UC Irvine. A grant from the National Science Foundation (SES-0094550) supported the research for Chapters 1 and 4. Li Zhang Li provided crucial help in completing the list of references.

We are happy to give full credit to our collaborators for the book's strengths and take full responsibility for its weaknesses.

Wayne Sandholtz
Irvine, California

Kendall Stiles
Provo, Utah

May 2008

List of Figures

List of Tables

Chapter 1

Explaining International Norm Change

Wayne Sandholtz

International norms are both static and changing. At any given moment, most rules appear fixed.[1] To the actors who are subject to them, the rule is a "given": it is a preexisting, external, social reality. Without that sense of fixity, norms would not provide what they must, namely, stable standards of conduct to guide the choices of those subject to them.[2] Yet, at the same time, rules are constantly evolving. Even law—the most codified, formal subset of norms—is a motion picture: the image is constantly moving, but at any instant it is frozen in a specific frame. For practical purposes, the legal frame at the moment is what matters; attorneys and judges must be able to identify and apply the law in a specific temporal context. This book focuses on the moving picture—how and why international rules change.

---

[1] Throughout this book we use the terms "norm" and "rule" interchangeably. Both are standards of conduct, indicating what behaviors are permissible for a given actor in a given situation.

[2] The work of lawyers and judges would be impossible without a presumption that the law has a fixed meaning at a specific time with regard to specific acts.

Custom [handwritten marginalia]

Scholars of international law take its constant development for granted. Indeed, customary international law is defined by patterns of state practice; as the conduct of states and their opinions regarding legal obligations change, the law also changes. International law journals are filled with articles evaluating how the latest events, disputes, and judicial decisions may have modified international norms. In the last fifteen years, international relations (IR) specialists have also taken a keen interest in international rules. The once dominant tradition in IR, neorealism, viewed norms as irrelevant. The interests and relative power of the major states explained all outcomes of importance in international affairs. The great powers established norms to shape the conduct of other states or to justify their own acts. More recently, a rich body of studies has demonstrated the effects of international norms in virtually every substantive domain, from security, arming, and war, to decolonization, apartheid, and human rights, to the environment and economic relations.[3] The present study takes as its starting point that international norms exert an influence on international relations that is partially independent of, and therefore not reducible to, material power. Norms shape the preferences of actors, influence their choices, and thus affect outcomes in international relations.[4]

Norms matter [handwritten marginalia]

Globalization makes international rules even more salient and more dynamic (Sandholtz 1999). Globalization comprises rising levels of interaction and exchange across borders, in multiple domains: goods and services, investment, communication, travel, news media, ideas, entertainment and the arts, even fashion and foods. The growing density of these cross-national flows requires an accompanying increase in international rules. The general logic is that transactors experience diverse (national) rules and standards as costs or hindrances to communication and exchange. Transnational rules facilitate international transactions (Stone Sweet 1999; Stone Sweet and Sandholtz 1998). But international rules also establish human rights standards with which all types of interactions—economic, social, political—must, in principle, conform. Just as market economies in the West were "embedded" in liberal social and human rights protections

---

[3] The following works represent only a sampling of this extensive literature: Barnett and Finnemore (2004); Crawford (2002); Finnemore (1996, 2004); Goertz and Diehl (1992); Jackson (1993); Katzenstein (1996); Klotz (1995); Legro (1995); Mueller (1989); Nadelmann (1990); Price (1997); Ray (1989); D. Strang (1992, 1996); Thomson (1990); Vincent (1984).

[4] Our primary purpose in this project is not to "prove" that norms exert an autonomous influence on outcomes in international relations. We accept that conclusion as sufficiently demonstrated by the studies already cited. Our objective is to account for change in international norm structures.

(Ruggie 1982), the emerging globalized world of communication and exchange is embedded in the postwar regime of international human rights norms. Of course, states and other actors too often ignore or violate international human rights law, but that law is just as important in a globalizing world as are the rules that sustain cross-border exchange. In short, globalization accelerates the emergence and development of international norms (Hurrell 2002, 146).

Not surprisingly, the problem of change in international rules has captured the attention of some IR scholars. Indeed, much of the early IR attention to international norms grew out of a recognition that rules have changed over time, sometimes dramatically. Slavery and colonization were, in previous historical epochs, entirely accepted features of international society; today they are not but are instead prohibited by international norms. War was formerly a matter of sovereign prerogative; today it is circumscribed by rules. Entire bodies of contemporary international law—human rights, environment—did not exist a century ago. But despite the recognition of constant international norm change, we are only beginning to understand how and why it occurs.

The present chapter offers three main arguments. The first is a claim that existing perspectives on international norms are limited by their focus on norms as outcomes. The main perspectives tend to view rules as the product either of utility-driven actor choices or of a transnational version of pluralistic politics. They take insufficient account of the dynamic tensions that are inherent in all normative systems and that generate constant development of the rules. The second main argument develops a general model of normative change. At the heart of the model is a cycle linking actions to disputes, disputes to arguments, and arguments to norm change. The inevitable gap between general rules and specific actions ceaselessly casts up disputes, which in turn generate arguments, which then reshape both rules and conduct. The final section of the chapter argues that the dynamic of international norm change over the past century exhibits an overarching pattern. Norm changes in diverse domains are neither random nor unconnected. Rather, the widening acceptance of a set of foundational values and ideas has channeled international norm change toward the interconnected rules that constitute a liberal world. Ours is not an argument that international rules are moving toward some historically inevitable endpoint, nor that the liberal world is fully consolidated and uncontested. We do, however, suggest that our approach goes a long way toward explaining broad patterns in the development of modern international rules.

Explaining Change

International law commentators routinely note that international legal rules undergo constant mutation but seldom seek to explain how or why international law changes. At its heart, and despite the growing volume of sophisticated legal theory, law is a practical discipline. Practitioners must know what the law is—what it prohibits, requires, or permits—before they can begin to argue or adjudicate specific cases. In domestic legal systems, identifying the law is relatively straightforward; it is codified in constitutions, statutes, regulations, and cases. What the rules mean or how they apply may not be clear at all, but at least the rules themselves are readily identifiable. In international law, the rules are frequently not easy to locate. Customary law, for instance, is, by definition, not codified. Documenting a regular practice of states and the accompanying *opinio juris* often requires substantial labor; it is not the same as opening a volume of the United States Code. Treaties might seem to lend themselves to more direct interpretation, but they sometimes evolve into customary law, binding on all states. Thus the sources of international law are a topic of perennial and live concern among international lawyers, who must routinely expend time and talent on identifying what the law is. Historically oriented international legal research charts major developments in international law over time. But documenting change is not the same as explaining change, and international law research frequently focuses on the former.

The social sciences do aim at causal explanation. International relations specialists, as they have taken an interest in international norms, have explored how and why those norms emerge. A recent research program on "legalization" in world politics, for example, seeks to explain the "move to law" in international relations (Goldstein et al. 2000). The "legalization" approach views the development of international rules, both hard and soft, as a matter of regime choice or institutional design. States and other actors seek international rules to order their interactions in a particular issue area. The content of those rules, as well as their degree of obligation, precision, and delegation, are the outcome of bargaining among interested actors. As a descriptive account, the "legalization" story is certainly plausible. But it stops at the moment of regime creation and has little to say about what happens after that. And what occurs after the moment of regime creation is relentless adaptation of rules to specific problems and changing needs. Actors attempt to apply the rules to new situations, with inevitable disputes and efforts to reinterpret or modify the rules.

The result is an incessant process of norm change, into which the legalization approach provides no insight.

To draw a domestic American analogy, the legalization framework would explain the creation of legal rules in the United States solely in terms of the legislative process. Laws, in this account, are the outcome of bargaining among members of Congress (the analog of states). But the passage of statutes is hardly the end of the story in terms of the development of legal norms. Indeed, what comes after the adoption of statutes is at least as important to the evolution of law as the legislative process. As people and organizations attempt to live under the laws, disputes inevitably arise as to what the law should mean or require in specific circumstances. Attorneys argue in court, and judges and juries decide. The outcome of each case modifies the law by clarifying its interpretation and application to specific categories of factual settings. A few major decisions—*Miranda, Brown vs. Board of Education*—entail far-reaching legal changes. Crucially, the ever-growing body of judicial decisions is law—case law—that is meticulously formalized and recorded. The case law shapes both behaviors (as people adapt their conduct to the rulings of the courts) and the resolution of subsequent disputes (the role of precedent). The legalization approach, as applied to the domestic setting, would stop with the passage of statute and miss the vital, dynamic adaptations of the law that inevitably follow.

An alternative (generally constructivist) account sees norm change as essentially a product of plural politics in which norm activists seek to rally support for a new rule. Domestic groups favoring the new norm establish coalitions with like-minded groups, sometimes within the same country but, increasingly, with foreign or international nongovernmental organizations (NGOs). These alliances produce transnational activist networks (Keck and Sikkink 1998), which are able to bring pressure on national governments from above (internationally) and below (domestically) (Brysk 1993, 2000). The result can be a "spiral" (Risse and Sikkink 1999) or "cascade" (Finnemore and Sikkink 1998) of norm acceptance. The constructivist approach to international norm change has generated useful conceptual tools, including the idea of "tipping points" and the notion of "norm entrepreneurs."

But the transnational networks approach also misses important dynamics of international norm change. Like the legalization project, it views norms essentially as outcomes. Whereas the legalization approach depicts norms as the product of interstate bargaining, the transnational networks perspective sees norms as the output of a more pluralistic political process. In both instances, norms emerge when they acquire sufficient support in the relevant political arena, whether that is an interstate negotiation (legalization) or an international process of pressure and persuasion (transnational networks). In a sense, the two approaches are quite compatible. Domestic and transnational activist networks can (and do) lobby governments before and during international negotiations. And interstate negotiations can be opened in response to the activities of transnational networks, as in the case of the conference that produced the Landmine Treaty. More crucially, both approaches ignore the ubiquitous and potent dynamic of change that is inherent to every normative system. At the heart of that dynamic are disputes about acts and arguments about norms.

The Cycle Theory of Norm Change

Dispute resolution is at the heart of governance. Every system of rules (which is to say, every social context) generates disputes, as general rules collide with the particularity of experience. The process of dispute resolution modifies the rules. Indeed, rule change through dispute resolution is necessary; it is the means by which societies adapt rules to the needs of those who live under them (Stone Sweet 1999). Normative systems are inherently dynamic, and it is that built-in dynamism that is missing from any analytical approach that sees rules simply as outcomes of bargaining or political processes.

Sandholtz has proposed a cycle theory of international norm change, building on the insight that normative change is continual, a product of the constant interplay between rules and behavior (2007). In every social system, the evolution of norms follows a cyclical, or dialectical, pattern. The cycle begins with the constellation of existing norms, which provides the normative structure within which actors decide what to do, decide how to justify their acts, and evaluate the behavior of others. Because rules cannot cover every contingency and because conflicts among rules are commonplace, actions regularly trigger disputes. Actors argue about which norms apply and what the norms require or permit. As actors seek to resolve disputes, they reason by analogy, invoke precedents, and give reasons, whether their audience is a judge or a set of other governments. The outcome of such discourses is always to change the norms under dispute, making them stronger or weaker, more specific (or less), broader or narrower.

In other words, rules may change in their substantive content (which acts are prohibited, permitted, or required), but they can also change along other dimensions (formality, specificity, and authoritativeness). Of course, weakening rules is also a form of change. The absence of consensus, or the proliferation of qualifications and exceptions, can indicate that a rule is becoming weaker or ambiguous. The process of disputing reveals the extent to which states and other actors agree on the international rules in question. The crucial point, however, is that the cycle of normative change has completed a turn and modified the norms underlying the dispute. The altered norms establish the context for subsequent actions, disputes, and discourses (Sandholtz 2007, chap. 1).[5] Figure 1.1 depicts the cycle of norm change in schematic form.

Clearly, our cycle model shares a number of basic theoretical under-pinnings with international society approaches to international law. We share the assumption that international norms constitute the framework of rules for international society (Bull 1995 [1977]; Buzan 1993; Dunne 1998; Watson 1992). Our theory also builds on the insight that a dialectical relationship links international rules and actors. Norms guide the choices and conduct of actors, but actors also modify and adapt the rules through their behavior and discourses. As Kratochwil puts it, "Actors are not only programmed by rules and norms, but they reproduce and change by their practice the normative structures by which they are able to act, share meanings, communicate intentions, criticize claims, and justify choices" (1989, 61; see also Kratochwil 2000).

Legal process approaches to international law do offer explanatory accounts of the evolution of rules. The New Haven School focuses on policy-making mechanisms and sees international law not as a complex of rules but rather as an authoritative decision-making process (McDougal 1987; McDougal and Reisman 1981; McDougal, Lasswell, and Chen 1980). The most powerful states dominate international decision making, so the New Haven School essentially equates law with fundamental goals or values of the dominant states. Normativity disappears, as rules *per se* have no genuine independent role. Our approach seeks to account for both normativity and power.

---

[5] This conception of a cycle of norm change is similar to that of Stone Sweet (1999), but whereas Stone Sweet's framework includes a third-party dispute resolver (and ties the construction of governance to the emergence of triadic dispute resolution), my framework excludes the dispute resolver and focuses on decentralized social persuasion as a mechanism of rule change.

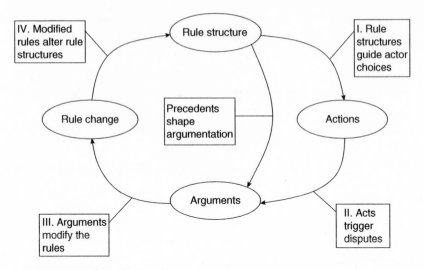

Figure 1.1 The cycle of norm change.

The International Legal Process school describes how law shapes decision making, as a constraint, as grounds for justifying choices, and as institutional structure (Chayes, Ehrlich, and Lowenfeld 1968). The "managerial approach" to compliance with international rules updates international legal process. Chayes and Chayes argue that reporting, monitoring, capacity building, and related policy tools can promote state compliance with regime norms (1995).[6] They propose that international regimes oversee an interactive, dialectic process of justification and persuasion that clarifies and elaborates norms. We too emphasize the intersection of rules and behavior and place importance on iterated processes of argumentation.

Our conception of international norm change also shares important affinities with Harold Koh's Transnational Legal Process framework. Like Koh, we argue that "one or more transnational actors provokes an interaction (or series of interactions) with another, which forces an interpretation or enunciation of the global norm applicable to the situation" (1997, 2646). We have suggested that disputed acts, in particular, constantly provoke normative arguments that modify norms. Koh's process of

---

[6] Slaughter offers a parallel argument, that transgovernmental networks can be an effective mechanism for constructing international rules and regimes that address global problems; Slaughter (2004). Whereas Slaughter emphasizes functional problem solving based on shared expertise and professional values, we focus on the centrality of disputes and arguments as engines of norm change.

internalization is perfectly compatible with our proposition that each cycle of norm contestation establishes the context in which actors make choices and frame normative arguments (Koh 1996). Indeed, we expect internalization to occur and find clear instances of it in our cases. For instance, international norms to protect cultural treasures in wartime have been internalized into the military regulations of many states; those rules guided U.S. targeting practices during the 1991 Persian Gulf War as U.S. forces sought to avoid damage to culturally significant sites (Chapter 4). Similarly, after the attacks of September 11, 2001, Security Council resolutions have impelled states to internalize international antiterrorism norms by adapting their internal laws and policies (Chapter 5). Many states have internalized international standards for the treatment of refugees, though they do not always abide by the spirit of those norms in practice (Chapter 9).

For more than a decade, international relations and international law (IL) scholars have called for greater bridge-building between the two disciplines. There has been some traffic in theoretical ideas and research methods between IR and IL, but the flow has been almost exclusively in one direction. International law scholars have borrowed theories and techniques from IR, but few international law theories and methods have found their way into international relations scholarship (Sandholtz 2007, 4). As Toope notes, "In reading most international relations literature, one looks in vain for the musings of international lawyers—even those who adopted theoretical stances closely allied to methodologies of the other social sciences" (2000, 91). This book seeks to integrate international law and international relations theories and concepts. The following paragraphs explain in greater depth the phases of the norm cycle.

Phase I: Rules and the Context of Choice

Begin, for the sake of argument, with the traditional rational maximizer. Because she is strategic, she attempts to foresee the costs and benefits of various courses of action, given the limits imposed by time, resources, and cognitive capacity. Her anticipatory calculation focuses on how other actors are likely to react to her choices. In other words, rational actors must anticipate which actions would be deemed (by other relevant actors) compatible with the rules and which would not, because, of course, various sanctions are likely to attach to acts judged incompatible with group norms. In order to make such determinations, the actor must understand not only the society's rules but also the community's current standards for interpreting and applying the rules. She must assess which justifying arguments tend to be successful, and which previous cases (precedents) carry persuasive force. Normative reasoning, then, shapes her choice of action.

As a consequence, people routinely and constantly engage in normative reasoning. Indeed, writers from Aristotle to the present have posited that the ability to reason about rules is inherently human (Aristotle 1988, Book I; Kratochwil 1989; Onuf 1998). Sugden points out that "ordinary people with limited rationality" find little difficulty in solving coordination problems that the fully rational players in game theory find intractable, and suggests that the ability to work with norms is innate, even biological (1989, 89, 95). If social norms influence not just our utility calculations but also our identities and preferences, then the basic point that rules shape actor choices is even more important.

Phase II: Disputes

Actors choose within a context of rules, but their choices routinely generate disputes. Two important features of rule systems guarantee a constant stream of disputes: incompleteness and internal contradictions.

Incompleteness arises because there cannot be a rule for every possible situation or set of facts. Rules must be general, whereas every action is, in its particularities, unique. Inevitably, some actions are difficult to assess in terms of rules; such acts are disputable, which is exactly the point. The classic statement of the problem is H.L.A. Hart's: "Nothing can eliminate this duality of a core of certainty and a penumbra of doubt when we are engaged in bringing particular situations under general rules. This imparts to all rules a fringe of vagueness or 'open texture' . . . " (1994, 123). Or, in MacCormick's words, "Almost any rule can prove to be ambiguous or unclear in relation to some disputed or disputable context of litigation" (1978, 65–66). In international relations, events routinely fall within the zone of ambiguity, where disputes arise.

Internal contradictions also generate disputes. Because there are multiple rule structures in any given society, tensions and contradictions between different rules are commonplace (Kratochwil 1989, 62, 190; Lowe 2000, 213–14; Schachter 1991, 20–21). Some actions can therefore evoke different rules, entailing divergent requirements (Kratochwil 2000, 48). For instance, the right of free speech sometimes clashes with the right to be protected from slander and libel. Rules to protect dolphins are in tension with rules of free trade. In international relations, actions commonly evoke different sets of rules, which are then seen to be in tension (e.g., nonintervention *vs.* protection of human rights).

Gaps and contradictions in the rules are, then, inevitable. But normative change does not occur as a process of abstract reflection. Rather, specific acts or events reveal the gaps and contradictions. Interested parties take opposing sides, offering divergent interpretations of which rules apply, and of what they require in the present dispute. The regular course of events continually tosses up disputes over the meaning and application of norms.

Certain types of international environments are likely to generate behaviors that challenge international rules and provoke disputes. Among these are:

1. **Wars**: The disputes triggered by wars ripple through numerous norm domains, including those regarding the use of force, the laws of war, refugees and displaced populations, human rights, regime change, and borders.
2. **Major technological changes**: New technologies (atomic power, space) generate new questions about what rules should apply.
3. **Major political changes**: Revolutions in important countries (France, Russia, China) always trigger a variety of international disagreements and disputes. The same is true when large political entities or empires collapse (the Ottoman Empire after World War I, the Soviet Union in 1990).

Thus we would expect to observe numerous episodes of norm change surrounding major changes or disruptions in the international setting. Such disruptions give rise to behaviors that test—or even shatter—international norms. As a result, disputes abound, which means that norm-changing arguments necessarily do also.

Phase III: Arguments

Sooner or later, despite her best efforts at anticipatory normative reasoning, the maximizer does something that triggers opposition. She finds herself embroiled in a dispute, and winning the dispute would provide a better payoff than losing. In order to win, she must persuade other relevant actors that her conduct complies with the group's rules, and therefore should not be sanctioned.[7] She must offer the most convincing arguments

---

[7] The audience that must be persuaded varies according to the context. In a legalized setting, the audience is the judge or a jury. In less formal contexts, like a dinner group, the audience is a

possible that her position in the current dispute best fits what the rules require and best conforms to the ways in which previous disputes were resolved (precedents). The determination of which arguments are likely to prevail depends on analogical reasoning, which involves shared standards of fit, similarity, and relevance. At this moment, the maximizer has entered the world of normative discourse, where payoffs depend on making persuasive arguments fitting situations to norms and precedents.

The same logic applies to international norms and disputes. Some state actions inevitably provoke criticism and opposition, and the arguments begin to fly. One side justifies its actions in terms of international norms and precedents; the other side marshals rules and precedents to argue that the acts in question were impermissible. Both sides argue to persuade other parties. Indeed, a growing body of research establishes the importance of argumentation and persuasion in international politics (Crawford 2002; Hawkins 2004; Risse 2000).

The notion of persuasion implies an audience that weighs the arguments and reaches conclusions. At the international level, judges are not usually the key dispute resolvers (except in substantially judicialized settings such as the WTO and the European Court of Justice). Therefore, whereas in a domestic court the litigants aim to persuade a judge or jury, in decentralized international society the parties to a dispute seek to persuade other states that have, or think they have, a stake in the matter at issue or in the norms being contested. In other words, international disputants must persuade what amounts to a jury of their peers. State officials will argue in fully self-interested ways and will draw selectively and strategically on rules and precedents that support their goals. But, as Schachter points out, the representative of a state "is able to do this successfully only to the extent that his positions are accepted (at least acquiesced in) by other States concerned" (Schachter 1991, 23).

Phase IV: Rule Change

The outcomes of arguments inevitably modify the rules. The rule may become more clear or less, more specific or less, more qualified by exceptions or less, but it cannot remain unchanged. Broad agreement among states, in favor of one side or the other, strengthens the norm being asserted

---

nonhierarchical set of peers. International relations usually resemble the less formal setting, in which actors must persuade their peers.

by the prevailing side. Absence of consensus leaves the norms in question subject to continuing contestation (Byers 1999, 154, 158).

At a minimum, each dispute adds to the pool of precedents. In international society, a small number of precedents can be crucial in establishing a norm. A sole precedent can be contradicted by a single subsequent contrary outcome. With two or three or more precedents, the weight of the emerging norm increases. A disputant acting in accord with the line of precedents can be more confident that her action will be accepted as legitimate by other actors. A disputant acting contrary to existing precedents will find it much harder to persuade others that her actions are justified (D'Amato 1971, 91–98).

In addition, to the extent that powerful actors internalize rules, their values, goals, and choices are shaped from within by normative structures that have been "domesticated." When international rules alter the terms of domestic policy debates, get incorporated into domestic legislation, affect the decisions of domestic judges, and become integrated in the organizational cultures and routines of domestic bureaucracies, then international rules have been absorbed into a country's own practices and institutions (Cortell and Davis 1996, 2000; Koh 1998).

Argumentation and Power

IR scholars sometimes assume that dominant states have no need for arguments and persuasion because they can rely on power. Yet not even hegemons are able to dictate international rules. Britain, at the height of is ascendance, did not impose the terms of the nineteenth-century Pax Britannica; it negotiated those rules with the continental European powers (McKeown 1986). Similarly, the United States has found that its status as sole superpower in the post-Cold War era by no means allows it to impose its preferred rules on the rest of the world, whether in trade, in humanitarian intervention, or in combating international terrorism.

A second common misconception is that because powerful states frequently escape punishment for violating international rules, they must also be able to create or change those rules. Naturally, the more powerful an actor is, the more it will be able to transgress rules without suffering adverse consequences. But two points require emphasis. First, it would be absurd to argue that, in normative systems generally, the capacity to break rules with virtual impunity is the same as the power to make rules. For example, in the American legal system, at least, wealthy and powerful citizens are more likely to avoid conviction or escape punishment than are the poor. Lawyers who fall asleep in court are a problem for destitute defendants, not for wealthy executives and famous athletes. Yet no one would argue that rich defendants who avoid jail terms are thereby making law. The same reasoning applies to international relations.

Second, escaping punishment for violations of international rules is not the same as making or changing the rules. Put differently, the claim that powerful actors in international relations can avoid sanctions for noncompliance with international rules is not equivalent to the claim that they are thereby remaking the rules. Rule breaking and rule making overlap at times, but they are not the same thing.

Even the assumption that violating international norms carries no costs for powerful states is mistaken. Naturally, the powerful are better able than the weak to bear those costs, but the costs are real. The 2003 U.S. invasion of Iraq provides a telling illustration. U.S. arguments that the invasion was justified failed to persuade most states. Neither the Security Council nor the broader international community was convinced that the invasion of Iraq was permitted by earlier Security Council resolutions or by the rules governing anticipatory self-defense. Much of the world, then, viewed the invasion as a violation of international law. When U.N. Secretary General Kofi Annan labeled the war in Iraq "illegal" (he had previously termed it "not in conformity" with the U.N. Charter), he was voicing a widely shared assessment ("The Primacy of International Law" 2004; Tyler 2004). The perception that the U.S. invasion of Iraq contravened international rules imposed significant costs on the United States. The war in Iraq has so far cost the United States more than 4,000 lives and hundreds of billions of dollars. In contrast, the U.S.-led military effort that ousted Iraqi forces from Kuwait in 1991 was on solid legal ground, and monetary contributions from other countries (such as Japan and Saudi Arabia) underwrote the massive U.S. involvement in that war. The widespread view that the 2003 war in Iraq was illegal also meant that fewer countries (as compared with 1991) contributed military forces to the effort. The United States has borne the burden of troop and hardware commitments that have markedly reduced the capacity of the U.S. military to respond to other threats or undertake other missions (Mazzetti 2005). In other words, even the most powerful country in the world pays the costs when its actions are seen as violating international rules.

Equally important, violation of an international rule by a powerful state does not in itself change the rule. The effect of a violation depends crucially on the justifications offered by the violator and the reactions of other states. If the violating state justifies its conduct as a permissible exception to a general rule, the effect is generally to strengthen the norm. As the International Court of Justice explained in its decision in the *Nicaragua* case, if a state breaks a rule of customary international law but "defends its conduct by appealing to exceptions or justification contained within the rule itself, whether or not the State's conduct is in fact justifiable on that basis, the significance of that attitude is to confirm rather than to weaken the rule" (International Court of Justice 1986, 98, ¶ 186). Similarly, the reactions of other states are crucial in determining the consequences of a violation for the development of international norms. In other words, when major states break the rules, norm change still depends on the ensuing arguments.

In the longer term, violations of international norms can lead to new or modified rules if other conditions are met. If an apparent violation provokes only mild or *pro forma* condemnation, that is evidence that the rule itself is weakening and possibly undergoing change. If, in addition, an apparent violation is followed in subsequent years by similar behavior on the part of other states, then the new pattern of conduct can be evidence of an emerging norm. In that case, the initial noncompliant act would be seen as not just a violation but as the first step in defining a new rule. Of course, such judgments can only be made in retrospect. To return to the Iraq war example, if international criticism of the 2003 U.S. invasion was more muted and if, over the next ten or twenty years, additional countries carried out preventive attacks and justified them in terms of a new rule of permissible preventive self-defense, then the U.S. conduct would be seen as initiating a process of rule change.

Powerful states can often impose outcomes on other states, but that does not necessarily mean that they are at the same time modifying international norms or making new ones. The difference is that whereas specific actions are individual, rules are social. Because norms are social, they evolve through collective processes of argumentation and persuasion.

Winning Arguments

The argument so far holds that actions in international relations constantly provoke disputes about the meaning and application of international norms. Actors favoring differing interpretations of the rules offer arguments designed to persuade others. Which arguments are likely to prevail? Certain features of the dispute context and of the arguments being offered increase the likelihood that a specific position will be more persuasive than its rivals. These factors fall into three categories: power, foundational norms, and precedents.

1. **Power**: The power that matters in normative arguments has to do with communications resources, as opposed to material (economic and military) power. Economic and military powers are more able than other states to violate international norms without suffering punishment. But their conduct, by itself, does not rewrite the rules. The rules change to the extent that the great powers are able to convince other actors (especially the other major states) to accept a new norm, or a modification to the existing norm. The capacity to persuade depends in part on shaping the transnational flow of ideas and communications. In other words, in arguments over international norms, what matters most is Gramscian, not Waltzian, power. Gramscian power implies preponderant influence over the production and diffusion of ideas and information (Ikenberry and Kupchan 1990; Murphy 1994). States that are able to "get their message out" are likely to sway others.

    The dimensions of communications power include:

    - *Worldwide diplomatic representation*: major powers have more embassies and consulates, with larger staffs, in more countries. The diplomatic corps carries the home government's message to other governments, media outlets, and societal actors.
    - *Presence in international organizations and negotiations*: major powers send larger missions to international meetings and negotiations. Their delegations frequently include more specialists and experts, not just in technical fields but in public and media relations.
    - *Mass media*: the world's largest and most influential news organizations (CNN, the Associated Press, Reuters, the BBC, Agence France Presse) are based in the wealthy and powerful Western countries. The Western news powers have reporters in, and disseminate their coverage to, virtually every part of the globe. The point is not that the news organizations faithfully parrot their governments' positions. But they almost inevitably cover the issues and ideas that are seen as important in the Western media markets. They are more likely to cover a speech by Condoleezza Rice than one by Nana Akufo-Addo (Foreign Minister of Ghana).

Of course, the world's economic and military powers are likely to possess the greatest communications resources. But material power does not translate directly into persuasive power. The United States was able to carry out the invasion of Iraq in 2003, but it has not been able to convince most of the world that the invasion was justified.

2. **Foundational metanorms of international society**: A number of scholars have noted that certain international norms are so fundamental that they underpin a huge variety of other rules. These foundational norms are affirmed across most, if not all, of the world's cultural and ideological traditions. Arguments that are grounded in one or more of these foundational norms are difficult to oppose, and therefore carry persuasive weight. Key foundational norms include:

   - *Universality*: international rules should apply universally, across cultures, nations, religions, and so on (Boli and Thomas 1998; Meyer, Boli, and Thomas 1987).
   - *Equality*: all persons should enjoy the same rights and protections (Keck and Sikkink 1998).
   - *Individual dignity*: a notion of the inherent dignity of each person undergirds a broad range of norms against behaviors that would be degrading to the individual. Rules to ensure bodily integrity and the prevention of harm (Keck and Sikkink 1998)—including norms against slavery, torture, cruel treatment, and sexual exploitation, for example—are grounded in a basic norm of the dignity of every person.

3. **Precedents**: Arguments are stronger when they can reference similar instances in which the norm being asserted was similarly applied. The idea is not that precedent is binding in international relations. Rather, as argued earlier, there is a powerful inclination for participants in normative systems to seek consistency; without consistency, rules do not fulfill their function of providing for stable expectations. Arguments based on analogous cases thus draw strength from the value attached to consistency. Two dimensions of precedent are important:

   - *Number*: A single precedent provides some minimum level of support to an argument, but just one contrary example can offset a single precedent. Two consistent precedents are therefore

substantially more persuasive than one, and three are more persuasive than two. In general, the larger the number of consistent
precedents, the stronger the argument (D'Amato 1971, 88–91).

- *Closeness in time*: Recent precedents tend to carry more argu-
mentative weight than historically remote ones. The more distant in time a precedent is, the less likely it will appear analogous
to current disputes, given the changes in social values and political systems that time inevitably produces. In contemporary
debates, the Persian Gulf War is much more likely to be a source
of persuasive precedents than are the Peloponnesian Wars.

To sum up, arguments inevitably lead to normative change. The substance of the rules may evolve (as with new rules that prohibited slavery or
war-time plunder), but rules can change in other ways as well. They can
become more specific, more formal, or more authoritative (backed by institutional mechanisms for monitoring compliance and applying sanctions).
Rules can also become less clear, more riddled by exceptions and qualifications, and less authoritative. In any case, the analytical framework leads us to
expect change. We also offer general expectations as to the outcome of arguments. Arguments are more likely to prevail to the extent that they: (1) are
supported by one or more great powers, (2) are consistent with foundational
metanorms (universality, equality, individual dignity), and (3) are supported
by multiple, recent precedents. As arguments modify norms, the cycle has
completed one turn. The modified rules establish the context for subsequent
choices of action and the precedents available in subsequent disputes.

The cycle theory of norm change offers important advantages over
both the legalization and the transnational activist approaches. To begin
with, both of the latter frameworks treat international rules as outcomes,
a perspective that is necessarily incomplete (Byers 1999, chap. 2; Hurrell
2000, 329; Kratochwil 2000, 52–54). Actors do modify social rules, but
rules also shape the range of strategic and discursive options available to
actors. The legalization and transnational activist frameworks emphasize
how actors shape rules but largely ignore what happens after that, as the
rules shape subsequent actions, disputes, and arguments.

Furthermore, the cycle theory can incorporate both interstate bargaining over rules and the activities of transnational norm entrepreneurs.
In fact, both kinds of events—international negotiations and transnational
activism—are frequently just episodes in longer, cyclic dynamics of norm
change. Viewing such events as relatively self-contained cases misses the

larger historical processes of norm development in which they are embedded. For example, in *Prohibiting Plunder*, Sandholtz explains the development of international rules that prohibit the wartime plundering of cultural treasures. The account begins with French looting during the Napoleonic Wars, and continues through the Nazi plundering of Europe, to the conflicts of the 1990s and the 2003 ransacking of the Iraqi National Museum. Antiplunder rules emerged and developed via multiple turns through the cycle of norm change over a period of some two hundred years. That development includes an important episode of transnational activism and a key instance of interstate bargaining.

The transnational activists were late-nineteenth century international lawyers and diplomats in Europe and the Americas who shared a desire to make warfare more humane. They established transnational networks and pushed for international rules to regulate the conduct of war. Their efforts culminated in the Hague Conventions of 1899 and 1907, which included protections for cultural monuments (Sandholtz 2007, chap. 4). The key episode of interstate bargaining took place in the wake of World War II and the massive Nazi cultural looting. Representatives of 56 countries gathered in the Hague in 1954 to finalize and sign the text of a Convention for the Protection of Cultural Property in the Event of Armed Conflict. The 1954 Convention was the first major treaty devoted specifically to shielding cultural and artistic treasures from seizure, damage, or destruction in war (Sandholtz 2007, chap. 7). Neither the work of the nineteenth-century international law activists nor the negotiations that produced the 1954 Convention would be fully intelligible as free standing cases. Both episodes are embedded in a larger, longer process of norm change. The cycle theory enables us to see that specific cases or episodes are linked forward and backward: each takes place in a context shaped by previous disputes, and each modifies the normative context for subsequent controversies. The chapters to follow include examples of international negotiations and transnational activism, but these are located within linked cycles of norm change.

The Emergence of the Liberal World

Each substantive domain examined in this book helps to establish our main proposition: that international norm change occurs in cycles driven by disputes and arguments. The chapters that follow identify major cycles of norm change and their phases (normative context, events that trigger disputes, arguments about the rules, and norm shifts). The cases also provide evidence for a second proposition: that the various arenas of norm development are interconnected elements of a broader pattern. The cycles we assess in the remainder of the book produce normative changes that are compatible with each other and are often mutually reinforcing. For example, the development of international norms prohibiting conquest is related to other rules governing the use of force, like those that forbid the wartime plundering of cultural treasures. Antislavery norms have an affinity with norms establishing the rights of refugees and asylum seekers; both are based on the notion of universal rights, even for people previously seen as less than full members of a political community. The development of modern international human rights norms is also connected to evolving rules for humanitarian intervention, which in turn overlap with the emerging right to democratic governance. In both humanitarian intervention and the right to democracy, international rules are based on the principle that how a government treats its own citizens is no longer a purely internal affair but can be subject to international monitoring and even forcible intervention.

Indeed, international norm developments seem to move together, like ships born along by the same ocean current. The vessels may not all have the same destination, but they move in generally the same direction. The major developments in international norms for the past two centuries are part of the broader flow of values and principles that have created, and continue to shape, a liberal world. Two powerful streams of values have given rise to the liberal world orders, one stream at the international level and one (at least for much of the world) at the domestic level.

Sovereignty Rules

The first, and still fundamental, stream of international norms is that which establishes sovereign states as the constituent units of international society. International society is based on formally autonomous and equal entities (states). States retain core rights and interact on the basis of rules to which they have assented.[8] Sovereignty—the idea that states possess

---

[8] As Onuf and Onuf have suggested, international society is "perhaps the first liberal society in the modern world" (2006: 50). It is the first because "the world became liberal, in just these terms, before Britain and the United States, the paradigmatically liberal societies, became liberal" (Onuf 1998: 61). Clearly, international society is not liberal in the same sense that France and Canada are liberal societies. A liberal international society, in other words, is not necessarily one whose rules and institutions are grounded in the essential value and dignity of each person and in universal human rights. The international society that emerged in the centuries before and after Westphalia was liberal at the level of states, not at the level of individuals. It was

exclusive authority over their territory and population—is meaningless outside the context of an international society because it defines a relationship among two or more units. Exclusive internal jurisdiction bars other states from taking action within my state but also prohibits my state from acting within others. As territorial states gradually emerged out of the hodge-podge of noncontiguous, overlapping political jurisdictions of the Middle Ages, the society of states began to develop. Westphalia did not create an international society of sovereign states, but it was a milestone along the way toward it. Westphalia began to codify the notion of exclusive internal jurisdiction that is the heart of sovereignty and the organizing principle of the society of states. The rights and prerogatives of sovereignty attached first to absolutist monarchs, but they later came to reside in states themselves, and subsequently in their peoples, with the rise of popular sovereignty (Bendix 1978).

Thus, the first powerful current that has shaped the development of international norms is that which defined, over a period of centuries, the international society of states. As shorthand, we refer to this stream of norms as "sovereignty rules." Sovereignty rules center on norms establishing exclusive internal jurisdiction and independence in external affairs. Related norms include nonintervention and legal equality in international organizations. These norms have continued to develop since Westphalia. The United Nations Charter, in fact, clarified and codified principles and rules that are at the heart of state sovereignty. For instance, the Charter declares as a foundational principle "the sovereign equality of all its Members" (Art. 2[1]). It also affirms the norm of nonintervention (Art. 2[7]). Even the

---

structurally liberal: its basic units were sovereign states, each possessing essential rights and prerogatives. Sovereignty meant that states retained, in principle, freedom to regulate their internal affairs as they saw fit. In their external relations, states could only be bound by rules to which they had assented. International society thus resembled the liberal society of Enlightenment thought in a structural sense. The state in international society is analogous to the individual in domestic society. Sovereignty for states parallels inalienable, universal rights for individuals. Just as rules in international society depend on the assent of states (at least, under the dominant positive view of international law), laws in a liberal domestic society require the consent of the governed.

Thus Hedley Bull's summary of the international society that emerged in the eighteenth and nineteenth centuries sounds strikingly like the liberal domestic society of Locke, Montesquieu, and Jefferson: the essential features of international society were "the idea that members all have the same basic rights, that the obligations they undertake are reciprocal, that the rules and institutions of international society derive from their consent . . ." (1995 [1977]). International society, then, is liberal as among states, not with respect to individuals. In the discussion that follows, "sovereignty rules" refers to the norms establishing a society of sovereign states. To avoid confusion, we reserve the word "liberal" for the set of rules establishing the rights and freedoms of individuals.

prohibition on the threat or use of force (Art. 2[4]) can be seen as strengthening sovereignty. Armed attack against another state not only violates its
exclusive authority over territory and population, it can threaten the continued existence of the state itself. The U.N. Charter also expresses key
norms that arise out of a second stream of values and principles, one tied
to individual human rights.

Liberal Norms

The second powerful current of normative development flows out of the
principles and values we typically associate with liberal individualism: the
essential value, dignity, and inherent rights of each person. Indeed, when
we refer to a "liberal world," we typically mean to invoke the constellation
of norms enshrining individual rights and liberties, at both domestic and
international levels. The stream of norms based on individual freedom
and rights has shaped liberal domestic orders (constitutional, representative democracy) but also opened new areas of international law (humanitarian law, international human rights law).

The flow of human rights norms emerged out of Enlightenment
thought (Locke, Rousseau), and with the American and French revolutions
began to find direct embodiment in political systems. The ideals of popular sovereignty and representative democracy, coupled with explicit constitutional protections for individual rights and liberties, subsequently
spread to most parts of the world, beginning in the eighteenth century and
continuing to the present. Indeed, liberal individualism underlies democratic political forms, which by now are seen as defining the only legitimate domestic political order, in principle if not in universal practice.
Market economies are likewise the embodiment of liberal norms, granting
primacy to individual choice and freedom of exchange. Liberal norms
thus inform current ideal (and, frequently, idealized) models for the political and economic organization of domestic orders. Of course, the spread
of liberal, human-rights-based norms has been uneven and incomplete
and continues to be contested. But liberal human rights principles are now
embodied in major international treaties and institutions, as well as in
domestic systems in every region of the world.

Norms of liberal individualism have also transformed international
law. International conventions—such as the Universal Declaration of
Human Rights, the International Covenant on Civil and Political Rights,
and the International Covenant on Economic, Social, and Cultural Rights—
enumerate and universalize personal rights and freedoms. The laws of war

(Geneva Law) likewise guarantee basic protections for individuals. A growing array of more specialized treaties codifies other human-rights-based rules, covering genocide, slavery, torture, racial discrimination, discrimination against women, and more.

The stream of values and principles tied to liberal human rights and freedoms has frequently collided with the stream of sovereignty norms. The inherent tension between sovereignty rules and human rights-based norms has been one of the primary motors of international norm change, especially since World War II. In explaining the inherent dynamism of normative systems, this chapter earlier noted that conflicts between different bodies of norms are inevitable (free speech vs. hate speech, free trade vs. the protection of endangered species). The norms of international society emphasize the sovereignty and rights of states; traditionally, international law, which developed to sustain the society of states, had nothing to say about the internal affairs of countries, including their form of government or their treatment of their own citizens. But international human rights norms challenged the traditional autonomy of states with regard to their internal arrangements and conduct. If international law enshrined basic and universal rights of individuals, then sovereignty could not shield abusive governments from international scrutiny and even sanctions. The tension between sovereignty rules and human rights norms has modified the sovereignty rules. For example, the nonintervention norm is no longer absolute. Forcible external intervention is now permissible in countries where the government engages in systematic or large-scale human rights abuses (see Chapter 10). With the emerging right to democracy, even the form of domestic political systems is becoming a valid concern of international society (see Chapter 11).

In short, international society has been shaped largely by two normative currents, one that emphasized the rights and freedoms of states and another that emphasized the rights and freedoms of individuals. The first generated sovereignty rules, the second produced liberal, human rights norms. The tension between these two main normative currents has produced numerous important changes in international norms. Figure 1.2 offers a graphic representation of those two major streams of norm development. The normative shifts in various domains have not been the product of abstract or theoretical dialogues between sovereignty and human rights. Rather, specific events and actions have triggered disputes, and the arguments generated by those disputes brought into play the tensions between sovereignty and human rights.

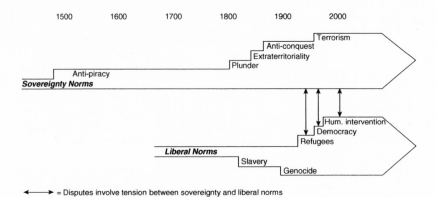

1500   1600   1700   1800   1900   2000

Terrorism
Anti-conquest
Extraterritoriality
Plunder
Anti-piracy
Sovereignty Norms

Hum. intervention
Democracy
Refugees
Liberal Norms
Slavery
Genocide

⟵⟶ = Disputes involve tension between sovereignty and liberal norms

Figure 1.2 Major streams of norm development.

The Plan of the Book

The following chapters test two main claims: (1) that international norm change occurs in cycles of disputation, and (2) that tensions between sovereignty and human rights norms have been at the heart of many of those cycles. The first claim takes up the argument Sandholtz advances in *Prohibiting Plunder*, which tests the cycle theory of norm change by analyzing the development of international rules against wartime art plunder. He examines a series of episodes, each of them following the cycle pattern. Cycles of disputation and norm change link backward and forward in time, making necessary the long historical view that the cycle theory offers. Each episode draws on previous cycles that established the normative context and the set of precedents; each episode also modifies the norms and adds to the stock of precedents for subsequent cycles. Chapter 4 assesses in abbreviated form the evolution of antiplunder norms, beginning with the Napoleonic Wars and ending with post-World War II developments. Sandholtz argues that the cycle theory should apply equally well to norm change in other substantive domains. The rest of the chapters in this volume test that proposition.

The empirical chapters also offer a plausibility probe of the argument that two major streams of international norms have shaped the international system. The first group of cases (Chapters 2–5) assesses developments along the stream of sovereignty rules. They examine cycles of norm change that extend, clarify, or specify rules relating to the rights and duties of sovereign states. The prohibitions of piracy (Chapter 2) and terrorism (Chapter 5), for example, are, in part, moves to consolidate states' monopoly on the use of force. The decline of the right of conquest (Chapter 3) strengthened the principle of sovereign equality; all states had the right to exist and no state could extinguish another via conquest. The traditional right of the victor in war to plunder the cultural treasures of the defeated was replaced by rules that prohibited such looting (Chapter 4). Again, anti-plunder norms established a right for states (not individuals), namely, the right states to retain their cultural patrimony. The decline of extraterritorial privileges (Chapter 6) represents a transitional case. On the one hand, the end of extraterritoriality reaffirmed sovereignty as the right of states to exclusive internal jurisdiction. On the other hand, the demise of extraterritoriality by the middle of the twentieth century was part of the larger normative movement toward recognition of the right of all peoples—not just those once considered "civilized"—to their own fully sovereign states. This broader development would subsequently lead to decolonization and self-determination for former colonies.

A second group of cases evaluates cycles of norm change along the second major stream of international norms, that based on individual human rights. These chapters cover the abolition of slavery and the slave trade (Chapter 7), genocide (Chapter 8), refugees and asylum (Chapter 9), humanitarian intervention (Chapter 10), and the emerging right to democracy (Chapter 11).

The cases selected for the book provide variation along a number of dimensions. First, they include norm developments relating to both sovereignty rules (centered on the rights and duties of states in international society) and human rights rules (centered on the inherent rights of individuals), as well as instances in which the two main streams of international norms are in tension. Second, the cases include variation in the substantive domain, from the monopoly on the use of force (piracy, terrorism), to the use of force by states against other states (conquest, plunder), to personal freedom and right to life (slavery, genocide), to basic rights for stateless persons (refugees), and preserving the rights of populations vis-à-vis their own governments (humanitarian intervention, right to democracy). Third, the cases cover a range of temporal contexts, from the sixteenth to the twenty-first century. Human societies have changed in every imaginable way over this span, yet we find cycles of norm change throughout it.

Finally, the cases share a basic format that highlights the cycles of norm change. Each chapter thus assesses the four phases of the norm cycle: (1) the existing normative context, (2) the event or action that triggers a normative dispute, (3) the ensuing arguments, and (4) the resulting modification of international rules. The chapters also illustrate the importance of linking norm cycles into longer, dynamic processes; all of them include multiple cycles of change linked across time. Some of them (slavery, plunder) have embedded within them instances of transnational activist groups that sometimes act to catalyze disputes and frame the arguments that lead to norm change. Finally, the chapters illustrate the connectedness of norm cycles to each other, as developments in one domain influence the disputes and arguments in other domains. Humanitarian intervention and the right to democracy, for example, show such connections.

This chapter advances the claim that normative systems are inherently dynamic. All normative systems, including international relations, ensure a continuous supply of disputes, which inevitably modify the rules in question. Norm cycles, we claim, must therefore be ubiquitous. If that claim is correct, we should observe cycles of norm change in all historical periods, in every substantive domain. It is time to test that proposition.

Part I

Sovereignty Norms

Chapter 2

Banning Piracy: The State Monopoly on Military Force

Kendall Stiles

New norms are more likely to establish themselves when powerful states embrace them. The case of piracy supports that claim and also illustrates how changes in technology can affect state capacity and power. In this case, we will see, for example, that rules governing piracy and privateering depended on states' ability to control crime at sea, which in turn required specific technical capabilities and resources (Pérotin-Dumon 2001). States that previously had an ambivalent relationship with pirates became increasingly hostile as their capacity to build and control navies increased (Becker 2005, pp. 134, 203). Caribbean piracy dropped precipitously in the early 1800s once new Latin American states were able to consolidate control over territory—especially the ports that had served as safe havens during the wars of independence. Privateering became illegal at roughly the same time it became obsolete, as states built large navies of steel ships in the mid-nineteenth century. Conversely, as state capacity has waned in recent years, piracy has increased proportionately.

Relations between the major seafaring states have also shaped the rules governing piracy. Rivalries between states with strong navies and those with weak navies called into question the role of piracy. Pirates had often been enlisted (or tolerated) by weaker states even as they were condemned by stronger states. Likewise, restricting piracy to nonpolitically motivated piracy has had much to do with whether particular actions were consistent with powerful states' foreign policy aims. For example, early rules governing piracy were tied to the maritime rivalry between Spain and Britain in the sixteenth and seventeenth centuries. In the early stages, Britain was more than willing to collaborate with pirates, but as Britain achieved dominance on the seas it was more eager to enforce a strict ban on piracy. The case of piracy is therefore important to our understanding of the nexus between power and norms and can be profitably compared with the cases on conquest, humanitarian intervention, and war plunder in particular.

To begin, piratical behavior was generally defined as robbery at sea and was looked upon as one of the risks of maritime commerce. Even so, it was not universally seen as criminal, as many states prospered by seizing other states' cargo at sea. In the early sixteenth century, Spain began to castigate piracy as criminal. The targets of Spanish opprobrium were British and French explorers and adventurers who often held "letters of marque" from their respective governments, giving them authority to plunder. States battled each other in the academy as well as at sea, as they recruited competing legal experts to articulate either a "closed sea" or "open sea" norm. Whether an actor was a pirate or a legitimate privateer was largely a matter of political interest. One would be hard-pressed to identify any governing norm at all between 1500 and 1700. More and more states outlawed piracy—not only off their coasts but also on the high seas—during the seventeenth and eighteenth centuries while at the same time employing privateers to engage in essentially the same kinds of conduct.

The unsettled status of piracy came to an end as Great Britain consolidated control of the seas in the Napoleonic era. At this juncture, the British Admiralty Courts became the source of international maritime law. Piracy was not tolerated and the United Kingdom (and the United States, for a time) claimed jurisdiction over all acts of piracy. Britain entered into a series of bilateral extradition agreements with European states and advocated universal jurisdiction over pirates. Most European states also outlawed privateering in the mid-nineteenth century. Such was the consensus on the new prohibitive regimes that by 1930, piracy and privateering were generally thought to be a thing of the past. The norm was stable until the 1980s, when the attack on the *Achille Lauro* prompted states to remove the political exception from the definition of piracy. Since then, high levels of state corruption and a shifting ratio of power between increasingly organized and well-funded pirate rings and developing country governments—many of which are mired in civil strife, corruption, and poverty—have led to an increase in piracy in the southern hemisphere and to renewed efforts to clarify and enforce the antipiracy norm. Such efforts, however, are running up against a vigorous defense of sovereign rights over adjacent seas.

Norms on piracy have moved through several distinct cycles of change (see Figure 2.1). These cycles involved intense disputes over definitions of piracy and over rules for the high seas. The trigger for the development of antipiracy norms, however, was not a specific disputed event but rather the emergence of naval technologies that allowed states to suppress piracy. The remainder of this chapter examines three cycles of normative development. In the first cycle, through about 1600, states moved from acceptance of privateering to contesting its legitimacy. The second cycle culminated in the nineteenth-century prohibition of piracy. A third cycle, embedded within the larger cycle of antipiracy norms, carved out in the nineteenth and twentieth centuries a political exception to the ban on piracy. Finally, the chapter assesses the still unresolved debate regarding universal jurisdiction over pirates.

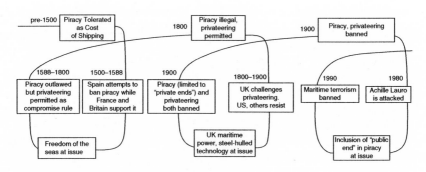

Figure. 2.1 Antipiracy norm cycles.

Piracy from Antiquity to the Renaissance: Acceptance to Contestation

Contemporary definitions of piracy generally refer to acts of theft or assault committed at sea which would be criminal on land under most states' laws. More specifically, as found in Article 1(1) of the 1932 Draft Convention on Piracy, piracy consists of "any act of violence or of depredation committed with intent to rob, rape, wound, enslave, imprison or kill a person or with intent to steal or destroy property, for private ends" (Harvard Draft 1932).

But as clear as this definition may appear, it was hotly contested for centuries. In antiquity, there was no single word that was equivalent to our modern concept of "piracy." Until 250 BCE, the Greeks referred to pirates as mere "brigands," making no distinction between theft on land and theft at sea. Thereafter, the term "*katapontistes*" was applied to those who committed violence at sea, although the term did not have a legal connotation (De Souza 1999, p. 41). Homer, when referring to pirates, apparently had in mind a relatively honorable profession of armed commerce (Rubin 1988, p. 3). Even when Rome undertook a systematic campaign to eradicate Mediterranean piracy in 68 BCE (under Pompey), the target was not so much those who attacked commerce for gain, but political rebels and religious heretics on the fringes of the Empire that threatened the Roman order. "The word . . . did not imply criminality under any legal system, Roman or law of nations" (p. 12). This is not to say that marauding at sea was permissible, simply that it was not treated as piracy or as a distinct crime.

Piratical acts became widespread during the Middle Ages and shipping in the Mediterranean and the North Sea was constantly under attack. But these acts were not generally considered criminal *per se*, and were as often as not an extension of the foreign policy of the various political entities along the Mediterranean and North Atlantic coastlines. This is not to say that states did not make every effort to protect themselves from marauders by pursuing them when possible—even from time to time "trying" them once captured (more typically executing them on the spot)—but this is better understood in the context of rules of war rather than any universal definition of piracy.

From the mid-ninth century CE (following the Muslim invasion of Sicily and its conquest from the Byzantines in 827) until roughly 1300, Muslim traders and caliphs dominated the Mediterranean (Khaliliel 1998, p. 133; Talarico 2003). Many Muslim ships were armed and engaged in depredations against a wide range of vessels, usually with the explicit support of their respective caliphs. Meanwhile, Norsemen spread across the North Sea and beyond, attacking English, Dutch and other vessels. Although the Hanseatic League was formed in 1159 in part to improve maritime security in the north of Europe (a largely unsuccessful endeavor), little coordinated effort was made in the Mediterranean, and states were left to deal with the so-called corsairs until 1830. By the mid-1400s, pirates came from virtually all the nations of Europe and North Africa. They numbered in the hundreds at a time when few states boasted navies of more than a dozen ships. Piracy ultimately threatened the survival of smaller states and contributed to the decline of Florence and Venice (Teneti 1967, p. 21). Still, there was no clear norm against piracy. Some states, including England, passed domestic laws against theft at sea. Henry VI of England adopted a policy of restoring pirates' prizes to their rightful owners in the 1440s, and Henry VIII labeled pirates as outlaws in 1511. These early declarations culminated in the codification of Rule 28 (1536), drawing a distinction between piracy, which was not sanctioned by the Crown, and privateering, which was (Rubin 1988, pp. 35–7).

Only in the early sixteenth century did a few states (particularly Spain and Portugal) explicitly define piracy in domestic law (as opposed to international treaty). The trigger was the 1494 Treaty of Tordesillas, which divided the New World (from Southeast Asia to the coast of Africa by way of the Americas) between Portugal and Spain, with the endorsement of the reigning pope. Once the line was drawn in the Atlantic (roughly at 46 degrees west latitude), Spain made clear that ocean navigation to the west of the line was exclusive to Spanish sailors. All others were declared "pirates" (Marx 1992, p. 5; Marcus 1961, p. 76). This bold assertion was like a gauntlet thrown at the feet of English, French, and Dutch mariners and rulers. English King Henry VII openly defied the Spanish ban as early as 1496 by commissioning Italian mariner Giovanni Caboto (renamed John Cabot) to explore the northern coastline of North America (he ultimately discovered Newfoundland) (Fowler 1965, p. 34). The French went a step further in the 1520s, launching direct attacks on Spanish treasure ships, prompting the latter to organize convoys to protect the movement of specie across the Atlantic (which would remain notoriously vulnerable) (Woodrooffe 1958, p. 63).

At the same time that Spain used military force to halt piracy, it also engaged in a diplomatic war of words with England and France. Throughout the sixteenth century, Spain repeatedly protested to the French and English governments over the actions of pirates, arguing for a doctrine of "closed seas." Spain called upon all Europeans to restrain their mariners, insisting particularly that they cease collaborating with privateers (Fowler 1965, 34; Richardson 1990, 145). In most cases, the other Europeans thus accused offered the diplomatic equivalent of a Gallic shrug. In 1575, for example, Philip II of Spain forwarded to British Queen Elizabeth I a list of English sailors to be tried as pirates and demanded they be arrested. The list included such luminaries as Francis Drake, John Hawkins, William Winter, Lewis Lader, and others (Kelsey 2003, p. 149). Elizabeth responded a few years later by bestowing a knighthood on Drake (Bevan 1971, p. 103). Ironically, this act of defiance so infuriated Phillip that it served as one justification for the attempted invasion of England in 1588, a disaster that contributed to Spain's naval decline and along with it the decline of the "closed seas" doctrine (Hattendorf et al. 1993, p. 148). In its placed rose the doctrine of "freedom of the seas" that was most forcefully articulated by Dutch jurist Hugo Grotius (Bevan 1971, p. 103). Spain's definition of piracy was never accepted as an international norm.

In fact, no new consensual definition emerged. Rather, during the next two hundred years it became customary to use the term "pirate" as an epithet against the enemy's privateers (although not against an enemy's royal fleet), and thus private and public assault were conflated. The result was that politics largely defined the norm.

Most states practiced a mixed strategy with pirates that did not presume their actions were inherently illegal. It involved confrontation, accommodation, and even collaboration and conscription. Spain was in the best position to confront pirates and had the greatest interest in doing so. After all, up to one-fifth of the country's wealth was derived from the flow of treasure (Woodrooffe 1958, p. 165). This mostly involved the forming of convoys once or twice each year. Later, Spain fortified bases in the Caribbean and created the Indies Fleet to strengthen its capabilities (Kelsey 1998, p. 45). At roughly the same time, England began to expand its navy, primarily to confront the many pirates sailing the English Channel (Fowler 1965, p. 26). It also established a sophisticated legal network centered on the Admiralty Courts to prosecute pirates that fell into their hands, particularly in cases of piracy near the English coast (Lydon 1970, p. 32).

Confrontation generally failed until the eighteenth century, as did attempts to criminalize piracy on the high seas. Pirates increased in numbers and success, sometimes seizing cargoes worth millions of pounds (Lane 1998, p. 57). Accommodation was therefore the most reasonable response. It involved both ad hoc and long-term deals consisting mostly of bribes and protection money being paid by shippers (including private companies and governments) to pirates. For example, Venetians routinely appeased the Muslim corsairs (later known as Barbary pirates) throughout the sixteenth century through payment of bribes (Tenenti 1967, p. 21; Irwin 1970, p. 140). Sometimes these payments were formalized as treaties or contracts. As recently as 1820, this was how U.S. leaders dealt with Barbary pirates after the failure of military confrontation (Irwin 1970, p. 174).

Pirates were often lionized and elevated to hero status. Christians who attacked Muslim shipping and Protestants who attacked Catholic shipping were praised as "defenders of the faith," and many pirates saw themselves as such (Loades 1992, p. 224). Many of them became extraordinarily wealthy and rose to prominence in their hometowns, as was true of slave traders during this period (many of whom also engaged in piracy). In the process, pirates sometimes enriched the surrounding community and the state (Gottschalk and Flanagan 2000, p. 19). Some governments argued that piracy was not inherently unlawful, so long as it was not aimed at their own shipping (Rubin 1988, p. 39).

This brings us to the last point: many if not most states actively engaged in piracy until the nineteenth century. Naturally, the practice was redefined for legal purposes as privateering or armed commerce. From an early time, then, states delegated certain aspects of military security to private actors. The practice of privateering had its origins in the notion of "reprisal," granting authority to private actors to obtain redress for some international wrong. Specific injuries could thus be remedied even by weak states during peacetime because private individuals could take action with state approval (when states lacked military capability) on a case-by-case basis (Starkey 1990, p. 20). Later, these specific reprisals were replaced with "general reprisal" orders—applicable only in wartime—through which a state could authorize private actors to attack all of the enemy's commercial shipping (Starkey 2001, p. 69). In addition to such ad hoc arrangements, monarchs sometimes created informal "naval reserves" of private ships. As early as the twelfth century, English kings entered into agreements with shippers in the Channel ports—the Cinque—to provide vessels to the Crown in the event of war (Marcus 1961, p. 14). Queen Elizabeth I informally endorsed and later funded the notorious ventures of John Hawkins, Sir Francis Drake (whom she knighted), and others who engaged in piratical practices (Lydon 1970, p. 28).

"Letters of marque" were the legal fig leaf that allowed pirates to claim authority from a state. This was a document issued by a government to a privateer (usually on payment of some sort of bond) that detailed what ships could be attacked, what could be done with the ship and its cargo, and so forth (Lane 1998, p. 165). Letters of marque varied little and were often drawn up in volume with blank spaces left for the name of the ship and its captain. Typically they forbade attacks on friendly and neutral shipping and spelled out the share of the cargo that would be awarded to the crew. Of utmost importance was the mandate that once a vessel was seized, it would be brought—preferably intact—to a court of some sort that would settle the distribution of the "prize." Strict rules were laid out to allocate the booty to the captain, the crew, and the Crown. The privateer who failed to comply could be considered a pirate (Rubin 1988, 78).

The Eighteenth and Nineteenth Centuries—Contestation to Ban

The line between piracy and privateering was very thin as of 1700, and the distinction was probably lost on most victims (Kontorovich 2004b, p. 231; Starkey 2001, p. 69) and on non-Europeans (Risso 2001, p. 294; Pennell 1989, p. 45; Kontorovich 2004b; Silverstein 2005, p. 187). But from the point of view of many European states, the line was clear. By this time, piracy was increasingly seen as taboo. Britain codified the law on piracy in 1698 and showed little tolerance for infractions (Keyuan 2000, p. 114). Public executions of pirates became common in the United Kingdom and the American colonies; in Rhode Island, the entire crew of a pirate ship was executed publicly in the 1720s (Lydon 1970, p. 80). This was possible because for the first time the British Navy, as well as the navies of other majors powers, were large enough to begin effectively controlling at least the coastline if not necessarily the high seas (Pérotin-Dumon 2001, p. 41).

The concern over distinguishing pirates from privateers was a matter of security: privateers in wartime were often pirates in peacetime. Governments drew from the same rather disreputable class of seamen who often found restrictions on prize taking a bureaucratic nuisance. Some even argued that pirates received their training on privateering ships. Failure to draw a clear line could lead to widespread violence at sea against a broad range of targets, with obvious national security implications.

The fact of the matter is that privateering, even when strictly regulated, created as many problems as it solved. Privateers drew able seamen away from state-run navies, tended to exceed their instructions by attacking neutrals and provoking reprisals from victimized states, and were usually not effective in organized combat anyway. These problems, balanced against the growing capacity of state-run navies, led to considerable disenchantment with privateering by the nineteenth century. When the Crimean War was fought entirely without privateers, in accordance with what had become French practice, the United Kingdom and a number of other states decided to formally outlaw privateering in 1856 (Stark 1967/1898, p. 88). The last time privateers served any country well was during the War of 1812 when Baltimore privateers played a pivotal role in harassing British shipping (Garitee 1977, p. 243). While the U.S. did not formally endorse international agreements against privateering (two were drawn up, in 1856 and 1907), its practice, along with that of virtually all states, consistently demonstrated support (Bowles 1910, p. 100; Wilson 1910, p. 311). Ultimately, technology was the key factor in the demise of privateers, since by the mid-1800s they could not acquire vessels capable of outdueling the steel-hulled ships of national navies (Winslow 1988, p. 245). In addition, as was the case with mercenarism, the consolidation of national identities in states across Europe made privateers appear less trustworthy (Thomson 1990).

The treaty banning privateering in 1856 provided for a compelling trade-off: policy makers reasoned that ending other countries' right to recruit privateers was worth abandoning their own right to attack neutral shipping that carried enemy goods (Stark 1967/1898, p. 140). The agreement was not universally accepted. The United States and Spain initially objected (as did Mexico) on the grounds that with small navies and long coastlines, privateers might still be needed, although they ultimately acquiesced to the new norm.

It is clear that power and transportation technology were critical to the norm on piracy. Until 1550, seafaring states encountered similarly equipped pirates who operated with relative impunity. At that point, Spain tried in vain to assert legal control of the Americas and adjacent seas by simply declaring all foreigners found there to be pirates. This prompted a debate over the law of the seas and an eventual consensus on a laissez-faire approach. For two hundred years, pirates and royal navies fought to a stalemate, with states engaging in both accommodation and co-optation to control the problem.

Once states were able to increase their naval power, however, piracy was increasingly viewed as criminal. By the late-eighteenth century, states could declare pirates outlaws without losing face. Law followed enforcement capacity rather than the other way around. From one point of view, controlling pirates and later privateers was one step along the path to state consolidation that has spanned modernity. Pirates, like highwaymen before them, could not compete against the power of modern states. And states had no use for them. The ban on privateering was thus a relatively superficial agreement, in that it required no significant change of practice on the part of states. Even those few states that rejected the 1856 agreement did not make use of privateers. One could argue that there was really no need for the treaty at all.

Scope of Piracy: Private versus Public Ends

Two issues have not been entirely resolved: the political exception and universal jurisdiction. These issues are worth separating because of their more contested status, but also because they overlap with other questions. With reference to our model, while the piracy and privateering norms cycled mostly within one framework (although considerations of freedom of the seas entered briefly into the mix in the sixteenth century), these next two issues were more directly linked to other cycles of norm development, namely, those relating to terrorism at sea and in the air and war crimes prosecution.

At the beginning of the nineteenth century, the definition of piracy was quite clear in that it involved all depredations at sea by private actors. Once privateering was outlawed, the question of state authorization became irrelevant. However, a critical issue was not immediately resolved and continues to bedevil policy makers and analysts. That is the problem of how to treat actors that are motivated by something other than greed or blood lust. Politically motivated attacks at sea present a special problem because they do not generally threaten any state other than the target. Such attacks often take place in peacetime and involve only a government and a rebel organization. In a sense, politically driven piracy on the seas would be similar to rebel assaults within the territory of the target state. Outside states would presumably be unaffected by such internal attacks, and would be prohibited from becoming involved by the rules of nonintervention. The only difference between rebels at sea and rebels holed up in the mountains is location, after all. States that attempt to disrupt such activities could justly be accused of meddling in the internal affairs of another sovereign entity (Halberstam 1988, p. 289).

This rule was not clear until a number of incidents in the mid-nineteenth century required action. By this point in history (as we see in Chapter 7, on slavery and the slave trade), the Admiralty Courts of the

United Kingdom were the final arbiters of the international law of the sea and, through their rulings, clarified the crime of piracy. Few states had the capacity or will to enforce piracy law and generally deferred to British authority. Even U.S. courts after 1820 generally endorsed British decisions (White 1989).

In 1851, Chilean rebels (and recently escaped convicts from a nearby penal colony) seized a British ship sailing in the Straits of Magellan, declaring themselves enemies of the sitting government in Santiago. After being recaptured by British forces, the ship eventually foundered and was later sold to a Portuguese interest. It finished its travels in Britain where the original owners sued to have the sale canceled. In the course of hearing the case, Dr. Stephen Lushington of the British Admiralty Court ruled in favor of the original owners (Rubin 1988, p. 233). In the process, he addressed the question of whether the Chileans were "pirates." He ruled that because another state's ship was involved in the attack, the perpetrators could be considered pirates, having met the "two ship" criterion. On the other hand, the British government had already turned the rebels over to the Chilean government—recognized by the United Kingdom—which had the right to prosecute Chilean nationals for an act that took place in Chilean territorial waters (p. 235). A similar case was heard in 1870 involving the seizure by local rebels of a British ship anchored in Venezuelan waters. The Admiralty Court ruled that because Britain did not recognize the rebels, they had no belligerent rights and could be treated as pirates (p. 244).

A turning point had been reached in 1873. An insurrection in Spain led to the seizure of vessels by rebels. Spain appealed to the states of Europe to seize the ships and extradite the rebels to Madrid, a policy that France was most willing to carry out. Britain, however, argued that France did not have the power to determine whether these rebel ships were pirates simply on the word of the Spanish government. As put by the Law Officers:

> The Spanish rebel ships have not committed and are not cruizing [sic] with the intent to commit any act which a foreign nation can properly call or treat as a piratical act.... [Therefore,] they cannot properly be visited or detained or seized unless the Government which orders or approves of such visit, detention or seizure is prepared to support the Government at Madrid against all persons and parties who may be in insurrection against that government. (McNair 1956, pp. 273–4, cited in Rubin 1988, p. 244)

This statement further implies that rebels may be entitled to treatment as belligerents rather than pirates. If they, as belligerents, considered England or France to be allied to the government in Madrid, they would have a legal right to attack their shipping as well, although this question was never directly tested.

A more controversial case arose in 1877, when Peruvian rebels took over a Peruvian flag vessel. They sailed to Chile in the hope of laying anchor, but were denied entry on the grounds that Chile did not want to become involved in an internal political matter (Rubin 1988, p. 260). Following the rebuff, the rebels attacked a passing British ship and stole its supply of coal. Chile refused Britain's request to take the ship when it again sailed into its territorial waters on the grounds that doing so constituted interference in Peru's internal politics. Britain at this point took it upon itself to seize the ship once it returned to international waters on the grounds that the rebels were in fact pirates and the United Kingdom could act in self defense, a rather strained logic by contemporary standards (Rubin 1988, p. 266). But the approach met with no recriminations from any other state.

At any rate, by the late nineteenth century, British admiralty law, and concurrently international law of the sea, was beginning to carve out a political exception in its definition of piracy. For the next fifty years, piracy gradually disappeared from the international stage and little active debate occurred on the topic. The only concerted effort to address the extent of this political exception came in the context of an academic debate Harvard Law School sponsored in 1932. Among other efforts, the assembled scholars endeavored to create a draft international convention on piracy and in the process applied themselves to its definition. Piracy, according to their Article 3, consists of "Any act of violence or of depredation committed with intent to rob, rape, wound, enslave, imprison or kill a person or with intent to steal or destroy property, for private ends without bone fide purpose of asserting a claim or right" (Harvard Draft 1932). How much debate focused on the "private ends" clause is not clear, but analyst Dubner is of the opinion that the exclusion of all but privately motivated piracy was done "for the sake of expediency" (1997, p. 19). As put in the explanation, "Although states at times have claimed the right to treat as pirates unrecognized insurgents against a foreign government . . . it seems best to [call pirates] offenders acting for private ends only" (Harvard Draft 1932, p. 798).

This language, which may have been rather casually drafted, was incorporated in the 1958 Geneva Convention on the High Seas

(Garmon 2002, p. 262). This is not to say that the negotiators were as blithe as the scholars appear to have been. On the contrary, during the talks, the Soviet Union objected to the political exception. Soviet bloc countries charged that the presence of the U.S. Seventh Fleet in the Taiwan Straits constituted piracy. Naturally, Western states firmly objected to this view (Morris 2001, p. 340). Ultimately the parties agreed to adopt the "private ends" language, in part because the problem of piracy seemed mostly hypothetical at the time and hardly worth the energy. This view carried the day when it was raised in the 1970s at the next meetings, and the "private ends" wording eventually found its way into the 1982 United Nations Convention on the Law of the Sea (Garmon 2002, p. 262). Interestingly, the standard view of insurance and shipping companies is that piracy consists of acts carried out for private ends (Kahn 1996).

Alongside the international conferences, state practice was also shaping norms on piracy. Efforts by Portugal to enlist general international support to apprehend a rebel ship in 1975 were rebuffed, confirming the private ends rule (Gottschalk and Flanagan 2000, p. 35). After President Gerald Ford labeled as "pirates" the captors of the SS *Mayaguez*, the State Department issued a clarification: these were not really pirates because they were politically motivated (Rubin 1988, p. 339).

The 1985 attack by Palestine Liberation Organization operatives against the Italian cruise ship *Achille Lauro* (anchored in Egyptian territorial waters) altered the parameters of the debate on the political exception. Because the attack was clearly political (it was intended to provoke a change in Israeli policy in the West Bank), none dared to call it piracy. This also meant that the enforcement provisions of the various Law of the Sea treaties did not apply. There was no clear means to prosecute the perpetrators. In the end, Egypt refused to prosecute and instead undertook to fly them out of the country. The aircraft was intercepted and forced to land in Italy at an American airbase. A bizarre scene unfolded as American troops surrounded the plane, which carried both terror suspects and Egyptian air marshals, only to find themselves in turn surrounded by Italian police forces (McGinley 1985). The U.S. troops were instructed to yield control of the aircraft and its passengers. Italy proceeded to prosecute and convict the terror suspects for murder (they were responsible for the death of U.S. national Leon Klinghoffer), but not for piracy. Furthermore, the United States never claimed that its interception of the aircraft was legal under existing law (p. 708).

This event exposed a gap in international law that states immediately set about filling. The result was the 1988 Rome Convention (formally

CHAPTER 2

the Convention for the Suppression of Unlawful Acts against the Safety of Maritime Navigation), sponsored by the International Maritime Organization (Halberstam 1988, p. 269). The Convention specifically provides for a much broader definition of piracy that includes politically motivated acts (Barrios 2005, p. 153; Stiles 2004, p. 310). Only 119 states have ratified the instrument (as of July 2005), and many East Asian countries, where modern-day piracy is most active, have declined (Hermann 2004, p. 24). The Convention also limits enforcement powers to those states with a direct interest in the attack, as opposed to the universal jurisdiction commonly applied to piracy (see next section). In other words, the Rome Convention did not resolve all of the problems raised by the *Achille Lauro*.

Some have argued that the Rome Convention was in fact redundant and that existing treaty language could be read to cover terrorist acts (Paladini 2004). Oppenheim, in particular, has argued that the parameters of what acts constitute piracy have been gradually broadened by successive cases (Oppenheim 1952–1955, pp. 613–4). For his part, Halberstam comments:

> [C]ustomary international law is not static; it is constantly evolving. . . . This evolution is exemplified by the customary law of piracy itself. At one stage, piracy was defined as robbery on the high seas and material gain was a necessary element; at a later stage *animus furandi* was no longer required. Just as Viscount Sankey and Justice Story held that actual robbery was not an essential element of piracy, so a judge today might reasonably conclude that the laws of piracy should apply to terrorist attacks even though the motive was something other than personal gain. The exemption for insurgents would not exclude present-day terrorists, since it applied only to insurgents who confined their attacks to a particular state. (1998, p. 289)

After the attack on the USS *Cole* in October 2000 and the September 11th attacks a year later, it became clear to Western powers that maritime terrorism was a clear and present danger that required multilateral cooperation. The United States has taken the lead in broadening the meaning of current agreements on piracy in the hope of covering these gaps without recourse to new negotiations. No specific rules governed the transshipment of weapons of mass destruction or the use of oil tankers to attack environmental targets, for example (Chalk 1998, p. 6; Becker 2005, p. 206;

Barry 2004; Kash 1993). The United States has also expanded statutory law to allow it to extend its powers of interdiction far beyond the territorial waters and even beyond the two hundred-mile Exclusive Economic Zone for the sake of combating drug trafficking and to defend the national security. U.S, courts have validated seizures as far as 700 miles off the coast, but other states are skeptical of the legality of these actions (Sorek 1983).

These efforts have met with tepid responses from governments—especially those in the developing world. Legal analysts also express skepticism about the legitimacy of US statutes that grant expansive prerogatives to intercept suspected terrorists on the high seas. As Buhler explains:

> First, there is still no clearly recognized right to pursue, seize and punish pirates irrespective of nationality of the victims, perpetrators and situs of the incident. Second, despite a U.S. statutory provision possibly encompassing the acts of political terrorists and guerillas in the definition of piracy, it is unclear if that broad coverage will be accepted by other participating states. (1999, p. 68)

The United States has recently promoted a new strategy for dealing with terror threats at sea. Dubbed the Proliferation Security Initiative, the program envisions a network of bilateral agreements between participants that would allow reciprocal searches of ships and extradition of suspects. Participants promise to amend domestic legislation to strengthen rules against the unauthorized shipment of nuclear materials and other weapons of mass destruction, albeit outside of the rubric of the nonproliferation treaty (U.S. Department of State 2005). The initiative involves mostly industrialized Western states and bypasses the cumbersome multilateral institutions the administration of George W. Bush has tended to disdain (Murphy 2004). Its legality is also questioned because it appears to violate traditional norms of freedom of the seas. Interception of suspect vessels may be acceptable under various provisions of fishing law (Becker 2005, p. 201), although Canada has met with opposition when exercising this authority. After intercepting Spanish fishing ships to stop them from overfishing endangered species, the European Union accused Canada of piracy (Teece 1997, p. 95).

In sum, the political exception to the definition of piracy appears to remain fairly strong. Rather than address politicized violence at sea under existing piracy laws, states created new instruments. Their origins can be found in decisions by the British Admiralty Courts to exclude attacks by politically motivated seafarers against their own governments on the grounds that intervention constituted inappropriate interference in domestic politics of foreign states. The rule congealed rather quickly and was codified without much debate, first in the tentative statement by Harvard-sponsored legal researchers in 1932 and later in the 1958 and 1982 Conventions on the Law of the Sea. It was not until the 1985 attack on the *Achille Lauro* that the political exception was scrutinized. The Rome Convention partially filled the gaps in existing law, but did not clearly remove the political exception—even for terrorism. As we will see, one of the unique provisions of piracy law is universal jurisdiction. This allows any state to apprehend anyone accused of piracy, regardless of the nationality of the attacker or the victim or its location (so long as the attack takes place on the high seas). Thus the Rome statute, by separating terrorism at sea from piracy, does not provide for universal jurisdiction. In fact, it provides for the conventional "prosecute or extradite" principle discussed in greater detail in the chapter on antiterror law.

Since 9/11, Western powers have sought a narrower interpretation of the political exception, such that pirates who attack a wide range of targets, and thus represent a threat to all humanity, could be considered "pirates." This view has not yet been accepted. Consequently, Western states are attempting to reinterpret enforcement provisions of other treaties that do not explicitly address piracy. This involves both multilateral and unilateral initiatives, informal and statutory.

Jurisdiction over Piratical Acts

Of central importance in defining the parameters of piracy has been the question of enforcement. Under international law, there are several different justifications for apprehending and trying a suspect in a crime. The territorial principle is the most frequently invoked because states are entitled to prosecute acts by anyone committed in their own territory. Territory has been understood to include some part of the coastal waters, although the extent has been disputed. The nationality principle allows states to request extradition of criminal suspects that carry their citizenship. Likewise, claims of jurisdiction based on the passive personality principle (the country of nationality of the victim of a crime exercises jurisdiction over the perpetrator) or the protective principle (a country asserts jurisdiction over the perpetrator of a crime that, though committed outside its territory, threatens its security or integrity). The latter two forms of jurisdiction require the cooperation of the state where the crime occurred. We have seen already that states may refuse such cooperation, even when relations between the countries are good and extradition treaties are in place (recall the refusal of Italy to extradite the *Achille Lauro* suspects).

A more rarely invoked principle is that of universal jurisdiction. It means that any state may try any criminal suspect that falls into its hands on the grounds that the crime in question falls into a limited category of crimes against mankind as a whole. This category includes piracy, slave trading, genocide, hijacking, war crimes, and, many would argue, torture (Garmon 2002, p. 260). In most cases, universal jurisdiction is based on customary law, although this has occasionally been codified (Randall 1988, p. 791).

Where piracy is concerned, until the eighteenth century the debate over jurisdiction primarily involved a debate over the extent of territorial waters. Because piracy was first and foremost a domestic crime, control over a territorial sea entitled states to arrest pirates found there (they were simply treated as coastal thieves). Almost all states claimed special prerogatives in that part of the sea closest to their shorelines. This typically was thought to extend two or three nautical miles. Even non-Western states made the same types of claims (Khaliliel 1998, p. 140). A few states attempted to extend this area unilaterally, although they invariably encountered resistance and at any rate found they lacked the capacity to act on the claim. England, for example, claimed the entire English Channel during the 1300s, although its neighbors disregarded the claim (Marcus 1961, p. 16). We have already addressed the world's reaction to the unrealistic claims of control over the oceans by Spain and Portugal in connection with the Treaty of Tordesillas.

Because states could generally control activities near their coastlines, especially by the eighteenth century, there was no need to draft international agreements on coastal theft. Piracy, from the beginning, was understood to involve acts beyond these coastal areas. And because piratical acts took place beyond the scope of national law enforcement, states began to adopt new understandings of their enforcement powers. Spain did not hesitate to apprehend and try pirates from any nation that attacked her vessels on the high seas. Spain also entered into a variety of bilateral agreements with other states, pledging mutual enforcement of antipiracy statutes (Richardson 1990). These agreements were routinely breached, however, as we have seen.

With England's assertion of the freedom of the seas, a new principle emerged. Because navigating the high seas was a right enjoyed by all, pirates were a threat to the interests of all seafaring states, regardless of which countries' ships were attacked. Over time, each major seafaring state enacted domestic laws banning piracy, classifying it as a capital offense (Kontorovich 2004a, p. 114). The global network of domestic laws gave pirates no safe havens. In addition, because pirates, by definition, repudiated their flag state, pirates did not have any defenders. Note that this was the key point of letters of marque—failure to secure them (a remarkably easy thing to do) placed the pirate outside the state system and made him an enemy of all. As stateless actors that threatened all, it was a fairly short step to infer that any state could take action against any of them. Kontorovich elaborates on the logic of universal jurisdiction over piracy:

> [A] combination of six characteristics allowed piracy to become and remain a universally cognizable offense against the law of nations. First, piracy was a crime in the municipal law of all nations; international law merely reflected an already ubiquitous condemnation of the conduct. Second, piracy had a narrow and universally agreed on definition. . . . Third, all nations made piracy punishable by death. Thus universal jurisdiction would not lead to forum shopping. . . . Fourth, and perhaps most importantly, pirates were private actors who had refused the protection of their home states by failing to obtain a letter of marque. . . . They could expect little succor from their home state, since they had turned their backs on it. . . . Fifth, piracy occurred on the high seas. While this did not make traditional jurisdictional limitations moot, it did make conventional enforcement difficult, and thus universal jurisdiction might seem an attractive auxiliary to domestic prosecution. Finally, pirates indiscriminately attacked the ships of all nations, as they were not constrained by ties of national loyalty or the limitations contained in a letter of marque. . . . (2004a, p. 114)

In the 1500s, exercise of universal jurisdiction typically involved seizure of offending ships and summary justice at sea (Paladini 2004, p. 41). England and Spain gradually moved to conduct formal trials in London, Madrid, and regional capitals during the 1600s but still focused primarily on cases where their own vessels were attacked or the pirates claimed English or Spanish nationality. It was not until the 1700s that states began to assert jurisdiction over foreign vessels and/or pirates. In 1701, the trial of William Kidd was a landmark in that he (a British subject) had attacked a French vessel even while he was sailing under a French commission. The crime consisted of his having exceeded the parameters of his commission, for which his status as privateer was revoked and he was hanged as a pirate (Rubin 1988, p. 96).

It was not until the 1800s, however, that the U.K. and France systematically exercised universal jurisdiction (Pérotin-Dumon 2001, p. 29). This stemmed in large part from their dramatically expanded naval capabilities. The Royal Navy nearly doubled in size between 1793 and 1805, from 500 to almost 950 vessels, and reached a peak strength of 150,000 seamen in 1810 (Royal Navy 2005). This put the U.K. in a position to defeat the Algerine corsairs in 1816 (Lowenheim 2003, p. 40). The strength of the French fleet allowed it to invade the area in 1830, thus bringing to an end the Barbary pirates (Silverstein 2005, p. 194). The United States was also expanding its own navy.

The United States was ahead of Britain with respect to assertions of universal jurisdiction during the early-nineteenth century. This stemmed from Justice Joseph Story's presence on the Supreme Court; he was a natural law advocate and strong believer in international law (Rubin 1988, p. 163). In a series of cases between 1818 and 1855, the Court considered the government's jurisdiction over pirates. Story consistently sided with an expansive view on the grounds that pirates were enemies of humanity and that any state could and should prosecute them (Paladini 2004, p. 42). Chief Justice John Marshall, a legal positivist, had urged the Congress to pass an antipiracy act (passed in 1819) to explicitly authorize seizure of pirates on the high seas (Buhler 1999, p. 64). Armed with this legislation, the Court ruled in favor of universal jurisdiction in *U.S. v. Klintock* (1820) and *U.S. v. Smith* (1820), in which Story wrote for a majority which included Justice John Marshall (White 1989, p. 732). In 1844 and 1855, however, Justice Story was unable to persuade his colleagues on the Court to extend US jurisdiction over piratical acts that did not in some way directly involve US actors (Rubin 1988, p. 148).

In 1832, the British Admiralty Court ruled that Spaniards who attacked an American ship on the high seas could be subjected to British law, although the suspects were eventually extradited as a gesture of good will (Rubin 1988, p. 138). In 1853, the Magellan Pirates case (mentioned previously) implicitly authorized the Royal Navy to engage in military enforcement against piratical acts, as defined (rather loosely) by the Navy. By the 1870s, the United Kingdom was asserting application of its own Admiralty Law around the globe. This included "hovering rights" at three-hundred miles from shore for the purpose of apprehending smugglers (Masterson 1929, p. 104). In an 1864 case, Britain tried British pirates in connection with their seizure of an American vessel, denying extradition to the United States in part on grounds of universal jurisdiction (Kontorovich 2004, p. 230). In 1871, the United Kingdom tried a Chinese national who had mutinied on a French ship (Rubin 1988, p. 241).

As we see also in the chapter on the slave trade, in the late-nineteenth century the Royal Navy knew no limits to its right to apprehend foreign ships engaged in illegal acts. This said, the Admiralty Court sided with the defendant in a case involving naval pursuit of a pirate up a river deep into Chinese territory (Rubin 1988, p. 249). For all practical purposes, the Royal Navy felt it had jurisdiction over piracy and the slave trade anywhere, from the shores of Britain to edges of the territorial waters of every other state (particularly weaker states in the developing world). One could argue that this was not so much universal jurisdiction as a global version of territorial jurisdiction, particularly since very few other states (notably the U.S.) respected and imitated the principle.

Once the United Kingdom began to lose its Empire in the 1930s, its expansive views could no longer be sustained in practice. This was reflected in the consensus among the Harvard Draft authors that pursuit of pirates into the territorial waters of foreign states could not occur without their consent (Rubin 1988, p. 315). With the end of the Second World War, the U.K. endorsed a narrow view of territorial waters for itself and the rest of the world. By 1958, general agreement was reached on a three-mile territorial waters limit within which the state had full sovereign rights with a few exceptions (innocent passage, e.g.).

Meanwhile, the United States was beginning to exercise universal jurisdiction—or at least claim it—in a manner reminiscent of Britain one hundred years earlier. Consistent with the Supreme Court's decision in *U.S. v. Flores* (1933), the official policy of the U.S. government in 1941 was that it held universal jurisdiction over piracy and all attacks against U.S. shipping (Buhler 1999, p. 76). This view was further supported by the Permanent Court of International Justice which ruled in the 1927 *Lotus Case* that "By [the] law of nations ... [as a matter of] universal jurisdiction, under which the person charged with the offence may be tried and punished by any nation into whose jurisdiction he may come. . . . [The pirate] is treated as an outlaw, as the enemy of all mankind—*hostis humani generis*—whom any nation may in the interest of all capture and punish" (Goodman 1999, p. 149).These crosscurrents left the issue of universal jurisdiction in a perplexing condition by the 1950s. Since the U.K. had clearly asserted this prerogative for nearly a century, and because the United States and the PCIJ endorsed this view, the argument could be made that it was international custom. Any doubt was removed when universal jurisdiction was enshrined in the 1958 Geneva Convention on the High Seas and again in the 1982 UNCLOS. But the practice of states belies this position and may lead one to the conclusion that it is more rhetorical than real. Some question whether, for example, the Lotus case was precedential (McGinley 1985, p. 709). More significantly, "universal jurisdiction over pirates was more a matter of theory than of practice. . . . [V]ery few criminal prosecutions for piracy can be found that depended on the universal principle. Moreover, some nations, such as the United States, did not allow their courts to exercise universal jurisdiction over piracy" (Kontorovich 2004, p. 192). It is, in fact, difficult (perhaps impossible) to locate a single case that was successfully prosecuted only on the basis of universal jurisdiction (Scharf and Fischer 2001, p. 228).

As mentioned earlier, in 1958, states agreed to a narrow band of territorial waters. Shortly after reaching this agreement, however, newly independent countries resented conceding control of waters just beyond this limit, noting that European and North American fishing interests were doing a strong business there. They began to claim additional territory in the high seas, up to twelve miles and sometimes beyond. Emboldened by the US claims over the continental shelf, many countries also claimed special prerogatives miles beyond these territorial claims—a special zone in which foreign states would be required to seek permission for economic activities. Some even claimed territorial waters rights out to two hundred miles from the shoreline. Ultimately, Western states conceded the creation of an Exclusive Economic Zone (EEZ) extending to two hundred nautical miles in exchange for a limit of twelve miles for territorial waters (Sebenius 1984).

The rights of states within the EEZ created some ambiguities with respect to piracy law. On the one hand, the EEZ is not, strictly speaking, the high seas. Coastal states may bar economic activity for the sake of resource preservation and environmental protection, for example, and may charge a royalty for activities that are approved (Garmon 2002, p. 265). On the other hand, it is clear that the EEZs are not territorial waters, in that states do not have the authority to enforce domestic criminal law as a general rule. To help clarify the rule, Article 58 of the 1982 UNCLOS states that Articles 88–115 (related to the law of the high seas, including piracy) apply to the EEZ "insofar as they are not incompatible with the provisions of the EEZ and comply with the laws and regulations adopted by the relevant coastal state" (Keyuan 2000, p. 111). According to Ethan Stiles, "The piracy provisions seem to apply to the exclusive economic zone as well as the high seas" (2004, p. 307). This said, it is unclear whether a state could try a pirate seized in another state's EEZ, a question that has yet to be tested in court (Keyuan 2000, p. 111).

In practice, governments have avoided arresting pirates in the territorial waters and even the EEZ of other states, which has created significant problems in those parts of the world where piracy is resurgent. Pirate attacks (including those taking place in port or within states' territorial waters) have risen from an average of just over 100 per year in 1991–94 to more than 215 per year in 1995–98 and 363 per year in 1999–2003 (Stiles 2004, p. 300). Roughly half of these have taken place in Southeast Asia, consistent with the fact that half of the world's shipping passes through this region (Barrios 2005, p. 151). The bulk of the attacks occur within territorial waters. Attacks around Indonesia occur, on average, just under twelve miles from shore (Dubner 1997, p. 26). In Bangladesh, the port operators in Chittagong are responsible for facilitating most attacks on shipping, the bulk of which take place while ships are docked. Attacks on the high seas are performed increasingly by arms of organized crime syndicates, and sometimes involve seizure of a ship and its cargo *in toto*. Ship manifests are often replaced and even the name of the vessel is painted over. Such "ghost ships" then unload their cargo in secret or even legitimate off-loading facilities (Chalk 1998, p. 3). Though the total cost of piracy for the shipping industry is relatively low, the human cost is rising (Dubner 1997, p. 8). Hundreds of crewmen and passengers have been killed in pirate attacks since 1990. Certain ports have earned the reputation of "pirate havens," leading shipping companies to simply avoid them wherever possible, with serious effects on the local economy (5). Considerable evidence shows that the People's Republic of China poses a threat to the region, not only because of its extreme territorial claims in the South China Sea and associated military operations but also because of indications it is aiding and abetting pirates in the region (Hunter 1999).

For much of the 1990s, the nations of the region resisted outside efforts to apprehend pirates and strictly enforced their territorial waters rights.

Because many of the most heavily trafficked straits in the region straddle international boundaries, it has been relatively easy for pirates to attack in one country's territorial waters and to simply travel ten or twenty miles to escape into the territorial waters of another country (see Figure 2.2). Until recently, states in the region have taken a very restrictive view of the "right of hot pursuit", which originally permitted states chasing pirates in their own territorial waters to continue the chase into another state's territorial waters to a certain point (usually ten miles or so). Now, the view developing countries advocate is that hot pursuit only applies to chasing pirates away from the coast into the high seas. As put by the Director of Malaysia's coast guard, "Under no circumstances would we intrude into each other's territory. If we chase a ship and it runs into the other side, we let the authorities there handle it" (Chalk 1998, p. 21). The result is a severe impediment to enforcement of piracy laws, creating a gap between treaty and reality (Becker 2005, p. 134).

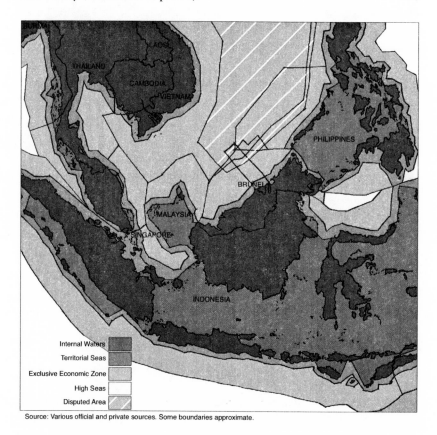

Source: Various official and private sources. Some boundaries approximate.

Figure. 2.2 Territorial Seas and EEZs in Southeast Asia.

UNCLOS is permissive with respect to regional initiatives to enforce the law of the sea (Goodman 1999, p. 158). Although such efforts have been slow to emerge, there are signs that some states are willing to coordinate intelligence sharing, clarify rules on hot pursuit, and even collaborate in seizures across borders. Several examples are noteworthy. Neighboring states Indonesia and Malaysia as well as Vietnam and Thailand have developed bilateral agreements on coordinated sea patrols in pursuit of pirates (Chalk 1998, p. 21). Hermann reports many other efforts: (1) ASEAN states have met regularly to coordinate security and law enforcement policies, beginning in 2000 in Mumbai; (2) Improved communication links between Singapore and Indonesia, allowing their respective navies to communicate in real-time; (3) Agreements between Indonesia, Malaysia, and Singapore on the mutual deployment of police forces to assist merchant shipping, a sort of "regional 9-1-1"; (4) Joint ocean patrols between Malaysia and the Philippines, and (5) An exchange of maritime liaison officers between Indonesia and the Philippines (Hermann 2004, p. 22). In late 2003, the PRC conducted joint naval exercises with India to train their respective naval patrol forces against piratical and other attacks (Hermann 2004, p. 22). Given the multiplicity of regional agreements in the developing world, the possibility of "piggybacking" security agreements seems high (Goodman 1999, pp. 162–3).

Finally, even as questions arise with respect to the practical use of universal jurisdiction in combating piracy, countries and legal scholars have often used piracy as an analogy to extend universal jurisdiction to other crimes. As we have seen in this chapter and in the chapter on slavery, the British government equated slave trading with piracy early in the nineteenth century, thereby helping to justify its campaign to apprehend slave traders from any country operating in any sea. In more recent years, jurists in Belgium and Spain have applied the piracy analogy to genocide and war crimes, claiming universal jurisdiction where no specific treaty language could be found. Their reasoning is as follows: piracy is a crime against the entire world because it is heinous and indiscriminate (Blakesley 1982, p. 1139). In the case of genocide and war crimes, the entire world is equally threatened since the crimes are also heinous and indiscriminate; therefore, every state has a right and a duty to arrest and prosecute suspects (Newton 1996, p. 63).

Where universal jurisdiction has been codified (see, e.g., the Torture Convention), this analogy is unnecessary. In other cases, however, it raises concerns. As we have seen, from the sixteenth century, states routinely authorized the use of force against enemy targets by private mariners even though their tactics and practices were essentially identical to those of pirates. The key distinction was that the captain had state license to carry out the attacks. Piracy, as pointed out by Kontorovich, was not considered "heinous" and could not be considered a "crime against humanity" because states had authorized it (Kontorovich 2004, p. 217). By and large, pirates were merely thieves at sea, and most states had no trouble adopting laws to regulate their behavior within territorial waters. It was the legal characteristics of the high seas that presented the problem, as we have seen. When genocide and war crimes take place within a state territory under the control of a government, the piracy story has no relevance.

In sum, the question of jurisdiction has moved along two paths: theoretical and practical. At the theoretical level, states have generally accepted universal jurisdiction over piracy, limited of course to acts on the high seas. This was done in the name of protecting freedom of the seas and because of the lack of national jurisdiction over the high seas and stateless pirates. At the same time, however, states showed remarkable reticence to act on this principle, based both on the lack of capability and on conflicting principles of jurisdiction. The result was that states prosecuted pirates when they or their victims were nationals. Even when the British prosecuted foreign nationals in the late-nineteenth century, it is not at all certain whether they did so with reference to universal jurisdiction or under an expansive view of national enforcement powers.

Ultimately, the decline of British naval power and the emergence of newly independent developing countries gave rise to significantly bolder claims of national jurisdiction over the seas. By implication, much less of the earth's oceans were high seas, which automatically limited the number of incidents at sea that could be safely called piracy. Since the recent rise in the number of piratical attacks, however, there are indications that developing countries are more willing to agree to ad hoc, regional arrangements to facilitate apprehension and prosecution of pirates.

Conclusions

Rules against piracy have always been the subject of considerable debate and challenge. Until the nineteenth century, many states employed or tolerated private navies. The prohibition of pirates and privateers was as much the product of power and technology as it was of consensus on values and principles. A key trigger for the development of antipiracy rules was the introduction of steel-hulled ships into national navies. More potent navies allowed states to exert more effective control over territorial seas and reduced the need to rely on privateers. At the same time, pirate ships could not compete with the larger, stronger steel ships of modern navies.

It seems ironic, in retrospect, that international law against piracy made considerable advances—in 1932 and 1958—at a time when the issue had been largely forgotten by the public. It was during this period that what had previously been rather informal and often ill-conceived policy statements in the United Kingdom, France, and the United States (many of which consisted simply of court decisions decided by majority vote) were codified as though sacrosanct. Such was the case with universal jurisdiction and the exclusion of political acts. By the end of the twentieth century, these rules proved virtually unworkable in practice, as states demurred from exercising universal jurisdiction but were prevented from protecting themselves against seafaring terrorists.

The model offered in Chapter 1 explicitly incorporates the role of power in the development and consolidation of norms, and this dynamic is readily apparent where piracy is concerned. This said, powerful states, seeking primarily to protect their own interests, were often guilty of defining the crime so narrowly as to expose themselves and their citizens to attack. Exogenous shocks thus exposed inconsistencies and contradictions in the formulation of international law. For example, powerful states sought permission to endorse the activities of oceangoing guerrillas, depending on relations with the target state. The result was that when Palestinian terrorists attacked the *Achille Lauro*, there was no international law governing the incident. Likewise, attacks by land-based mobs against foreign ships in port were not unlawful under the various antipiracy conventions. Nor was the seizure of a ship containing nuclear weapons by a mutinous crew considered piracy.

States have improvised in order to remain faithful to existing rules while still protecting the security of shipping. In the case of sea-based attacks for political purposes, new legal instruments drew on the incipient law against terrorism, rather than on existing antipiracy norms (see Chapter 5 on terrorism). Arrangements to seize WMDs on the high seas have been ad hoc and of questionable legality. As far as the onshore mob, the response is generally left to the market as shipping companies seek out safer harbors.

Chapter 3

The End of Conquest: Consolidating Sovereign Equality

Brook Gotberg

One of the most dramatic ways in which actors challenge the international status quo is through aggressive war, particularly when states annex territory by conquest. Conquest has at times been applauded, at times tolerated, and eventually condemned. In other words, norms regarding the rights of conquest have altered substantially from the beginning of the state system to the present. Whereas earlier conquerors, such as Marc Antony, Alexander the Great, and Napoleon enjoyed international acclaim for their military prowess, today would-be conquerors such as Saddam Hussein face broad, and potentially forcible, international opposition. Modern norms of self-determination and territorial integrity have replaced the right of conquest; conquest is no longer legitimate. The development of norms against conquest exemplifies the cycle of actions, arguments, rule change, and consolidation of new norms. Key developments in the emergence of rules prohibiting conquest occurred in response to disputes triggered by specific wars.

Conquest was, for much of history, the victor's right to annex or control territory captured in war (Korman 1996, 8). Until the end of World War I, the classical system of international law validated claims for territory annexed as a result of aggressive warfare (106). Under international norms, conquered territory was legally acquired, and had to be so recognized by third parties (Langer 1947, v). Typically, the two warring parties signed a peace treaty and drafted a decree of annexation signifying legal transfer of sovereignty (Korman 1996, 99). A conquest was complete when the surrendering state no longer claimed the lost territory and did not continue to fight for its recovery (Hyde 1922; Oppenheim 1952–1955; Wilson 1935). Philosophical thinkers such as More, Vattel, and Kent all justified conquest in the name of advancing civilization (Korman 1996). As stated by Heinrich von Treitschke, "the great strides which civilization makes against barbarism and unreason are only made actual by the sword" (61).

In recent history, states have become less tolerant of conquest and in some cases dedicate both military and financial resources to stop aggressors. The behavior of would-be conquerors also provides evidence of the new norm. Whereas in the more distant past, expansionary states would have invoked a right of conquest, more recently they tend to characterize their behavior as a justified exception to the rule against conquest. Especially in the United Nations era, those seeking gain international recognition for acts of aggression face an uphill battle. Generally, attempts at justification revolve around assertions of self-defense, prior or superior territorial claims, and occasionally the contention that the conquered "country" was not a sovereign entity. The level of success that belligerent states have in convincing the international community that their actions were an exception to the rule also contributes to shaping the norms.

A set of case studies examines the cycle theory of international norm change with respect to rules on conquest. Each case represents a key cycle of norm change. The cases include Germany's 1870 annexation of Alsace-Lorraine, World War I, Japan's transformation of Manchuria into the puppet state "Manchukuo" during the early years of the League of Nations, the Nazi invasions of Czechoslovakia and Poland leading up to World War II, North Korea's 1950 invasion of South Korea at the beginning of the Cold War, and the 1990 Iraqi invasion of Kuwait at the Cold

War's end. The cases are not just wars (which, of course, have been more numerous), but wars for the purpose of annexing territory. Each demonstrates the evolution of international responses to conquest: the sometimes uneasy acceptance of justifications gives way to definitive rejection of conquest and nonrecognition of forcible annexations. The United Nations Charter codified the international norm against conquest and aggression. Although initially rejected by some of the world's most powerful actors, including the Soviet Union and China, by the end of the Cold War, the norm against conquest was firmly established. Figure 3.1 depicts the cycles of development of norms against conquest.

Alsace Lorraine

Our examination of rights surrounding territorial acquisition begins at the point where the right of conquest began to conflict with norms of self-determination and territorial integrity. The development of arguments challenging the right of the victor to conquered territory was slow, almost imperceptible. However, as states embraced the norms of territorial integrity and self-determination, they were more hesitant to recognize the legality of acquiring territory by military means.

Otto von Bismarck annexed the French provinces of Alsace and Lorraine following the Franco-Prussian war of 1870. Though powerful states ultimately accepted Bismarck's justification or at least ceased to protest it, the annexation raised questions within the international community regarding a victor's right to territory, particularly when conquest was against the wishes of the land's inhabitants. The normative background for the conflict of 1870 was influenced by ideals brought forth in the French Revolution almost a century before, in particular, the right of self-determination for nations and peoples. On May 22, 1790, the new National Assembly of France ratified Title VI of their recently drafted Constitution, which read, "the French nation renounces the undertaking of any war for the purpose of conquest, and . . . will never employ its forces against the liberty of any people" (Korman 1996, 121). This renunciation of conquest did not last long; Napoleon shortly thereafter conquered most of Western Europe. However, the arguments against conquest had been introduced into international discourse. Indeed, Napoleon felt compelled to seek explicit recognition from the international community for his territorial acquisitions (Langer 1947, 3).

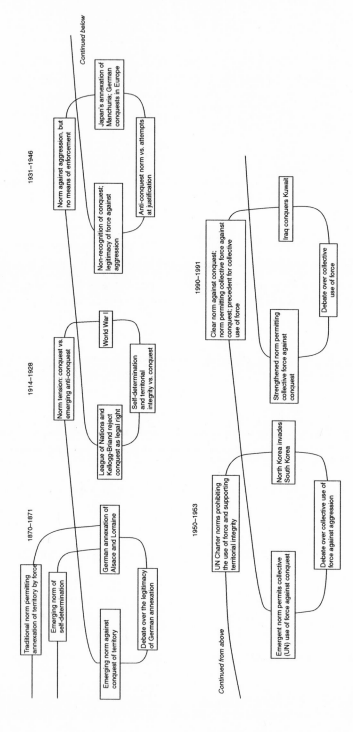

Figure 3.1 Anticonquest norm cycles.

Still, at that time, there were no international rules in Europe forbidding conquest. As Brownlie notes,

> Apart from the functioning of the public law of Europe, which
> had some characteristics of a constitutional law, the right of
> states to go to war and to obtain territory by right of conquest
> was unlimited although some qualifications to this position
> had appeared by 1914. Situations resulting from resort to force
> were regarded as legally valid as in the case of the Prussian
> annexation of the Danish duchies and the annexation of
> Alsace-Lorraine by the German Empire. (Brownlie 1963, 20)

However, the legal right to conquest was countered by an emerging "anti-
conquest" norm, based on the right of self-determination. The tension
between these two principles led to norm change, as events triggered disputes about international rules. Though the international community in
the end accepted Bismarck's annexations, it questioned his motives and
demanded justification.

As remarked by Emile Ollivier, the French prime minister during
the Franco-Prussian war, "the real author of the war, he who willed it,
sought it, premeditated it, prepared it, rendered it inevitable at the
appointed moment, was Bismarck" (Lord 1966, 4). Bismarck himself reaffirmed this statement by boasting in his memoirs of how he strategically
reworded the famous "Ems Telegram" to goad the French into declaring
war (Lord 1966, 5; Wetzel 2001, 151). Bismarck revised the telegram,
describing a meeting between King Wilhelm and the French Ambassador,
to create a version of the story that was insulting to both sides. He then
published his revision without informing the French. Bismarck used the
subsequent German indignation to unify and strengthen the state,
responding to French hostility by creating a German empire and acquiring Alsace and Lorraine as a buffer against France.

The initial debate between the King of Prussia and Napoleon III,
Emperor of France, was over the candidacy of a Hohenzollern-Sigmaringen
prince for the throne of Spain. Disagreements over the claim appeared ame-
nable to a peaceful resolution, but Bismarck exploited the conflict as a pretext
to increase German territory and to assert Germany's military supremacy.
He and others in the German government pressured King Wilhelm of Prussia
not to give in to "French insolence" and even to hold back from compromis-
ing with the French (Lord 1966, 34–5). Indeed, Bismarck pushed the quarrel

in the hopes that the French would—as they eventually did—declare war. He considered advising the Prussian King to begin hostilities even though this would decrease Prussia's moral legitimacy in the war later on. By not attacking, Prussia escaped the label of aggressor in the eyes of the international community, a factor that proved to be important in Bismarck's eventually successful conquest. For this reason the French were also slow in declaring war, much to Bismarck's frustration: when it appeared that there might be no war, Bismarck threatened to summon the North German parliament for the purpose of submitting his resignation (Wetzel 2001, 140).

In truth, conquest of Alsace-Lorraine was not Bismarck's primary goal. Instead, he was focused on the unification and security of Germany, and the nationalistic cause of "liberating" Alsace-Lorraine, a region that had some linguistic and cultural ties to Germany, was a useful tool to achieve that goal (Lord 1966, 11; Silverman 1972, 29). Alsace did have some remote historical linkages to Germany (Bankwitz 1978, 4; Silverman 1972, 9); Lorraine's ties to Germany were even more remote than those of Alsace (Silverman 1972, 8–9).

In spite of their somewhat tenuous claims to the territories, the German people were enthusiastic about reclaiming Alsace and Lorraine. Calls for annexation were circulated extensively in the German press (Feuchtwanger 2002, 172). German academics laid claim to the territories on the basis of ethnic and racial similarities. Bismarck privately ridiculed this argument, calling it a "professorial idea" (173), and claimed the territories in the name of security (Silverman 1972, 29). As the German nationalist historian Heinrich von Treitschke indicated, the ethnic basis for reclaiming the territory was a ruse; even if the Alsatians had been Japanese, Germany would have annexed them to capitalize on their strategic position in relation to France (Monod n.d., 151, quoted in Silverman 1972, 30). Bismarck felt that annexation would support the creation of a German empire (Silverman 1972, 34). The idea was strongly supported by German public opinion, and France's arguments against the transfer were undercut by its having initiated the war.

Still, though earlier centuries saw annexation of conquered land as expected and commonplace, increasing opposition to conquest caused some discomfort among European nations at the time: "to the nineteenth century, with its growing belief in national self-determination and plebiscitary voting, the process, carried out in defiance of the wishes of the populations, seemed an open flouting of that public law on whose development Europe was beginning to pride itself" (Korman 1996, 92). Great Britain, in particular, worked to involve the international community during the siege of Paris, and Prime Minister Gladstone expressed his abhorrence of the idea of annexing Alsace-Lorraine (Feuchtwanger 2002, 175). As he states in a memorandum, "My opinion certainly is that the transfer of territory & inhabitants by mere force calls for the reprobat[ion] of Europe, & that Europe is entitled to utter it" (Millman 1965, 211).

According to letters from King Wilhelm to his wife, the neutral powers, particularly Russia, also complained about Prussia violating France's integrity by annexing the territories. Although these complaints were never backed with any threat of force, they were enough to make King Wilhelm uneasy about the process. To avoid international criticism, Crown Prince Friedrich Wilhelm sought a way to punish France by taking the territory away without adding on to the territory of Prussia or Germany, avoiding too great a breach of the status quo (Silverman 1972, 30, 32).

Bismarck, on the other hand, had no patience for the King's hesitation or the Crown Prince's suggestion. Despite the criticisms, the general sense in Europe seemed to be that France only received her just desserts as the initial aggressor. There was a tacit consensus that Germany had the right to possess the territories as protection against further French aggression, hence the annexation was legally valid (Korman 1996, 93). The seizure was, in part, "justified by the consideration that France was a nation with a record of constant aggression which she could not be trusted not to renew at the first opportunity" (90). Even Gladstone, although he later opposed the annexation, initially reacted to the idea impassively: "You know that if it [the war] had been successful France would have demanded territory, and got it. . . . She cannot plead the doctrine of inviolability" (Millman 1965, 211). Instead, Gladstone sought to promote the standard of self-determination on behalf of the Alsatians and Lorrainians, the standard that would be most frequently used in later disputes surrounding conquest.

Germans, of course, tended to defend the legality of the annexation. The views of German general and military writer Friedrich von Bernhardi may not have been extreme within Germany: "since almost every part of the globe is inhabited, new territory must, as a rule, be obtained at the cost of its possessors—that is to say, by conquest, which thus becomes a law of necessity" (1914, 21). Bernhardi wrote that "the right of conquest is universally acknowledged," and "might gives the right to occupy or conquer. Might is at once the supreme right, and the dispute as to what is right is decided by the arbitrament of war" (21, 23).

Europe and most of the world accepted the inevitability of conquest and the rights of the victor at the Peace Treaty of Frankfurt (10 May 1871), which gave the territories of Alsace and Lorraine to the victorious Germans. Europe had been introduced to the right of self-determination but the principle did not prevail over the longstanding international norm that legitimized conquest. Still, the complaints of neutral countries expressed disapproval of conquest, and the Treaty of Frankfurt gave expression to the emerging norms. Article 2 of the Treaty responded to demands for self-determination and rights for the inhabitants of the conquered territories. Even though Alsace and Lorraine were now part of German territory, under the Treaty, German citizenship was not required of inhabitants. In fact, residents were permitted to move to France if they wished to maintain their French citizenship, at the cost, of course, of giving up home and property (Tomczak 2002). An important shift had taken place. Prussia's annexation of Alsace-Lorraine was justified not in terms of a right to conquest, but as punishment for France having initiated hostilities and as necessary for German self-defense.

World War I and Versailles

Within a few decades of Bismarck's successful conquest, international norms made a dramatic shift against conquest for territorial gain. In fact, after a long period of peace in Europe, World War I shocked many countries into condemning all forms of aggression. Nations adopted an attitude of peace at all costs, "an idea whose time had come" (Mueller 1991, 1–28). European states came to a tacit agreement to respect one another's territorial integrity and moved toward colonialism instead, acquiring territory in non-European parts of the world.

By the late nineteenth century, states had begun to discuss methods for limiting aggression and establishing common security, but it was not until the end of World War I that these discussions created a shift in international norms (Langer 1947, 12, 16). In the decades prior to the war, states participated in a series of international conferences and treaties that began to address the subjects of conquest and the sanctity of territory. For example, at the Second Hague Peace Conference in 1907, Brazil submitted a proposal denying the right of conquest, "except where the other state had refused a proposal to arbitrate or disobeyed an award" (Brownlie 1963, 24). Still, the Hague Conferences concluded without prohibiting conquest and annexation.

Thus traditional norms of conquest remained in place up to World War I. As one legal scholar wrote during the war, "[o]f all the titles by which sovereigns hold and govern territories, title by conquest is now generally considered the least desirable. Nevertheless, having regard to international practice and to the fact that modern international law contains no provision to the contrary, it must be admitted that such a title is juridically valid. . . . [F]orcible annexation, however it be deprecated and condemned by international morality, is not forbidden by international law" (Phillipson 1916, 19, 31).

Only a year after this work was published, the Russian Revolution made a symbolic statement against conquest to the international community. The Russian Provisional Government stated on 10 April 1917 that, "Free Russia does not aim at dominating other nations, at depriving them of their national patrimony, or at occupying by force foreign territories; . . . its object is to establish a durable peace on the basis of the rights of nations to decide their own destiny" (Korman 1996, 136). In his speech at the All-Russian conference at the end of April that same year, Lenin made it clear that conquest was not in the interest of a proletariat state (Lenin 1964, 236–37). Russia offered the first international document to renounce all aggressive wars soon after at the Second All-Russian Conference on 8 November. This Decree of Peace denounced conquest as a crime against humanity (Rifaat 1979, 32–33). Russia's statement against conquest hinted at a shift in attitudes about annexing territory.

The entry of the United States into the War contributed to this transformation. Wilson expressed the U.S. attitude toward annexation and conquest of territory in his request for war made to Congress on 2 April 1917: "We desire no conquest, no dominion; we seek no indemnities for ourselves" (Wilson 1917). British Prime Minister Lloyd George also relinquished the right to conquest and promoted self-determination on behalf of Great Britain in his speech on war aims given 5 January 1918. He proclaimed that a "just and lasting peace," England's goal in the war, required "a territorial settlement . . . based on the right of self-determination or the consent of the governed" (George 1918). France joined the United States and Great Britain in denouncing conquest. In a memorandum to Italy, dated 9 December 1919, France stated that "it is neither just nor expedient to annex, as the spoils of war, territories inhabited by an alien race, anxious and able to maintain a separate national State" (Korman 1996, 144).

The rejection of conquest as a legal right became part of international law through the Covenant of the League of Nations in 1919. Article X of this Covenant stated that "[t]he Members of the League undertake to respect and preserve as against external aggression the territorial integrity and existing political independence of all Members of the League. In case of any such aggression or in case of any threat or danger of such aggression the Council shall advise upon the means by which this obligation shall be fulfilled" (League of Nations Charter IX). The norm of territorial integrity was thus established, and legitimacy denied to the former right of conquest (Brownlie 1963; Eagleton 1932; Wright 1935).

Less than ten years later, the Kellogg-Briand Pact of 1928 (also called the General Treaty for the Renunciation of War) outlawed all war. The first and second articles asserted, "the High Contracting Parties solemnly declare, in the names of their respective peoples, that they condemn recourse to war for the solution of international controversies, and renounce it as an instrument of national policy in their relations with one another . . . the settlement or solution of all disputes or conflicts of whatever nature or of whatever origin they may be . . . shall never be sought except by pacific means" (Kellogg-Briand Pact 1928).

Manchuria

The 1922 Nine-Power Treaty, signed during the Washington Conference of 1921–22, obligated its signatories "to respect the sovereignty, the independence, and the territorial and administrative integrity of China" (U.S. State Department 1922). Along with the League Covenant and the Kellogg-Briand Pact, the Nine Power Treaty would be the point of reference for arguments against the Manchurian campaign launched by Japan in September 1931. While each of these three documents figured in the debate over Manchuria, the Covenant bound the greatest number of nations and was referred to most extensively. It shaped the environment of the invasion and the subsequent debates by making war an international concern (Brownlie 1963, 57). As specified in Article XI:

> (1) Any war or threat of war, whether immediately affecting any of the Members of the League or not, is hereby declared a matter of concern to the whole League, and the League shall take any action that may be deemed wise and effectual to safeguard the peace of nations. In case any such emergency shall arise the Secretary-General shall on the request of any Member of the League forthwith summon a meeting of the Council. (2) It is also declared to be the friendly right of each Member

of the League to bring to the attention of the Assembly or of the Council any circumstance whatever affecting international relations which threatens to disturb international peace or the good understanding between nations upon which peace depends. (League of Nations, Charter XI)

Manchuria served as the "acid test" for the League of Nations and its condemnation of conquest, redefining the law and revealing the extent to which it would be enforced (Tohmatsu and Willmott 2004, 39).

In 1931 Manchuria was a large, underpopulated, fertile region inhabited mostly by workers from China, Japan, and Korea (Wiloughby 1935, 19). Despite its backward character, the territory had been a fundamental part of China since 1644, and the Chinese regarded it as integral to their nation (Wiloughby 1935, 20–21; Young 1928, 6). However, the land had been a bone of contention between China, Japan, and Russia for decades (Langer 1947, 50). By 1930, Japan, a rising power internationally and the undisputed leader in the Far East, coveted Manchuria (Tohmatsu and Willmott 2004, xxv, fn.8). Japan attacked on 18 September 1931, under the pretense of defending Japanese interests after an explosion damaged a Japanese railroad. By some accounts, the explosion had been planted by two Japanese junior officers (Mitter 2000, 4). A League of Nations Committee sent to investigate concluded that the Japanese attack was completely unprovoked and a surprise to the Chinese (Smith 1948, 21).

China decided not to declare war against Japan. In later statements to the Council of the League of Nations, the Chinese Representative indicated that China wished to uphold the League rules and keep its commitment to peace (Wiloughby 1935, 83–4). It is also likely that China feared utter defeat, following which, as rightful victors, Japan would be able to not only keep the territory they had claimed but also demand reparations (39). For whatever reason, neither side formally declared war throughout the duration of the Sino-Japanese disputes (27).

Almost immediately after the attack, the Chinese Representative to the League requested assistance under Article XI. Some question why China did not invoke Article X, which directly addressed aggression (Kuhn 1933, 96). Only after Japan had shown a determination to keep troops in Manchuria did China invoke Article X and Article XV of the Covenant (Wiloughby 1935, 38). But there was international precedent for using Article XI. In the Greco-Bulgar conflict of 1925, League Members had taken action under Article XI and effectively halted Greece's invasion.

Additionally, Article XI was flexible enough to give the League unqualified discretion in the course of action to take.

As a member of the League, Japan took great pains to convince the Council that its actions in Manchuria were not inconsistent with the League Charter. Rather than deny the validity of Article X and the law against conquest, Japan accepted and endorsed it. Japan saw the League of Nations as "an instrument for preserving territorial integrity," in particular Articles X and XXI (Fujii 1925, 59). Its defenses to the League were designed to legitimize Japanese behavior by making Manchuria an exception to this rule.

Japan's initial defense, maintained even after the release of the Lytton Report, was that Japanese armies had acted in self-defense and that the occupation had continued out of concern for Japanese nationals who were being targeted by anti-Japanese bandits (Smith 1948, 68–9). The mass demonstrations in China against Japanese involvement in that country lent some credence to this claim (Mitter 2000, 43). The argument was initially accepted by the League, which declined to intervene in the conflict.

Japan invoked other defenses that proved unconvincing for League members. One argument, directed particularly to the Western European members, was that the controversy was between China and Japan alone and that premature involvement from the League would only complicate the situation (Wiloughby 1935, 50). Japan argued that Western European members of the League were not qualified to judge actions that took place in the Far East (53). Japan also claimed that China, as a fairly new and disorganized entity, could not actually qualify as a state and therefore did not merit the League's protection. Although Britain accepted this argument, (Langer 1947, 60), its validity was questionable because Japan had voted along with all the other members to include China as a state-member of the League four days before the invasion (Wiloughby 1935, 29). Japan also attempted to deflect attention away from Manchuria by pointing blame at Russia for its conquest of Mongolia (260).

Japan's final line of defense, which worked to a large extent despite its obvious deviation from the truth, was a statement released to the League on September 25, after the matter had already received some discussion. The statement was an affidavit that Japan did not hold territorial designs on China and was not seeking to conquer Manchuria (Langer 1947, 62). The Japanese representatives frequently referred to this statement in subsequent discussions and, for the most part, the League Council took them at their word (Wiloughby 1935, 131, 242). As evidence of

Japanese sincerity, Japan argued that had it really intended to take Chinese territory, it would have done so immediately after the Russo-Japanese War when it had the chance (259).

Despite the League's investigation following the initial attack, Japan was not deterred from making further advances into Manchuria. On October 3, Japan bombed the city of Chinchow, where Chinese authorities had established a provisional government to replace the one forced out of Mukden. In so doing, Japan was blatantly seeking to destroy the civil administration, planning to replace the administration with a more "Japan friendly" regime (Smith 1948, 83). Following this attack, the Chinese Representative to the Council, Mr. Sze, made a statement to the League questioning its lack of commitment to keeping the peace and ensuring China's territorial integrity. He expressed the view that if the League did not act on this occasion, it would lack the legitimacy needed to act in the future (98).

In response, the League produced a Draft Resolution on 24 October, declaring that the Pact of Paris, the Covenant of the League of Nations, and the Nine-Power Treaty all required that Japan leave China (Smith 1948, 117). Spain, with other smaller nations in the League, including Czechoslovakia, Sweden, Poland, Peru, Panama, and Guatemala, condemned Japan's actions. As stated by the Spanish representative, "The League of Nations is based on respect for the territorial integrity and political independence of its Members . . . I would state that Article 10 is one of the most important articles of the Covenant" (Wiloughby 1935, 125). The smaller states expressed concern that lack of response to Japan's actions might damage respect for the rule, and expressed the importance of setting a good precedent in this case (191–94). As the representative from Romania indicated, "any weakening with regard to Article X, any fumbling in its unqualified application, would be a death-blow to the League" (292). Some of the larger states were more equivocal. Within the League, Canada and Great Britain seemed to favor the Japanese side at first but ultimately declared that it was impossible to justify permanent occupation of Manchuria (455). Outside the League, the United States applauded the League's resolution against Japan, extolling its "modern and enlightened methods" (187).

Japan recognized the importance placed on the norms of territorial integrity, and the negative view League-member states held of aggression. In a declaration read to the League on 26 October 1931, Japan expressed the "fundamental points" it required before reconciliation with China.

These were: (1) mutual repudiation of aggressive policy and conduct, and (2) respect for China's territorial integrity (Smith 1948, 135). The presumed intention for this declaration was to show that Japan respected the League norms against aggression and for territorial integrity, but that the conquest of Manchuria should be seen as an exception for the sake of Japanese security, an argument reminiscent of Bismarck's justification for annexing Alsace-Lorraine.

China's goal was to insure that the League saw Manchuria as a case of the very form of aggression that the Charter was written to control. On November 24, the Chinese representative to the League read a statement from his government calling on international law, specifically the League Covenant and the Pact of Paris, to condemn and resist the Japanese attacks:

> The Japanese Government should have, in observance of her obligations under international law, the League Covenant, and the Treaty for the Renunciation of War, as well as in fulfillment of her undertakings under the Resolution adopted by the League Council on September 30th, and that adopted on October 24, which has full moral force, completed withdrawal of her troops within the specified time-limit long ago, and no room is left for further argument. (Wiloughby 1935, 159)

The most conspicuous player missing from general debate on Manchuria was the United States. U.S. officials feared getting too involved. Secretary of State Henry Stimson explained U.S. foreign policy by saying, "we are not taking sides . . . we are 'playing no favorites'" (Clyde 1948, 195, 197). The Chinese Nationalist Government was irked by the "apathy" of the U.S. in the face of Japanese military action, and felt that "the American Government [was] in some way accountable for the apparent lessening of the League's first eagerness" (194).

However, by 7 January 1935, even the fence-sitting United States had announced the so-called Stimson Doctrine of Non-recognition, thereby accepting a norm adopted two years earlier by the League of Nations:

> The American Government deems it to be its duty to notify both the Government of the Chinese Republic and the Imperial Japanese Government that it can not [sic] admit the legality of any situation de facto nor does it intend to recognize any treaty or agreement entered into between those governments,

68 INTERNATIONAL NORMS AND CYCLES OF CHANGE

or agents thereof, which may impair the treaty rights of the United States or its citizens in China, including those which relate to the sovereignty, the independence, or the territorial and administrative integrity of the Republic of China, commonly known as the open-door policy; and that it does not intend to recognize any situation, treaty, or agreement which may be brought about by means contrary to the covenants and obligations of the pact of Paris of August 27, 1928, to which treaty both China and Japan, as well as the United States, are parties (Current 1954, 524).

This doctrine was referred to by American Under-Secretary of State Castle as a "new dictum of international law . . . the strongest moral sanction the world has ever known . . . [as] a means of depriving a conqueror of the fruits of his conquests" (Korman 1996, 239). It was enormously popular on an international level. Under the doctrine of nonrecognition, states were not obligated to recognize *de facto* situations, thereby denying them *de jure* status. Legitimacy was hence no longer attainable through naked force (Wright 1935, 439–46).

League Members had adopted nonrecognition doctrine as an expression of disapproval before its recognition by the United States and christening as the "Stimson Doctrine." In a Declaration presented on 11 March 1932, the League declared, "[i]t is incumbent upon the Members of the League of Nations not to recognize any situation, treaty or agreement which may be brought about by means contrary to the Covenant of the League of Nations or to the Pact of Paris" (Korman 1996, 240). Some of the Great Powers including Britain, the Netherlands, France and Italy did not support the Stimson Doctrine at first (Clyde 1948, 202), but eventually the League as a whole accepted it as "a statement of the course of action to which the parties to the Covenant and the Pact are legally obliged by their ratification of those instruments" (Wright 1935, 439–40). By 24 February 1933, the Report of the Assembly of the League of Nations declared that members should "exclude the maintenance and recognition of the existing regime in Manchuria, such maintenance and recognition being incompatible with the fundamental principles of existing international obligations and with the good understanding between the two countries on which peace in the Far East depends" (441).

Although the Stimson Doctrine proved to be ineffective in preventing the continued occupation of Manchuria and the establishment of

Japan's puppet state, Manchukuo (Wiloughby 1935, 256), it did catalyze international condemnation of Japan's conquest (Leang-Li 1935, 186). By March 27, 1933, Japan could no longer shrug off the condemnation of other members of the League, and decided to withdraw from the organization (Wiloughby 1935, 493).

In sum, the case of Manchuria reflects the redefining of a norm in the international community. The right to conquest was rejected by members inside and outside the League of Nations, who expressed disapproval through the principle of nonrecognition. This principle, although it received only qualified support from some countries and proved ineffective at preventing Japan's *de facto* annexation of Manchuria, eventually became the means for expressing international disapproval. Though the League did not act to compel Japan to relinquish Manchuria, it was, in the words of Sir John Simon, "far better for the League to proclaim its principles, even though it failed to get them observed, than to forsake these principles by meaningless compromise" (Langer 1947, 65). The League's stance against conquest would strengthen future positions concerning annexation by force in later international organizations.

Hitler, Czechoslovakia, and Poland

Further development of the norm against conquest involved not just moral condemnation but also a pragmatic consideration of what unrestrained conquest could mean in a world of modern technology and methods of warfare. World War II was a crucial turning point in the development of the norm of territorial integrity. Whereas previous international opinion had rejected conquest in largely moral terms, the emergence of fascist expansionism in the 1930s demonstrated that prohibiting conquest was necessary for maintaining world order. Even major powers such as Britain and France confronted not just a threat to the international system but to their own survival.

As the model and prior chapters have shown, norms evolve at times when general rules conflict with specific actions, inviting dispute and reexamination of accepted norms. Following Manchuria, the norm for dealing with conquest was to formally ignore the aggressor's claim over conquered territory. However, what constituted conquest was not fully explicit. Japan's claims of necessity for self-defense were without foundation, but it was unclear based on the League's response how other justifications for annexation would play out. Germany's brazen annexations preceding

World War II gave the international community an opportunity to redefine international norms for responding to conquest.

The development of norms, as we saw in the chapters on piracy and slavery, is in many ways shaped by those who embrace and enforce those norms. The League of Nations had proven ineffective in preventing annexations and in punishing those who attempted them. Shortly after Japan's exit from the League of Nations in March 1933, Germany exited the League in October on the pretense of a dispute over disarmament (Crozier 1997, 13). In 1935 Mussolini's Italy also estranged itself from the League by invading Abyssinia (today's Ethiopia). The League failed to protect the territorial integrity of Abyssinia, a League member, although it condemned Italy and imposed sanctions. Italy subsequently exited, further diminishing the League's ranks (Crozier 1997, 105).

The summer before Mussolini's October invasion, the newly appointed Minister of League of Nations Affairs for the British government, Anthony Eden, sought to convince Mussolini that the Abyssinian prize was not worth the quarrel its seizure would inevitably provoke between Italy and Britain (Rothwell 2001, 61). Mussolini went forward nonetheless, and in spite of the League's economic sanctions, Italy retained a comfortable supply of oil and other military necessities through trade with America, a country not bound by League decisions (Crozier 1997, 109). France and Great Britain took no further steps, seeing conflict over Abyssinia as "the wrong war with the wrong enemy at the wrong time" (Rothwell 2001, 62). The appropriate response to conquest continued to be formal disapproval and nonrecognition without the backing of force.

By that time the real concern of the western powers was Germany. Germany's revanchism and growing military capacity threatened to plunge the world into chaos and violence. Britain adopted a policy of appeasement to forestall (or at least delay) global war. Though many have castigated the tactic as mere capitulation, in truth it was rooted in progressive norms against war and in favor of self-determination. Initial steps taken by Hitler to expand German boundaries were frequently rationalized under the doctrine that Germans should govern themselves. In March of 1938, Hitler completed the Anschluss of Austria, following a long debate and a threatened plebiscite over who should govern the country. Many Austrians supported joining "greater Germany," but Hitler, unwilling to risk losing a plebiscite, preempted the vote with his invasion (Cowling 1975; Crozier 1997, 140). The peaceful nature of the Anschluss, which Austrians largely supported, kept most countries from asserting any opposition. The absorption of

Austria could be seen as consistent with the norm of self-determination and did not appear as a serious threat to other, non-German nations.

Hitler's next step was to claim the Sudetenland, a part of Czechoslovakia with a large German minority.[1] In conversations with English Prime Minister Neville Chamberlain, Hitler indicated that he wanted to unify the German people by assimilating ethnic Germans living in neighboring countries as a result of border changes following WWI (G. B. Strang 1996, 725). Thirty percent of those he wanted to include in the Reich were in the Sudetenland, where the population generally was eager to join with Germany (Cowling 1975, 188). The struggles regarding language differences, education, and representation were real concerns in Czechoslovakia, and Hitler was able to make a convincing case for German self-determination (Beneš et al. 2002, 101). He told Chamberlain that he did not want to bring a lot of Czechs to Germany, "all he wanted was Sudeten Germans" (Cowling 1975, 188). He pressed the issue of violence being inflicted on Germans in Czechoslovakia, and stated that he was determined to settle the issue at once, even if it meant risking a world war (189).

Following this interview, Chamberlain returned to the Cabinet with the report that Hitler intended to resolve the question through use of a plebiscite (Cowling 1975, 190), invoking the norm of self-determination. Chamberlain believed that Hitler's goals centered around "racial unity, and not the domination of Europe," and giving Germany the Sudetenland "might be a turning point in Anglo-German relations" and the end of Hitler's "territorial ambitions" (197). As one historian explained, "[t]he Nazi lie that the well-being of the Sudeten Germans was of central importance to them was . . . extremely successful with international opinion and not least with the British government" (Rothwell 2001, 83).

To resolve the question of the Sudetenland and prevent a war between Czechoslovakia and Germany, on 29 September 1938 England, France, Germany, and Italy met and agreed on a transfer that would involve a ten-day occupation and an international commission to supervise the transfer of territory, together with a plebiscite in areas of greatest uncertainty (Cowling 1975, 202; Crozier 1997, 144–45). The result was a guarantee that what was left of Czechoslovakia would be bound to the former Franco-Czech Treaty, which provided for mutual assistance in accord with the Covenant of the League of Nations, should either France

---

[1] Approximately 23%, but much higher nearer the German border.

or Czechoslovakia be "attacked without provocation" (Wright 1936, 489). This conference also produced the famous Munich Agreement, in which Hitler declared that Germany and Britain should never go to war with each other again (Cowling 1975, 202). The agreement spelled the doom of Czechoslovakia, which after its forced concessions could offer little resistance to Hitler when he invaded in March 1939. With pacifism strong in both Britain and France, and with neither country prepared to oppose Germany militarily, British and French leaders saw few alternatives (Caputi 2000, 26; Imlay 2003, 31–32, 142, 148; Kennedy 1940, 184; Thomas 1996, 148–49).

Following Germany's invasion of Prague, however, British and French policy shifted dramatically toward deterrence of further expansionism by Nazi Germany (Imlay 2003, 154, 165; Rothwell 2001, 6; G. B. Strang 1996, 723–26; Sword 1991, 82). By the end of March, Britain had entered into a mutual defense pact with Poland. Germany invaded western Poland on 1 September, and the U.S.S.R. followed suit, invading eastern Poland on 17 September. Britain and France, honoring their agreement with Poland, declared war on Germany on 3 September but hesitated to declare war against the Soviet Union (Sword 1991, 82–84, 88). Britain and France condemned the Soviet move but at the same time hesitated to alienate a potentially crucial ally against Nazi Germany (89–93). The Western powers made no effort to enforce the anticonquest norm against the Soviet Union.

In short, France and Britain forcefully challenged Hitler's conquests after the annexations could no longer be explained away in terms of "self-determination" or "race unification." Equally important, resistance to Hitler's conquests emerged when Nazi aggression challenged the security of norm-building states such as Britain and France. Indeed, security concerns provoked by Germany's power and hostile intentions were primary motivations for asserting the norm against conquest. World War II became a vast struggle for national survival in the face of fascist aggression. The war thus gave a new impetus to the development of norms against conquest.

Korea

In response to the catastrophe of World War II, states established the United Nations to promote international peace and stability. The United Nations Charter enunciated rules that prohibited not just conquest but any aggressive use of force. The Charter declared "that armed force shall not be used, save in the common interest" (Preamble) and enjoined states to "refrain in their international relations from the threat or use of force" (Article 2(4)). The Charter also codified a set of positive norms that precluded any right to conquest, establishing "the principle of equal rights and self-determination of peoples," (Article 1(2)), mandating the peaceful settlement of disputes (Article 2(3)), and affirming the territorial integrity and political independence of all states (Article 2(4)).

Within a few years of its founding, the United Nations faced a serious challenge to the norms against conquest. When North Korean troops invaded South Korea in the summer of 1950, the United Nations responded with a series of Resolutions supporting the intervention of a coalition of Member forces, led by the United States. The international norms prohibiting conquest and the emerging U.S. foreign policy priority of containing communism motivated these Resolutions. The international response to North Korea's invasion continued a shift in international norms that began with European responses to Nazi aggression.

Korea had been the meeting point for U.S. and Soviet troops in the last days of World War II, as both eagerly stepped forward to accept Japan's surrender (Middleton 1965, 24). Stalin considered Korea part of his "political compensation" (along with the return of Port Arthur and the southern Sakhalin) for staying with the Allies even after the end of the European conflict (Kim 1993, 20; Middleton 1965). U.S. goals, in contrast, were (1) to prevent the Soviet Union from occupying all of Korea, (2) to put the United States in a good position to implement Korean independence, (3) to provide security for both U.S. and Japanese forces during military occupation, and (4) to limit the area of communist control (Goodrich 1956, 11–12).

As early as 1947, the United States encouraged the newly formed United Nations to take up the subject of government in Korea (Potter 1950, 709). To facilitate national independence and report developments, the United Nations created a Korea Commission, with representatives from Australia, Canada, China, El Salvador, France, India, the Philippines, Syria, and Ukraine. The Soviets protested U.N. involvement, and the U.N. Commission was barred entry to North Korea (Middleton 1965, 26). By late 1948, Korea was definitively divided between North and South. Kim Il-Sung, in the north, enjoyed extensive support from the Soviet Union. Stalin secretly arranged for Kim to come to Moscow to work out preparations for war and supplied massive infusions of military equipment (Thornton 2000, 101, 110). Stalin gambled that the U.N. would see the conflict as between two regions of the same country and elect to stay out of the conflict due to lack of jurisdiction.

With increased military capacity, the strategic backing of the Soviet Union and the anticipation of possible Chinese involvement, Kim declared war on South Korea and invaded on 25 June 1950 (Middleton 1965, 31). Fourteen hours after the invasion began, the Security Council met for a special session, resulting in Resolution 82, which stated that "the armed attack upon the Republic of Korea by forces from North Korea constitutes a breach of the peace." The Resolution called for immediate cessation of hostilities and recommended that "the Members of the United Nations furnish such assistance to the Republic of Korea as may be necessary to repel the armed attack and to restore international peace and security in the area" and noted that the General Assembly Resolution 293 had concluded that the Government of the Republic of Korea is a "lawfully established government . . . based on elections which were a valid expression of the free will of the electorate" (U.N. Security Council 1950, Res. 82). The Soviet Union representative, Jacob Malik, was nearby but did not attend the meeting to enter a Soviet veto (Thornton 2000, 189). The U.S.S.R. was boycotting the United Nations because Communist China had not yet been recognized as a Member (Middleton 1965, 22). As a result of the boycott, the Resolution against the Soviet-sponsored North Korean aggression passed 9 to 0, with Yugoslavia abstaining.

Again, normative and strategic considerations intermixed. Armed conquest was by now viewed as antithetical to worldwide norms and international law, as manifest by the United Nations' response. The strategic interest of the United States in preventing Soviet control of the Korean peninsula coincided with the international norm. Truman acknowledged the normative and strategic dimensions of the confrontation: "If this was allowed to go unchallenged it would mean a third world war, just as similar incidents had brought on the second world war. It was also clear to me that the foundations and the principles of the United Nations were at stake unless this unprovoked attack on Korea could be stopped" (Thornton 2000, 189).

On 27 July 1950, the Security Council adopted a second resolution reiterating prior demands for a cessation of hostilities, and calling for international intervention. This Resolution was crucial to garnering support for the deployment of ground troops (Thornton 2000, 210). The General Assembly of the United Nations responded to the Security Council Resolutions with a declaration on 7 October, that

> there has been established a lawful government (the Government of the Republic of Korea) having effective control and

jurisdiction over that part of Korea where the United Nations Temporary Commission on Korea was able to observe and consult and in which the great majority of the people of Korea reside: that this government is based on elections which were a valid expression of the free will of the electorate of that part of Korea and which were observed by the Temporary Commission; and that this is the only such government in Korea. (U.N. General Assembly 1950, Res. 376)

To drive the message home, the Assembly passed an additional resolution on 3 November, commonly known as the "Uniting for Peace" Resolution. In it, the Assembly reaffirmed the importance of the Security Council's ability to take action in the maintenance of peace and security. To ensure the maintenance of peace, and obviously mindful of the threat of a Soviet veto, the Assembly granted itself the authority to counter aggression in the case of a Security Council deadlock (U.N. General Assembly 1950, Res. 377). This determination allowed the United States to lead forces from 15 Member-states into Korea. Troops came from Australia, Belgium, Canada, Columbia, Ethiopia, France, Greece, Luxembourg, New Zealand, the Netherlands, the Philippines, South Africa, Thailand, Turkey, and the United Kingdom. During the war, the General Assembly also passed Resolution 500, imposing economic sanctions against North Korea as part of the war effort and encouraging what amounted to an embargo enforceable by all Members (U.N. General Assembly 1951, Res. 500).

In sum, the United Nations responded with force against North Korea's attempt to annex its southern neighbor. Recently codified U.N. norms against conquest—or, more precisely, supporting self-determination and territorial integrity and prohibiting the use of force—clearly played a role, as did a United States powerfully motivated to contain communism.

Kuwait

During the Cold War, the United States and the Soviet Union backed opposing sides in a variety of regional conflicts and internal wars. With each superpower wielding a veto, the Security Council was essentially unable to act on questions of peace and conflict. After the collapse of the Soviet Union, the Cold War deadlock in the Security Council vanished, and the United Nations suddenly found itself capable of forcible intervention in a variety of humanitarian and security crises (see Chapter 10 on "Humanitarian Intervention" and Chapter 11 on "The Right to Democracy").

An early test for the emerging "new world order" came with Iraq's invasion of Kuwait in August 1990. The U.N. reaction to the Iraqi annexation of Kuwait clarified international law on conquest, as the Security Council expressed unanimity on the subject. Virtually total cooperation within the Security Council, coupled with a strong coalition of countries providing financial and military support to reverse the invasion, allowed the international community to affirm the norm against aggressive conquest. The timing of the invasion was crucial: Gorbachev's new policy of *perestroika* encouraged increased international cooperation and dependence on international institutions, such as the United Nations, for resolution of international problems (Gow 1993, 121). Soviet need for Western economic aid during the period of transition was an additional incentive to cooperate (Matthews 1993, 53). Thus, rather than addressing regional violence through unilateral superpower pressure, as the U.S.S.R. had done historically, Gorbachev encouraged the international community to take police action. At the same time, China was trying to regain approval in the West following the massacre in Tiananmen Square. China thus promised not to veto a Security Council resolution that would use force to free Kuwait (Miller 1994, 109). Shifting political priorities in the two major communist powers thus created an opening for Security Council action in support of the norm against conquest.

Saddam Hussein's invasion of Kuwait on 1 August 1990 was quick and successful (BBC World Service 1991, 1). In one day, Kuwaiti forces had been obliterated and Iraqi troops were massed at the Kuwait-Saudi Arabia border (Matthews 1993, 33). One week following the invasion an Iraqi government spokesperson announced the "formal union" of Iraq and Kuwait, or in other words, Kuwait's annexation (BBC World Service 1991, 10). Saddam justified the invasion and the annexation as a recovery of lost territory. Kuwait, he claimed, was the "nineteenth province" of Iraq, a title he based on the geography of former Ottoman provinces. The land comprising both Iraq and Kuwait used to be part of the single province of Basrah; Saddam's logic was that splitting the two countries following World War II was an error he had corrected (Matthews 1993, 132).

Territorial claims based on old maps were only part of Saddam's reasons for invading. Iraq had long sought political supremacy in the Gulf area. Many speculate that Saudi Arabia was his true target and that had the international response not been so quick, Saddam would have continued

to sweep past Kuwait and into the large, powerful, and oil-rich Saudi kingdom (Matthews 1993, 44). However, Kuwait itself was a "target of opportunity" for Iraq: it presented a variety of economic incentives including
sole ownership of Iraq and Kuwait's shared Rumaila oil field (41), cancel-
lation of the debt Iraq owed to Kuwait, and stimulation for the Iraqi economy through the liquidation of Kuwait's assets, including, for example, its
gold reserves (Bulloch and Morris 1991, 10). Following Iraq's long and
costly war with Iran, Saddam Hussein's government was in dire financial
straits, and rather than liberalize the economy, which could threaten
Saddam's political hold on the country, he looked to the spoils of conquest.

As fast as the occupation was, international outrage was equally
rapid. Within twenty-four hours Washington, Moscow, and London had
condemned the invasion and called for Iraqi withdrawal (BBC World
Service 1991, 1–3). The United Nations Security Council[2] passed
Resolution 660 the next day, also condemning the invasion and demanding "that Iraq withdraw immediately and unconditionally" (U.N. Security
Council 1990, Res. 660). The European Community was not far behind in
adding its condemnation on 3 August (BBC World Service 1991, 4). As
U.S. President George H. W. Bush expressed to the Congress in September
1990, resistance to the invasion was "not, as Saddam Hussein would have
it, the United States against Iraq. It is Iraq against the world" (1990). Bush
also asserted that the international response to the Iraqi invasion had the
potential to create a world in which "the rule of law supplants the rule of
the jungle [and] . . . nations recognize the shared responsibility for freedom and justice, a world where the strong respect the rights of the weak"
(1990). Joe Clark, Canada's Secretary of State for External Affairs, expressed
similar aspirations: "in the Persian Gulf, the UN is acting as it has not been
able to act for decades. It is acting to bring the authority of the international community to bear on a country which has grossly and clearly contravened the UN Charter's prohibition on aggression" (Miller 1994, 142).

Even Iraq's purported allies could not defend the invasion in the
face of international condemnation, particularly when it came to the proposed annexation of Kuwait (Bulloch and Morris 1991, 110). The day following its announcement, the U.N. Security Council, including at that
time Iraq's allies Cuba and Yemen, unanimously adopted Resolution 662,

---

[2] At the time the Security Council was composed of the five permanent members, the U.S.S.R.,
the U.S., the U.K., France and China; and nonpermanent members Canada, Colombia, Côte
d'Ivoire, Cuba, Ethiopia, Finland, Malaysia, Romania, Yemen, and Zaire.

declaring the annexation null and void (U.N. Security Council 1990, Res. 662). All U.N. members had an interest in preventing Iraq's absorption of Kuwait; if they allowed one country to be annexed out of existence, then any of them might also be vulnerable to annexation. Iraq's invasion of Kuwait thus presented a difficult position for many Arab states that disliked the United States (the leaders of Iraqi opposition) and yet could not justify Saddam Hussein's behavior. As stated by the president of Libya, Colonel Muammar Quaddafi:

> The presence of Iraq in Kuwait is illegal and it is unacceptable. The presence of US troops in Saudi Arabia is legal in terms of international law, because an independent country has asked another independent country for troops to defend it. However, it is unacceptable in pan-Arab terms and in terms of the region's security. (Gow 1993, 62, 68)

U.S. leadership in the resistance to the Iraqi invasion was distasteful to others as well. Many if not all of the other countries eventually involved in the coalition to free Kuwait wanted a clear separation between the U.N. interests, which they supported, and U.S. interests, which they did not. At one point, the Soviet Union criticized the United Nations' involvement as being "hijacked by the Americans" (Gow 1993, 6). However, this criticism did not prevent the U.S.S.R. from backing Security Council resolutions calling for Iraqi withdrawal (Resolution 660), imposing an economic and military embargo (Resolution 661) and condemning Iraq's annexation of Kuwait (Resolution 662) (125). In Canada's House of Commons, a motion to condemn the invasion and affirm support for Canada's involvement was amended several times to ensure the motion would express Canada's intent to work and fight under United Nations command, explicitly authorized by the Security Council, and not under the United States (Miller 1994, 129).

It is significant that Bush referred so frequently to the international order and the importance of opposing aggression. Concerns about "energy resources"—oil—were obviously and inevitably a strategic issue as well. Regardless, U.S. rhetoric, even to domestic reporters, consistently referred back to the "world order," implying a concern and respect for the developing international law, based on common norms. One author suggests that it is unlikely that Bush could have rallied support in any other way. Concerns about oil, while legitimate and persuasive to some extent, would not have convinced democratic nations that the Persian Gulf War was just.

To garner the support of the American population and the international community, Bush needed to point to international norms and commonly held security concerns (Gow 1993, 193).

In Great Britain, the response to the Iraqi invasion was just as vigorous in defending international order and opposing aggression. Britain supplied the largest military contribution from a European country: 45,000 troops along with warplanes, helicopters, and support ships (Bennett, Lepgold, and Unger 1997, 70). Foreign Secretary Douglas Hurd explained British involvement by saying:

> Saddam Hussein has set the world on a crucial test. If we pass it, there will be a chance for a new order of peace embracing the whole Middle East. If we fail it, would-be aggressors would rejoice, potential victims despair. No small country could ever again feel safe from the expansionist whim of a mighty neighbor. (72–73)

Prime Minister Margaret Thatcher described Iraq's invasion as a return to "the law of the jungle"; unless Iraq was stopped, small countries such as Kuwait could never feel safe (73). By the middle of October 1990, eighty-six percent of the British public approved of the government's war aims and strategy, a number that remained steady throughout the duration of the ground war. Even opposition party members who favored economic sanctions over military intervention indicated seventy nine percent of them were "satisfied" or "very satisfied" with government policy 82).

The so-called middle powers Australia and Canada played little role in the development of diplomatic strategy, but they would prove to be highly supportive members of the coalition. Support was due in large part to Bush's close personal relationships with Australia's Prime Minister Robert Hawke and Canada's Prime Minister Brian Mulroney (Miller 1994, 111). Each prime minister defended his support for the United Nations coalition by referring to the strategic and moral need to preserve international order and build up international law. Hawke explained, "[w]e are not sending ships to the Gulf region to serve our allies; we are going to protect the international rule of law which will be vital to our security however our alliances may develop in the future" (Lenczowski 1987). Mulroney stated:

> We do not have the might and the reach of some others. Canada is, however, capable of making a contribution to the containment

of aggression and to the integrity of nations, as we have done effectively throughout our history . . . our peacekeeping role neither excludes us nor excuses us from the call to resist aggression. The roles are complementary, as both serve the larger political purpose of preserving *international order* and both are very much in *Canada's interest* (Miller 1994, 148).

Addressing the Security Council, Mulroney explained, "Our position is one of integrity and dedication to the upholding of international law and the universally recognized norms of conduct in the relations between states" (129).

Even the Soviet Union, which in an earlier era had carried out a de facto annexation of Eastern Europe, indicated a definite reversal in policy regarding the right of conquest. Following a five hour summit meeting in Helsinki, Finland, President Bush and Mikhail Gorbachev brought a statement to the press regarding the Kuwait invasion:

Our preference is to resolve the crisis peacefully. But we are determined to see this aggression end and if current steps fail to end it, we are prepared to consider additional ones consistent with the United Nations charter. We must demonstrate beyond any doubt that aggression cannot and will not pay. (Miller 1994, 108)

However, even if Gorbachev was willing to take military action under the United Nations Charter, commentators in the U.S.S.R. opposed the use of force, seeing it as "a recipe for disaster" and "playing second fiddle" to U.S. policy (Gow 1993, 129). The Soviet Union did, nevertheless, favor "the immediate and unconditional withdrawal of Iraqi troops from Kuwaiti territory" and the restoration and defense of the "sovereignty, national independence and territorial integrity of Kuwait" (123).

The ensuing war was quick and decisive. After weeks of intense bombing by the coalition, allied forces drove Iraqi troops out of Kuwait over a period of days in February 1991. The United Nations oversaw the return of Kuwaiti prisoners and assets, imposed a set of restrictions on Iraqi weapons programs, and established "no-fly zones" in the north and south of Iraq to protect Kurdish and Shiite minorities. In short, the international community, acting through the Security Council, enforced international norms against aggression and conquest with economic sanctions and military power. The right to conquest had completely vanished, to be replaced by norms of self-determination, sovereign independence, and territorial integrity. International law condemning aggression and conquest was firmly established, and the United Nations was becoming the organization to uphold those rules.

Conclusions

The right of conquest was uncontested in its day. What nations could seize by force of arms was rightfully theirs. However, beginning with the emergence of the norm regarding self-determination during the French Revolution, this right of conquest began to be questioned and weakened. Specific acts of conquest and annexation provoked disputes about the content and meaning of international rules. Bismarck's conquest of Alsace-Lorraine triggered debates about self-determination. Though Bismarck's claims of self-defense were dubious, he was allowed to annex the two areas, with a few countries making hesitant complaints about the rights of the people in Alsace-Lorraine to determine their own destinies.

These complaints and others came up again in the case of Manchuria. In the intervening years, the League of Nations Charter had enunciated a norm of territorial integrity of states, in opposition to the right of conquest. Japan accepted the norm and attempted to excuse its seizure of Manchuria as an exception. But the international community rejected Japan's claims that outside (Western) countries did not understand the situation, and that Japan harbored no territorial designs. The Stimson Policy of Non-Recognition, endorsed by League members, dismissed Japan's justifications and affirmed the norm against conquest and annexation.

World War II provided the impetus for codifying, in the United Nations Charter, international rules against aggression and conquest. Hitler's expansionism forced states to recognize that territorial acquisition was not simply wrong in principle but posed a threat to international order and the survival of states, even major powers. In practice, the norm against territorial conquests could not always be applied: when the Soviet Union seized the remainder of Poland in September 1939, Britain and France reluctantly accepted the move as a diplomatic necessity in light of pending war with Germany.

With the formation of the United Nations and its prohibition of the aggressive use of force, the world had a clear and codified standard, and world leaders, most prominently the United States, used Charter norms to justify military resistance to attempts at conquest. In South Korea, Western states and their allies, driven in part by the desire to limit the spread of Communism, opposed the North Korean invasion. Years later, following *perestroika* and the move toward greater international cooperation and collective security, nations around the world, including many non-Western states, decisively opposed Iraq's invasion of Kuwait. In Kuwait, the United Nations reaffirmed, and enforced by strength of arms, the international norm forbidding conquest.

The international norm against conquest developed through a series of cycles, each triggered by an aggressive war. The prohibition of conquest is, perhaps, the backbone of sovereignty norms that have developed over the past three and half centuries. It aims to guarantee the continued survival of existing states. By ruling out the forcible annexation of territory, the norm against conquest protects the most fundamental right of states—their right to continued existence within existing borders.

Chapter 4

Protecting Cultural Treasures in Wartime

Wayne Sandholtz

For centuries, the aphorism "to the victor go the spoils" offered a pithy summation of international law.[1] The accepted norm was that the winners in war were entitled to carry away the artistic and cultural treasures of the vanquished. Thus art plunder has long been a symbolic dimension of war. By appropriating the greatest artistic and cultural artifacts of the defeated, the victors symbolically absorbed "lesser" cultures. Or, as Hugh Trevor-Roper puts it, to the extent that cultural valuables confer prestige upon a polity, its rivals in war will seek to destroy that aura and appropriate it for themselves, "like cannibals who, by devouring parts of their enemies, think thereby to acquire their *mana*, the intangible source of their strength" (1970, 7). For instance, the ancient Romans made the display of plunder a central feature of the public celebration of their victories. The practice apparently dates from the early period of Roman expansion, as "Rome became a vast museum where the masterpieces of Greece, Egypt and

---

[1] Parts of this chapter appeared previously in Sandholtz (2008).

Asia Minor were crowded together." Roman plundering was not primarily driven by the monetary value of the objects taken; rather, the importance of the looted art was as "tokens of triumph" (Treue 1961, 13, 18).

After the collapse of Rome, art plunder was a regular feature of European wars. In modern Europe, the most exorbitant instances of art plunder have been those of revolutionary France and Nazi Germany. Though personal enrichment has always provided a motive for the looting of art objects, Napoleonic and Nazi plundering were not solely eruptions of greed. In both cases, the carrying away of artistic treasures was massive, systematic, and organized by the state, with the stated purpose of demonstrating the political and cultural superiority of powers aspiring to be the new centers of civilization.

Recent events and controversies—the destruction of significant cultural sites during the 1990s in the ex-Yugoslavia,[2] recent negotiations between Russia and Germany on the return of cultural objects seized at the end of World War II,[3] a growing body of litigation over artworks seized by the Nazis,[4] and, most recently, the looting of the Iraqi Museum in April 2003[5]—demonstrate that the problem of wartime protection of cultural property is not merely of historic interest. Rules on the wartime protection of cultural property are an actively developing area of international law. This chapter assesses the evolution of international norms against cultural plundering, focusing on two crucial turns through the cycle of normative change: the Napoleonic Wars and World War II (see Figure 4.1).[6] The empirical account, based on both secondary and archival sources, clearly depicts cycles of normative change as posited in Chapter 1. International rules prohibiting plunder are part of the stream of sovereignty norms; antiplunder rules protect the right of states to their cultural patrimony, a right that states retain even in defeat or under occupation.

The Normative Context

The empirical analysis should produce two key kinds of evidence. First, it should show that the rules did in fact change. We can identify, *a priori*,

---

[2] See Detling (1993), United Nations Commission of Experts (1994).
[3] See Gattini (1996), Hochfield (2000).
[4] See Palmer (2000), Bazyler (2003), chap. 5.
[5] See Paroff (2004), Sandholtz (2005).
[6] For a more comprehensive account of the development of antiplunder norms, including analyses of developments in World War I and recent events in the Balkans, Kuwait, and Iraq, see Sandholtz (2007).

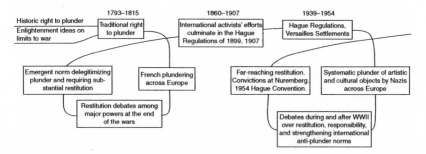

Figure 4.1 Antiplunder norm cycles.

the kinds of situations that would offer the strongest evidence of the existence of a new norm against plunder. Against the backdrop of hundreds of years in which plundering was considered the normal reward for victory, compelling evidence of the antiplunder norm would consist of countries that: (1) prevail in war, (2) were not plundered themselves, (3) oblige defeated plunderers to effect restitution to third countries, and (4) do not engage in plundering of their own. The two episodes I examine produce two clear instances: Great Britain in 1815 and the United States in 1945. Second, the empirical analysis should show that normative change occurred in the cyclical or dialectical process proposed in Chapter 1, in which actions trigger disputes about rules, actors argue, and the outcomes of those arguments modify the rules.

Existing norms provide the context in which actors choose among options and frame arguments in justification of their choices. A brief summary of international rules regarding wartime plunder is therefore the appropriate starting point. In the seventeenth and eighteenth centuries, war-making was one of the sovereign prerogatives of states (Oppenheim 1952, 178). The right to initiate war was virtually unlimited, though some limitations on permissible means of prosecuting war were beginning to emerge. Even Grotius acknowledged that the law of nations permitted belligerents in just war to seize or destroy enemies and their possessions (though he also noted that what is lawful is not necessarily also morally laudable) (1901, Book III, chaps. 1–5). Cornelius van Bynkershoek, writing in the Netherlands in 1737, held that "everything is lawful against enemies as such . . . . We make war because we think that our enemy, by the injury done us, has merited the destruction of himself and his people. As this is the object of our welfare, does it matter what means we employ to accomplish it?" (1930 [1737], 16). International law writers into the eighteenth century generally held that any means were justified in war and that combatants possessed "unlimited right" over the person and property of their enemies (Williams 1978, 5).

But liberal ideals on the value and the "natural" rights of individuals were beginning in the 1700s to make their way out of the philosophers' treatises and into politics and law, both domestic and international. Some law scholars were beginning to argue that humanitarian considerations established bounds on the conduct of armies fighting wars. Some began to argue that, though international law permitted plunder, cultural monuments enjoyed unique and protected status. Vattel, for instance, in *The Law of Nations* (first published in 1758), sustains the doctrine that states are justified in doing what they wish with enemy properties. Indeed, Vattel defines enemy property as broadly as possible, including the possessions of the sovereign, the state, and all its subjects, and asserts that a belligerent has the right to confiscate enemy property or to destroy "what he can not conveniently carry off." Thus, "it is not, generally speaking, contrary to the laws of war to plunder and lay waste to a country," Vattel affirms. "But," he quickly adds, "the deliberate destruction of public monuments, temples, tombs, statues, pictures, etc., is . . . absolutely condemned even by the voluntary Law of Nations, as being under no circumstances conducive to the lawful objects of war" (Vattel 1916 [1758], Book III, chap. 5, §73).

Furthermore, Vattel articulates general principles that justify exempting cultural treasures from the right to plunder:

> For whatever cause a country be devastated, those buildings should be spared which are an honor to the human race and which do not add to the strength of the enemy, such as temples, tombs, public buildings, and all the edifices of remarkable beauty. What is gained by destroying them? It is the act of a declared enemy of the human race thus wantonly to deprive men of these monuments of art and models of architecture . . . (Vattel 1916 [1758], Book III, chap. 9, §§161–173)

Thus Vattel asserts two ideas that are fundamental to the development of international rules against art plunder: first, the Renaissance notion that masterworks of art and architecture occupy an exalted station in the panoply of values; and second, that such treasures belong not only to their legal owners but also in some sense to all (the "human race"). Given Vattel's influence across Europe, these ideas entered the international discourse on art plunder. Still, in practice, plunder was the prerogative of the victor.

Napoleonic Plunder

Against this backdrop, French armies carried out a systematic confisca-
tion of art treasures across Europe. As they crossed the continent, they
sent back to Paris convoys laden with Europe's most celebrated
masterpieces. The plundering was officially organized. For instance, the
Committee of Public Instruction in 1794 and 1795 began assigning commissioners to travel with the armies in order "to identify and to have
removed with care the masterpieces that are found" (Müntz 1895, 377;
my translation). By October 1794, the Temporary Art Commission had
established a subcommittee to compile lists of artistic and scientific
objects in countries where the French armies were expected to enter
(Gould 1965, 41).

Napoleon began his illustrious career in art plunder as general of
the French forces in Italy. Both the general and the *Directoire* in Paris
assigned art experts to accompany the army. In contrast with the art
requisitions in the Low Countries and the Rhine cities, those in Italy were
generally formalized in the treaties imposed on the various Italian states.
The haul from Italy was immense, culminating with the Treaty of Tolentino
(February 1797), in which Pope Pius VI agreed to hand over one hundred
treasures from the Vatican, to be shipped immediately to France (Müntz
1895, 385–92; 1896, 481–502).

The art trophies became part of the public rituals of victory.
A triumphal procession in Paris in July 1798 included a parade of art treasures on twenty-nine carts—including the Apollo Belvedere, the Laocoön,
the *Transfiguration* of Raphael, the *Saint Jerome* of Correggio, and paintings of Titian and Veronese—accompanied by troops, dignitaries, a military band, and wagons with caged bears, lions, and camels. Preceding the
carts was a banner whose inscription explicitly placed France alongside the
great ancient civilizations: "La Grèce les cèda; Rome les a perdus; Leur sort
changea deux fois, il ne changera plus" (Saunier 1902, 35, 37).[7] The parade
ended at the Champ-de-Mars and moved on the next day to the Louvre,
which had become the preeminent collection of art in Europe (Gould
1965, 65; Lanzac de Laborie 1913, 236). It would subsequently be enriched
by plunder from the German states, Austria, Spain, and (for a second
time) Italy.

---

[7] "Greece gave them up; Rome lost them; Their fate changed twice; It won't change again."

French Rationales

The policy of acquisition of art trophies enjoyed enthusiastic support within France. The justifications for plunder took three main forms. One was that the masterpieces of European art could only reside appropriately in the seat of liberty—France. For instance, upon returning to Paris, one of the French commissioners in Belgium declared that "these immortal works are no longer on foreign soil; they are today in the fatherland of the arts and genius, in the fatherland of liberty and freedom, of the French Republic" (Saunier 1902, 26, 29, 33). Later, in May 1796, the *Directoire* explained to Napoleon, then commanding the army in Italy, "The time has arrived when the reign of the fine arts should pass to France, to strengthen and embellish the reign of liberty. The National Museum should contain the most celebrated monuments of all the arts" (Lanzac de Laborie 1913, 234).

A second argument held that France should by right be the capital of art and culture, sometimes drawing a comparison with the great centers of ancient civilization (Greece and Rome). Indeed, much of official France, both Republican and Imperial, held the view that through its conquests France was making itself the political and cultural center of civilization. The conquered countries were therefore simply parts of a larger and more glorious realm whose capital was Paris. Napoleon took this mode of thinking to an all-encompassing extreme, declaring that "all men of genius, all those who have earned a distinguished rank in the republic of letters, are French, whatever their land of birth" (Müntz 1895, 393).

A third rationale, sometimes also citing ancient precedent, referred to the customary practice of nations, by which plunder was the appropriate reward for military virtue and victory. One member of the Institute of France justified the looting of the "principal riches" of the libraries of Liège and other Belgian cities, writing that "the Republic used its right, in choosing among the spoils of the vanquished those objects with which it wanted to enrich itself" (Müntz 1895, 378). Thouin, an art commissioner in Italy, wrote in a letter to Napoleon that the French plunder there was the reward of "military virtue" and compared it to how the Greeks had treated conquered Egypt and how the Romans had dealt with vanquished Greece (Gould 1965, 65). The director of the Musée Napoleon, Vivant Denon, also wrote often to the Emperor, to keep him apprized of developments at the museum, and to offer advice on how best to enrich it further. In a letter of 13 December 1805, he writes, "Sire, there should exist in

France a trophy of our victories in Germany as there was for those in Italy" (Chatelain 1973, 169).[8]

In one instance at least, a victim of plunder may even have recognized the preexisting international norm that allowed the victors to control the spoils. Pius VII visited Paris to perform the marriage of Napoleon to Marie Louise (1810) and visited the Louvre. When one of his guides remarked that some of the pieces on display might cause him some discomfort, the Pope reportedly responded, "These objects have always followed victory; it is very straightforward for them to be here" (Chatelain 1973, 245).[9] Finally, even the restored Louis XVIII appealed to the rights of conquest and the example of Rome in arguing that France was entitled to retain art works taken from the Vatican. In a letter to Pius VII (whose position had clearly changed from that attributed to him in 1810), the French king wrote, "If France pushed too far the right of conquest, in extending it to objects of art and science, this was perhaps simply to imitate both ancient Rome and modern Rome" (Malamani 1914, 198).

Allied Responses

Though many of the states despoiled by France demanded a comprehensive return of all plundered art, there were significant divisions within and among the allies, and positions changed from 1814 to 1815. After the defeat of Napoleon in 1814, the Prussians in particular insisted on the return (not necessarily immediate) of art works, as did the Duke of Brunswick and the king of Bavaria (Saunier 1902, 87). But the other Allies did not support the German demands. A note of May 29, 1814, from Castlereagh, the British minister, communicated the English crown's opposition to restitution and left it to Louis XVIII to determine the amount of compensation to be offered to the prior owners of the art (Treue 1961, 188). The British feared that a wholesale emptying of the Louvre would incite the Parisian public against the king and destabilize the restored monarchy, an outcome the other monarchies clearly preferred to avoid. This reasoning was later spelled out by Castlereagh: the Allies used "their influence to repress at that moment any agitation of these claims [for restitution]," in

---

[8] In this instance, Denon suggested that Cassel could yield at least 40 paintings, including some by Dürer and Holbein. He also recommended a collection of medallions in Vienna.

[9] The account is not entirely reliable, as the source is an anonymous document published in Paris in 1815. At that date, the French were vigorously resisting restitution. It is at least conceivable that the words attributed to Pius VII were manufactured in order to undercut the Pope's current demands for restitution.

hopes of preserving the peace that had been established "as a bond of reconciliation between the nation and the King" (Castlereagh Memoir 1815).

Czar Alexander offered the same interpretation. The Czar argued
that, in 1814, the Allies could have relied upon their right of conquest to
reclaim the works of art seized by France during the wars. "But at that time
the necessity of treating with care a newly established government, and of
avoiding any measure that might discredit it in the eyes of the nation,
compelled a rejection of that proposition" (Russian Memoir 1815; my
translation from the French). The czar helped to arrange an agreement,
confirmed by Louis XVIII, whereby only those art works held in storage at
the Paris museums would be returned to their previous owners; pieces on
regular display would remain (Chatelain 1973, 221).

In the end, the documents of the First Peace of Paris (30 May 1814)
were silent on the question of art restitution. Talleyrand considered the
treaty a diplomatic success for France. In his *Mémoires*, he listed the points
that were favorable to France, concluding, "And finally, we have retained
all of the admirable pieces of art conquered by our arms in nearly all the
museums of Europe" (Talleyrand-Périgord 1957 [1807–1815], 343; my
translation).

Everything changed after Waterloo. This time, according to Baron
von Müffling, the military governor of Paris, the allies resolved to repos-
sess the stolen art "without any diplomatic negotiations, and to disregard
any protestations" (1997, 264). Still, the fate of the looted art was the subject of intense debate in the ensuing negotiations in Paris. The Allied
plenipotentiaries, gathered again to negotiate the terms of the second
peace, received demands from various sides for the complete restitution of
artistic treasures plundered by France during the wars. On the very day
the Prussians entered Paris, they had sent a contingent to the Louvre
demanding the restoration of plundered artworks; the French demurred
(Chatelain 1973, 226).

For instance, the ministers received a long note from Antonio
Canova, a famous sculptor commissioned by Pope Pius VII to petition
for the return of masterpieces taken by the French from Rome and the
Vatican. Canova had to refute the contention, offered by the French, that
the treasures from Rome were ceded to France by the Treaty of Tolentino
(1797). Canova argued that the Pope had been forced to conclude an
armistice with burdensome conditions to save his states from devastation
and pillage. To respect the treaties would be to "respect that which
the wolf dictated to the lamb." Furthermore, to permit the French to retain

the precious objects from Rome would be to approve the principles of spoliation and rapine, and would set "a disastrous example for conquerors and usurpers to follow in the future." The pope was thus not reclaiming the works of art solely for the Romans but also for the utility and advantage of all the civilized nations of Europe (Canova 1815; my translation from the French).

The envoys of the King of the Netherlands submitted to the French minister, Prince Talleyrand, a request that France return art objects that had belonged to the family of the king as well as to various towns and churches (Netherlands letter 1815). After receiving no response from the French, the Dutch appealed to the Allied plenipotentiaries. The minutes of the ministers' meeting of 6 September 1815 record that the Dutch envoys had received from their court repeated orders to obtain the restitution of paintings taken from the Netherlands. "The return of the products of the fine arts to the places where they had been, for the inhabitants of the Kingdom of the Netherlands, the object of national attachment and of religious worship, is of high importance . . . " (Minutes, 6 September 1815; my translation). The Elector of Hesse similarly requested the return of forty-eight paintings taken from Cassel (letter from Baron Carlshausen 1815).

In response to the various demands, the Allied ministers sought to agree on general principles regarding the looted art (Protocol of the Conference, 6 September 1815). The initiative in this regard came from Britain, which had not been a victim of art plunder. If anything, British dealers and collectors had benefited from the sales and auctions that flooded art markets across Europe during the Napoleonic Wars. In fact, Lord Liverpool, the Prime Minister, had already in July 1815, at the request of the Prince Regent (future George IV), floated the idea to Castlereagh of obtaining for England some of the Louvre treasures (Gould 1965, 120–21). In formulating the British position in Paris, he had to bury that idea before he could propose a policy of complete restitution. In a letter dated 11 September 1815, Castlereagh informed the Prince Regent that he had already submitted to the Allied ministers a note clarifying that the British crown had no wish to acquire any of the looted artworks. Interestingly, Castlereagh was not asking permission; he was explaining to the Prince Regent a step already taken. Castlereagh had felt compelled to take this action given "insinuations that were circulated here, as to the motives" of the British government. He had been "rather anxious" to avoid "the imputation of any interested motive" on the part of England. Certainly, neither the Prince Regent nor the government could "have endured thus to participate in the plunder of Europe." Castlereagh concludes by declaring that it was "necessary to place His Royal Highness on the high ground of desiring to see Justice done," which would in any case "do Honor to His Royal Highness in the Eyes of Europe" (Castlereagh Letter 1815).

The memoir Castlereagh submitted to the conference in Paris had been drafted after "full consultation with the Duke of Wellington" and in light of communications received from the Allied Ministers (Castlereagh Letter 1815). In the note, Castlereagh argues that the Allies had not insisted on restitution of the artworks in 1814 not because they wished to approve of the plunder; in fact, they "uniformly refused" to recognize any French title to the art objects. Their forbearance the previous year was based on a desire to solidify the position of Louis XVIII by not provoking the French public. The situation in 1815 being different, Castlereagh declares, the Prince Regent "deems it to be the duty of the Allies Sovereigns . . . to facilitate the return" of the art treasures to "the places from whence they were torn." His Royal Highness further believed that the removal of the objects from the Louvre should not provide the occasion for the allies to bring "within their own dominions a single article which did not of right, at the period of their conquest, belong either to their respective family collections, or to the countries over which they now actually reign." The restitution had to be complete, for otherwise it would "recognise a variety of spoliation under the Covers of Treaties" (Castlereagh Memoir 1815). The Prussian minister, Prince Hardenberg, quickly expressed, in a note to Castlereagh, complete agreement with reasoning contained in the memoir (Hardenberg Note 1815). Metternich (the Austrian minister) had earlier submitted a note similarly calling for full restitution (Metternich Note 1815).

Castlereagh made a further assertion in his memoir, namely, that the French art seizures were "contrary to every Principle of Justice, and to the usages of Modern Warfare" (Castlereagh Memoir 1815). Wellington had similarly written that the plunder had been "contrary to the practice of civilized warfare" (quoted in Gould 1965, 131–35). The two British leaders invoked what they saw as a "usage" or "practice," what modern international lawyers might refer to as "customary international law." But, in fact, art plunder had been a feature of European warfare for centuries, with striking instances of it occurring in the 1600s (Trevor-Roper 1970). It is true that the mid-1700s saw some instances of restraint; for example, the contestants in the Seven Years' War (1756–63) seem to have refrained from plundering each others' art collections (Treue 196, 117–18). Still, in the partition of Poland in 1795, Prussia, Austria, and Russia helped themselves to the art collections and royal treasures of Stanislaus Augustus (155–57). In short, it would have been a stretch in 1815 to argue that the usages and practices of war prohibited the plundering of cultural treasures; the claims of Wellington and Castlereagh should therefore be seen as argumentation tactics, asserting an antiplunder norm that did not yet exist but which they wanted to emerge.

In any case, there was not agreement among the great powers in 1815 that victors in war were not entitled to appropriate the artistic treasures of the conquered. Talleyrand, responding on behalf of Louis XVIII to Castlereagh's memoir, offered several arguments. Because the war of 1815 was not against France but against Napoleon himself, a usurper, there was no need for a new treaty, and the Treaty of Paris of 1814 had famously not required the French to return the art treasures. In addition, many of the art objects belonged to France by virtue of solemn treaties. And, since treaties did not cover all of the loot, a "right of conquest . . . has been admitted by all nations in all times." Finally, if the king were to return the art objects, it would be seen by the nation as a crime even more than the cession of territories, and would be felt as a vital injury to the national pride (Talleyrand Note 1815; my translation from the French).

The Emperor of Russia, Czar Alexander, largely agreed with the French. Through his ministers in Paris, the czar argued that "the military success of allies gave them no right to profit from their current position by demanding concessions from France contrary to the treaty of Paris." The Emperor believed that the same principle should apply "equally to the art objects in France's possession." In fact, the czar believed that the Allies could have, the previous year, "in all fairness exercised their rights of conquest to reclaim the art objects that France had taken from other countries." But the Treaty of Paris had in effect approved France's possession of them. Furthermore, as in the previous year, forced restitutions might undermine the new government (of Louis XVIII). The czar would, however, welcome any partial and voluntary restitution agreed to by the Kind of France (Russian Memoir 1815).

In the end, the Allies, without the concurrence of Russia, required France to surrender the looted art treasures. The Prussians enforced a restitution of artworks to many of the German states. German and British troops supported the Belgian and Dutch demands for restitution (Saunier 1902, 101–118), though the Austrian restitution proceeded more smoothly.

In the end, a new norm had taken an important step forward: art plunder was not acceptable conduct in the European society of states. Even Talleyrand, in his *Mémoires* written years later, conceded that the right of conquest was a tenuous justification for the art seizures: "perhaps the monuments of art should never have entered the domain of conquest" (Talleyrand-Périgord 1957 [1807–1815], 463). Initially, at least, the Prussians, Austrians, Russians, and British held divergent views regarding the disposition of the plundered art. The British, who had not been despoiled, were in a position as victors to claim some portion of Napoleon's cultural loot. The fact that they did not is evidence of a shift in norms, one that even a great power chose to respect.

Emergent Rules

The dynamic of norm change is continuous and ubiquitous, as actions trigger disputes that modify rules. Yet the next episode I examine occurred nearly 150 years after the conclusion of the Napoleonic wars. By no means do I intend to suggest that nothing was happening in terms of rule change during that interlude. The wars of 1793–1815 triggered a cycle of normative evolution and World War II produced a decisive turn through that dialectical loop. In a sense, the two episodes serve as first and last chapters in a longer account. However, to reinforce my contention that the dialectic of normative change is continuous, I briefly describe some of the key developments that occurred between 1815 and 1938.

During the U.S. Civil War, officials in the War Department asked Francis Lieber, then a professor at Columbia College in New York City, to draft an authoritative statement on the rules of warfare for use by the Union armies. As a young man in 1815, Lieber had joined a German regiment to fight against Napoleon and was seriously wounded in battle at Namur in Belgium. After the war, he became a passionate proponent of liberal politics and international laws to humanize warfare. The document he drafted was approved by the Secretary of War and by President Lincoln, who issued it as General Orders No. 100, *Instructions for the Government of Armies of the United States in the Field*. The "Lieber Code," as it became known, contained rules for the protection of works of art and cultural, charitable, and educational institutions, including "museums of art." The Lieber Code exercised a powerful influence on a network of law scholars and jurists in Europe and America; many of these international law activists played key roles in the development of rules of war.

96   INTERNATIONAL NORMS AND CYCLES OF CHANGE

In the latter half of the nineteenth century, European governments, which the international law activists commonly served as legal advisors or foreign ministry officials, undertook a variety of efforts to limit the destructiveness of warfare. States entered into treaties designed to protect sick and injured soldiers (1864 Geneva Convention) and to ban specific types of weapons (1868 Declaration of St. Petersburg). The 1874 Brussels Declaration, explicitly inspired by the Lieber Code, included articles prohibiting the seizure or destruction of historic and artistic monuments and institutions (the Declaration was never ratified)(Schindler and Toman 1973, 38). The same principles, however, did appear in the conventions that emerged from the 1899 and 1907 Hague Peace Conferences. Convention IV (1907) included the following provision (Art. 56):

> The property of municipalities, that of institutions dedicated to religion, charity and education, the arts and sciences, even when State property, shall be treated as private property [protected from damage or confiscation].
>
> All seizure of, and destruction or wilful [sic] damage done to institutions of this character, historic monuments, works of art and science, is forbidden, and should be made the subject of legal proceedings. (Schindler and Toman 1988, 91–92)

World War I witnessed the destruction of historic buildings and collections; Germany was compelled by the treaties concluding the war to make reparations for damage to renowned cultural sites (like the library of Louvain) and to return to Belgium certain artworks that had made their way to Germany in previous decades. In the 1920s and 1930s, there were several efforts to produce an international convention for the protection of cultural objects and monuments during wartime. But events in Europe in 1938 and 1939 interrupted the latest of these projects.

Nazi Plunder

Hitler and the Nazis surpassed even Napoleon as relentless plunderers of Europe's artistic patrimony. Of course, the Nazis could exploit tools and technologies that Napoleon never imagined. Where the French relied on carts and barges, the Germans could loot on a scale made possible by trucks, trains, and aircraft. But the same spirit that drove Napoleonic plundering inspired the Nazis. In both cases, the looters gathered (what they saw as) the highest expressions of artistic genius and civilization, to what were meant to be the capitals of new empires. In fact, from the plundered art, Hitler expected to stock what he envisioned would be the greatest collection of art in the world, housed in an immense museum planned for Linz, Austria (Roxan and Wanstall 1964, 8–15; Plaut October 1946, 73).

In Eastern Europe, Nazi looting was systematic and ruthless. In addition to seizing valuable pieces of art, the Germans razed important cultural sites; in Russia alone they destroyed some 427 museums (Roxan and Wanstall 1964, 115). The story in Western Europe was quite different, not in outcome but in technique. Though the Germans left public collections alone for the most part, they meticulously took possession of privately owned art, especially collections Jews owned.[10] In addition, the Nazi plunder machine also acquired artworks through purchases that presented a semblance of legality[11] but that amounted to forced sales.[12] The total haul from France was immense. According to German records, presented as evidence at the Nuremberg trials, the major looting organization, the Einzatstab Reichsleiter Rosenberg (ERR), through July 15, 1944, had sent to Germany 21,903 items, including 10,890 paintings, 583 sculptures and statues, and 583 tapestries (U.S. Chief Counsel 1946, vol. 3, 666–70).

Nazi Justifications

The Nazis felt some compulsion to explain or rationalize their plundering, which demonstrates that even they were conscious of international norms and aware that others would find their plundering objectionable or illegal. The justifications for seizing the cultural properties of other countries and private individuals fell into three categories. First, the Nazis claimed to be reclaiming Germany's own artistic patrimony, of which it had been despoiled in earlier wars. For instance, a three-volume report, submitted to Hitler in 1941, listed thousands of German cultural items then to be found in various countries (including the United States and the Soviet Union), though France bore the brunt of the document's indignation. In addition, the report condemned and sought redress for two

[10] The story of Nazi art plundering in France and the rest of Western Europe is expertly told by Nicholas (1994), Feliciano (1997), Simon (1971), and Roxan and Wanstall (1964).
[11] On the activities of the agents and dealers, see Nicholas (1994, chap. 6), Roxan and Wanstall (1964, chap. 6), and Simon (1971, chaps. 6, 7).
[12] Much of the German art acquisition activity in the Low Countries followed this pattern. See Nicholas (1994, chap. 4) and Roxan and Wanstall (1964, chap. 5).

historic wrongs: Napoleon's plundering in Germany and Austria and the Versailles Treaty.

Second, the Nazis asserted a right to objects produced by Germanic artists or under the influence of German culture. Anything that could be tied to German artists, or even a "Germanic spirit," should be reintegrated into the Reich (Petropolous 2000, 9–10). For example, the German claim on Poland's artistic treasures was expressed with brazen clarity by one of Mühlmann's assistants:

> Due to the comprehensive safeguarding of works of art in the Occupied Polish territory, there are today again available to us works which Polish scholars have falsely claimed as the achievements of their own artists. Their place in the true context of the mighty Germanic cultural tradition in the East can now be assured. (Quoted in Nicholas 1994, 71)

Third, the Nazis saw themselves as establishing the Third Reich's rightful cultural supremacy. That was, for instance, a guiding motive behind Hitler's Führermuseum in Linz, which would house the greatest collection of paintings in the world.

Opposing Plunder

The Allied countries considered Nazi art seizures an additional outrage against international norms. Their response consisted of measures to preserve Europe's cultural patrimony during the war and a massive restitution effort at its end. Naturally, some French officials sought to oppose or obstruct Nazi plundering efforts. They referred to international law; in a June 1941 letter, the French Treasury ministry explicitly raised Article 46 of the 1907 Hague Convention that declared private property inviolable (Simon 1971, 54).

Word of Nazi cultural plundering eventually reached the West. In the fall of 1942, prominent American art museum leaders proposed the creation of a commission for the preservation of fine arts and monuments in war zones. One rationale for the proposal was that it would counteract Axis propaganda that depicted the Allies as looters and despoilers (additional evidence that the Nazis understood that plunder was widely regarded as illegitimate). Creating the commission would "bear witness that these things belong not only to particular peoples but also to the heritage of mankind" (American Commission for the Protection and

Salvage of Artistic and Historic Monuments in War Areas 1946, 33). The American Commission for the Protection and Salvage of Artistic and Historic Monuments in Europe (known as the Roberts Commission after its chairman, Supreme Court Justice Owen J. Roberts) came into being in August 1943. In the words of the State Department press release announcing the creation of the Roberts Commission, it was "evidence of the Government's intention that, when military operations have been concluded, there shall be restitution of public property appropriated by the Axis Powers" (U.S. Department of State 1943). The Roberts Commission, in conjunction with a pair of nongovernment committees, produced and supplied to the armed forces more than seven hundred maps identifying churches, palaces, museums, historic buildings and monuments to be shielded from war damage (American Commission for the Protection and Salvage of Artistic and Historic Monuments in War Areas 1946, 4).

The Roberts Commission also lobbied the War Department's Civil Affairs Division to establish a Monuments, Fine Arts and Archives Branch (MFA&A), which it did in autumn 1943. Among the early MFA&A officers were academics, architects, sculptors, painters, and museum curators (Flanner 1947, 269; Simon 1971, 155). Not surprisingly, qualified personnel for the MFA&A were in chronic short supply; there were seldom more than twelve officers in the field in Europe. The British created a parallel structure, in October 1943, naming the renowned archaeologist, lieutenant colonel (Sir) Leonard Woolley, as Architectural Adviser to the War Office. Woolley staffed a Monuments and Fine Arts branch and, with the help of outside experts, compiled a list of monuments, collections, and historic sites to be protected in Europe and Asia (Woolley 1947, 7, 9). One of the first challenges for the MFA&A personnel and their British colleagues during Allied offensives in Europe was to prevent, as much as possible, unnecessary damage to cultural sites. Though winning battles was the Army's overriding concern, General Eisenhower conveyed general orders prior to the invasions of Italy and Normandy regarding the preservation of cultural treasures. For instance, the May 1944 order, issued days prior to the Normandy landings, said, among other things:

> Shortly we will be fighting our way across the Continent of Europe in battles designed to preserve our civilization. Inevitably, in the path of our advance will be found historical monuments and cultural centers which symbolize to the world all that we are fighting to preserve.

It is the responsibility of every commander to protect and respect these symbols whenever possible . . .

Civil Affairs Staffs and higher echelons will advise commanders of the locations of historical monuments of this type, both in advance of the front and in occupied areas. (Eisenhower Order 1944)

As the Allied offensives pushed into Germany, and it became clear that the war was nearing an end, the mission of the MFA&A units changed. With the help of information from captured Germans, Allied forces located the mines, monasteries, and castles where the Nazis had stored both German cultural treasures and the plundered objects from all across Europe. By consensus, it was clear that the heart of Allied policy would be restitution—returning cultural properties stolen by the Nazis to their rightful owners.[13] A few high-profile cultural treasures were returned almost immediately; for example, the stained glass windows from the Strasbourg cathedral arrived home in November 1945 amidst considerable ceremony (Standen n.d.).

The planning for restitution had begun much earlier. As early as 1942, discussions on restitution took place in two bodies. The first was a subcommittee of the Comité Interallié pour l'Etude de l'Armistice (the organ of the governments in exile). The Comité's draft proposals regarding restitution of and compensation for cultural objects was accepted by the Committee of Ministers of Foreign Affairs in September 1943. The second was the Conference of Allied Ministers of Education (CAME), which in April 1944 created the Commission for Protection and Restitution of Cultural Material (chaired by Paul Vaucher and known more commonly as the Vaucher Commission). The Commission began to collect data on the losses of cultural properties in the occupied countries (Sutton 1945).

The general restitution policy was enunciated in the January 1943 *Inter-Allied Declaration Against Acts of Dispossession Committed in Territories Under Enemy Occupation or Control*, signed by sixteen governments (including those of Britain, the Soviet Union, and the United States) and the French National Committee. The declaration announced that transfers of ownership of or interest in properties from the occupied lands would be void, even if they took place under apparently legal cover

---

[13] My account of Allied restitution policies and the U.S. role in them relies on the excellent work of Michael J. Kurtz (1985) and Wojciech Kowalski (1994; 1998).

(Kowalski 1998, 40–41; Kurtz 1985, 58). The disposition of looted properties also figured in the agenda for the Bretton Woods conference of July 1944. The Bretton Woods *Final Act* referred to the 1943 *Declaration* and endorsed the measures taken by the Allies to recover and restore to their owners looted properties, even when found in the territory of neutral countries (Kowalski 1998, 42).

To carry out restitution, the Allies established "collecting points" at Munich, Wiesbaden, and seven other locations (American Commission for the Protection and Salvage of Artistic and Historic Monuments in War Areas 1946, 135). The Allies continued to conduct the restitution effort until 1951, when they turned it over to the Germans (Roxan and Wanstall 1964, 173–74).

The Soviet Exception?

The exception to the Allied policy of restitution was the Soviet Union. Already in 1942 the Soviets had established a special commission to calculate the value of art the Nazis seized from Soviet institutions. The commission quickly settled on the notion that Soviet losses should be compensated by replacements of equivalent value from German museums and collections. Special trophy brigades traveled with the armies. The first trainload of artworks from Germany left for Moscow in March 1945. Subsequent shipments included treasures from Berlin, Potsdam, and the Dresden museums, as well as a major collection of Impressionist and Post-Impressionist paintings, which went into a storeroom at the Hermitage. The Hermitage received in total four trainloads of plunder from Germany; the Pushkin Museum in Moscow took in 2,991 crates of art (Akinsha and Kozlov 1995, 142–73).

Two aspects of Soviet policy reveal an awareness that other countries would consider Soviet seizures of cultural properties illegitimate: secrecy and justification. First, the Soviets kept secret their art removals from Germany and did not make them part of the Allied restitution or reparations processes. The Soviets did not officially admit to the possession of German art until two art scholars, Konstantin Akinsha and Grigorii Kozlov, discovered long-buried archives relating to the World War II trophy brigades. Only after they published their findings did the Ministry of Culture, in October 1991, publicly acknowledge the truth. The Hermitage "trove" of Impressionist and Post-Impressionist art was finally opened to public viewing in 1995 (Akinsha and Kozlov 1995, 234, 239, 257). Second, even when the Soviet possession of looted art became public knowledge, some Soviet officials sought to justify retention of the plunder. Justification amounts to an acknowledgment of the rules. When the Soviets finally did reveal the existence of the artworks seized in the war, many Russians argued that Russia should keep the treasures as compensation (restitution in kind) for the hundreds of thousands of cultural objects the Nazis destroyed in the Soviet republics. The argument was not that plunder was acceptable, rather that what the Soviets had done was to carry out a form of restitution (235, 253–54).[14]

An American Exception?

In one instance, the United States also flirted with the possibility of taking German cultural properties as compensation for war losses. The denouement of that story strengthened the norms against plunder. The U.S. military government in Germany had in July 1945 prepared a memorandum outlining three categories of cultural properties, the last of which (Category C) was eligible to be shipped to the United States. An important rationale for such transfers was that "neither expert personnel nor satisfactory facilities are available in the US zone to properly safeguard and handle these priceless works of art" (U.S. Group Control Council n.d.) However, some American officials supported the idea that artworks from German collections could be used as restitution in kind or for reparations. For instance, a letter from political adviser Robert Murphy to General Lucius Clay (Deputy Military Governor in the U.S. zone) quoted from a State Department message declaring that "the Department of State . . . is disturbed by the view that Germans should not be required to replace looted art not found or destroyed." The State Department message also referred to a statement agreed upon by the State-War-Navy Coordinating Committee and the Roberts Commission, envisioning replacement in kind from German collections for cultural property known to have been looted and not found within two years of Germany's surrender (Murphy Letter 1945). In addition, Edwin Pauley, advisor on reparations to the U.S. military government and U.S. delegate to the Allied Reparations Commission, wanted to use art for reparations (Kurtz 1985, 126).

As plans developed to transport at least some major artworks from German collections to the United States, opposition erupted in

---

[14] The Soviet government had returned artworks to East Germany (by then, of course, a Soviet satellite) in 1955 and again in 1958–59. But millions of trophy art objects remained in the Soviet Union.

many quarters. The first MFA&A officers to hear of it were appalled. John Nicholas Brown, a civilian assigned as arts advisor to the U.S. military government, strongly protested to General Clay. He contradicted the memo's assertion regarding the lack of facilities and personnel and argued that moving masterpieces across the ocean was quite as risky for their wellbeing as leaving them in Germany. More importantly, Brown opposed the idea on normative grounds: shipping Germany's artistic patrimony to the United States "seems to the writer, and to his associates in the MFA&A Branch not only immoral but hypocritical." Brown further declared:

> All through the operational phase of the MFA&A it was constantly said by our officers in the field that the US Army had established this service in order to preserve and protect works of art and not for the purpose of carrying them off to the USA, as was often accused by our Allies as well as by enemy propaganda. To have the German propaganda turn out to be true would indeed be humiliating. (Brown Letter 1945)

The British and Russian foreign ministers argued vigorously against the removals (Kurtz 1985, 126–27). By mid-August 1945, Pauley, supported by General Clay, was recommending that U.S. authorities make a public announcement along the following lines: the United States was "moving these [artworks] to the United States for the sole purpose of safeguarding and is holding them only as trustee for the German people and other rightful owners and will keep them in its possession only as long as it is necessary from the standpoint of physical safety or until the rightful owners may be determined" (Clay Note 1945; Pauley Cable 1945).

Finally, on September 26, 1945, the State Department and the National Gallery announced that German artworks would be brought to the United States "with the sole intention of keeping such treasures safe and in trust for the people of Germany or other rightful owners" (National Gallery Press Release 1945). The MFA&A officers in Germany were ordered to select 200 paintings from among those being stored at the Wiesbaden Collecting Point and begin preparing them for shipment. The order ignited immediate opposition among the American monuments personnel. Lieutenant Craig H. Smyth, Officer-in-Charge of the Munich Central Collecting Point, wrote to the Chief of the MFA&A unit, Major L. Bancel La Farge, that the plan was "entirely without justification" and would "only weaken our influence for good in Europe" (Smyth Letter 1945).

Thirty-two (out of thirty-five) of them either added their names to a strongly worded protest or expressed support for its content (Standen Letter 1945). The protest became known as the Wiesbaden Manifesto. The Manifesto declared that the shipment of German paintings to the United States would be "neither morally tenable nor trustworthy" and stated that facilities and personnel for the protection of works of art were open and functioning in Germany. The Manifesto also pointed out that the Allies were preparing to prosecute individuals for the seizure of cultural treasures under the pretext of "protective custody," and argued that U.S. personnel would be "no less culpable" in carrying out the removal of the German paintings (Wiesbaden Manifesto 1945). The Manifesto was never forwarded to the Army hierarchy (several MFA&A officers had been reminded that they could be court-martialed for refusing to carry out orders) (Flanner 1947, 289).

In the meantime, the plan to bring 200 paintings to the United States had been reported in *The New Yorker*. In a story by Janet Flanner, the magazine reported that the project was "already regarded in liberated Europe as shockingly similar to the practice of the ERR [Hitler's looting task force]" (quoted in Nicholas 1994, 395). An incident reported by Edith Standen in her essay on MFA&A activities illustrates the sensitivities involved. Drawing on reports filed by MFA&A officers in Baden-Württemberg, Standen relates how the "greatest painting in the Land, the 'Stuppach Madonna' by Grünewald," was found in the Heilbronn salt mine and returned in perfect condition to the small church in the village of Stuppach on 23 March 1946. "At the time it returned, the memory of the 202 great German paintings, taken to Washington for safe-keeping in the previous November, was still fresh, and Lt. Koch reported that the home coming of the Grünewald was most re-assuring to people who knew that the Nazis never 'stole,' but always removed for safe-keeping" (Standen n. d.).

In the end, 202 paintings left Wiesbaden and went into storage at the National Gallery in Washington, D.C., in December 1945. Newspapers published letters of protest. The President of the College Art Association of America wrote to Secretary of State James F. Byrnes that "the integrity of United States policy has been questioned as a result of this action" (Lee Letter 1946). Petitions opposing the transfer flowed into the Roberts Commission and government offices. Former MFA&A officers published the text of the Wiesbaden Manifesto in the *Magazine of Art* and a highly critical article in the *College Art Journal*. Ninety-five art historians petitioned President Truman.[15] Later, the paintings went on display at the National Gallery and then traveled to New York, Philadelphia, Chicago, Boston, Detroit, Cleveland, Minneapolis, San Francisco, Los Angeles, St. Louis, Pittsburgh, and Toledo. Ten million people saw the paintings. By the spring of 1949, they were back in Germany (Nicholas 1994, 405).

Conclusion

The case of antiplunder norms conforms to the cycle theory of norm change. Actions—in this case, massive plundering by Napoleon's armies and by the Nazis—triggered disputes. Actions— plundering by the French armies—triggered disputes about what kinds of conduct were permissible in war. Actors offered arguments on both sides. The consensus that emerged in 1815 was that the art treasures brought to Paris should be returned. The policy of restitution was, however, not included in the treaties negotiated at Paris and Vienna, nor was it comprehensively implemented. The principle that cultural properties should be protected in war was subsequently more fully developed, and found expression in the Hague Conventions. World War II produced another turn through the cycle. Nazi plundering triggered outrage and argument. This time, consensus quickly emerged among the Allies that seizures of cultural goods were impermissible and would be undone. The outcome of the debates was a policy of thorough-going restitution. Antiplunder norms were strengthened by the inclusion of cultural property crimes in the Nuremberg trials and by the peace treaties, which mandated the return of cultural objects. The 1954 Convention for the Protection of Cultural Property in the Event of Armed Conflict codified international norms against wartime art plunder.

The prohibition of plunder also demonstrates how cycles of norm change are linked across time. In the Napoleonic case, the French argued that they were exercising the historic right of conquering armies. The allies were not unanimously opposed to this claim; some, in fact, were resigned (at least initially) to leaving the confiscated artworks in France as a fact of war. But others (led by Prussia) insisted on restitution, which, after Waterloo, became the general policy. The outcome of the arguments

---

[15] A few notable figures from the art museum world, such as Francis Henry Taylor (the Metropolitan Museum) and John Walker (the National Gallery) supported the presence of the German paintings in the United States and hoped to acquire German-owned pieces for their galleries (Nicholas 1994, 400-1).

in 1815 supported subsequent development of the antiplunder norm. The case of Nazi looting shows how earlier disputes had shaped the normative context. During and after World War II, there was no ambivalence or disagreement among the Allies on the illegality of plunder and the imperative of restitution. They could cite a developed body of international norms and precedents, including the Hague Conventions. Even German justifications for the plundering offered backhanded acknowledgment of the international normative context. For instance, the Nazis argued that their seizures in France were justified because the restitution of 1815 had not been complete, that they were reclaiming German artworks seized by Napoleon and still in France.

Not surprisingly, international norms for the protection of cultural treasures in wartime continue to evolve. And developments in this area of international law continue to emerge out of disputes triggered by specific acts. The wars in the former Yugoslavia produced hundreds of cultural atrocities, most famously the shelling of the Old Town of Dubrovnik and the destruction of the bridge at Mostar. The international community responded with outrage and efforts to restore the damaged sites. The Iraqi looting of Kuwait's cultural treasures in 1990 provoked a similar international response. These events triggered international debate about the inadequacy of protections for cultural treasures in wartime. One outcome of those arguments was an additional Protocol (II) to the 1954 Convention for the Protection of Cultural Property in the Event of Armed Conflict. International rules prohibiting plunder are part of the stream of sovereignty norms; antiplunder rules protect the right of states to their cultural patrimony, a right that states retain even in defeat or under occupation.

Chapter 5

Terrorism: Reinforcing States' Monopoly on Force

Kendall W. Stiles

The international regulation of terrorism has invariably confronted two major challenges. First, as nonstate actors, most terrorists have no clear standing under international law (O'Connell 2005, 454). Because international law traditionally has regulated state-to-state interaction, it is ill-adapted to regulating private activities. These fall more naturally under domestic law. Second, because terrorism is inherently political, it invariably provokes varied responses from states. The age-old notion that "one man's terrorist is another man's freedom fighter" still holds. Even regimes known for their opposition to terrorism, such as the Reagan Administration, have provided support to irregular military forces in the name of "national liberation" or "self-determination" (Kerstetter 1978, 535).

This chapter shows how states have coped with these two challenges and how they have reframed the struggle to suppress terrorism using diverse legal structures and principles. In particular, we will see that the scope of what could be termed "justifiable" terrorism has narrowed dramatically, especially over the last decade, and the scope of justifiable responses has broadened proportionally. At the same time, the status of terrorist groups has changed in fits and starts over the years as states seek greater control over what may well be uncontrollable.

International norms on terrorism have developed through three distinct cycles. Prior to the mid 1950s, terrorism was not considered a separate crime of special interest to the international community. In most respects, it was viewed as either a matter for domestic law enforcement or an issue of international intervention. In any case, no rule required states to suppress terrorism. The fact that a 1937 draft terrorism convention received only a single ratification is evidence of the lack of interest in the topic.

During the 1960s and 1970s, interest in terrorism increased dramatically, mostly in direct response to the number and scale of attacks taking place around the world. As hijackings, bombings, abductions, and assassinations spread across both the developed and developing world, governments struggled to categorize and respond to these acts. From the beginning, terrorism defied definition because of its political nature. On the one hand, many states were inclined to view terrorism as a particularly egregious case of criminality, subject to domestic law enforcement. On the other hand, since political goals and motives clearly colored these attacks, many states argued that attention should be paid to the merits of those goals. As an increasing number of colonies achieved independence—many as a result of violent insurrection—a number of treaties expressly carved out political exceptions for terrorists and urged states to address underlying grievances and oppression. States were even enjoined to support legitimate violence (especially movements of national liberation or struggles against unlawful occupation).

A dramatic shift of attitude emerged in the 1980s, however, the result of which was a push by developed countries to remove these political exceptions and treat all terrorists as international criminals regardless of motive. The September 11, 2001, attacks served to remove most of the remaining resistance to this approach, although the Organization of the Islamic Conference continues to seek an exception for Palestinians fighting Israeli occupation. Antiterrorism norms thus evolved through three main cycles, each triggered by specific clusters of terrorist acts that provoked debates over appropriate state responses. Rules to suppress terrorism are part of the stream of sovereignty rules, as they consolidate the control of states over the use of force by seeking to suppress the use of force by alternative (nonstate) actors. These cycles are represented in Figure 5.1.

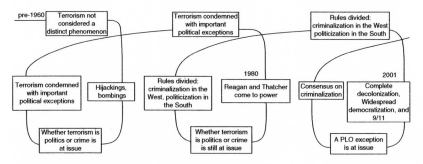

Figure 5.1 Antiterrorism norm cycles.

The Context of Antiterror Law Circa 1960

Terrorism is generally understood to be violence perpetrated by individuals and small groups aimed at instilling fear in the target society and government apparatus with the aim of inducing changes in policy. Though definitions vary widely in academic writings and treaty language, one typical definition is provided by the US Department of Defense: terrorism is "the calculated use of unlawful violence or the threat of unlawful violence to inculcate fear; intended to coerce or intimidate governments or societies in the pursuit of goals that are generally political, religious, or ideological" (Kastenberg 2004, 100). This said, one important variant is the notion that only states commit acts of terror, a position held by the U.N. General Assembly for a time in the mid-1970s, as we will see below. Other observers deny that motivation is a defining characteristic, with the implication that not only states but also criminal organizations, gangs, and others may engage in terrorism (Kronenwetter 2004, 24).

Depending on one's definition, then, the number of terrorist incidents varies widely. Some trace terrorism back to the Jewish Zealots of Antiquity, while others begin with the anarchists of the late-1800s. All agree, however, that during the 1960s a new wave of what could be termed "modern" terrorism emerged. This new phenomenon had several characteristics that required a multilateral response. To begin, the attacks tended to be transnational, involving organizations from Palestine or Cuba, for example, attacking targets in Europe and North America. Many of the targets, such as aircraft on international flights, were also transnational in nature, prompting comparisons with piracy and other *ius cogens* crimes (Evans 1978, 4; Kronenwetter 2004, 30). The clear implication was that unless states collaborated in controlling the behavior of these actors across national boundaries, no one would be safe.

Prior to 1960, violent political dissent was more often than not treated as mere crime (Bhoumik 2005, 294). Where guerillas and terrorists have become too powerful for ordinary police forces, states have formed paramilitary units within the police (such as SWAT teams in the US and the CRS in France) and special forces groups within the military (such as Delta Force) and have deployed them, sometimes alongside conventional military units. In such situations, states generally deny both military status and full due process rights to the unconventional fighters. At the peak of IRA terrorism in the United Kingdom, British authorities resorted to torture, for example (Stiles and Wells 2007). This said, in some situations, governments have also resorted to negotiations, coupled with grants of amnesty and other exemptions from criminal culpability. These "softer" approaches at least implicitly acknowledge the legitimacy of the terrorists' political goals (Wilkinson 2000, 114).

Where the violence has had a transnational dimension, states have engaged in disputes over jurisdiction and responsibility. In 1934, the King of Yugoslavia was assassinated in Hungary, and many states blamed Budapest for failure to control the terrorists' movements (Mellor 2002, 367). The League of Nations issued a formal rebuke to Hungary and passed a resolution calling upon all states to take action against terrorists operating within their borders. France moved that a full-fledged antiterror Convention be drafted and an international court be created to try terrorists and other "enemies of mankind" (*hostis humani generis*; Kastenberg 2004, 103; Wilkinson 2000, 188). The result was the 1937 Convention for the Prevention and Punishment of Terrorism and a Convention for the Creation of an International Criminal Court (Blakesley 1992, 141). The Terrorism Convention was signed by twenty-five states—essentially the entire League membership—and ratified by India before World War II broke out and diverted attention from the issue. The United Nations did not include the treaty among those passed to it from the League and lack of interest in the topic in the 1940s left it a "dead letter" (Franck and Lockwood 1974, 69).

The 1937 Terrorism Convention was ahead of its time in many ways, and its provisions anticipated language that would be used in future agreements. It defined terrorism as "criminal acts directed against a State and intended or calculated to crate a state of terror in the minds of particular persons, or a group of persons or the general public" and enjoined states to cease and desist from providing encouragement and solace to the perpetrators (Franck and Lockwood 1974, 79). Jurisdiction over such acts would be granted to a multilateral criminal tribunal on the basis of the universality principle (Lillich 1982, 175), a form of jurisdiction that states have since rejected in favor of the "prosecute or extradite" principle, to be discussed later. Today's International Criminal Court, for example, does not have jurisdiction over terrorism (Wilkinson 2000, 189).

After World War II, terrorism was far from the minds of most governments until the 1950s when a series of hijackings-most carried out by private individuals for private motives-prompted efforts to improve security. It was noted, for example, that the framers of the Warsaw and Chicago Conventions on air travel did not anticipate hijacking—especially politically motivated hijackings—and had made inadequate provisions for its prevention (Evans 1978, 15).

In sum, at the end of the 1950s, terrorism had been categorized as both an indigenous issue to be addressed by domestic criminal law or political negotiation, as well as a global issue warranting universal jurisdiction. This left those who would respond to modern terrorism with an extremely wide array of legal alternatives.

Modern Terrorism: Initial Responses

Kronenwetter traces modern terrorism to the hijacking of an El Al flight in 1968 by Palestinians (2004, 30; Evans 1978, 7). In addition, foreign diplomats came under increasing attack in Venezuela and elsewhere. Such attacks were complicated by the fact that not all states objected to the political objectives of the perpetrators and some were willing to provide them refuge, resources and training.

As early as 1962, the United States and Venezuela began to press for tougher international rules on hijacking in the context of negotiations on the International Civil Aviation Organization's (ICAO's) Tokyo Convention. Originally intended to address general safety standards, the United States succeeded in introducing new standards on preventing hijacking per se (McWhinney 1987, 36). This dovetailed with new measures adopted in the United States to outlaw hijacking (calling it "aircraft piracy") in 1961 (Evans 1978, 4). Western governments were increasingly intent on setting standards to ensure that every state from which international air travel originated provided minimum guarantees against hijacking. Since at this point in history these states dominated the ICAO membership, they were able to dominate the negotiations producing the 1963 Tokyo Convention. It was ratified rather quickly and entered into force in 1969. But the attacks on aircraft and diplomats in the late 1960s spurred even more agreements, most of which were primarily reactive (Anderson 2000, 228). This pattern of reacting dramatically to isolated events would come to characterize the evolution of international antiterror law. The more dramatic the attack, the greater the tendency of states to further criminalize terrorism.

Another pattern that emerged early on was the "sectoral" approach to antiterror agreements. Once African colonies began to achieve independence in large numbers in the 1960s, they added to an overwhelming majority of developing countries in the U.N. General Assembly. United in hostility to Western colonialism and sympathetic to radical ideologies, the developing countries adopted a new approach to terrorism, namely by making an exception for any attacks that were motivated by a quest for self-determination (McWhinney 1987, 138). This had the result of almost paralyzing efforts at negotiating a comprehensive agreement on terrorism. Rather than settle for complete stalemate, enterprising and resourceful states argued instead for agreements on very narrow issues around which there was considerable agreement.

One area that prompted the least opposition was the effort to further protect diplomats from terror attacks. Their symbolic role as state representatives was not lost on those who sought to send a political message, and so they were especially vulnerable to attack. However, even states that were sympathetic to the terrorists' goals acknowledged that diplomats deserved special protection in order to ensure ease of interstate communication. This is known as the functional theory of diplomatic immunity (Murphy 1978, 279). The first attempt to provide special protections was the Organization of American States' 1971 Convention to Prevent and Punish the Acts of Terrorism Taking the Forms of Crime against Persons and Related Extortion That Are of International Significance. As it happened, the ideological divide in the OAS was already too severe to allow the creation of a coherent agreement. The Convention provided for states to agree to either prosecute or extradite any persons that came into their custody and were suspected of attacks on diplomats (Lillich 1982, 79). At the same time, however, it also provided for grants of asylum to anyone a state thought might be persecuted by the requesting state on the basis of his political views (the so-called political exception; Cassese 1996, 77; Freestone 1997). These two provisions naturally conflicted with each other—a problem in future agreements on terrorism.

This conflict was reflected in the response of OAS member states to the final text, which only thirteen supported and only six ratified in the first ten years. Another six countries had opposed the entire negotiation on the grounds that the causes of terrorism—namely colonialism, poverty, hegemony, and so forth— should be the focus (Murphy 1978, 300). In the final analysis, the OAS Convention has served little purpose. Even where states were willing to ratify the treaty, they could opt out of the "extradite or prosecute" provision.

The United States pressed the U.N. General Assembly to develop a new global convention to protect diplomats. The initiative was rather warmly received, in part because of détente between the United States and U.S.S.R. and the fact that the proposed convention had little that was controversial (McWhinney 1987, 134). Most governments had passed specific laws protecting diplomats at any rate (Murphy 1978, 283). The International Law Commission drafted the agreement, which incorporated both the principles of "prosecute or extradite" as well as the political exception (McWhinney 1987, 134). Algeria, speaking for both the OIC and the developing country caucus more generally, insisted that national liberation movements be exempted, with the result that some Western states worried that their diplomats were no better protected than before (Murphy 1978, 312).

In the ICAO, the United States and Canada introduced new treaty language in 1971 that would allow states to sanction other signatories that failed to adequately protect international air travel (Evans 1978, 79). France and others objected to the automaticity of the U.S.—Canada proposal, arguing for greater flexibility. They also sought to amend the Chicago Convention rather than draft a new agreement (McWhinney 1987, 53). Ultimately, the lack of hijackings in the early 1970s, which more than likely stemmed from new national initiatives to screen baggage and passengers, led negotiators to suspend the talks for a new treaty (Wilkinson 2000, 113). Note that just as new treaty negotiations have been spurred by exogenous shocks, a return to normalcy has tended to blunt interest in further agreements.

The debate that erupted in the U.N. General Assembly following the attacks on Israeli athletes by PLO gunmen at the 1972 Munich Olympics and the response to Israel's raid on the hijackers in Entebbe, Uganda quickly came to dominate international actions on terrorism. The United States put forward a draft terrorism convention and urged its acceptance. The draft provided for the criminalization of terrorism and mutual agreement to prosecute or extradite (Franck and Lockwood 1974, 85). This was an extension of U.S. bilateral negotiations to include specific provisions for extraditing terrorists by removing the "political exception" provision of existing treaties (Kerstetter 1978, 537). Though Western states generally supported the U.S. initiative and developing states opposed it, Western governments were not united at this time. Canada, for example, argued for an emphasis on the continued validity of the political exception to prevent human rights abuses. Other governments were inclined to acknowledge the legitimacy of certain terrorists' aims, including those of the PLO, having elsewhere condemned Israeli occupation. Israel objected to the U.S. definition of terrorism as exclusively involving violence against persons rather than property as well (Franck and Lockwood 1974, 76). Even the European Convention on the Suppression of Terrorism, negotiated in the mid-1970s, provided for the political exception even as it aimed at strengthening antiterror cooperation. France refused to extradite Basque suspects to Spain and Ireland refused to extradite IRA members to Britain (Wilkinson 2000, 120). Several European states harbored members of the PKK—a rebel Kurdish group operating in Turkey (Aktan and Koknar 2002, 296). As of 1974, there was no consensus on rules among Western states.

Developing countries, including especially member-states of the Organization of the Islamic Conference, opposed the US proposal and countered it with considerable relish. With the support of the Soviet Union and China, the General Assembly Sixth Committee passed a resolution in 1972 that, rather than condemning the terrorists, condemned "the continuation of repressive and terrorist attacks by colonial racist and alien regimes" (Luck 2004, 88). In 1973, the General Assembly passed Resolution 3103 (XXVIII)—over Western objections—declaring that national liberation movements were 'international combatants' under the Geneva Conventions and therefore were permitted considerable latitude to engage in acts of violence (Verwey 1981, 81).

In this context, the U.N. General Assembly in 1972 commissioned a study of terrorism, with a focus on its causes. A thirty-five member Ad Hoc Committee of state representatives was created for the purpose. Syria became a spokesman for the developing countries, arguing that any discussion of criminalizing terrorism should be set aside in favor of a discussion of actions that were "worse than terrorism," namely aggression, hegemony, nuclear weapons, imperialism, colonialism, attacks on civilians by occupying powers, poverty, and so on (McWhinney 1987, 138). All of these fell under the broad category of "state terrorism" (Franck and Lockwood 1974, 73). Naturally, national liberation movements were exempted from any antiterror measures. The final report that emerged in 1979 was the high-water mark for the political exception, granting as it did blanket exemptions for victims of Western imperialism, exploitation and apartheid, among other things (Cassese 1996). Meanwhile, in the Security Council, a relatively weak draft resolution condemning terrorism in general was vetoed by the USSR and China and rejected by four other elected members (Luck 2004, 87).

The Declaration on the Granting of Independence to Colonial Countries and Peoples, which called upon states to abandon colonial rule and support genuine national liberation movements, was unanimously approved by the U.N. General Assembly in 1960. Likewise, the International Covenant on Civil and Political Rights, which received widespread support from Western countries, enjoined state parties to "promote the realization of the right of self-determination" (Article 1 (3); Honoré 1996, 141; Rosenstock 1971). Of course, consent to a General Assembly resolution does not carry the weight of a binding legal commitment. The same could be said of some signatures to conventions. Some agreements were simply left unratified by the vast majority of states after the initial vote and signature so that they never came into force. Only the conventions on the protection of diplomats and airports were ratified by a majority of states as of mid 2001, while most other conventions had fewer than seventy ratifications (UN GA 2001a).

The Hostages Convention illustrates the international debate over the handling of the terrorism question during the 1970s. Nonaligned countries in general and members of the Organization of the Islamic Conference (OIC) in particular pressed for special treatment of certain national liberation groups—especially the PLO. The OIC submitted the following language at the beginning of the debate:

> For the purpose of this Convention, the term 'taking of hostages' shall not include any act or acts carried out in the process of national liberation against colonial rule, racist and foreign regimes, by liberation movements recognized by the United Nations or regional organizations. (Verwey 1981, 72–3)

This proposal met with strong opposition from the US, which was now joined by other Western states that had grown weary of the impunity granted to perpetrators of terrorism. However, unlike earlier agreements, the developing country sponsors sought consensus. To achieve this, a compromise was reached. The legitimacy of the struggle for self-determination was explicitly acknowledged in the Preamble while the "prosecute or extradite" clause found its way into the body of the treaty (Verwey 1981, 76). The result was a relatively weak (but widely accepted) agreement that had no enforcement provisions and numerous escape clauses (Freestone 1997; Downs, Rocke, and Barsoom 1996).

While much ink was being spilt defending the political exception, another current flowed through the United Nations. In 1974, the the General Assembly passed Resolution 33/14, which condemned states that supported "armed bands, groups, irregulars or mercenaries, which carry out acts of armed force against another State" (Maogoto 2005, 249). The resolution passed largely because the term "terrorist" was omitted from the text, even though it was clear that most terrorist groups were covered. In 1979, the Sixth Committee drafted another resolution—approved in its essence in 1985—that condemned "all acts of terrorism that endangered human lives or fundamental freedoms" and appealed to states to endorse existing antiterror conventions.

International policy toward terrorism, even on the part of Western countries, evinced considerable ambivalence and contradiction until the mid-1980s. Terrorism was both condemned and officially tolerated, depending on the motives of the perpetrators and the political interests of states. Self-determination and prevention of persecution of suspects for ideological or other reasons largely trumped the principle of protecting innocents. It was not even clear whether anyone could be considered innocent where the target was global patterns of exploitation and oppression (Franck and Lockwood 1974, 80). Even U.S. policy during this period—among the most aggressive among Western states—has been described as "passive, reactive and patient" (Maogoto 2005, 280).

Removal of the Political Exception, 1980–2001

During the period 1980–2001, the international community struggled with the question of eliminating political exceptions for terrorism. At the initiative first of the United States, then Europe, then Japan, an increasing number of instruments removed any justification for acts of terrorism. Opposition came primarily from the Organization of the Islamic Conference which still opposes any definition of terrorism that might condemn Palestinian violence against Israeli occupation. But over the course of twenty years, opposition in the developing world gradually evaporated—culminating in the emergence of a virtual consensus on a definition of terrorism after the attacks on September 11, 2001.

In April 1984, Ronald Reagan signed National Security Directive 138, signaling to the world a new strategy to deal with terrorism and the states that sponsor it. The United States would from this point on take offensive action when warranted to punish and deter terrorist attacks by striking the states that sponsored it (Maogoto 2005, 280). This policy led to the military strikes on Libya following the Berlin discotheque attacks in which Libyan agents were implicated. In 1986, after gradually tightening laws against terrorism (Leich 1984), the United States substantially expanded its jurisdiction over terrorists implicated in attacks on the US and US interests through the Omnibus Diplomatic Security and Antiterrorism Act (Blakesley 1992, 93).

The law became a model for other Western states and coincided with a new interest in a "military" approach to supplement the "criminalization" model (Bhoumik 2005, 294). It involved a commitment to deprive terrorists of safe havens, both in developing countries and Western states. In 1984, governments withdrew the political exception for Interpol investigations, making it easier for states to share intelligence (Wilkinson 2000, 191). They expanded the powers of police forces to conduct searches (Italy in particular) and asserted jurisdiction over criminal acts (Germany, e.g.) (Anderson 2000, 238; Blakesley 1992, 202). European states gradually improved their collaboration by removing the political exception from bilateral extradition treaties, culminating in its deletion from the European Terrorism Convention in 1996 (Wilkinson 2000, 121). They were also instrumental in pushing for a Security Council resolution (748) that condemned providing shelter and support to terrorist organizations and imposed sanctions on Libya (Kastenberg 2004, 119).

Of special interest is the shift of attitude in France and Japan where policies had tended to emphasize accommodation with militant political groups during the 1970s. Following a spate of attacks in both countries in the early 1990s (especially the Aum Shinrikyo sponsored sarin gas attacks in a Tokyo subway in 1995 that killed twelve and injured six thousand), both countries adopted a more inflexible approach. They were generally persuaded that political accommodation was likely to be ineffective in many cases and had generally failed. Japan passed a new law in 1997 which, although narrow and limited, gave the state enhanced powers to deal with irregular groups that engaged in mass killing (Alexander 2002, 361). In 1999, it passed new laws against money laundering in response to recommendations by the newly created Financial Action Task Force (FATF—see below) and generally endorsed new multilateral instruments (367).

France went a step further by hosting a meeting in mid-1996 of the Group of Seven (plus Russia) and guided the drafting of a toughly worded statement calling for all states to strengthen antiterror measures, including attacking their sources of funding and negotiating stronger extradition agreements (G7/P8 1996). This roughly coincided with the establishment of "financial intelligence units" and the "Egmont Group" to create specialized governmental investigations of money laundering and improve information-sharing—also at France's instigation. The Group created the FATF, whose functions included assessing member-states' laws governing money laundering and other illegal financial transactions and making recommendations for revision. Finally, France was instrumental in crafting language for the International Convention for the Suppression of the Financing of Terrorism (see below) that ultimately provided much of the language for Security Council resolution 1373 (see also below) (France, Ministère de l'Intérieur 2003).

International response to this shift in Western policies was mixed but became gradually more tolerant and even sympathetic over time. The U.N. General Assembly condemned the United States' attack on Libya, but a similar initiative in the Security Council was vetoed by the United States, United Kingdom, and France (Maogoto 2005, 279). The landmark General Assembly resolution 40/61, passed in December 1985, condemned imperialism, colonialism, apartheid and other global ills as the causes of terrorism, while at the same time unequivocally criminalized terrorist acts themselves (McWhinney 1987, 143).

> The significance of this resolution lay in the fact that after thousands of terrorist orchestrated injuries and deaths, affecting nations across the world, the United Nations had moved to take away the "shield of legitimacy" behind which terrorists hid. The world had officially accepted terrorism, not as an expression of political ideologies, but as a crime. (Maogoto 2005, 257)

A key reason for this shift in tone was a shift in the policies of the Soviet Union. Under Mikhail Gorbachev, the Soviet Union reversed its

Cold War policy where national liberation movements in general and terrorism in particular were concerned. The Soviet Union signaled a shift in attitudes as early as 1985 when it endorsed a Security Council resolution (579) condemning hostage taking and reminding all states of their obligation "to secure the safe release of the hostages" and prevent future incidents (Luck 2004, 90).

The end of the Cold War even led to a shift in the decision-making procedures of the United Nations, with significant implications for anti-terror law. Consensus became the norm in both the General Assembly and the Security Council (Hulton 2004; Wallensteen and Johansson 2004). Seizing the opportunity, Secretary-General Javier Perez de Cuellar urged the five permanent members to collaborate informally to resolve long-standing issues, thereby establishing a pattern that has continued, particularly since the 1991 Persian Gulf War (Mahbubani 2004, 256).

Other shifts in the global system contributed to the new U.N. approach. With the end of blue-water colonialism in the 1980s, newly independent states saw their new role as defenders of the status quo rather than fomenters of revolution. They found terrorist organizations particularly threatening. Most states were disinclined to give these nonstate global actors any standing in world affairs. The spread of democracy also meant that most aggrieved minorities now had nonviolent means available to express their complaints. A large number of countries shifted to a pro-Western orientation and were inclined to accept the West's interpretation of international law and terrorism.

Finally, with the end of the Cold War, U.N. members believed that the General Assembly could expand its role as the creator of new international law by means of consensus resolutions. For the General Assembly's Sixth Committee (Legal), in particular, this principle has become a central code:

> For the Sixth Committee, it's effectively taboo to bypass total agreement among its membership. Traditionally, it strives to embrace the opinion of every member and include it within the final body of opinion. This Committee, like the Second (Economic and Financial), runs on consensus. It has to, if its resolutions on international legal issues are to have more universal validity. (Talwar 2004)

With respect to antiterror law, new initiatives were being entertained in rapid succession. In 1994, the General Assembly approved

Resolution 49/60, the "Declaration of Measures to Eliminate International Terrorism," around which a new consensus crystallized. Although its principal purpose was to prepare the way for further study and discussion, it served to highlight international agreement on the need to eliminate terrorism in part by reducing the number of exceptions to previous rules. The key contribution of this resolution was a consensus definition of terrorism that would find its way into several subsequent documents:

> Criminal acts intended or calculated to provoke a state of terror in the general public, a group of persons or particular persons for political purposes are in any circumstances unjustifiable, whatever the considerations of a political, philosophical, ideological, racial, ethnic, religious or other nature that may be invoked to justify them. (GA Res. 49/60)

In 1996, the Sixth Committee was tasked with conducting negotiations on a comprehensive convention on terrorism through Resolution 51/210. Although work began on the comprehensive convention in 1996, this was eclipsed by the rapid success of other terrorism-related negotiations. By 1997, the General Assembly had already produced the International Convention for the Suppression of Terrorist Bombings, and in 1999, it approved the International Convention for the Suppression of the Financing of Terrorism without a vote. The final language was approved less than a year later. The convention repeated several familiar clauses ("prosecute or extradite") but broke new ground with Article 5 that clearly states bombings are "not justifiable by consideration of a political, philosophical, ideological, racial, ethnic, religious, or other similar nature" (Witten 1998, 777). The treaty specifically exempts the acts of armed forces during combat (they are covered under the Geneva Conventions). No references to self-determination can be found in the text, although Article 19 reaffirms existing international laws, including humanitarian law.

The Convention on Financing Terrorism has nearly identical provisions. Its pro-Western language would later become the anchor for Security Council actions in 2001. What is perhaps most surprising is that members of the the Organization of the Islamic Conference reluctantly endoresed these agreements. This decision can in retrospect be ruled an error in judgment. The OIC has since repudiated key provisions of the Financing of Terror convention in its own Convention on Combating International Terrorism of 1999, particularly with respect to the right of peoples to use terrorism to combat occupation and achieve self-determination (Hafner 2003, 157). In fact, much of the OIC members' efforts in the Sixth Committee beginning in 1998 were devoted to undoing what had been done previously by asserting the narrowest possible interpretation of the language and preventing its reuse in subsequent agreements (Interview with OIC member representative). Given the requirement of consensus, as we will see, they were largely successful in blocking objectionable clauses. This explains, for example, the stalemate in negotiations on both a convention against nuclear terror and a comprehensive convention on terror.

Negotiations on a comprehensive convention against terrorism, also begun in 1996, moved more rapidly toward a final draft with language supplied by India and Australia. Although some of the familiar disagreements emerged, it appeared for a time as though they would be solvable. Most governments had resigned themselves to setting aside a definition of terrorism and settling instead on a laundry list of specific prohibited acts. They agreed on "extradite or prosecute" and other familiar language. As of August 2001, the chair of the talks optimistically predicted completion of the draft within weeks (Interview with OIC member representative). The only sticking point appeared to be the question of scope, as in the Nuclear Terrorism text.

The Security Council went on record on the question of terrorism during the 1990s, although what was decided came as something of a surprise. A new consensus emerged that permitted the joint use of force against aggression (Wallensteen and Johansson 2004). But even though most of the cases involved some degree of transnational terrorist activity, the Security Council approached them as primarily internal or interstate conflicts. Only in reference to Iraq's sponsorship of terror (condemned in passing in SC Resolution 687 (1991)) did the Security Council take action.

Continuing the initiative of 1985 on hostage taking, the Security Council began to address the problem of terrorism as a general phenomenon. The Five permanent members were able to agree on condemning certain acts and practices, but stopped short of defining terrorism or sanctioning particular organizations. Two general resolutions were passed in 1989 (SC Res. 635 and 638) that called for the marking of plastic explosives (subsequently codified in a treaty sponsored by the ICAO) and that condemned hostage taking (Resolution 638, passed in the wake of abductions of mediators in Lebanon). Resolution 638 simply reaffirmed the principles of the Hostage Convention and urged all states to ratify it. In 1999, the Council approved Resolutions 1267, calling for a global compact to fight terrorism, and 1269, condemning all actions by states to protect or support terrorists (Bantekas 2003, 317).

In 1992, however, the Council addressed terrorism with respect to the Pan Am/Lockerbie attack in 1988. The United States and United Kingdom demanded the extradition of two Libyan nationals to Western courts and imposed economic sanctions and issued veiled threats of military strikes. After these gestures failed to bring about the surrender of the individuals, they took the matter up with the Security Council, which passed Resolutions 731 and 748 condemning Libya's sponsorship of terror and demanding the extradition of the suspects (Frank 2002, 533). Resolution 748 initiated a sanctions regime, including an air travel ban, arms embargo, and diplomatic isolation. A settlement was ultimately negotiated and the two suspects were tried in The Hague. The International Court of Justice later affirmed the validity of the Security Council's actions (UN GA 2001).

The Security Council imposed mandatory sanctions on governments charged with sponsoring terrorism in the late-1990s. This reflected a shift in attitudes toward military responses to terrorism (Maogoto 2005, 282). Sanctions were imposed on the Sudan in 1996 (Res. 1054) and later on the Taliban in Afghanistan (Res. 1267, 1333 and 1363). At the same time, the Security Council sent mixed messages regarding the legitimacy of the struggle for self-determination. It supported the East Timorese, Bosnian and Eritrean movements in spite of their use of violence while at the same time it established criminal courts on Yugoslavia and Rwanda (Daudet 1997, 211).

By September 11th, however, it had become clear that the Security Council and the General Assembly had reached different places on the issue of terrorism and self-determination. The Security Council was establishing for itself, case by case, the power to intervene against states that sponsor terrorism. The Permanent 5 became increasingly comfortable with informal consultations prior to the tabling of draft resolutions, making the use of the veto far less necessary. This said, the Council was not yet ready to invoke Chapter VII provisions that would justify military intervention, despite pressure from the United States. The Clinton administration became exasperated with the Council's unwillingness to endorse American air strikes against Al Qaeda training facilities in 1998 and opted instead to fight terror unilaterally (Luck 2004, 93). International reaction against the attacks was muted, although subsequent attacks on Sudan were criticized—mostly because of the unconvincing evidence that the targets represented a threat. Neither attack was the subject of a formal GA resolution, however (Maogoto 2005, 283).

The General Assembly, for its part, operated on the basis of consensus, with the result that a relatively small group had considerable sway over the final content of the agreements. Although two conventions on terrorism had emerged from the tortuous process, these seemed by 2001 to be the exceptions to the rule of deadlock. The OIC made it clear that it was through making concessions (interview with Perm-5 representative).

The OIC ambivalence was reflected in the language of the Convention of the OIC Conference on Combating International Terrorism which explicitly exempts national liberation movements and those combating Israeli occupation (Hafner 2003, 157). Likewise, the African Union's Convention on the Prevention and Combating of Terrorism of 1999 exempts "the struggle waged by peoples . . . for their liberation or self-determination, including armed struggle against colonialism, occupation, aggression and domination by foreign forces" (Article 3(1)). The AU's ambivalence is reflected in the language of the next clause: "Political, philosophical, ideological, racial, ethnic, religious or other motives shall not be a justifiable defense against a terrorist act" (Article 3(2)).

Before discussing international responses to the September 11th attacks, a word on ongoing American and European cooperation is warranted. In 1992, the members of the European Community transformed the institution into the European Union via the Maastricht Agreement. In addition to strengthening European institutions and deepening commitments to open markets, Maastricht provided for improved cooperation on security issues. Naturally, these commitments are among the more shallow of those made at the time, given the high priority all member-states have placed on security and the means to protect it (Anderson 2000, 230). Wilkinson goes so far as to say that the Maastricht arrangements are "toothless" (Wilkinson 2000, 119).

The "Third Pillar" of Maastricht provided for the so-called K-4 Committee, named after the relevant clause in the agreement. It consists of a coordinating body of senior government representatives with authority over security issues, including counterterrorism (Chalk 2000, 178). Because Maastricht does not provide for a specific definition of terrorism, states have considerable discretion with regard to coordinating specific actions. In general, Third Pillar provisions build on existing domestic legislation, all the while aiming for enhanced domestic legislation and improved coordination. The results have been relatively meager, however, which may have prompted the creation of EUROPOL in 1996 (it came into effect when the UK ratified the agreement). Finally, continental EU members forged a more informal arrangement, known as the Schengen partnership, to better monitor border crossings (Deb Boer 2000, 215).

Even in the context of more aggressive policies against terrorism, European states were still somewhat hesitant to collaborate closely on antiterror measures. Portugal, for example, declined to extradite individuals who might be subject to life in prison since it had no such penalty, and Belgium objected to Spain's so-called double incrimination whereby a suspect could be convicted of both conspiracy and membership in an illegal group (Chalk 2000, 213). As we will see, several provisions of the UK's antiterror laws were found to be incompatible with the European Convention on Human Rights (Stiles 2006).

The conflicts that emerged between asylum rights and other human rights on the one hand and antiterror cooperation often required states to choose between principles. Until September 11th, many Western states erred on the side of human rights. This was also true of Japan, which had a policy of negotiating with terrorists during the 1970s and found itself unprepared both in terms of police capacity and powers to deal effectively with the attacks that occurred in the 1990s (Itabaski and Ogawara 2002, 361). Further, states such as Colombia, Argentina, Israel and Turkey that resorted to extraordinary violence and some repression to address terrorists were routinely chastised by the international community (Alexander 2002, 383–96).

September 11th and Antiterror Law

With the attacks on New York, Washington, and Pennsylvania, the urgency of combating terrorism made it easier for many states to set aside their concerns about due process rights of suspects and protecting state secrets. Within hours of the attacks, both the Security Council and General Assembly passed almost identical resolutions condemning the attacks as cowardly, barbaric and unjustified and expressing sympathy with the United States and its citizens (GA Resolution 56/1 and SC Resolution 1368 of September 12, 2001).

For a brief time, the international community had reached consensus on a definition of terrorism—especially its exclusion of any political justifications. This was the culmination of twenty years' effort begun with the Reagan Administration. As later became clear, however, the consensus was more apparent than real and the OIC continues to object to removing political justifications for the acts of Palestinian combatants in their struggle against Israeli occupation. But during that relatively brief period after the attacks, the precedent was set for a much more muscular and inflexible approach to combating terrorism.

Following the issuance of initial statements of revulsion at the United Nations, the United States engaged in capital-by-capital diplomacy to build an antiterrorism coalition, beginning with the Perm-5 countries and Japan, Germany, Saudi Arabia, and Pakistan. Once the evidence pointed to Al Qaeda and Osama Bin Laden, the United States began orchestrating a military response targeting Afghanistan, but not without approaching the Security Council for approval. A few governments had expressed reluctance to join the coalition in the absence of a formal U.N. statement, and Bush administration decided to acquiesce in spite of its profound ambivalence about multilateralism in general and the United Nations in particular. With U.N. approval in hand, the United States was able to secure the support of NATO allies, who invoked Article Seven activating the organization's mutual defense provisions. It secured the support of China, Japan, South Korea, and Southeast Asian states (Tay 2004, 121). It also received support from India, Pakistan, Turkey, and other South, Central, and West Asian states in and around Afghanistan (Aktan and Koknar 2002, 295).

Beyond this initial flurry of activity, U.S. policymakers sought a long-term global policy against terrorism. But because there had never been an effective multilateral offensive against terrorism, could any U.N. agency make this possible, and if so, which one? On the one hand, a comprehensive convention on terror, such as was being drafted in the 6th Committee, would have considerable authority and legitimacy and could perhaps be enhanced with enforcement provisions along the lines of the International Convention on Civil and Political Rights. On the other hand, the Security Council's Chapter VII powers might be expanded to authorize strikes against nonstate actors. Ideally, the United States wanted a bit of both: a broad statement on combating terror plus a capacity for enforcement. U.S. officials decided to begin with the Security Council. Its open-ended agenda made it possible to quickly raise the issue (the GA 6th Committee was not scheduled to meet for several weeks). Its Chapter VII authority and a latent provision of the Charter—Article 25—allowed the Council to adopt rules that could be made binding on all U.N. members.

The question was whether this assertion of authority could also be seen as legitimate.

Security Council Actions

John Negroponte, US Permanent Representative, presented a draft resolution on September 27th calling upon all member-states to "deny financing, support and safe haven to terrorists," as well as expand information sharing. It also called upon all states to sign and ratify all existing antiterror conventions (even though the USA itself had not yet signed a number of them). The demands would be mandatory ("All members shall . . . "), based on Chapter VII and Article 25, which reads: "The Members of the United Nations agree to accept and carry out the decisions of the Security Council in accordance with the present Charter." Article 48 (1) further states: "The action required to carry out the decisions of the Security Council for the maintenance of international peace and security shall be taken by all the Members of the United Nations . . . "

The heart of the resolution states:
The Security Council...
1. *Decides* that all States shall:

   (a) Prevent and suppress the financing of terrorist acts;
   (b) Criminalize the willful provision or collection . . . of funds by their nationals or in their territories with the intention that the funds should be used . . . to carry out terrorist acts; . . .
   (d) Prohibit their nationals or any persons and entities within their territories from making any funds, financial assets or economic resources or financial or other related services available, directly or indirectly, for the benefit of persons who commit or attempt to commit or facilitate or participate in the commission of terrorist acts; . . .

2. *Decides also* that all States shall: . . .

   (e) Ensure that any person who participates in the financing, planning, preparation or perpetration of terrorist acts or in supporting terrorist acts is brought to justice and ensure that . . . such terrorist acts are established as serious criminal offences in domestic laws and regulations

and that the punishment duly reflects the seriousness
of such terrorist acts;...

(g) Prevent the movement of terrorists or terrorist groups
by effective border controls

It is important to note that this use of Article 25 was unprecedented in its scope and magnitude. As Szasz explained, the Security Council has historically avoided imposing sweeping rules for all member-states (2002, 902). Rather, Security Council mandates have been limited to narrow sanctions against particular states (viz., South Africa, Yugoslavia, Iraq) for limited times, allowing for some latitude. This new use of Charter powers constitutes what some have called the first-ever legislative acts of the Security Council (Alvarez 2003; Szasz 2002). By this they mean that the action is legally binding and enforceable, even upon states that did not directly participate in the decision making, and has broad scope and indefinite temporal applicability. SC Res. 1373 could thus be seen as a constitutional breakthrough. The resolution was adopted almost immediately by unanimous vote with almost no alterations to the original draft. Clearly, it was brought about by the energy and creativity of the United States and its allies—although it is likely that setting a constitutional precedent was not their intent (905).

Compliance was to be monitored by an ad-hoc committee that would collect reports from every U.N. member-state attesting to their efforts to strengthen domestic legislation and practices. Implicit in the resolution was the authorization to use force against states that sponsor and/or aid and abet terrorists (interview with U.N. staff). Note the perambulatory clauses that read as follows:

> The Security Council . . . reaffirming . . . its unequivocal condemnation of terrorist attacks . . . reaffirming further that such acts, like any act of international terrorism, constitute a threat to international peace and security, reaffirming the inherent right of individual and collective self-defense as recognized by the Charter of the United Nations . . . reaffirming the need to combat by all means, in accordance with the Charter of the United Nations, threats to international peace and security caused by terrorist acts. (SC Res. 1373)

Subsequently, representatives of the United States made several appearances before the Security Council during the bombing campaign in

Afghanistan, each time receiving unanimous—if private—support for its strategy and tactics (interviews with Perm-5 representative).

Of special interest is the behavior of IOC members who served on the Council during this period (Bangladesh voted for Res. 1373 and Syria and Pakistan—who joined later—supported all of the follow-up resolutions and were active in the CTC). Though, as we have seen, the OIC has adopted a formal position requiring its members to oppose certain positions in the GA 6th Committee, it appears that no such constraint was applied to its members sitting on the Security Council. Several procedural and political factors may account for this discrepancy—approaching schizophrenia in some instances. For one, although the General Assembly has embraced the consensus approach, this does not mean that participants are required to moderate their rhetoric. Just as was the case during the Cold War, it is widely understood that what is said in the General Assembly need not be taken too seriously. On the other hand, it is more difficult for countries to wax polemical in the Security Council. The presence of the Perm-5 at each meeting can be somewhat intimidating and it is more difficult to dismiss strongly worded statements as mere grandstanding (it is easier to hold countries accountable for what is said in such a setting). The Security Council's agenda, as pointed earlier, is case specific and as such deals with concrete and usually urgent problems rather than vague philosophical issues. Polemics are generally considered a waste of time under such circumstances. Members of the Council value instead constructive contributions aimed at finding practical solutions to intractable political problems (US official familiar with negotiations). This helps to explain why OIC members on the Council have been eager supporters of what were clearly American initiatives to deal with mostly Islamic terrorists.

In spite of its unprecedented character, as the first effort by the Security Council to invoke Chapter VII to strike at a nonstate actor, much of the language had precedents. The use of the Council to punish state sponsors of terrorism began with the Libya resolutions in the 1980s. The language regarding financing was lifted almost verbatim from the recently approved Convention on Financing of Terrorism mentioned earlier. The reliance on familiar phrases and principles was a deliberate attempt to increase the legitimacy and acceptability of the actions (Laurenti 2002; interviews with U.N. diplomats). That said, the fact of the matter was that few states had ratified the Financing of Terror Convention, and there was considerable doubt about its future. Resolution 1373 essentially bypassed the standard process of signature and ratification, making many of the treaty's provisions immediately and irrevocably binding on all states in defiance of the long-standing tradition of consent.

To make it clear that 1373 was not a fleeting, emotional response to a crisis, the Security Council immediately set about creating the enforcement structures it provided for. The Counter-Terrorism Committee (CTC), initially under British leadership, was tasked with collecting antiterror plans from each U.N. member-state. Its members generated guidelines for states, established a strict timetable for submission and review, and hired experts to assist in evaluating the plans. Five Security Council members were assigned to each of three committees, along with a few experts; the committees began to allocate review of the copious volume of national plans that began to arrive. By the end of 2001, 112 states had submitted reports, and 140 had done so by mid-March 2002 (UN CTC 2002a). To the surprise of Security Council members, the greatest obstacle to submitting reports was the lack of professional staff in the capitals of member states to draft a summary of the country's statutes regarding terror-related crimes (interviews with CTC staff). The committee has therefore reoriented its focus in the direction of technical assistance and capacity building rather than rooting out terrorists' havens as originally expected (UN CTC 2002b).

The 1373 standard is so high that every state has been forced to amend its legislation and ratify a few more treaties to come into technical compliance. When the resolution was passed, for example, only four states had ratified the convention on financing or terror, although forty-six more had signed it and all have endorsed it in the General Assembly. The USA Patriot Act and the Anti-Terrorism Act (2001) of the United Kingdom were both passed in part to comply with 1373 and to provide a model for other states. Taken together, the tone of the meetings taking place between CTC staff and U.N. member-states to review the national plans have assumed a collaborative, nonconfrontational character. At this point, there is no indication that any states are incriminating themselves (although as of January 2003, Liberia was singled out for having failed even to begin the process of drawing up its report. UN CTC 2004).

The overwhelming majority of states have submitted initial reports on the status of their antiterror legislation and resources. The second phase involves providing evidence that laws and enforcement capacity have been strengthened, and the upcoming third phase will involve an assessment of implementation and performance (Cortright et al. 2004). From the beginning, the CTC has opted not to make use of the latent enforcement powers at its disposal but instead to approach the report-writing process in a nonconfrontational, collaborative spirit (CTC 2004, SC Res. 1526 [2004]). In 2004, the CTC's institutional status was upgraded with the creation of the 'CTED' (Counter-Terrorism Committee Executive Directorate) with a larger budget and more permanent status.

One might reasonably ask how the US managed such a shift in institutional culture at the Security Council. Consider the remark by Ambassador Joe Legwaila, Permanent Representative of Botswana in 1995:

> Suddenly the Council began to meet Monday, Tuesday, Thursday, even on Sunday to consider a stream of resolutions coming from the Contact Group. Some took umbrage. But the Group was inclined to suggest it would be irresponsible for the other members not to accept their proposals. Also there was the pressure of time to move on to the next item. So the rest of us tended to go along. (Grey 2000, 36)

In addition, more and more Security Council meetings are held in secret—a right that is enshrined under rules 51–57 of the Council's rules of procedure but which can naturally lead to abuse (UN SC 1982; Mahbubani 2004). Some have argued that the CTC proceedings are too secretive as well (Alvarez 2002), although others praise its transparency (Rosand 2003). One thing is clear—some groups on the list of Al Qaeda supporters have not had the opportunity to defend against the accusation, with the result that their assets have been frozen without due process.

In the final analysis, it is clear that when faced with a choice between institutions, the United States believed—correctly—that the Security Council offered more procedural levers at its disposal. One senior U.S. official familiar with the proceedings explained that the Security Council's rules of procedure are remarkably flexible, and once the members have decided to do something, they are usually able to find some rule that allows them to do it (2005 interview).

General Assembly

In the General Assembly, two developments are noteworthy, aside from the passage of GA Res. 56/1 on September 12. To begin, the GA called a special session on terrorism, held in early October. During the meetings, well over one hundred member-states spoke out against terror, in sympathy for the United States and in support of Resolution 1373. Regimes as diverse as France, Cuba, Syria, North Korea, and Canada repeated virtually the same outrage and resolve. Only Tanzania expressed concern that the Security Council may have overstepped its bounds with 1373. By the end of the session there was no question of the U.N. membership's commitment to supporting the Security Council's resolution. This said, the GA opted not to sponsor a specific resolution of support, but left that task to UNESCO (Laurenti 2002, 27).

The second major item on the GA's agenda was the negotiation on the comprehensive convention against terrorism. The Security Council paid scant attention to this endeavor in its passage of 1373. During deliberations, only China made reference to the twelve antiterror conventions (UN SC 2001). In particular, although the United States continued to press for a comprehensive convention, it clearly had cast its lot with the Security Council. The General Assembly's leadership quickly recognized that it risked becoming utterly irrelevant if it did not produce results soon.

This left the negotiations on the comprehensive convention on terrorism in an awkward position. Meetings were scheduled for mid-October 2001 and early February 2002 for completion of the text. At the October meetings, many amendments and proposals were withdrawn for the sake of creating consensus quickly. Observers noted a high degree of passion following the events of September 11th, which seemed to bode well for an early completion of the treaty (interviews with U.N. staff and diplomats).

Two voices of opposition were raised, however. On the one hand, supporters the Indian text complained that 1373 had to a large extent trumped their work. Res. 1373 conveniently glossed over all of the nettlesome aspects of the GA 6th Committee debate, offering member-states a "take-it-or-leave-it" solution to the problem (with veiled threats to those who choose to "leave it"). To them, this undermined the efforts to create a consensus document that could carry the force of universal law (interviews with U.N. staff and diplomats). It was further personally disheartening for those who had labored during the previous five years to craft universally acceptable language to see their efforts overridden.

On the other hand, opponents of the Indian draft—particularly OIC members, strengthened their determination to hold firm on the question of scope and justification for fear that SC 1373 would entirely sweep away the legal nuances they wanted protected. They drafted alternative language for the Preamble and Article 18 and refused to compromise. Their proposed language for paragraph two read:

> The activities of the parties during an armed conflict, *including in situations of foreign occupation*, as those terms are understood under international humanitarian law, which are governed by that law, are not governed by this Convention (emphasis added).

Note the difference with the language proposed by the Coordinator (Australia) which has the approval of the USA and the EU:

> The activities of armed forces during an armed conflict, as those terms are understood under international humanitarian law, which are governed by that law, are not governed by this Convention.

Considering this was the principal sticking point (other than some vague preambulatory language about self-determination), it is understandable why delegates said they were "tantalizingly close" to completing the convention (UN GA 2001).

There was some added drama at the close of the February meetings involving an Australian proposal of new language, lifted from the bombing convention, and presented at the last minute to the OIC delegates. They objected to the lateness of the offer and also reiterated that the bombing convention language was a one-time offer given in a moment of weakness (interviews with U.N. diplomats). The result was the passing of the deadline without resolution of the differences. As of mid 2007, the negotiations, while still formally ongoing, could be described as moribund. Delegates continued to be deadlocked over Art. 18 (on scope), Art. 2 (on precedence), and the Preamble and its definition of terrorism, and although the plans were still in place to call an international conference once these disagreements were resolved, delegates were beginning to wonder openly whether the negotiations were worth pursuing any further (Talwar 2004; UN Press Release 2004). What is perhaps ironic is that although the veto is a less and less significant feature of Security Council voting, the rule of consensus has created a de-facto veto for the General Assembly—raising the possibility of deadlock on all controversial issues of import.

In this situation, one might ask whether the United States or any other Western power has considered breaking from the norm of consensus to call for an up-or-down vote, as provided for in the Charter. The answer is no, for two reasons, according to senior U.S. officials. First, it is unclear exactly how many countries would vote in favor of the draft convention as it now stands. Given the strident opposition of the OIC (more than fifty countries), some countries that oppose the treaty appear to have opted for silence. A vote would force them into view. Secondly, once a vote has begun, members are free to add amendments. It is difficult to predict either their content or popularity, and so taking a vote may jeopardize the substance of the convention. Finally, US representatives are concerned that breaking from the norm of consensus would create an unwelcome precedent for other countries—most of which oppose the US position on most issues. The rule of consensus, in other words, is as much a truce between rivals as an agreement to cooperate (interviews with U.S. officials).

National Policies

Since 9/11, many states have amended their domestic laws to more effectively combat terrorist threats. In Australia, Japan, the United Kingdom, and especially the United States, measures have been drawn up and quickly passed that allow police forces to monitor private communications, detain suspects without charge, enhance information sharing between intelligence and police agencies, and so forth (Kirby 2005). These actions have generally redefined terrorist acts more broadly to include not only acts against the state but also acts against civilians and to include not only actual violence but also threats of violence (Alexander 2002, 387).

In the United Kingdom, the ink on the 2000 Terrorism Act was barely dry when the Blair government responded to 9/11 with the Anti-terrorism, Crime and Security Act of 2001. The Act dramatically expanded police powers, particularly with respect to interrogation, surveillance, and detention. Fenwick has argued they are "in some respects more authoritarian than much of the legislation passed in the recent years" (2000, 840). The Joint Committee on Human Rights, created by the Human Rights Act to advise Parliament on the validity of pending legislation under the Act, reported its judgment that these bills would likely fall short with respect to European human rights norms that had been recently incorporated into U.K. law (JCHR 2001, iv). Given the obvious contradiction between its crime and terror policies and its commitments under the Convention, the Blair government formally notified the Council of Europe that it was derogating its commitment under Article 5 of the Convention. It thus acknowledged publicly that it was setting aside some human rights while it concentrated on domestic security matters.

In the United States, the USA Patriot Act was also passed shortly after 9/11 with large majorities in both houses. It gives federal authorities greater powers to intercept communications, track the flow of foreign money through banks, and restrict immigration to bar entry of terrorist suspects. It also expands powers to deport and detain suspects on lesser charges and suspicions than before. Critics have attacked the legislation as a violation of privacy rights of law-abiding citizens, citing provisions that allow federal agencies to investigate law-abiding citizens for "intelligence purposes." It also allows for detention of suspects without charge for six month renewable periods (ACLU 2005).

In both cases, new antiterror legislation and policy have been challenged in court—both international and domestic. In the United States, George Bush categorized Taliban and Al Qaeda fighters picked up in Afghanistan as "unlawful enemy combatants" to make it easier to disregard the Geneva Conventions and U.S. civil rights law. It allowed unlimited detention without charge and without full due process anywhere in the world—even where there is not "combat" (O'Connell 2005, 454). Many such combatants have been housed at the Guantánamo Bay Naval Station. This ultimately led to a Supreme Court test in *Rasul v. Bush*, which rejected some of the Bush administrations broad claims (Kirby 2005, 334). Esam Hamdi, a U.S. citizen, filed a suit arguing that he was entitled a hearing before an impartial judge. The Court agreed in June 2004, prompting the government to create a Combatant Status Review Tribunal where Guantánamo detainees will be able to challenge their status, albeit under serious restrictions (AI 2005). In 2006, in the case of *Hamdan v. Rumsfeld*, the Court further ruled that the military commissions failed to protect detainee due process, whether based on the Universal Code of Military Justice or the Geneva Conventions. The administration asked Congress to create new tribunals through the Military Commission Act of 2006 to bring them in line with Court demands. But critics charge that the government is still interpreting the protections of the Geneva Convention too loosely and jeopardizing the safety of detainees for the sake of national security (Kelley and Turner 2007).

In the United Kingdom, the detention without charge of certain foreign terror suspects under provisions of the 2001 Act prompted an unprecedented challenge by the Law Lords. A full-blown constitutional crisis erupted in December 2004 when the Law Lords ruled that a key provision of the Anti-Terror Act—the power to detain foreign terror suspects without charge indefinitely—was incompatible with the European

Convention on Human Rights which had been incorporated into British law in 1998. Lord Hoffman wrote:

> The real threat to the life of the nation . . . comes not from terrorism, but from laws such as these. It calls into question the very existence of an ancient liberty of which this country has, until now, been very proud—freedom from arbitrary arrest and detention. (Hinsliff and Bright 2005)

Detainees were released to house arrest in March 2005. At roughly the same time, the Blair government faced a political crisis as it submitted language to extend provisions of the 2001 law that were due to expire. Instead of a rubber stamping the bill, the House of Lords challenged the law on constitutional grounds. Even Lord Irvine, Blair's one-time mentor—voted against the government. Unable to reach a compromise in time, Blair was forced to allow parts of the law to expire (Stiles and Wells 2006).

Other countries have sought legal shelter under the post-9/11 crisis environment for their own struggles against domestic insurgents. Chief among these are Russia and India. Russia has been combating an insurrection in Chechnya for several decades, although it has been most intense since 1994 when Russian troops invaded the area without success. After a period of lawlessness and confusion, Russia invaded again in 1999. Throughout this period, the government in Moscow generally referred to the rebels as "bandits" and "criminals," making no explicit reference to their Muslim heritage. The government's often brutal methods for dealing with the Chechens were often criticized abroad, although even the U.N. Secretary-General acknowledged that this was a strictly internal affair (Hollis 1995, 793). After 9/11, however, Vladimir Putin was quick to claim links between the Chechen rebels and Al Qaeda and Islamic fundamentalism generally. The links were tenuous at best, but the charge forced Western powers to further mute their criticisms (Cornell 2003, 168).

Likewise, the Indian government's fifty-year struggle against Kashmiri rebels was characterized not so much as a proxy war between India and Pakistan, as it had in the past, but rather as a struggle against Islamic fundamentalism. Here again, while there were certainly some fundamentalists operating in Kashmir with links to Al Qaeda, the bulk of the anti-Indian forces received support either from Pakistan or indigenous nationalist movements. It is clear that both Russia and India hoped that by linking their long-standing struggles against nationalist movements with the American war on terror that they could receive Western support—or at least minimize criticism. Such efforts have naturally undermined peaceful negotiations for a change in the legal status of the territories and peoples in question.

Regional efforts at cooperation against terrorism have generally been fruitful, as was the case prior to 9/11. In addition to cooperation with respect to the Afghan situation, governments in various areas have strengthened regional cooperation in areas such as extradition, border control, control of transshipments of suspicious goods, information exchange, and so forth. Japan in particular has become an important instigator of new arrangements among ASEAN members (Itabaski and Ogawara 2002, 367). Europeans are taking more seriously the requests by Spain and Britain to extradite terror suspects and formally listed ETA as a terrorist organization in 2003 (Kirby 2005, 331). In some cases, however, regional efforts at combating terrorism have been constrained by other regional commitments. For example, the participation by some European states in the American-led Container Security Initiative provoked disciplinary action by the European Commission on the grounds that the policy led to discrimination against nonparties (Romero 2003, 604).

Conclusions

Antiterror norms have been essentially reactive, developing through cycles triggered by specific sets of events. The norms remained undefined until the 1950s, when attacks began to multiply. At that point, new instruments were created that outlawed hijacking, kidnapping diplomats, attacking airports and so forth with injunctions to states to collaborate on the apprehension of the perpetrators. Until the mid-1990s, however, these agreements generally included exceptions for those committing acts of violence against occupation forces, colonial powers and so forth—which covered almost all suspects. A new round of terrorist acts in the 1990s launched a new cycle of debates and norm development. As car bombings and suicide bombings—particularly those committed by Islamic fundamentalists—took a greater number of lives in the developing world, other states began to join and crafted instruments that removed the political exception. The attacks of September 11th triggered a new cycle, channeling and intensifying this approach and leading to more rapid ratification of existing treaties as well as to the use of the Security Council as an antiterror instrument.

The development of antiterror norms has also involved conflicting principles—law enforcement versus the political exception, for example.

The attacks on September 11th brought to a head many controversies regarding global rules on terrorism. In particular, it ended the political exception for extradition among most Western countries, as well as many others. Violent groups and individuals generally cannot find shelter in Western countries, no matter the merit of their political objectives. States have therefore benefited from labeling all violent regime opponents as "terrorists" (all the better if links to Al Qaeda can be insinuated). September 11th significantly weakened the position of the pro-Palestinian camp at the U.N., although sentiment in favor of protecting certain insurrection movements persists, especially in the OIC. Given the rule of consensus in the U.N. General Assembly, this vestige of support has resulted in a veto for the OIC on a comprehensive convention on terror. Specifically, it means a lack of full consensus on the definition of terrorism itself.

The OIC remains the "persistent objector" to these efforts and will likely remain so for the foreseeable future. It is conceivable; nonetheless, that the eventual establishment of a state of Palestine—made somewhat more likely by the withdrawal by Israel from the Gaza Strip in September 2005—will trigger a shift in OIC policy. If it becomes apparent that only outlaw Palestinian groups still employ violence—a scenario made less likely by the electoral victory of Hamas in early 2006—it will be easier for regimes such as Saudi Arabia's to endorse a definition of terrorism that no longer exempts groups fighting foreign occupation. Otherwise, such a consensus appears unlikely.

Ultimately, international law on terror cannot be separated from the specific political context. Antipiracy policy during the early eighteenth century offers a useful comparison (Chapter 2). Pirates served as irregular naval forces for many states, including some of the great powers. Somewhat analogously, states lacking conventional military might have at times tolerated or even supported terrorist groups with which they shared political objectives. When eighteenth-century states were able to release themselves from the need for pirates and privateers through the construction of large, technologically sophisticated navies, they began to ostracize and then outlaw pirates. In a similar way, until terrorist organizations find themselves utterly without sympathizers, some states are likely to continue to tolerate them. Rules to suppress piracy and terrorism have evolved as states have sought to enforce their monopoly on the use of force. Both norms have thus been part of the larger historical development of sovereignty rules.

Chapter 6

Extraterritoriality: Expanding Exclusive Internal Jurisdiction

Titus Chih-Chieh Chen

Extraterritoriality disappeared from international relations in the twentieth century, resolving a long-term tension between two contending bodies of norms. Extraterritoriality refers to an international norm that allowed Western powers to exercise various judicial functions (consular courts, mixed courts, admiralty courts, and international courts) within certain non-Western countries.[1] These extraterritorial courts placed resident

---

[1] In recent decades, other forms of extraterritorial jurisdiction have produced controversies in international law. Current debates have focused on extraterritorial application of securities regulation, rules of corporate governance (including anticorruption laws), and trade restrictions regarding specific countries (the most publicized being U.S. efforts to force non-U.S. companies to comply with the American ban on trade with Cuba under the Helms-Burton Act). This chapter addresses extraterritorial judicial jurisdiction, which ended with the Second World War.

foreigners, with or without diplomatic or official capacity, under the jurisdiction of their own states and thus exempted them from the jurisdiction of
the host state (Chang 1984, 3).[2] Exclusive internal jurisdiction has been a
foundational element of state sovereignty in the modern international
system. Exclusive internal jurisdiction holds that no state may exercise governmental authority—legislative, executive or judicial—within the territory
of another state. Yet, up until the late 1940s, extraterritorial justice was a
parallel, even contending, norm. As much as the norm of exclusive internal
jurisdiction had been observed among Euro-American states, the principle
and practice of extraterritorial justice had also been frequently installed and
defended in the West's global engagement with the non-Western world.

The delegitimation and disappearance of the Western-imposed
extraterritorial judicial system in the post-WWII world emerged out of
the tension between two sets of foundational norms. On the one hand, the
Western powers justified the norm and practice of extraterritoriality by
appealing to the principle of individual and property rights protection
and by emphasizing the cultural and legal prerequisites of modern statehood. On the other hand, the ruling and intellectual elites of non-Western,
weaker, or colonized states, after embracing and internalizing the institutions of modern Western governance, scrambled simultaneously to set up
Western-style national legal and judicial structures and to rid themselves
of the Western-imposed justice system.[3] They defended the exclusive right
of territorial jurisdiction by highlighting the Westphalian norm of legal
equality among independent sovereign states (which implied equal treatment
of all recognized states) and the norm of nonintervention.

As argued in the introductory chapter, norm change frequently
occurs (1) when norms are in tension with each other and (2) when the
"fit" between norms and concrete experience is disputed. This chapter
provides historical case studies in support of that proposition. It begins
with a concise discussion of the formation of the two temporally coexisting

---

[2] Western courts were entitled to prescribe binding rules and legal procedures, adjudicate civil
litigation and criminal cases, set judicial precedents, and enforce rules and judgments.

[3] The constructivist attention to national identity formation offers additional insight into the
process of international norm change. The efforts of the subordinate, non-Western states to
imitate and internalize the Western model led to changes in national identity. The reform
enabled non-Western states to claim recognition as independent sovereign entities fully
competent in exercising complete jurisdiction within their territory. Their arguments amounted
to a campaign for the abolition of extraterritoriality. Witnessing the transformation of non-
Western states in their self-understanding and judicial systems, Western treaty powers became
more receptive to the campaign for abolishing judicial privileges because Asian states were
becoming more "modern" and Westernized.

yet inherently contending norms—exclusive territorial jurisdiction and extraterritorial justice—as the dual normative structures guiding state policies and generating interstate disputes. The second section summarizes the justifications for, and the establishment of, extraterritorial justice through imperial expansion and colonization. Section three analyzes the cases of Japan, Turkey, and China to reveal the contentious processes in which concrete practices of various forms of extraterritorial justice triggered disputes not only between the West and non-Western states but even within and among Western capitals. Countries involved in the debates over extraterritoriality invoked opposing reasons, precedents, and analogies to make their arguments more persuasive. The two World Wars significantly changed the context in which the logic and practice of extraterritoriality evolved and triggered cycles of normative change. Both World Wars created an opportunity for the subordinate states to assert their demand for an end to extraterritoriality. The World Wars enhanced non-Western states' relative status vis-à-vis the Western treaty powers (particularly China during the 1940s) as the former negotiated for a relationship based on sovereign equality. The chapter concludes by suggesting that the abolition of extraterritoriality modified international normative structures by promoting the principle of self-determination and paving the way for post-WWII decolonization. The demise of extraterritorial courts thus contributed substantially to the consolidation of sovereignty norms, extending the principle of sovereign equality to non-Western states. Figure 6.1 depicts the cycles of change that led to the abolition of extraterritorial justice.

Normative Context

Prior to the consolidation of the Westphalian principle of exclusive internal jurisdiction, it was "race or nationality rather than territory [that] formed the basis of a community of law" (Liu 1969 [1925], 23). In addition, a religious identity "seems to have been during this period a necessary condition of a common system of legal rights and obligations" (23). In ancient civilizations and medieval Europe, subjects of a political entity were bound by different legal systems according to their social status, nationalities, or faiths.[4] By the end of the fifteenth century, it had become

---

[4] Examples include the practice of *proxenus* among Greek city-states, the institution of *prætor peregrinus* of the Roman Empire, and the special *comtes* of Ostrogoth that settled disputes between Goths and Romans in the 6th century.

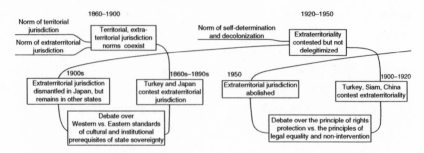

Figure 6.1 Extraterritorial jurisdiction norm cycles.

an international norm that, through bilateral agreements, foreign consuls or special magistrates were invested with judicial capacities (i.e., "consular jurisdiction") to decide cases of compatriots residing in the foreign land. The mixed court (with local and foreign elements) also appeared in bilateral agreements between European nations (34–36). The practice of extraterritorial jurisdiction also existed in the Byzantine Empire and later on the Ottoman Empire (Al Barhana 1998, 16). Furthermore, consular jurisdiction of a reciprocal nature was a feature of the treaties the East Asian states signed with European powers prior to the nineteenth century (Fishel 1952, 2). Until the early part of the nineteenth century, legal jurisdiction was based not only upon the principle of territoriality but also upon religion and nationality.

The process by which contending forms of political organization gave way to the sovereign state—a process that the Peace of Westphalia consolidated and partially formalized, but which began earlier—set Western Europe apart from the rest of the world. Nonterritorial jurisdiction among European Christian states had been gradually abandoned (Spruyt 1994). As Liu summarizes, sovereign states in Europe "awakened to the fact that what had once been a normal practice [extraterritorial jurisdiction] had become a distinct limitation and derogation of their sovereignty. They have come to realize that the system is regarded as a humiliating sign of backwardness, which the Christian States had seen fit to put an end to" (1969 [1925], 103). Thus European Christian states abolished the practice of extraterritoriality among themselves. However, the elimination of extraterritoriality in Europe was not unconditional. The dismantling of extraterritoriality required, as a precondition, that a state's domestic legal-political institutions be recognized by other states as compatible with the dominant norms of sovereignty. A state had to be perceived as a "like unit" in the eyes of the European powers before she could be treated as one of them.

Justification of Extraterritorial Jurisdiction

The abolition of extraterritorial jurisdiction in Europe did not apply to the rest of the world. In fact, different forms of extraterritorial regimes had spread in tandem with imperial expansion and colonization. The elimination of extraterritoriality in Europe and its imposition upon Africa, Asia and the Middle East were actually the two sides of one coin—both practices were characterized as evidence of the competency, progress, and civilization of Western imperial powers.[5] On the one hand, the imposition of extraterritoriality upon others testified that a state was able to protect its subjects even beyond its borders and to bring another political entity under its tutelage.[6] On the other hand, Western observers argued that the local justice system of a non-European (and mostly non-Christian) nation was inadequate for protecting the life and property of resident foreigners. To be sure, Western legal experts and diplomats recognized the achievements and sophistication of non-Western civilizations (Willoughby 1966, 555); the argument for the necessity of extraterritoriality was based less upon cultural or social backwardness than on the incompatibility between Western jurisprudence and non-Western legal conceptions (Al Barhana 1998, 18; Chang 1984, 78; Liu 1969 [1925], 84).

The discourse of the Westerners on law and judicial administration in China and Japan during early years of the nineteenth century is the most representative of this discrediting effort. Euro-Americans resident in China and Japan in the nineteenth century declared that local justice systems were unsuitable for them. They pointed to three deficiencies. First, Westerners asserted that European and Chinese laws developed

---

[5] A critical, postcolonial perspective would suggest that the constructed identity of the nineteenth-century West needed a less advanced counterpart to validate its progressive image and superior status, and extraterritoriality was perfect for this purpose. It operated as a display on foreign lands that served both political and pedagogical goals—manifesting the superiority of the Western sociopolitical institutions and educating local peoples about the logic and operation of the "civilized" judicial system (Fishel 1952, 3; Hevia 2003; Said 1979, 1993). It also explains why European publicists and international lawyers of the nineteenth century, almost without exception, endeavored to classify different countries and nations into different categories (civilized, semicivilized/barbarous, and savage). See Gong (1984, especially chapters 2 & 3) for a detailed description of the efforts at categorization.

[6] *The Standard of 'Civilization' in International Society* by Gerrit Gong (1984, particularly Part I) rightly illustrates the interrelationships between the rising of the "standard of civilization" among European imperial powers, the concept of sacred trust of civilization, and the evolution of international law during the heyday of imperial expansion and colonization.

from "two conflicting sets of juristic principles" (Keeton 1928, 120; see also Willoughby 1966, 554–5). Several fundamental principles constitutive of European law were nonexistent in the Chinese legal codes. For instance, Keeton (1928, 118) argues that "English law considered that the essence of a criminal act was the wrongful motive of the wrongdoer. Chinese law applied the *lex talionis* to a number of cases. . . . [I]t failed to recognize the validity of the plea of self-defence, and purely accidental homicide involved criminal liability."[7] The legal implication was that Europeans involved in a dispute might be held liable for the injury without examining the intention and circumstances of the injurious act. Similarly, Western observers found that the principle of equality before the law was missing in Chinese criminal codes; instead, local magistrates took sociopolitical status and familial relations of litigants into consideration, which granted the upper classes and senior family members a privileged position at trial.

In addition, the right of private property was not absolute in non-Western systems. Both the civil law and the penal code of China's Qing dynasty were devised in line with the neo-Confucianism that highlighted the supreme political authority and universal dominion of the Chinese emperor over each person and his possessions regardless of nationality. Civil liberties and private property rights were thus alien concepts to Chinese law, and local authorities at Canton could confiscate the commodities of Western merchants without due process or redress. More frustrating to the Westerners was the lack of separation of powers. Local magistrates in China assumed the roles of executive, lawmaker, and judge at the same time, allowing them to select, interpret, and even make up the legal codes at their convenience. Keeton hence complained that "[t]hey (local authorities) were not bound by the provisions of the code, for they had the power at all times of creating new offences and punishing for their breach" (1928, 100). The discretionary power of local authorities made legal proceedings exceedingly unpredictable. Following the same argument, Lord Granville, the British foreign secretary, when dealing with an opium-related dispute between England and Japan in October 1881, insisted that "the system of ex-territorial jurisdiction . . . must remain a necessary condition of the relations between Western nations and those of

---

[7] *Lex talionis* refers to the law of retaliation; it is a law permitting equal and direct retribution conducted by the plaintiff or victim.

the East so long as their judicial systems are widely dissimilar" (quoted in Chang 1984, 78).

The second aspect of the problem of the Chinese legal system, as Westerners staying in China pointed out, revolved around the charge that in the Chinese judicial system there was no such thing as "due process" in the Western sense. In other words, procedural justice was not highlighted in the Chinese legal order. Investigation of the validity of witnesses, testimonies and confessions was not required for conviction and sentencing, and the practice of cross-examination was rarely applied in proceedings. Xenophobic magistrates usually imposed personal opinions and preferences in their decisions. Most unbearable was the prescription of torture in Chinese penal codes (Willoughby 1966, 552–3). Keeton indicates that "the provisions of the code were systematically ignored, cruel and violent tortures being habitually employed, not only on the prisoner, but on the witnesses, and in some cases on those not involved in any way in a criminal proceeding, presumably for purposes of extortion" (1928, 135). He then concludes that "[c]learly it was impossible for the Western nations to recognise a jurisdiction in which such grave abuses flourished" (136). By the same token, Sir Henry S. Parkes, while negotiating with the Japanese government concerning the importation of medical opium in 1880, criticized proposed regulations that would bring foreign importers of drugs and medicine and apothecaries under Tokyo's jurisdiction. In his view, Japan's laws and law enforcement were degrading, unnecessarily restrictive, and abusive (Chang 1984, 53, 75).

The third category of Western grievances concerned law enforcement. The Chinese prison system was known for its miserable conditions to the extent that even the Chinese themselves drew an analogy between the prison and hell. Even worse was the outrageous corruption and condoned misconduct of the bureaucracy at all levels (Fishel 1952, 4–5). Bribery, extortion, and fraud were justified and rampant among Chinese law enforcement officials (Willoughby 1966, 552). The British foreign office held a similar perception of Japan's law enforcement, that "no Japanese regulations framed unilaterally by the Japanese government met the quality standards of a 'civilized' state" (Chang 1984, 74).

Such an assessment of Chinese legal codes and judicial institutions unsurprisingly led to a judgment among the Euro-American communities that Chinese law "violates the laws of God, the human reason, and the universal commonsense" (Keeton 1928, 105). The disappointing quality of

Chinese jurisprudence and judicial administration had provoked the Westerners in China during the early nineteenth century to call for the establishment of some kind of consular jurisdiction that would exempt them from the defective and inhumane Chinese law (Fishel 1952, 4–6; Liu 1969 [1925], 83; Willoughby 1966, 554–5).[8] Not surprisingly, similar criticisms could also be heard from foreign communities resident in Japan around the same period.[9]

Opinions of Western business communities, scholars and news media prior to the 1840s confirmed the social constructivist proposition that states tend to develop and apply different norms, rules, and customs for intercourse with those of different "kind."[10] The Westphalian principle of territorial jurisdiction and the customary practice of extraterritorial jurisdiction therefore coexisted in parallel in the nineteenth century, for application to different categories of states. The norms of sovereignty were not violated as Krasner (1999) suggests, because the exercise of sovereign rights was not unconditional, and the application of norms of sovereignty was always contingent upon how the Western states perceived and categorized the domestic legal-political attributes of individual non-Western nations.[11]

The differentiation of state attributes was aptly illustrated in the Western discourse of international law and diplomacy of the nineteenth century. William E. Hall argued that "[i]nternational law is the product of the special civilization of modern Europe and forms a highly artificial system of which the principles cannot be supposed to be understood or

---

[8] Such a request could even be heard among the China experts, for instance Sir George Staunton (the interpreter of Chinese penal codes), and missionaries, for example, Dr. Robert Morrison (the first Protestant missionary to China and the long-time chief interpreter for the British East India Company) and Dr. Elijah Bridgeman (a medical missionary and the founder of *The Chinese Repository*).

[9] For example, Jones (1931, 77) summarized the Western perception of the Japanese law by indicating that "the distinction it draws in favor of the military caste, its scheme of family gradations, and its lack of provision for mercantile affairs are more important than even its scale of punishments in illustrating the gulf between occidental and oriental conceptions of social and legal relationships."

[10] Recall the efforts of categorization and labeling by European publicists and international lawyers as the domain of international law was expanding into the non-European world. In other words, different codes of conduct were devised to regulate interactions with states of different categories.

[11] Therefore Gong (1984, 25) indicates that "[t]he international legal texts record the efforts of the era's leading international lawyers (publicists such as Henry Wheaton, William E. Hall, and T. E. Holland) to determine if and when the international law could recognize non-European countries as 'civilized' countries with full international legal personality."

recognized by countries differently civilized" (quoted in Fishel 1952, 3).[12] This argument justified the imposition of extraterritoriality by hinting that Asian and African nations, due to their incompatible cultural and political systems, were not qualified to exercise jurisdiction over resident Westerners (Jones 1931, 72).

The argument of "immiscible character" was not just echoed by Western merchants and publicists but also embraced by government officials. For instance, Caleb Cushing, envoy extraordinary, minister plenipotentiary, and chief commissioner of the United States to China in 1844, expressed his conviction regarding the necessity of extraterritoriality in China in his letter to the American consul at Canton:

> The nations of Europe and America form a family of states, associated together by community of civilization and religion, by treaties, and by the law of nations. By the law of nations, as practised in Europe and America, every foreigner, who may happen to reside or sojourn in any country of Christendom, is subject to the municipal law of that country, and is amenable to the jurisdiction of its magistrates on any accusation of crime alleged to be committed by him within the limits of such country . . .
>
> In the intercourse between Christian states on the one hand and Mohammedan on the other, a different principle is assumed, namely, the exemption of the Christian foreigner from the jurisdiction of the local authorities, and his subjection (as the necessary consequence) to the jurisdiction of the minister, or other authorities of his own government.
>
> In my opinion, the rule which obtained in favor of Europeans and Americans in the Mohammedan countries of Asia is to be applied to China. Americans are entitled to the protection and subject to the jurisdiction of the officers of their Government.

---

[12] In a like manner, Sir Travers Twiss declared that "amongst the Mohammedan and Buddhist nations there is so essential a diversity in the sanctions, which religion and morality attach to human conduct, as contrasted with those which prevail throughout Christendom, that from the oldest times an immiscible character between Europeans and Orientals has been maintained" (Fishel 1952, 3). And Sir Robert Phillimore even suggested "the vital and ineradicable differences which must always separate the Christian from the Mohametan or Infidel, the immiscible character which their religion impressed upon their social habits, moral sentiments, and political institutions, necessitated a departure from the strict rule of territorial jurisdiction" (Fishel 1952, 3).

The right to be protected by the officers of their country over them are [*sic*] inseparable facts. (Fishel 1952, 5)[13]

It then came as no surprise that in 1855 Cushing admitted, "I entered China with the formed general conviction that the United States ought not to concede to any foreign state, under any circumstances, jurisdiction over the life and liberty of a citizen of that United States, unless that foreign state be of *our own family of nations*—in a word, a Christian state" (Fishel 1952, 12, emphasis added). By the 1840s, governments of the Western states came to a consensus that the acquisition of extraterritorial rights was an important national interest indispensable for the management of diplomacy and interstate commerce in the Orient.

Establishment of Extraterritorial Justice

Western powers established extraterritorial jurisdiction through both armed conflict and coercive diplomacy. China's Qing Dynasty, defeated by the British expeditionary fleet in the Opium War, signed the Treaty of Nanking in August 1842 and a series of supplementary agreements in 1843. The Treaty opened five Chinese ports for commercial intercourse with the West, ceded Hong Kong to Great Britain as Her Majesty's colony, and conferred on British subjects extraterritorial jurisdiction exercised by the British consuls in treaty ports and Hong Kong. The United States and France in 1844 signed treaties with the Qing court that conceded almost identical provisions of extraterritoriality, and a host of other Euro-American countries followed suit (Willoughby 1966, 560–9). During the next decade the Euro-American powers attained extraterritorial jurisdiction of various degrees through bilateral treaties from almost all independent countries of East, Southeast, and Pacific Asia, including Borneo (1850), Japan (1855), Siam (1855), Samoa (1878), and Korea (1883).

Besides the Far East, European powers since the sixteenth century onward had acquired and sustained the rights of consular jurisdiction from the Ottoman Empire and Mediterranean and African nations, including Egypt, Algiers, Morocco, Tripoli, Tunis, Persia, Muscat, Zanzibar,

---

[13] In his letter in September 1843 to then Secretary of State John C. Calhoun, Cushing stated that the request of extraterritorial jurisdiction of the American consuls over U.S. citizens in China should be understood not as a concession made by China, but as a legitimate application of an established international law, which was the consular jurisdiction European nations exercised in the Ottoman Empire. In other words, the Chinese empire until the nineteenth century "was not entitled to assert the general principle of territorial sovereignty in order to retain jurisdiction over foreigners within her borders" (Willoughby 1966, 555–6).

Senna, Congo, Ethiopia, and Madagascar. By the middle of the nineteenth century, the acquisition of extraterritorial privileges from non-Western/non-Christian nations had become a constituting quality and defining character of the "enlightened" nations. Those joining the "family of civilization" (namely, the United States and Japan) later also eagerly secured and exploited this judicial privilege from weaker states.

By the end of the nineteenth century, extraterritoriality in Asia and Africa had developed into a well entrenched, yet poorly coordinated and decentralized exercise of treaty powers. Various forms of consular courts and mixed courts had become the symbol of Western expansion and domination. However, because treaty powers constructed extraterritorial regimes of their own without consultation and multilateral coordination, unforeseen yet consequential shortcomings emerged, to the extent that powers had to keep revising treaty provisions and amending the extraterritorial rules (Fishel 1952, 8–9). This phenomenon confirms the proposition in the introductory chapter that although rule structures establish contexts for individual choice, they also, and inevitably, generate disputes about specific choices.

One major defect of the extraterritorial regime was the multiple and contending claims of jurisdiction, which created judicial inconsistencies between consular courts of different treaty powers. Al Barhana points out that in "a criminal case the Consul of the accused was competent, and in a civil case the Consul of the defendant was competent. . . . [T]he incapacity of the local Governments to pass any legislation affecting foreigners, except with the approval of the Powers who exercised Capitulations, resulted in legislative confusion" (1998, 18). An implication of this judicial confusion was that the judges and law enforcement authorities of extraterritorial structures had to invest a considerable amount of time and resources in clarifying and defending their decisions regarding which sets of laws and precedents could be adopted before a pending case was adjudicated.

In addition, because nationality—not territory—determined which courts, procedures, and statutes applied in an extraterritorial litigation, those involved in the legal proceedings (prosecutors, attorneys, judges, assessors, plaintiffs, defendants, and police) had to be familiar with a wide variety of dissimilar statutes, procedural rules, judicial principles and precedents stipulated by various treaty powers and China. The diversity of rules rendered judicial proceedings and the enforcement of decisions costly and inefficient (Fishel 1952, 11). Trial decisions tended to be less predictable and more arbitrary. Precedents under this condition became less binding and nonauthoritative, and expectations of disputants diverged. From the very beginning, these problems weakened the legitimacy and persuasiveness of the extraterritorial justice system, generated resentments not just among Western communities but also in the host country, and significantly reduced incentives of disputants to settle their disagreements through the courts. In other words, the major problem of extraterritoriality was not that no rule structure existed; the problem was that there were multiple but incompatible rule structures applicable in each case.

Also, the quality of consular justice had been questioned not just by the host country but even by governments of treaty powers, primarily because diplomatic delegates did not receive proper legal training (Fishel 1952, 13). To the host state, an even more pressing issue was that the rights of extraterritorial jurisdiction had been abused by various consular or mixed courts and had been unduly extended to whatever cases affected the interests of subjects of the treaty powers (24–5).

Disputes and Arguments

The more non-Western states participated, voluntarily or by coercion, in world politics, the more their political elites and public opinion became familiar with international law, and thus the more they realized that their country was treated differentially.[14] As soon as the subordinated began to see themselves through the eyes of the West, they internalized the perception and evaluation of the West, and through this "mechanism of reflected appraisals" (Wendt 1999, 338) they came to perceive extraterritoriality and other foreign privileges as humiliating and adverse to national development (Zhang 1991, 23).

It then follows that the states subject to extraterritorial concessions shifted their attitude from either ignorance or acquiescence to resentment and resistance (Gong 1984, 65). Non-Western states, through interactions with Western powers and other states, learned a great deal about and were able to define their national interests in accordance with, the operating principles of modern interstate relations. Hence, from the 1860s onward, states in Asia, Africa, and the Middle East began to request the revision and eventually the complete repealing of extraterritorial provisions (Zhang 1991, 23).

---

[14] Richard T. Chang (1984) persuasively reveals this sentiment widely held among the nineteenth-century Japanese intellectuals and officials who were familiar with Western culture and politics.

Abolishing extraterritoriality became a national interest and even a symbol of national liberation.

To get rid of extraterritoriality, states had to break the conviction collectively held by treaty powers, and this goal could not be achieved without a comprehensive makeover of jurisprudence and judicial institutions. By conforming to, and internalizing, Western legal concepts, judicial procedures, and methods of law enforcement, non-Western states endeavored to make a case before treaty powers that they were no longer what they used to be and that they had actually become "like units" with Western powers in political and judicial institutions. As modern states, they qualified for being treated as such and for exercising complete territorial jurisdiction. In short, non-Western states asked to be recategorized by treaty powers as full members of the modern state system.

However, it took more than identity transformation and institutional conformity to have extraterritoriality abolished. Substantial modernization in legal-political attributes did not guarantee immediate changes on the part of the West. Treaty powers had to recognize the changes made by non-Western states, and this recognition involved the arduous process of issue framing, contestation, and persuasion in bilateral and multilateral settings. The introductory chapter suggests that the chances of winning an argument over time improve when actors possess and wield powers of communication and when they invoke foundational metanorms as the basis for their claims. Power here refers not only to relative economic and military capabilities but also to the capacity of communication and persuasion because "[t]he rules change to the extent that the great powers are able to convince other actors (especially other major states) to accept a new norm or a modification to the existing norm" (Chapter 1). Therefore, power struggles in this context play out in the arena of diplomatic interaction, international bargaining, mass media, and even public opinion. States controlling resources of, and access to, communication (generally the economically and militarily powerful ones) certainly have a better chance of winning a debate. But the outcome of normative arguments is also shaped by actors' capacity to frame issues and to direct persuasive arguments to both domestic and international audiences.

Foundational metanorms refer to the rules that constitute the essential logics of modern international relations. These norms are almost uniformly accepted and observed worldwide; therefore, arguments based upon these norms "carry persuasive weight" (Chapter 1). Notwithstanding their foundational nature, metanorms do not necessarily work harmoniously with one another. Sometimes an international dispute becomes difficult to solve exactly because parties invoke competing metanorms. The history of abolishing extraterritorial justice reflects such a dilemma. The two sides appealed to two contending sets of metanorms that endorsed their arguments: non-Western states invoked the foundational principles of self-determination, nonintervention, state dignity, and sovereign equality to justify their right to exclusive territorial jurisdiction. Western treaty powers on the other side highlighted the essential principles of cultural-legal prerequisites, individual dignity, property protection and domestic legal-political attributes that supported the continuation of extraterritorial justice. Treaty powers resisted changes in their privileges by arguing that the norm of territorial jurisdiction must be balanced with the principle of protection: the right of territorial sovereignty should not hamper the duty of other states in protecting foreign subjects and property (Al Barhana 1998, 23). In other words, the notion of territorial sovereignty was not absolute and unconditional, but existed in a dialectic relationship with other norms.

Furthermore, Western treaty powers suspected the competence of native judges to discharge judicial functions for the protection of Western subjects' safety and property.[15] Occasionally, Western representatives promised to inquire into the legal and judicial progress made by the host state and look into the prospect of revising consular jurisdiction, but their concessions turned out to be nothing more than a dead letter. The Ottoman Empire in 1856 and the Republic of China in the 1920s experienced this lip service. More often, the petition for abolition was politely but firmly turned down, accompanied by Western advice of further and more thorough reforms in jurisprudence and judicial administration, modeled on either the Continental or the Anglo-American legal system.

In addition, the treaty powers urged non-Western states to employ Western legal experts or jurists as advisors on legal reforms (or even co-magistrates) and to submit to the treaty powers the draft versions of new codes of civil, criminal, and commercial law before their promulgation and enforcement.[16] Also, Western representatives on a number of occasions

---

[15] Read Jones (1931, chapters 5–7) and Liu (1969, chapter 10) for further understanding of the standing of Western treaty powers concerning treaty revision.

[16] The Conference at Tokyo in July 1887, in which Japan presented to the treaty powers the achievements of her legal and judicial reforms for the abolition of extraterritoriality, broke up on the Western request of prepromulgation inspection: Western delegations insisted that Japan's new criminal code must be examined by treaty powers before promulgation.

proposed the establishment of mixed courts as a transitional phase leading to the complete judicial autonomy of the host state.[17] The mixed courts
system of Egypt since 1875 had been mentioned as a success that "imposed
the rule of law and thus began the transition of Egypt from a feudal country into a modern and structured state with a legal climate conducive to
commercial and social progress" (Al Barhana 1998, 19). Mixed courts
existed also in the Ottoman Empire and China.

As Western powers delayed the process of relinquishing the rights
of consular and mixed courts, every non-Western state upon which extraterritorial jurisdiction was imposed endured numerous rounds of pains-
taking and frustrating negotiations (bilateral and multilateral), preceded
by domestic reforms in jurisprudence, judicial administration, law
enforcement, and political institutions.[18] The substance of these reforms
was no less than a comprehensive legal-political makeover that substituted
the transplanted concepts of law and politics for the traditional establishment. The cases of Japan, Turkey and China illustrate the extent of the
difficulty that non-Western states confronted in the process of abolishing
the capitulatory judicial regime.

Norm Change

Japan

Japan signed a Treaty of Amity and Commerce with the United States on
July 29, 1858, followed by a string of treaties with other European states.
Treaty provisions granted the rights of extraterritorial jurisdiction to foreign
powers, which established consular courts in treaty ports. The jurisdictional
rights claimed and exercised by treaty powers gradually extended "beyond
what the treaties warranted" (Jones 1931, 31), and Japanese politicians came
to realize their judicial autonomy had been chipped away bit by bit.

---

[17] Acknowledging the incompatibility of extraterritoriality to the modern norms of state sovereignty and the harm the capitulatory regime had inflicted upon Turkey's autonomy, the Allies
during the First Conference of Lausanne (November 1922–February 1923) were concerned
with the personal status of foreigners especially in criminal procedures. They thus proposed
that Turkey allow foreign judges and legal experts to participate in further legal reforms. The
suggestion was strongly opposed by the Turkish delegation, and the Conference ended without a satisfactory conclusion on this matter. It then took almost half a year before delegates
reconvened at Lausanne where both sides made concessions.

[18] For instance, it took Turkey 67 years (1856–1923), and Japan 28 years (1871–1899) to get rid
of extraterritoriality.

Chang suggests that the Japanese ruling elite "freely and willingly—though out of ignorance—conceded extraterritoriality to the Western 'barbarian,' reasoning as it did that it would be better for them to deal with their own criminals and scoundrels and to settle disputes between them" (1984, 77). Yet the more the Japanese learned about Western notions of sovereignty, the more they realized the discriminatory nature of extraterritorial privileges. Several widely publicized cases decided by Western consular courts in the 1870s sparked much resentment among Japanese intellectuals who reached the conclusion that "no Japanese could expect justice in the Western consular courts" (Chang 1984, xii).

The collapse of the Tokugawa Shogunate and the subsequent *Meiji* Restoration after 1868 brought forth Japan's comprehensive Westernization. Under the banner "wealthy country and strong arms" (*fukoku-kyohei*), the emperor *Meiji* and his chief advisors resolved to change national identity from a Confucian, feudal, decentralized polity to a modern, sovereign, and unified state. Such identity transformation brought a series of political, military, economic, judicial and administrative reforms. The emperor promulgated the Chief of the New Fundamental Laws in 1870, announcing significant alterations of criminal punishments. In December 1871, the emperor dispatched the Iwakura Mission to the United States and England to examine Western sociopolitical institutions and to probe the likelihood of treaty revision. The government promulgated the reformed penal code in May 1873, modeled on a European pattern. A committee under the ministry of justice took on the task of proposing a new penal code and a code of criminal instruction. A French legal advisor participated in the undertaking, and the Code Napoleon was the model (Jones 1931, 84). The new penal code came into force in 1882. Another committee was established in 1875 to work out a civil code, and the French law was once again the object of learning and imitation. Reforms of law enforcement and the prison system were also set in motion in 1876. In addition, the Council of State entrusted a committee in 1881 to compose a commercial code modeled on the German law.

However, treaty powers were not impressed with the extent and intensity of Japan's endeavors in legal and political reforms, and they repeatedly turned down Tokyo's requests for treaty revision. The Conference at Tokyo in July 1887 broke up on the Western insistence that the treaty powers be allowed to examine the new criminal code before promulgation.

Negotiations between Japan and Great Britain concerning treaty revision resumed in 1894. The British delegation withdrew the previous insistence on the pre-promulgation inspection in response to Japan's concession that the revised treaty would not be effective until the legal reform was complete, and the new laws would be translated into English or at least some European language. The British negotiators agreed to Japan's suggestion that left the issue of foreign ownership of real estate in interior Japan to the legislation the Diet adopted later, and Japan in return allowed the leasing system within the foreign settlements to remain untouched. The two sides reached agreement, and on July 16, 1894, the Aoki-Kimberley Treaty was signed. All British extraterritorial jurisdiction and accessory privileges in Japan ended, and Japan won the longed-for judicial autonomy and equal status among the powers. Other states soon followed the British example. The exercise of extraterritoriality officially came to the end in Japan in 1899, even though various forms of discrimination and double standards remained during succeeding decades.[19]

Turkey

At the Congress of Paris in 1856, Great Britain, France, and Italy agreed to hold a conference in Constantinople to consider the modification of the Western rights of consular justice in the Ottoman Empire. The conference never took place. As a result, the Ottoman Empire tried at least twice (in October 1881 and in September 1914) unilaterally to abrogate extraterritoriality, only provoking disagreements and protests by European powers. Although Germany (in 1917), Austria-Hungary (in 1918), and the Soviet Union (in 1921) had revoked the rights of consular jurisdiction in Turkey, the Turkish delegation at the Conference of Lausanne (convened from November 1922 to February 1923) had to persuade the Allies to reach a comprehensive abrogation of the capitulatory regime.

The Turkish delegation emphasized to the Allied plenipotentiaries the legal and judicial reforms the Turkish government had achieved since 1856. A set of reformulated and secularized laws (including, *inter alia*, the commercial code, the penal code, the codes of civil and penal procedure, and the various administrative and regulatory laws), modeled on the jurisprudence and law of advanced European countries, had been brought into effect. In addition, forty years of learning and internalization in Turkey

---

[19] For example, Japan was frustrated with the 1895 Triple Intervention where Russia, Germany, and France forced Tokyo to return the Liaodong peninsula to China. Furthermore, various discriminatory anti-Japanese immigration laws of the United States and failed diplomatic efforts at the League of Nations all strengthened Japan's complaints about the double standard of "civilization" (Gong 1984, 198).

had produced a body of qualified and competent judges and attorneys acquainted with the concepts and procedures of modern Western law. Ismet Pasha, the Turkish plenipotentiary, then argued that the moment of abolishing the defective capitulatory regime had come.

The Allies, however, were not convinced. Though acknowledging the incompatibility of extraterritoriality with modern norms of state sovereignty, the Allies were concerned with the personal status of foreigners, especially in a criminal procedure (Gong 1984, 118). They thus proposed that Turkey allow foreign judges and legal experts to participate in further legal reforms. The suggestion was strongly opposed by the Turkish delegation, and the First Conference of Lausanne ended without a satisfactory conclusion on this matter. It then took almost half a year before delegates reconvened at Lausanne, where both sides made concessions.

The Treaty of Peace signed on July 24, 1923, confirmed the complete abrogation of the capitulations in Turkey. Attached to the Treaty was a joint declaration in which Turkey announced the employment of European legal councilors as Turkish officials under the ministry of justice for a period of "no less than five years" to observe and report on the implementation of new laws and legal procedures. In a separate treaty signed in August 1923, the United States also officially revoked its rights of extraterritorial jurisdiction in Turkey. Turkey thereby won complete judicial independence.

In fact, what Turkey achieved during the 1920s was not an isolated or random event but should be seen as the beginning of something even larger, namely, a seismic shift in the requirements for membership in the community of modern states. The Western insistence on the fulfillment of certain cultural and institutional standards of "civilization" before non-Western/non-European countries could be granted full sovereignty began to lose its persuasive force after WWI (Gong 1984, 84). Active participation of a number of non-Western countries (the Ottoman Empire, Japan, China, Siam, Persia, among others) as parties during the War and the following Peace Conference emboldened them to ask for equal treatment and hastened Western reevaluation of their international status. Furthermore, non-Western states' acquisition of full membership in the League of Nations, followed by their engagement in various disarmament and arms control conferences in the post-WWI period, also severely challenged the standard of "civilization" argument and brought forth a sustained debate among leading Western publicists and lawyers concerning the necessity and legitimacy of the standard of civilization as a scale by which to measure state sovereignty and autonomy.[20] Gong suggested that "[t]he global expansion of the domain of international law appeared to impose a choice between the universality of the Family of Nations and strict adherence to the standard [of civilization]" (1984, 84).

On the other hand, World War I exposed what non-Western states called the hypocrisy of Western civilization. Contrary to their self-description, the most "civilized" states were no less willing than their non-Western counterparts to conduct unconstrained warfare and inflict maximum casualties on their enemies. The brutal war efforts of leading Western states therefore sparked large-scale peace movements in Western countries and led ruling elites of non-Western countries to question the validity of maintaining a distinction between the "civilized" and the others.

By the end of the 1920s, prominent Western legal experts and publicists gradually came close to a consensus in which the cultural standard of sovereign statehood was "increasingly considered anachronistic and insulting" (Gong 1984, 84). The norm of cultural and institutional requirements for state sovereignty, as Sir John Williams maintained, "no longer corresponds with the main facts of contemporary life" (85). World War II only reconfirmed the inadequacy and obsoleteness of the standard and its extraterritorial apparatuses.

China

The Manchu dynasty that ruled the Chinese empire conceded extraterritoriality in 1843 to Great Britain. A number of other states acquired the rights of consular jurisdiction in the following forty years. By the early twentieth century, extraterritorial jurisdiction had evolved into a complicated and confusing multiplicity of legal orders in Chinese territory, leased lands, international settlements, and colonies on the Chinese mainland. Great Britain and the United States even set up their own district courts and courts of appeal in China. Extraterritorial jurisdiction in China, as in other places visited by colonialism and imperialism, had gradually seized judicial rights not stipulated in the treaties. Hsu thus pointed out the "lamentable fact that in the case of China, the foreign assessor, instead of stopping with the treaty rights of attending to watch the proceedings in the interest of justice, gradually arrogated himself the role of the principal

---

[20] Oppenheim in the 1928 fourth edition of International Law suggests that because Abyssinia, China, Persia, and Siam became founding members of the League of Nations, it was "impossible to deny that they [were] International Persons and Members of the Family of Nations" (Gong 1984, 83).

magistrate" (1949, 32). The historical development of the Shanghai Mixed Court at International Settlement was the most illustrative of the overextensive and abusive nature of extraterritoriality (Stephens 1992).

Two armed conflicts, namely, the 1894 Sino-Japanese War and the 1900 Boxer Incident, both resulting in embarrassing defeats for China, severely challenged the physical survival and political legitimacy of the ruling Qing dynasty. Equally important, the defeats also forced Chinese ruling elites and intellectuals to realize that, for the survival of the dynasty, China had no choice but to pursue comprehensive modernization in her legal-political institutions through constitutional and institutional remodeling. Sinocentrism and the Sinocentric world order collapsed in the face of Western advancement in the Asian continent (Zhang 1991). Therefore, by the end of 1901, the grand debate between the conservatives and the reformists within the court eventually came to an end. The Qing court finally adopted the Westphalian notion of sovereign statehood and its corresponding norms, which implied comprehensive modernization in politics, law, economy, education, national defense, and other areas. Legal and judicial reforms finally became a crucial element of the New Policy Campaign beginning in 1902. Determined to be recognized by Western powers as one among the equals, the changed self-understanding of the Qing dynasty eventually hastened the pace of domestic reforms.

From 1902 until the Republican Revolution of 1911, the Qing court achieved substantial progress in law codification, law enforcement, and judicial administration. A 1902 Imperial Law Codification Commission set up a subordinate Legal Revision Office, headed by Wu Tingfang and Shen Jiaben, the two most prominent legal scholar-officials of the time in the Qing court. During the following years, the Commission, assisted by prestigious Japanese scholars and judges, completed the modern Qing Criminal Code (promulgated in 1909), the Qing Draft Civil Code, the Draft of Procedural Criminal Code, and the Draft of Procedural Civil Code (Fishel 1952, 28; Gao 2003, 187). Also, the court established the ministry of commerce in 1903, which drafted a series of commercial laws and relevant regulations to facilitate the development of industry and trade. The reorganized ministry of agriculture, industry, and commerce completed the Qing Draft Commercial Code in 1910. The more important development was the Qing announcement of the Outline of Imperial Constitution in 1906. The Qing Draft Constitution, which imitated the cabinet system of Japan and Britain, was completed in September 1911.

With respect to law enforcement and judicial administration, the modern police department was established in 1905 at central, provincial, and local levels. In November 1906, the Qing court began to reorganize the central government and guaranteed the autonomy of the judiciary from the executive branch. The Provisional Regulations of the High Courts and the Subordinate Courts went into effect in 1907, and the Law on the Organization of the Judiciary in 1909. A new court system and a corresponding prosecutorial system soon followed.

On the other side, the treaty powers recognized the determination of Qing officials in the New Policy Campaign, and most Western diplomats came to consider extraterritorial justice as transitory. In 1902 Great Britain, in the Sino-British Mackay Treaty, agreed to relinquish extraterritorial rights: "China having expressed a strong desire to reform her judicial system and to bring it into accord with that of Western nations, Great Britain agrees to give every assistance to such reform, and she will also be prepared to relinquish her extraterritorial rights when she is satisfied that the state of the Chinese law, the arrangement for their administration and other considerations warrant her in so doing" (Reynolds 1993, 181). Japan and the United States in October 1903 agreed to the same plan (Hinckley 1906, 192). Sweden agreed in 1908 to renounce her jurisdictional privilege in China "as soon as other Treaty Powers have agreed to relinquish their extraterritorial rights" (Fishel 1952, 27). Still, the majority of Westerners resident in China considered the abolition of extraterritoriality too hasty because of "continued dissension within the country, a consequent delay in the perfecting of a reformed Chinese judicial and administration and legal codes, and a weakened central administration whose tenure was never assured" (28). In other words, the West took notice of, and welcomed, the empire's reforms in law and judiciary but expected more before agreeing to give up extraterritoriality.

The project of legal reforms accelerated after the Republican Revolution of 1911. Aided by French and Japanese advisors, Chinese legal experts and jurists by 1919 had promulgated the civil code, the criminal code, the code of civil procedure, the code of criminal procedure, and the commercial code for the nascent Republic of China. Three grades of courts, with the institution of procuratorship, were consolidated, with Western rules of evidence and examination. China created the legal profession from ground up, with legal training and a bar examination required for judicial officials.

Though Westerners viewed China's judicial reforms over the following twenty years as shallow, fractured, and ineffective, the modernization effort did empower Chinese diplomats to request more frequently and assertively the abolition of extraterritoriality (Chou 1923). The Chinese delegation at the Paris Peace Conference of 1919 refused to sign the Versailles Treaty because the Allies turned down China's request to abolish several nonreciprocal privileges exercised by treaty powers in China, extraterritoriality included. Just a few years later at the Washington Conference (November 1921–February 1922), the Chinese delegation, pressed hard by the rising nationalism of domestic and overseas Chinese, demanded again the abolition of extraterritorial jurisdiction. The General Committee of the Washington Conference, composed of the delegates of the Nine Powers, adopted a resolution on November 27, 1921, that authorized the Conference to organize a Commission with a mandate of investigating extraterritoriality and legal reforms in China.

On January 12, 1926, the Commission on Extraterritoriality convened for the first time at Peking; nine months later the final report of the Commission concluded that "there could be no relinquishment by the Powers of their extraterritorial rights until the judiciary of China was effectively protected against any unwarranted interference by the executive or other branches of the government, civil or more particularly, military" (Hsu 1949, 95). Apparently, China's sociopolitical development through the 1920s did not persuade treaty powers, particularly Great Britain and the United States, to put their subjects under Chinese jurisdiction. The unceasing fighting between belligerent warlords and divided and extremely unstable governments had frustrated the efforts of legal and judicial reforms, and obstructed the road to judicial independence. It was not until national unification in spring 1928 that the effort to revoke the extraterritorial regime gained new momentum.

Yet around the same time, principles of self-determination and sovereign equality began to pick up in Western states, particularly England and the United States. Social consciousness, prompted by domestic and transnational peace movements, led public opinion, mass media, and a growing number of legislators to adopt a sympathetic attitude towards China's efforts to liberate herself from discriminatory treaties. Acknowledging China's nationalist fervor and the shifting attitude of its domestic audience, officials at the U.S. Department of State (and their counterparts at the British Foreign Office) also began to admit that extraterritoriality and other "special privileges" currently enjoyed by foreigners in China had become "socially unfashionable" and had to be radically revised.[21] The Nanking Nationalist Government of China took a radical step in December 1929 to abolish unilaterally all extraterritorial jurisdictions. Though the treaty powers immediately denounced the move, China's unilateral action reminded Great Britain, France and the United States that the termination of extraterritoriality would be only a matter of time. The Western powers then proposed a gradual relinquishment of the regime; accordingly, China signed an agreement with the delegates of extraterritorial powers (except Japan) in February 1930 that established a special district court and a court of appeal in Shanghai to replace the existing international mixed court.

British and American negotiators then requested a transition period of ten years, during which China would set up "Special Chambers" in designated large cities to try foreigner-related cases and staff these Chambers with specifically trained judicial officials. The Chinese government had to employ foreign legal experts as advisors and assessors during the transition. Treaty powers during the transition would retain criminal jurisdiction over foreign subjects. China in a counterproposal declared that the Chinese government agreed to the foreign advisor and special chamber clauses but declared that both civil and criminal jurisdiction must be returned.

The Sino-British negotiation reached a draft treaty in June 1931, made possible by concessions of both sides. American delegates followed suit by signing a draft treaty with China in July. Then the process of revoking extraterritoriality was halted in September when Japanese troops invaded and occupied Manchuria. As a result, the priority of the Chinese government's foreign policy shifted from abolishing extraterritoriality and other humiliating treatments to winning international support against the Japanese incursion, postponing indefinitely further negotiations over extraterritoriality.

However, the Japanese intrusion produced unexpected effects that ironically hastened the delegitimation of extraterritorial justice. Japan's disregard for and frequent violations of Western extraterritorial rights in occupied Chinese territory (Manchuria and part of northern China) provoked constant protests from the treaty powers (particularly England and

---

[21] Nevertheless, the majority of Western career diplomats stationed in the field held a quite opposite opinion from those at metropoles because their top concern remained the safety of foreign residents and protection of their properties in the host country after extraterritoriality and other preventive arrangements were abolished.

the United States). But Japan's flouting of extraterritorial privileges revealed to both the Japanese and the Chinese that the ability of the Western powers to safeguard their treaty rights was waning. On the other hand, extraterritoriality proved to be a nuisance when Japan attacked and took over Western settlements, leased lands, and international concessions after all-out war broke out in 1941. For Western powers, it was pointless to cling to extraterritoriality knowing the right could no longer be retained. Its only remaining utility was to become a bargaining chip to keep China in the Allied camp, and that was exactly what England and the United States governments did in 1942.

The release of China from the extraterritorial regime came along with its alignment with the Allies in WWII. In October 1942, Great Britain and the United States informed China of the resumption of negotiations concerning foreign privileges. On January 13, 1943, China and the United States signed at Washington the Treaty for Relinquishment of Extraterritorial Rights and the Regulation of Related Matters. The Sino-British version was signed on the same day at Chungking, China's wartime capital. By the end of 1946, extraterritoriality was completely lifted. It took China forty-four years (1902–1946) to reach this goal.

Conclusion

Besides Japan, Turkey, and China, Siam (1920) and Egypt (1949) were able to reclaim judicial and administrative autonomy. By 1950, extraterritoriality had vanished from the world scene. The end of extraterritoriality involved changes on both sides of the institution. Given power asymmetries, non-Western nations could not achieve the goal of exclusive territorial jurisdiction without being recognized by Western powers as competent modern states. Western powers based that recognition on their assessments of comprehensive reform of domestic institutions. Therefore, the modernization of judicial, administrative and law enforcement systems became crucial national interests for non-Western nations. The degree of norm internalization gradually progressed from forced compliance to active learning and voluntary embracing. On the other side, the Western powers gradually came to view extraterritoriality as incompatible with foundational norms of international society, like sovereign equality and self-determination.

Extraterritoriality died, but only after intense disputes between the Western powers and the subordinated states. Thus we highlighted the debates and negotiations that led to the change. Western recognition never took place automatically but emerged out of exhausting processes of bilateral (or multilateral) contestation. The disputes and discourses eventually constructed a collective identity of sovereign states shared by Western powers and non-Western ruling elites. In those debates, the non-Western states grounded their arguments in the cornerstone norm of international society: sovereignty. They claimed, with increasing insistence, the same sovereign privileges enjoyed by the Western powers, in particular, exclusive internal jurisdiction. The Western powers responded that they would not abolish extraterritorial judicial arrangements until the legal systems in the receiving countries adhered to the norms and standards of the "civilized," that is, Western, states. In other words, the subordinated countries could not be fully sovereign until their institutions and practices conformed to Western model of statehood. Thus, initially, there was no compromise on the norm of extraterritoriality.

World War I, as in several of the other cases, proved to be a watershed, triggering a cycle of change that brought about the end of extraterritorial justice in Turkey and other countries. Woodrow Wilson made self-determination one of the prominent themes of the peace negotiations, raising the hopes of subject nations around the world. The new world body being created at Versailles was, significantly, to be not a League of *States* but a League of *Nations*. The aspiration to independent statehood of peoples that saw themselves as nations thus received a measure of legitimation. The notion that some states were entitled to maintain special authority over, or within, others was entering its decline. In a way, values that Western elites had proclaimed since the Enlightenment—equality, self-determination, national independence—were undermining arrangements that did not conform to those principles. Extraterritoriality was one institution that was on its way out, to be followed in fairly short order by colonialism. World War II launched the decisive cycle of change that finally abolished extraterritorial courts.

A counterargument to the one offered here might be that shifting power relations would account for the decline of extraterritoriality and of colonialism as well. It is true that the World Wars weakened the imperial powers, and thus altered the distribution of state capabilities. In this account, extraterritoriality disappeared and the colonies attained sovereign independence because the Western powers no longer possessed sufficient power to hold on to them (Horowitz 2004). But that argument is inadequate, for two reasons. First, if extraterritoriality were simply a function of power disparities—something imposed by the strongest on the "backward" and "underdeveloped"—then we would observe it in the period since 1950. If anything, the power gap between today's great powers (the United States, China, Russia, Japan, Germany, France) and the weakest states is larger than ever. Second, the gap between Western legal and judicial standards and those existing in some states is as great as ever. Today's Myanmar or the Democratic Republic of Congo have judicial systems no more advanced than those of Japan, Turkey, and China were during the era of extraterritoriality. Thus both of the gaps that were associated with extraterritoriality in the past—in state power and in legal systems—continue to exist today, but extraterritoriality does not.

Instead, extraterritorial judicial institutions are simply not on the policy menu. In the post-WWII era, states, regardless of their military capabilities, not only exclude consular justice from the list of foreign policy options but define the practice as illegitimate. Under today's norms, a person who is within the territory of a foreign country is subject to that state's judicial system should she violate its criminal laws. On the commercial side, contracts between parties from different states normally specify in advance which country's courts will have jurisdiction in case of a dispute. Or, increasingly, such contracts obligate the parties to submit disputes to private arbitration. In neither criminal nor commercial realms do states today claim extraterritorial judicial jurisdiction.[22]

Extraterritoriality became illegitimate and obsolete. Through identity reconceptualization, institutional renewal, and unabated contestations that eventually changed Western perceptions, non-Western states became recognized members of the "society of nations," and hence changed a norm that had partially defined the concept of sovereignty. Once considered as a parallel norm to territorial jurisdiction, extraterritorial justice has been discarded. Abolishing Western special privileges thus paved the way for the tide of decolonization that swept the globe after World War II.

---

[22] Some states, including the United States, do on occasion claim the extraterritorial application of their laws, but that is a separate topic.

Part II

Liberal Norms

Chapter 7

Slavery: Liberal Norms and Human Rights

Kendall Stiles

Between 1760 and 1920, the institution of slavery went from being an accepted social institution to being taboo. Not only was slavery banned, but with it the trade in slaves, indentured servitude, trafficking in persons, and other ancillary practices. Though this shift was in part a victory of principles of human dignity over traditional paternalism and exploitative capitalism, the fact is that various different ideas contributed to the demise of each of these institutions.

The theory proposes that some norm cycles can be understood as part of larger "metanorm" cycles. We will see that the norm against chattel slavery was primarily a product of the broader Enlightenment struggle to guarantee fundamental rights for all (though evangelical Christianity helped to advance the cause from time to time). The abolition of slavery thus contributed to the growing stream of liberal norms. We have also argued that norm cycles coexist and borrow from each other. Thus, while the norm against slavery drew on ideas about rights and the proper structure of domestic society, norms against the slave trade also borrowed from the law of the sea and the regulation of commerce. And modern efforts to mitigate human trafficking draw on still other principles on the rights of women and children in particular and workers in general. This chapter will therefore address three related cycles of normative change—the ban on slavery, the ban on the slave trade, and the struggle against human trafficking—to illustrate more clearly the utility of various elements of our model. Figure 7.1 depicts the cycles.

Finally, the model points to the role of power in advancing certain types of norms, and each of these three norm cycles helps to clarify this connection. In the case of the slave trade, Great Britain's naval power is decisive, while this is less true with respect to the institution of slavery itself, especially where the Arab world is concerned. At the same time, the United Kingdom devoted considerable effort to persuade states to suppress the slave trade through a succession of detailed and progressively stricter bilateral agreements, the provisions of which are not predictable on the basis of power relations alone.

The chapter will begin with a brief review of slavery through the late-eighteenth century, with an emphasis on the broad consensus over the legitimacy of the institution and its centrality to international economic life. Next, we explore the origins of the ban on the slave trade and its subsequent implementation. This will lead to a discussion of the ban on slavery itself which progressed in tandem but as a result of somewhat different forces. Finally, we will consider how the modern struggle against human trafficking is informed by and yet departs from these normative origins.

Antiquity to the Renaissance

Slavery has been pervasive in human society across time and space. By slavery we generally refer to the legal ownership of human beings or the exercise of the rights of ownership, and there is evidence of the practice by the first settled humans in Mesopotamia in 2000 BCE. The world's first codified legal system—the Hammurabi Code (Meltzer 1993, 12–15)—addressed it. Today, slavery also encompasses such slave-like conditions as serfdom and indentured servitude. The concept is still alarmingly relevant. Conservative estimates put the number of persons trapped in slavery and slave-like conditions today at roughly twenty-seven million (Bales 2004, 5; Reinhardt 2001, 52).

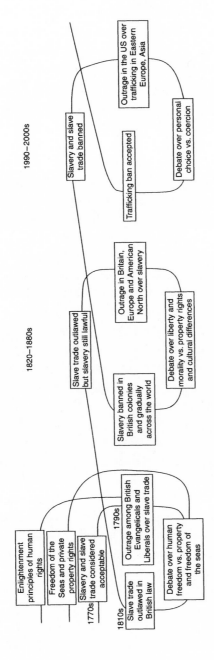

Figure 7.1 Antislavery norm cycles.

Until the Middle Ages, the legitimacy of slavery and the powers of masters were rarely questioned. In antiquity, the typical justification for slavery was that it was part of the natural order of things: the powerful used the labor of the weak. Plato and Aristotle both defended slavery as not only an inevitable social order but also one that benefited both slave and master. Aristotle argued that "from the hour of their birth some are marked out for subjection, others for rule" (Meltzer 1993, 93) As an inferior, the slave could benefit from his status by providing useful service. Plato advocated strong powers for masters, although he objected to the enslavement of Greeks by other Greeks.

This is not to say that the rights of masters were limitless. Even in Antiquity, there were those who sought to limit their power to inflict harm on slaves, starting with a ban on the capricious taking of slave life (Sawyer 1986, 2). Caesar Augustus gradually limited the rights of masters, banning the torturing of female slaves, the use of slaves as prostitutes, and the mutilation of slaves (Meltzer 1993, 177). Some in Ancient Rome (including Epictetus, Florentinus, and Ulpian) went so far as to argue that men are naturally equal and that slavery therefore violated the laws of nature.

During the Middle Ages, ancient forms of slavery mutated into debt peonage, serfdom, and bonded labor whereby individuals were obligated to work particular plots of land throughout their lives. But as canon law replaced Roman law, the justifications for slavery remained remarkably constant. The Roman Catholic Church noted that slavery was sanctioned in the Bible and was therefore not inherently sinful (Ericson 2000, 19; Maxwell 1975, 49). Both St. Augustine and Thomas Aquinas argued that slavery was the natural outgrowth of Adam's transgression in the Garden of Eden (Meltzer 1993, 211). The Church itself owned slaves, for that matter.

Over time, however, various popes expressed concerns about Christians enslaving other Christians and, by 1433, condemned the practice as a cardinal sin (Maxwell 1975, 51). Oddly enough, one penalty for owning Christian slaves was enslavement. This said, at no point was the capture of non-Christians—particularly of those who fought against Christian kings—considered anything but honorable by the Church's senior hierarchy (Ray 1989, 408).

Non-Christian peoples also practiced slavery as a matter of tradition and social ordering. Of them, Muslims had perhaps the most ambivalent perspective because the teachings of the Prophet Mohammed were some-what contradictory. On the one hand, slavery was justified as a necessary evil to maintain production and social order. But a "higher law" called for masters to allow slaves to purchase their own freedom or to emancipate them directly (Freamon 1998, 31–44). At any rate, Muslims were enjoined to never bring another Muslim into slavery and to limit their captures to infidels.

In the 1430s and 1440s, Portuguese explorers made contact with vulnerable African peoples. In 1441, the first Africans were taken into captivity and transported to Lisbon to work as household servants. By 1540, one-tenth of Lisbon's population consisted of African slaves. In 1454, Pope Nicholas V granted formal approval for this first wave of slave trafficking, based in part on the false claim by slavers that the Africans in question had allied themselves with Muslims who were fighting Christians (Maxwell 1975, 53). After Christopher Columbus landed in Hispaniola in 1492, it quickly became apparent that while the climate and soil were suited to plantation agriculture, the local inhabitants were not. Their virtual extinction from smallpox and other European diseases left the new fields without workers. The first African slaves (who had developed immunities to European plagues) were shipped across the Atlantic within less than a decade after Columbus' first voyage. By 1530, slaves were arriving at the rate of ten thousand each year.

At the same time as Africans were being shipped to the Americas with the Pope's blessing, other local Indian populations—more resistant to European diseases but not to their weapons—were enslaved with the blessing of Spain's Queen Isabella. Spain instituted the "Requerimiento" in 1503 to justify the enslavement by announcing to the local peoples (in Spanish) that the conquistadors operated under the secular power of the papacy, as delegated to the Spanish crown. Their refusal to accept conversion at this point was taken to mean they were enemies of Christendom and therefore deserved to be destroyed or enslaved—a status imposed on the vast majority (Maxwell 1975, 57).

Before long, the immense scale of slavery in the Americas prompted a reconsideration of the policy. Stories of abuses of local populations and African slaves were conveyed by Jesuits and other missionaries as early as 1511, raising concerns in Madrid (Maxwell 1975, 61). King Charles V went so far as to suspend the enslavement of native peoples from 1530 to 1534 out of concern for their welfare. In 1537, Pope Paul III declared that Indians were humans and entitled to redemption (although they could still be enslaved if they made themselves enemies of Christianity). Catholic clerics Jean Bodin and Bartolomé de las Casas began to articulate an alternative theology of slavery that stressed every Christian's obligation to treat other humans as children of God (Meltzer 1993, 12; Sawyer 1986, 6).

Ultimately, these concerns were drowned out by the possibility of tremendous profits from both the sale of slaves and their work on the plantations. By the mid-1500s, Spain's attempt to maintain a monopoly on slave trading in the Caribbean was under attack. One of the first to challenge it was John Hawkins, an English pirate whose greed and violent tendencies proved extremely valuable to his queen, Elizabeth I. Although Elizabeth had expressed deep reservations about the slave trade—fearing God's punishment for participating in it—she set aside her qualms and directly contributed to Hawkins' voyages (Jackson 1924, 15; Kelsey 2003, 18). For her, the key issue was one of freedom of navigation (see Chapter 2 on piracy). Sir Francis Drake's first voyage in 1562 led him to slaving almost by accident when he stumbled upon a Portuguese ship full of slaves on his way to the Caribbean. He secured the ship and ran the Spanish blockade to find an eager clientele of Spanish planters eager to purchase his discounted merchandise (Herman 2004, 2; Kelsey 2003, 69). He returned to pay his queen a tax on his profits and secure assistance from her in the form of the *Jesus of Lubeck*, a royal ship which he used for a subsequent voyage. Elizabeth received Drake and other slavers with open arms, showering them with wealth, homage, and social respectability (Jackson 1924, 16). France, Sweden, Denmark, the Netherlands, and every state where slaving took place repeated this pattern (Anstey 1975, 403).

As Spain's power waned during the late sixteenth and seventeenth centuries, its monopoly on the slave trade became untenable. Britain entered into a contractual arrangement to provide Spain its African slaves from 1707 on (Muhammed 2004, 897), and with the Treaty of Utrecht in 1713, replaced Spain as the sole provider of slaves through means of an *asiento* (Herman 2004, 237). The Crown was heavily involved in the slave trade, both directly and by means of its grant of authority to the slave trading Royal African Company. Slaves became the most heavily traded good in the world (2), followed closely by sugar and other plantation crops. Sugar consumption in England had risen to the point that each individual consumed hundreds of pounds a year, although the supply and price fluctuated wildly (239). In time the Royal Navy provided security for shipments of slaves and sugar. By the mid-1700s England was by far the world's major slaver, and its national economy was deeply dependent on the profits. Slavers were tightly linked economically and politically to the cities of Liverpool and Bristol as well as the financial centers of London

(Mackenzie-Grieve 1968, 254). As put by Porter, "[With] agents, officials, MPs, and merchants: the London West Indian interest was so widespread, so well organized, and so powerfully represented in Government that it needed little assistance to defend the slave trade" (1970, 25).

Slaving supported the Anciens Régimes and mercantilist trading systems in Spain, Britain, France, and Portugal. Competition between these powers was intense, as France dramatically increased its production of sugar, becoming a serious rival to Britain in the 1780s (Mathieson 1967, 7–14). Spain addressed its continuing decline with piecemeal liberalization, making it easier for Spanish planters to gain access to less expensive slaves (Flint and Alfaro 2003, 785). French slavers took advantage and made serious inroads into the market (Porter 1970, 15). By the 1790s, the total number of slaves being trafficked to the Americas rose to 80,000 per year (Lloyd 1974, 230).

In each of these four countries, governments and royal families actively supported the slavers, providing subsidies, tariff protections, and monopoly rights to assure their continued prosperity and that of the aristocracy and other elites that had grown dependent upon them (Porter 1970, 109). In Spain, planters and the aristocracy could scarcely imagine an alternative to protectionism and the slave traffic (Schmidt-Nowara 1999, 133). Even in the United States, a country without an aristocracy *per se*, slavery and the slave trade were so integral to the economic and political unity of the country that attempts to end the slave trade in 1776 and 1787 were abandoned (Julius 2004, 2–5). In fact, the U.S. Constitution formally legalized the slave trade.

It should be clear at this point that, in spite of concerns about the treatment of slaves—both as children of God and as investments—the major powers were heavily invested in the institution and considered it not only legitimate but honorable. Principles that supported this belief included a view of humanity as inevitably hierarchical, a belief in freedom of commerce and navigation by mercantilist states, and a commitment to the security of private property. Those opposed to slavery and the slave trade were a small minority and rooted their opposition in beliefs about the inherent value of all human beings, first as children of God and later as human beings endowed with inalienable rights.

The Enlightenment, Christian Revivalism, and Slavery

Given the status of slavery in the late-eighteenth century, it is nothing short of amazing that between 1790 and 1841 the opinions of so many people and the policies of so many states would utterly reverse themselves (D'Anjou 1996, 194). We explain the shift by a combination of international and domestic factors in the major slave trading states, as well as by the exertion of power by the United Kingdom to alter the norm through persuasion, inducements, and coercion. These factors have their own sources in deeper political-economic trends, including the emergence of free-market capitalism, the rise of the middle class, the advent of industrialization and urbanization, for example (Jennings 1997, 132; Ray 1989, 410). As seen in Figure 7.1, the movement to emancipate the slaves was part of a broader push toward civil liberty generally, what we have described as the stream of liberal norms. In this sense, it is useful to imagine the slavery norm cycle as "nested" in this overarching norm cycle. The figure simplifies reality, of course, because there were still other norm cycles that affected the movement, including the Christian Evangelical movement.

To begin, we should consider the Enlightenment and the new conceptions of freedom and human dignity proposed by the great European thinkers of the late-eighteenth century (Anstey 1975, 404). Beginning with critiques of slavery found in Montesquieu's *L'Esprit des Lois* (LaFontant 1979, 7; Maxwell 1975, 97), we find Rousseau and the Scottish Enlightenment thinkers building on the notion that all people enjoy basic, inalienable rights, including freedom from ownership by another human (Walvin 1986, 99). One of the earliest policy statements to incorporate this perspective is the judgment by Lord Mansfield in the 1772 case of *Somerset v. Steward*: "the state of slavery is of such a nature, that it is incapable of being introduced on any reason, moral or political; but only positive law, which preserves its force long after the reasons, occasion, and time itself from whence it was created, is erased from memory; it's so odious, that nothing can be suffered to support it but positive law" (Redman 1994, 767). In this judgment, the British Courts emancipated all African slaves living in the mainland of the United Kingdom (numbering 15,000 at the time).

The notion that slavery could not be grounded in any natural law theory of the origins of social norms was repeated frequently during the debate over slavery. For example, in the 1822 US case of *La Jeune Eugénie*, Supreme Court Justice Joseph Story ruled that the slave trade, while legal under positive law, violated international custom and natural law (Clark 1999, 400; Muhammed 2004, 919). The 1825 case of *The Antelope* reiterated this position (922). In France, the United States, and later Spain, this idea that slavery violated fundamental rights was central to abolitionist initiatives in the eighteenth and nineteenth centuries and still drives contemporary initiatives against trafficking in humans (Sawyer 1986, 220).

In Britain, however, another strain of thought animated the abolitionist movement: evangelical Protestantism (Anstey 1975, 405). Nonconformists, such as Quakers, Baptists, Methodists and Congregationalists, believed in a more egalitarian and personal form of Christianity in which all people were children of God and deserving of salvation (Oldfield 1995, 127). In the 1750s, Quakers in the United Kingdom, who were in contact with Quakers in the United States, reached a decision as a group to emancipate their slaves and begin organizing an abolitionist movement (D'Anjou 1996, 137). In addition, a group of Anglicans from Clapham, in some cases as a result of personal epiphanies and religious conversions, became convinced of the need to abolish the slave trade and slavery (Merrill 1945, 387). Members of these religious groups formed the core of the London Abolition Society, created in 1787 at roughly the same time as similar groups were springing up around the country. The importance of these associations cannot be underestimated. As put by Lyons, the London Abolition Society was "perhaps the first transnational moral entrepreneur—religious movements aside—to play a significant role in world politics generally and in the evolution of a global prohibition regime specifically" (Lyons 1963, 5).

While ideological reformers were intent on opening the political system and improving the human condition for the sake of freedom, evangelicals also believed that helping others was absolutely essential if Britain were to return to God's good graces. They believed that God was displeased with the nation's support of slavery and the slave trade and that the loss of the United States was only the first divine punishment (Jennings 1997, 130; Kaufman and Pape 1999, 648). Therefore, abandoning these practices was the first step to the spiritual redemption of the nation. In the final analysis, the two strands of reformism—secular and sacred—merged in the abolitionist movement. Some of the early founders of the London Abolition Committee, such as Thomas Clarkson, were political radicals, sympathetic with the Leveller movement (Oldfield 1995, 42). Their sympathy for the republican ideals of the French Revolution would later earn them the epithet of Jacobin by British conservatives (Walvin 1986, 114).

The Abolitionist Committee was fortunate to count among its own a Member of Parliament, William Wilberforce, who was eager to take the lead in drafting an Act of Parliament that would end the slave trade. The Committee coordinated its propaganda efforts closely with his parliamentary maneuvers in a way that would set a precedent for mass political movements for centuries to come (Drescher 1986; Jennings 1997, 126). The Committee began with the publication of inexpensive books and pamphlets that articulated the abolitionist credo. The Committee sold these throughout the country for a small profit, thereby not only spreading the word but also keeping the Committee solvent (Jennings 1997, 130). The abolitionists also collected information (Clarkson traveled 35,000 miles on fact-finding tours) and disseminated it through speeches and small rallies. They produced posters depicting the deck of a slave ship, packed with slaves like cordwood (Oldfield 1995, 165). They even created a Committee "logo"—a small piece of artwork designed by the legendary Josiah Wedgewood—depicting a manacled, kneeling slave with clasped, raised hands asking "Am I not a man and a brother?" Eventually, thousands of the logos appeared in cameos and became a minor fashion craze among England's burgeoning and well-intentioned middle class (1992, 334). As expected, the almost universal reaction to learning of the conditions of slaves was revulsion and outrage (Walvin 1986, 24). Clearly, the Committee understood its bourgeois audience (Jennings 1997, 134).

The table was now set. Not only were there ideas afloat that pronounced slavery an intolerable evil, but there were activists with the capacity and skill to do something about it in the capital of the most powerful nation in the world. Add to this a rather unique economic situation that appears to have made ending the slave trade (and perhaps slavery itself) a reasonable business move for Britain.

The Ban on the Slave Trade

In the end, the ban on the slave trade was a compromise between abolitionists and slave owners that ultimately affected only the slave traders—a more narrow constituency. Further, banning the slave trade folded into Britain's general war against piracy and lawbreakers on the high seas. The government was already firmly committed to improving the safety of maritime navigation and was developing the capacity to patrol the seas unilaterally. Finally, the movement to end the slave trade was seen primarily as a matter of international law, which was far more promising than actually ending the practice of slavery itself. British elites and abolitionists felt confident that they could persuade and pressure states into helping end this particularly odious form of commerce, even though reversing centuries of local traditions might have to wait.

The initial salvo in the battle against the slave trade was fired in 1788. In the year, the Committee orchestrated a national petition drive to persuade the Commons of the need to end the slave trade. The petition drive was handled mostly through face-to-face contacts in dozens of towns across England—particularly in the north-central and northern regions (Manchester was a key hub of activity). By 1789, hundreds of petitions were received in London with a total of nearly 100,000 signatures (D'Anjou 1996, 166). To put this figure in perspective, it was larger than the total number of votes cast in the previous parliamentary election.

The result of this initiative, and Wilberforce's tactical objective, was the creation by the Prime Minster, William Pitt, of a special investigatory committee. The committee, staffed with some members of the Abolitionist Committee, was tasked with gathering information about the slave trade with a view to revising current law on its regulation or abolition in the next session (Oldfield 1992, 338). The tasked proved too great and the issue carried over another year. Testimony came from slavers in Liverpool and Bristol and from several European capitals (Porter 1970, 36). The report ultimately provided considerable grist for the abolitionist side of the debate and provided momentum for Wilberforce, who submitted a proposal for abolition of the slave trade in 1791.

At about the same time, the Jacobin leaders of revolutionary France embraced the cause of emancipation, and Thomas Clarkson had developed a very friendly relationship with the regime. When the slaves revolted in Haiti demanding their freedom, the Jacobins acquiesced. British Abolitionists were accused of recklessness and radicalism because of their ties to France (Jennings 2000, 3; Walvin 1986, 117). It is perhaps not surprising, then, that against this backdrop the Commons voted 163-88 against Wilberforce's motion (Mackenzie-Grieve 1968, 205).

In 1792, the government of Denmark took the unexpected, although relatively uncontroversial, step of banning its participation in the slave trade, effective January 1, 1804 (Mathieson 1967, 20). Denmark's shippers were better known for their tea smuggling at the time, which naturally brought the country into conflict with Great Britain. In 1801, the Royal Navy attacked Copenhagen and destroyed its fleet in 1807. But in the meantime the Danes had claimed the moral high ground—a galling turn of events that encouraged the House of Commons to reconsider the question of banning the slave trade (Porter 1970, 120). This time, Wilberforce and Pitt operated without massive public mobilization and succeeded in winning an initial vote for abolition in 1804 by a vote of 124 to 49 in the

Commons (Walvin 1986, 121). The Lords, where banking and slaving interests were better represented, tabled the action and in 1805 it was defeated in the Commons by a 77-70 vote, as the Irish MPs swung their vote the other way (Merrill 1945, 395).

With the death of Pitt in 1806, a coalition government was formed that included Charles Fox, an ardent abolitionist, and Lord Grenville in a triumvirate. Fox opted for a mere resolution stating the Parliament's intention to ban the slave trade in 1806 (Jennings 1997, 128). Such a maneuver avoided the cumbersome "three readings" process that had proven difficult to overcome in the past. The resolution sailed through on a 114 to 15 vote (Mackenzie-Grieve 1968, 275; Porter 1970, 135). An election in December of that year brought a Parliament in which abolitionists outnumbered slavers by nearly four-to-one (Kaufman and Pape 1999, 654; Porter 1970, 136). Lord Grenville (Prime Minster since the death of Fox) took the bold step of beginning the formal debate on banning the slave trade in the House of Lords in the hope that he could secure passage of an act that declared the trade a misdemeanor. His three-hour speech was a tremendous success and he won a vote of 100 to 34 (Anstey 1975, 396). The motion later sailed through the Commons and, effective January 1, 1808, Britain was out of the slave-trading business. This meant that any slave trader sailing under the Union Jack was liable to seizure by the Royal Navy which would, under the authority of Admiralty Courts, impound the vessel and release the slaves back to Africa (Sierra Leone was available for this purpose). Slave patrols began operating as early as 1811 to carry Parliament's will into effect (Herman 2004, 420). Because no investors could insure these ships (Rice 2003, 63), slave trading became the riskiest of all English businesses and quickly died off. In the United States, abolitionists in Congress still held a slim majority at the turn of the century, and they were able to secure a series of significant victories. The slave trade was ended on the same day as Britain's ban went into effect, but with no provisions for enforcement—a concession to Southerners and a pyrrhic victory at best for abolitionists (Ward 1969, 126). By 1808, then, three states had formally approved a ban on slave trading and France had flirted with emancipation (Wanquet 1998). But Denmark's role in the slave trade was negligible, and the United States went on to become the world's leading slaver in spite of the laws on the books. Had it not been for the fact that one of the countries to ban the slave trade was also the ruler of the seas, it seems likely that little would have come from this initial flurry of debate. That said, the ideological and religious concepts that gave rise to the debate in the first place would continue to vex slavers for the rest of the century and beyond.

The United Kingdom's commitment to ending the slave trade has already received the attention it deserves, both from a legal and political point of view (DuBois 1970/1896; Kaufman and Pape 1999; Lloyd 1968; Ward 1969). Feeling constrained by the principles of freedom of navigation and sovereignty over flag ships, the Foreign Ministry took several approaches in succession to deal with the problem. First, the United Kingdom attempted to forge a multilateral commitment to banning the slave trade in a series of global conferences. When these failed to produce binding commitments, she approached each of the major slave trading states—persuading, bribing and threatening in turn—to reach agreement on a ban coupled with enforcement provisions. The reasoning is clearly articulated by Wilberforce in an 1817 address:

> Every consideration impelled us to stop a traffic like this. If it were not put an end to, any hope for our colonies selling their produce beyond our own possessions would be at an end. He should not hesitate, if the two powers [France, Spain] would not put an end to the Slave Trade, to advise a recourse to an expedient the prospect of which had been held out, viz., a treaty with the great powers of Europe to prevent the purchase of colonial produce from colonies of those states which had not abolished the Slave Trade. (Williams 1970, 64)

As the early treaties failed to produce satisfying results, the UK sought stronger provisions in new treaties—particularly with the addition of an "equipment clause" that would allow seizure of slave ships that were empty of cargo. Finally, in a few cases where weak states were still out of compliance with treaty law, Parliament was called upon to grant the Navy the authority to take unilateral action against slavers. This cumbersome and tortuous process cost the United Kingdom dearly in lost revenues, increased taxes and loss of life at sea (Kaufman and Pape 1999, 636; Ray 1989, 413). But it brought an end to the Atlantic slave trade by 1865 (Herman 2004, 422). The overall process is summarized in Table 7.1.

In spite of his early reticence about the ban on slaving (Ward 1969, 16), Foreign Minister Lord Castlereagh became an ardent advocate of the government's goal of a multilateral treaty (Mathieson 1967, 22). In 1814 and 1815, at the Congress of Vienna, he managed to persuade the crown

Table 7.1 Progressive changes in domestic laws and treaties regarding the slave trade

	UK	France	Spain	US	Portugal	Brazil	Cuba	Ottoman Empire	Multilateral Conventions
Status of Slave Trade:									
Slave trade abolished in principle	1808	1818	1817	1808	1818	1829	1830	1857	Vienna 1815
Slave trade legally abolished	1815	1850	1820		1830	1855	1865	1877	
Slave trade effectively stopped			1845	1862	1865			1890	
Status of Agreements with the UK:									
Treaty with UK providing partial mutual searches of slavers	x	1833	1817 1835		1815	1826	1831	1880	
Treaty with UK providing full mutual searches of slavers	x		1845	1862	1842				Quintuple Treaty 1840 Berlin 1885 Brussels 1890
Treaty with UK providing joint cruising for slavers	x	1845		1842					

princes assembled to accept language endorsing a ban in principle. They agreed that the practice was "repugnant to the principles of humanity and universal morality" (Meirs 2003, 14). The effort to secure agreement on a limited right of mutual search and seizure of suspected slavers found on the high seas did not fare as well. In 1818, a U.K. proposal for such a treaty failed (Adams 1925, 610). France opposed U.K. visits on French vessels on principle, a position which she would hold for many decades.

At this point, Britain set aside further efforts toward a multilateral treaty in favor of a series of bilateral agreements. By the end of the century, there would be dozens of these arrangements, a patchwork intended to cover every country and every contingency (Sawyer 1986, 217). The first major agreements were with Spain and Portugal (although a less significant pact—the Treaty of Paris—was concluded with France in 1814) (Van Bueren 2004, 239; Williams 1970, 68). Spain and Portugal were central to the slave trading issue because almost all traded slaves ended up in their colonies in the Americas. The bulk of trading took place under their flags, especially since the 1807 ban (Williams 1970, 69). However, neither country was inclined to alter the status quo. Abolitionist sentiment in Portugal was very muted, and even the more enthusiastic abolitionists still opposed a sudden end to the traffic (Schultz 2005, 278). Abolitionist sentiment in Spain would never figure prominently in Madrid's policies and did not emerge until the 1850s at any rate (Schmidt-Nowara 1999, 74). In Brazil, at most a third of policy elites favored abolition in the 1820s (following Brazil's independence from Portugal in 1822) (Adams 1925, 624). If anything, British pressure tended to provoke a nationalist backlash, particularly over the issue of search and seizure, bringing even liberals in line with conservatives with respect to the slave trade (Marques 1995).

But Britain could exert considerable leverage on the Spanish and Portuguese regimes by virtue of its relative power, both material and diplomatic. This is consistent with predictions made in the Introduction to this volume. Major powers clearly have a greater capacity to make their positions known and respected. Britain had helped liberate Portugal and Spain from Napoleon's armies in the 1810s, even rescuing the Portuguese royal family and carrying it to Rio in 1807 (Adams 1925, 614). The Iberian governments thus owed their very existence to Britain. Neither Spain nor Portugal had the naval power to back up any assertions of autonomy, and both were finding it increasingly difficult to control their colonial domains (Spain lost many of her possessions in the 1810s and Brazil was growing restive). Furthermore, Portugal was growing increasingly dependent on

British loans and goods. In some respects, she was turning into a British protectorate (Smith 1969).

For all its power, Britain was able to secure only a tentative commitment to ending the slave trade in exchange for hundreds of thousands of pounds of indemnity (Lloyd 1968, 45; Redman 1994, 772). The treaties signed in 1817–1819 with Spain and Portugal provided for mutual search and seizure and hearings at jointly operated indemnity courts (located in the Caribbean, Brazil and the West African coast). However, they only covered ships seized north of the Equator, which had little effect on trade with Brazil (the number of newly arriving slaves actually increased during the 1820s as smugglers resorted to extremely creative methods to avoid detection by British patrols) (Adams 1925, 616). The same was true in Cuba (Lloyd 1968, 45). Once the tribunals—formally known as "mixed commissions"—began operating, it became clear that the English judges would play the role of prosecutor while the Spanish or Portuguese judges played the role of defense attorney (Bethell 1966, 86). In some cases, the Spanish or Portuguese judges would simply "take ill" and stop attending the sessions, bringing the work to a halt. The English judges in Rio and Havana were so unpopular that they took to hiring armed body guards to travel the streets of the city (84). In spite of this, the commission in Sierra Leone was able to dispose of more than five hundred slave ships—including 240 Spanish and 140 Portuguese—between 1819 and 1845 (83).

With respect to the United States and France, British policy depended almost entirely on the countries' domestic politics. Neither government was inclined to give the British what they most wanted—a treaty providing for mutual search and seizure—although neither government supported the slave trade overtly. Napoleon abolished the slave trade during the "Cent Jours" in 1815 in the hope of garnering support for his brief reappearance on the world stage, and his successor Louis XVIII could not help but ratify the move in 1818 (Jennings 2000, 6). For that matter, Louis needed international recognition as well. Penalties were fairly light and enforcement measures at sea were limited (Mathieson 1967, 23). Many French became involved in slave smuggling. French newspapers challenged British sincerity and wondered openly whether its ban on the slave trade (and later slavery itself) was just a ruse to guarantee British supremacy over commerce (Kaufmann and Pape 1999, 640). Such criticisms may have even prompted Britain to attack Algiers in 1816 to prove its consistent antipathy toward slavery in itself (in this case attacking the "white" slave trade) (Lowenheim 2003).

In the United States, appeasement of Southern sentiments was the first order of business. Although slave trading was banned, enforcement was left to local jurisdictions, which guaranteed that slavers arriving in Southern ports had nothing to fear. This was in spite of the fact that Congress had declared in 1820 that slavers were pirates and therefore subject to hanging (the first slaver would not be hanged until 1861; Lloyd 1968, 175). With regard to the issue of mutual search and seizure, the War of 1812 was fought in part over British impressments of American sailors on the high seas. As explained by Secretary of State John Quincy Adams to the British representative in 1814, any treaty providing for mutual search and seizure would be met with the universal repudiation by the American people (Lloyd 1968, 51). Even a fairly weak treaty on slave trading was blocked by Congress in 1817 (DuBois 1970/1896, 135). In the courts, U.S. judges consistently ruled in favor of slavers and returned several slave ships to the flag countries on the grounds that since slaving was not illegal in these places, the United States had no right to intervene (Hawkins 2000, 12; Muhammed 2004). Before long, Americans flying under both U.S. and Spanish flags dominated the trans-Atlantic slave trade.

During the first three decades of the nineteenth century, the United Kingdom was clearly on the defensive with respect to its desire to ban the slave trade. Although it secured a few bilateral treaties providing for mutual search and seizure, and many European governments had officially banned the slave trade, implementation of these laws was resisted at every step of the way. And Britain found it difficult to persuade France and the United States that freedom of the seas did not mean impunity to allow scoundrels and criminals to fly one's flag (Ward 1969, 77). A mere 135 slavers were captured between 1817 and 1830, and the average number of slaves arriving in the Americas was up to 135,000 each year (Lloyd 1968, 275). During the next three decades, the United Kingdom grew impatient with those who refused to comply with the new norm, eventually deciding to attack slavers within the territorial waters of foreign states.

Britain continued to seek stronger treaties against slave trading with France, seeing it as a key player in the system. As mentioned previously, the shifts in French policy over the next decades stemmed almost entirely from domestic political upheaval, rather than British pressure (which was probably counterproductive). The French Revolution of 1830 brought to power a pro-abolition government, and much as in 1794, it precipitously passed a law banning slavery (Jennings 2000, 32). Although the law was not enforced by Louis-Phillipe, the incoming regime sought a new treaty with Britain in the hope of securing its diplomatic recognition (Lloyd 1968, 48). The 1833 treaty provided for a limited right of search and seizure of French ships sailing in the Atlantic between longitudes 15 degrees north and 10 degrees south and between 30 degrees west and Greenwich (Ward 1969, 121). It was not until the establishment of the Third Republic in 1848 that slaves were freed across the French Empire and slave trading under the French flag came to an end. The French abolitionist society was largely uninvolved in this shift and even opposed it as reckless (Jennings 2000, 279)!

To address the problem of cheating where Spanish and Portuguese ships were concerned, Britain pressed the two governments for two major changes to the 1817 agreements: expansion of the geographical scope of the treaties and acceptance of the so-called equipment clause, meaning subjecting to seizure any ship equipped for slaving. Slave ships were unusual in that they had barrels to supply far more food and water than an ordinary crew of a dozen of so men could need. They usually had empty shackles, unique "shelving" below deck to place slaves, and a stench that could be detected more than a mile away (Lloyd 1968, 46; Ward 1969, 119). An agreement with the Netherlands in 1826 that included the equipment clause resulted in an almost immediate end to the slave trade under the Dutch flag (1969, 120).

The Spanish and Portuguese complied with British demands beginning in 1822—to a point. With regard to the equipment clause, for example, they agreed that searches and seizures could be made only if there was absolutely no doubt that the ship was only used for slaving (Lloyd 1968, 46). In 1835, the standard of proof was relaxed in a new round of treaties. The last of the treaties between the United Kingdom and Spain and Portugal were signed in 1839 and 1842, respectively. The result was a virtual end to Spanish-flagged slaving by the mid-1830s (47). The situation with Portugal was not resolved, however, in large measure because of conditions in Brazil.

Where Brazil was concerned, the United Kingdom hoped to stop the slave trade by eliminating the demand for the slaves. The Brazilian government after independence (1822) was only willing to go so far, however. Treaties in 1820, 1826, and 1831 provided apparently strong measures to combat slaving, but the government had neither the capacity nor the will in the first decade after independence to enforce the measures. Many protested British measures as cynical and sneaky, claiming that as "her colonies were fully stocked, . . . she wishes to accomplish the abolition among other nations who are not so well provided with laborers" (Adams 1925, 619). Britain approached the problem with still more proposals for new treaties, submitted in 1835, 1840 and 1841. In time, the Brazilian government asked that no further proposals be proffered (628). Foreign Minister Lord Palmerston was reduced to a string a verbal assaults on the regime for breach of its obligations.

At about the same time, British patience with Portuguese attitudes came to an end and in 1839, the government sought authority from Parliament to act unilaterally (Kaufmann and Pape 1999, 659). This entailed authorizing the Royal Navy to search and seize Portuguese vessels without the consent of the Portuguese government, anywhere on the high seas. Needless to say, the measure directly challenged the norm of freedom of the seas, but in British thinking, because slaving was such an abomination and because considerable diplomatic effort had not yielded sufficient results, the move was warranted (Bethell 1966, 89). Portugal protested the move but could do little to stop it, and for the next three years, the Royal Navy operated against Portuguese slavers with impunity, suspending the operation in 1842 when the Lisbon government consented to a new treaty.

But since Brazilians were still receiving smugglers—often with open arms—the government asked Parliament to issue the same declaration in 1845 with respect to Brazilian shipping (Adams 1925, 629). The United Kingdom announced that it intended to activate a clause of the 1826 agreement declaring that slavers were pirates, thereby justifying universal jurisdiction over slavers. Foreign Minister Lord Aberdeen proposed legislation to that effect to the House of Lords:

> Your lordships are aware that the Brazilian government have always declined to fulfill their general engagements to cooperate with the British government for the abolition of the slave trade. With rare and short exceptions, the treaty has been by them systematically violated from the period of its conclusion to the present time. (Adams 1925, 629)

In defiance, Brazil increased its importation of slaves from 51,000 in 1845 to 60,000 in 1848. As put by the Brazilian Minster of Marine, "You cannot expect us to assist England, or consent to stop the trade, whilst you are seizing Brazilian vessels, insulting our flag, and illegally condemning them" (Adams 1925, 630). But the Royal Navy went on the offensive anyway, and in 1850 patrolled not only the high seas off Brazil but also in its territorial waters and even coastal rivers. As it happened, the British policy was supported by elements of the Brazilian Navy, and as the central government was able to defeat a variety of insurrectionist movements in the late 1840s, it was in a position to provide better coastal patrols. In 1852, the British withdrew their patrols and slaving dropped to insignificant levels.

The last area in the Caribbean that still defied a growing global consensus against the slave trade was Cuba. But because almost all ships sailing to and from Cuba were under American flags or manned by American crews, the real problem was US policy. As discussed earlier, although American statutes called for the execution of slave traders, these were not enforced. Further, the United States resisted proposals by the UK to patrol the waters off the U.S. coastline. It was not until 1829 that the country openly debated slavery, beginning with an attack on the institution by William Lloyd Garrison in a public address in Boston (Julius 2004, 39). The country split almost evenly on the issue, such that changes to the status quo were virtually impossible. Van Buren was the only President prior to 1850, other than father and son Adams, not to have been a slave owner. His effort to persuade Congress to provide for enforcement of the slave trade ban in 1839 failed miserably. He later left the Democratic Party to lead to abolitionist Free Soil Party in the 1848 Presidential race (Earle 2004, 141; Julius 2004, 250). Many Secretaries of State were slave owners and contributed to the country's intransigent foreign policy. John Forsyth, who served from 1834 to 1841, was particularly obstructionist, as was John C. Calhoun, who took office in 1843. Forsyth defended the government's position in the Supreme Court case involving the famous slave ship *Amistad* against the position argued by the slaves' attorney John Quincy Adams (being a mere Congressman, Adams was more free to act on his abolitionists instincts than when he had been President) (Muhammed 2004, 928). Forsyth was also responsible for persuading France not to ratify the 1841 Quintuple Treaty it had signed, whereby the United Kingdom, Russia, Austria, Prussia, and France agreed to strong mutual search and seizure provisions (Ward 1969, 121). He was especially concerned about the Treaty's statement that slavery was piracy and loudly protested the implication for the United Kingdom's jurisdiction over foreigners at sea (Redman 1994, 773). It did not help matters that during this time, British Foreign Minister Lord Palmerston took to berating and lecturing American representatives for allowing the U.S. flag to be shamed by the slavers who flew it (Lloyd 1968, 52). British frustration with the widespread use of the American flag by slave smugglers led Palmerston to ask Parliament for the right to search U.S.-flagged shipping unilaterally (having failed to secure a firm commitment from the US) to confirm the authenticity of the registration (Kaufmann and Pape 1999, 659; Ward 1969, 140). For a time, it seemed to many that open warfare with Britain was inevitable (Lloyd 1968, 51).

Daniel Webster, who served from 1841 to 1843 and was an abolitionist, was able to defuse the situation and negotiate one of the few diplomatic breakthroughs during the first half of the century—the Ashburton Treaty—which provided for more vigorous US patrols along African and American coastlines, although it stopped short of joint patrols (Lloyd 1968, 55). But Calhoun was able to block implementation of the agreement when he took office. In the 1850s, some Southern politicians even made a concerted effort to rescind the ban on the slave trade, but they settled for smuggling instead (Bernstein 1966).

As late as 1858, the United States again appeared to move closer to the British position on joint patrols only to reverse itself under pressure from proslavery newspapers (DuBois 1970/1896, 147; Lloyd 1968, 170). Then in 1861, as a direct and immediate result of the election of Abraham Lincoln, U.S. policy toward the slave trade did an about-face. In 1861, the first American slaver was sentenced and hanged under the 1820 law declaring slavery to be an act of piracy. In 1862, the United States signed an agreement allowing joint patrols with the British Navy—even off the US coastline. This had the effect of bringing the slave trading in the Caribbean to an abrupt halt by 1863 (17). In 1865, the Thirteenth Amendment abolished slavery in the United States.

Spain, Portugal, and Brazil experienced liberal openings in the 1860s and 1870s, resulting in a lively debate on the status of slavery. In 1874, the short-lived First Republic abolished slavery in its remaining Caribbean territories, and in Portugal, the liberal reformer Peter V (1853–61) moved resolutely toward abolition, which was ultimately accomplished in 1875. Cuba outlawed slavery in 1886, Brazil in 1888— both through a long process of step-by-step emancipation (Lamounier 1995, 191). In these cases, emancipation was the product of an elite debate between conservatives and liberals, with the liberals ultimately winning the day (Schmidt-Nowara 1999, 123). Even the Ottoman Empire— responsible for much smaller scale slave trade and slavery—ultimately moved in the same direction for some of the same reasons. In 1877, the new constitutional monarch Abdullah II affirmed the ban on the slave trade after ongoing pressure from the UK, and in 1908, the liberal "Young Turk" regime outlawed slavery itself (Erdem 1996, 125, 141).

It may seem ironic that another mechanism used to halt the slave trade was the very thing that had given rise to it in the first place: colonialism. In 1830, France invaded and annexed Algiers in part to halt the white slave trade practiced by the Barbary Pirates. In 1861, Britain took control of the port of Lagos to bring an end to its role as a center of slave trading (Herman 2004, 423; Temperley 2000, 9). David Livingston's horrifying tales of the brutal slave trade in East Africa contributed directly to Britain's decision to invade the region in the 1880s (Meltzer 1993, 252). Britain brought the practice of slavery to an end in Nigeria, although it took several decades (Ubah 1991).

By 1880, it seemed clear that slave trading and slavery were violations of customary international law. The linking of slaving with piracy implied that slave trading, and perhaps slavery itself, involved peremptory norms (although in fact universal jurisdiction was rarely asserted; U.K. policy toward Portugal and Brazil between 1839 and 1852 stands out as a dramatic exception) (Van Bueren 2004, 191). The next task for Great Britain was to codify the slavery ban by way of binding, enforceable multilateral treaties.

In 1885 at Berlin and in 1889 at Brussels, the leaders of most European states (including the Ottoman Empire, Persia, and France) gathered to negotiate the status of Africa, among other things. British representatives placed the question of slavery and the slave trade on the agenda and put forward a sweeping plan of action. The proposal called for multilateral enforcement of a global ban on slaving, although the conferees eventually focused on the Congo and the East African coast from Cape Town to the Arabian Peninsula (Sawyer 1986, 217). Along with a statement declaring unequivocally that "trading in slaves is forbidden in conformity with the principles of international law," the conferees established agreements on effective search and seizure of slavers with bases set up for this purpose in Brussels and Zanzibar (the Sultan had committed to fighting the slave trade in 1873 under threat of British bombardment) (Meirs 2003, 16) under the authority of a new International Slavery Bureau (ISB) (Redman 1994, 775; Sawyer 1986, 217). Although the ISB did not directly control naval patrols, it was able to collect and disseminate information, particularly to the Royal Navy which still carried most of the burden of interception (Meirs 2003, 20). These conferences and the ISB proved fairly effective at controlling the slave trade in the Indian Ocean—a region that had been neglected during much of the nineteenth century—although trade in and to the Congo actually increased over the next ten years (Sawyer 1986, 217). Nonetheless, these agreements and the ISB in particular stand out as a high water mark in multilateral cooperation on the issue of slavery and the slave trade. As early as 1919, where the signatories endeavored to restart the system suspended during World War I, they found it was not possible to secure the same degree of commitment to multilateral enforcement, and the British Navy was already beginning to question its capacity to go it alone (Meirs 2003, 62; Sawyer 1986, 218).

The Ban on Slavery

The norm prohibiting the slave trade did not, as shown above, simultaneously abolish slavery itself. In fact, it makes sense to conceive of separate, though linked, cycles of norm change. The two cycles overlapped in time, with the prohibition on the slave trade usually (but not always) preceding, and paving the way for, the proscription of slavery.

Abolitionists in the United Kingdom in the 1780s often spoke of their dream of ending slavery across the Empire. But although serfdom within England had been abolished by Lord Mansfield in *Somerset v. Steward* in 1772, the prospect of banning slavery outright was remote (Redman 1994, 767). The first nation to address this issue directly was France. The French Revolution of 1789 put in power a small cadre of liberal intellectuals whose ideological commitment to freedom included abolition of the slave trade and slavery. Among them were the founders in 1788 of *Les Amis des Noirs* (Friends of Black People) —the Abbé Gregoire, Count Mirabeau, Condorcet, and the Marquis deLafayette (Jennings 2000, 1). They took as their inspiration the London Committee and endeavored to bring about changes in public policy through their lobbying and petitioning.

News of the Revolution quickly reached French colonies in the Caribbean, fueling demands for emancipation. A slave uprising broke out in Haiti in 1791, led by the charismatic Toussaint L'Ouverture. The slaves were outraged by the decision on the part of the Revolutionary government to extend the rights articulated in the Declaration of the Rights of Man to nonblacks living in the colonies (blacks at this time made up ninety percent of Haiti's population). The rebellion proved too much for the unstable government, and an emissary was sent in 1793. He agreed to grant the rebellious slaves their freedom in exchange for an alliance with the Paris regime in its war with monarchical Europe (Jennings 2000, 3; Meltzer 1993, 120). In 1794, the National Assembly ratified the action and quickly passed a law emancipating all the slaves in France's Caribbean colonies.

Less than a decade later, the government of Napoleon Bonaparte moved to suppress the slave uprising in Haiti, reversing the abolitionist policies of the First Republic. The fight ended in stalemate and Napoleon acquiesced to Haitian independence in 1803, although he was more successful in restoring slavery in other Caribbean islands. Eventually, the British Navy seized several of these islands, and the status of the local slaves remained in doubt (Meltzer 1993, 120).

The British abolitionist movement reorganized and revitalized itself during the1820s under new leadership. As early as 1823, MP Foxwell Buxton declared to Parliament the movement's desiderata:

> The object at which we aim, is the extinction of slavery—in nothing less than the whole of the British dominions—not, however the rapid termination of that state—not the sudden emancipation of the negro—but such preparatory steps, such measure of precaution, as, by slow degrees, and in a course of years, first fitting and qualifying the slave for the enjoyment of freedom, shall gently conduct us to the annihilation of slavery. . . . We are far from meaning to attempt to cut down slavery in the full majority of its vigour. We rather shall leave it gently to decay—slowly, silently, almost imperceptibly, to die away and to be forgotten. (Williams 1970, 94)

This gradualist sentiment was well received by the sitting government, which decided to put pressure on the local assemblies in British colonies in the Caribbean in the hope that they would move toward emancipation on their own. Though some argued that Parliament had every right to assert its powers over these assemblies, restraint might produce consensus (Mathieson 1967, 139). By 1828, however, it was becoming clear to the abolitionists that the local assemblies did not intend to move forward, and so the Anti-Slavery Society began to lead street rallies in favor of immediate emancipation.

In 1830, the Whigs won a sizeable majority in the Commons and quickly passed the Great Reform Act that substantially expanded the suffrage in Britain (Kaufmann and Pape 1999, 632). With their new law in place, they requested the dissolution of Parliament and ran for reelection in 1833, winning an even broader majority. This is not to say that the new leadership was unequivocal—the preference was still for piecemeal reform, if at all possible, by consensus (Mathieson 1967, 199). The fear was that forcing emancipation down the throats of the planters could lead to defiance, unrest and perhaps even the splintering of the Empire.

In time this gradualist sentiment gave way to a sense of urgency. For those on the fence, the slave rebellions in Jamaica in 1831, while prompting more repressive measures in the short term, made it clear to many observers that maintaining slavery would be too costly (Walvin 1986, 163). By 1833, the government was ready to submit an abolition bill to the House of Commons. The new Colonial Minister, Lord Stanley, acknowledged that "the only course left to you is to advance. The only dangerous course is happily impracticable—you cannot recede—you cannot stand still" (Mathieson 1967, 231). The bill called for an end to the legal status of slavery, although former slaves were still expected to work for free for three-fourths of the day. After twelve years, the last of these former slaves would have completed apprenticeships for trades and would thereafter be their own agents. The government would provide them loans to get started, and compensate planters as well, to the tune of twenty million pounds (Meltzer 1993, 247). Though many criticized the bill as a half-measure, the end result was that legalized slavery came to an end in the British Empire by the late-1830s, well before most other states in the world.

During this time, Americans openly struggled with abolition, particularly as territories and states were added to the Union. But although the abolitionist arguments are well known, it is interesting to note that slave holders also made reference to Christian and Enlightenment principles. Southerners argued that Southern states had a right protected by the Constitution to forge whatever type of society they liked based on democratic sovereignty. And they argued that the institution of slavery had proven a beneficial one that deserved protecting. As put by John C. Calhoun:

> Experience had shown that the existing relations between them [the two races in the South] secured the peace and happiness of both. Each had improved; the inferior greatly; so

much so, that it had attained a degree of civilization never before attained by the black race in any age or country. Under no other relation could they coexist together. To destroy it was to involve a whole region in slaughter, carnage, and desolation; and, come what will, we must defend and preserve it. (Ericson 2000, 3)

Some even went so far as to say that African slaves were being uplifted and empowered by the opportunity to learn about freedom as found in the United States (Ericson 2000, 19). At any rate, they argued, liberal thinking places the protection of private property at the center, and because slaves were property, their emancipation would violate this tenet. Ultimately, this helps to demonstrate that Enlightenment principles had won the day and were reshaping the discourse on slavery, even if its principles were often applied inconsistently (see Table 7.2).

As mentioned in the previous section on the slave trade, the emergence of liberal regimes in France in 1848 and in Spain, Portugal, and Cuba in the 1860s and 1870s spurred forward the ban on slavery. Emancipation in the United States was also the product of domestic struggle, although in this case it pitted two versions of liberalism, as mentioned above. Even in Turkey, the rise of a new, more western-oriented regime led by the so-called Young Turks made possible a ban on the practice (although to term this government "liberal" would be an exaggeration; see the chapter on genocide in this volume). Thus by 1890, it seemed as though chattel slavery was fading into history.

Be this as it may, the unbridled exploitation of man by man persisted. Slaves were renamed but still required to work under almost identical conditions. In Haiti, dictatorial regimes emerged soon after independence and reinstituted gang labor under state control (Temperley 2000, 4). Portugal reclassified slaves as "libertos" in 1869 and "serviçaes" in 1878 without

Table 7.2 Formal abolition of slavery (domestically and in overseas colonies) in selected countries

United Kingdom	1834
France	1848
United States	1865
Portugal	1869
Spain	1874
Cuba	1874
Ottoman Empire	1908

changing their working conditions or the substance of their relationship with their former masters (Grant 2005, 22). The French colony of Réunion renamed slaves "engagés" after the 1848 abolition and continued import slaves from East Africa (Lloyd 1968, 201). Institutions such as "debt peonage" and "indentured servitude" came under increasing scrutiny at the turn of the century (Meltzer 1993, 258). Clearly, emancipation did not lead directly to fair labor contracts. In some cases, slaves were treated worse after emancipation. As put by Haraksingh: "[F]reedom of contract was designed to allow one party to take advantage of the straightened circumstances of the other, and to permit the shark to swallow the sardines" (1995, 227).

Slavery, Similar Practices, and International Treaties

The application of antislavery norms to cognate practices did not begin until after World War I. With the establishment of the League of Nations, the United Kingdom began to press for a new multilateral convention that would begin to address this broader problem of slave-like working conditions and eradicate the last vestiges of slavery in Asia. In 1921 and 1922, the United Kingdom, New Zealand, and a German antislavery NGO began to press for such a convention, which led to the establishment by the League of Nations of the Temporary Slave Commission (TSC) in 1924, tasked with drafting a general convention against slavery. Members of the TSC, led by Frederick Lugard, a well-known British expert on slavery, agreed rather quickly to broaden the definition of slavery beyond chattel to encompass debt peonage, indentured servitude, serfdom, and forced labor (Meirs 2003, 113). The inclusion of forced labor, however, met with resistance from colonial powers that commonly used forced labor to carry out major public works projects (Redman 1994, 780). The language was therefore tempered to permit forced labor for public projects but not for private enterprise (Meirs 2003, 122; Rassam 1999, 331).

Governments preferred a definition of slavery that was brief and deliberately vague. The final language defined slavery as "the status or condition of a person over whom any or all of the powers attaching to the right of ownership are exercised." Although the definition does not explicitly cover slave-like practices, language in the Convention that calls upon states to end slavery "in all its forms" was interpreted by some to mean that these other practices were thenceforth unlawful (Meirs 2003, 130). It is apparent from the discussion, though, that the signatories intended to limit the scope of the definition (Grant 2005, 161; Rassam 1999, 331).

To their credit, the negotiators accepted the notion that freedom from slavery was a fundamental right under customary law (Redman 1994, 764). The League Covenant already included words to that effect, giving some reason to believe that the prohibition of slavery was a peremptory norm (Van der Anker 2004, 15). However, the convention did not establish universal jurisdiction over slave trading, and no state claimed such jurisdiction afterward (Rassam 1999, 309; Redman 1994, 760).

Of special interest is the parsing of words to the effect that although slavery was illegal, this did not mean that all slaves should be immediately emancipated. Lugard in particular had strong reservations about a proposal to liberate slaves immediately around the world:

> [S]udden emancipation would dislocate the whole social fabric. Men wholly unaccustomed to any sense of responsibility and self-provision would be thrown on the streets to fend for themselves. Slave concubines would become prostitutes. Masters, albeit with money in their pockets, would be ruined; industry would be at a standstill; and plantations would be wrecked before the new order could adjust itself. (Grant 2005, 157)

This naturally troubled abolitionists, who found the enforcement provisions of the 1926 Slavery Convention inadequate. The treaty required states merely to "undertake to communicate to each other and to the Secretary-General of the League of Nations any laws and regulations they might enact with a view to the application of the provisions of the present Convention" (Sawyer 1986, 219). States were not even required to submit the typical annual report on their progress. It took the United Kingdom six years to persuade the League to create a standing, autonomous body to monitor compliance with the 1926 Convention. The Standing Advisory Committee of Experts on Slavery was formed in 1932 but closed shop with the outbreak of World War II (219).

This preference for a weak agreement, especially regarding an end to forced labor, was repeated in the negotiations over the International Labour Organization's convention on forced labor, negotiated shortly after the Slavery Convention. At the insistence of France, Portugal, Spain, Italy, and Belgium, the ILO convention also failed to ban forced labor. Even its rather lenient restrictions came with long implementation schedules and were not ratified by these states for many years (Portugal did not ratify until 1956) (Meirs 2003, 146–8).

After World War II, the issue of slavery arose again, albeit with little urgency because the issue seemed to have only historical importance. A 1955 U.N. drafting committee undertook to expand upon the 1926 agreements. Although most colonial powers were engaged in dismantling their empires, there was still reluctance on their part to end practices analogous to slavery in their domains. Even the United Kingdom was dragging its feet on the issue and opposed any proposals to ban slave-like practices in colonies (Meirs 2003, 326). Meanwhile, the Soviet bloc hoped to make slavery a Cold War issue by linking it to imperialism and capitalism, while at the same time stonewalling on the issue of its own use of forced labor (319). Given the existence of forced labor in its penal system, the United States sympathized with Soviet concerns and succeeded in removing the item from the agenda. The 1956 Supplemental Convention on the Abolishment of Slavery, the Slave Trade, and Institutions and Practices Similar to Slavery was a conservative document, broadening the definition only slightly. That said, it represents the state of the art and continues to provide the basis for current work on slavery at the United Nations (Herzfeld 2000, 1).

The Current Debate: Trafficking in Human Beings and Slave-like Practices

International discourse on the question of slavery became a casualty of the ideological divide at the United Nations during the 1960s and 1970s. Western countries generally sought to strengthen monitoring and enforcement provisions of existing treaty language, whereas the Soviet bloc and the Group of 77 saw in the slavery debate an opportunity to attack oppressive institutions such as colonialism and *apartheid* (Meirs 2003, 374; UN 1984, vii). In 1966, a debate over the creation of a U.N. body on slavery became an occasion for what Sawyer calls "instinctive, rather than rational," position taking (1986, 233). Developing countries such as Peru, India, and Iran charged that creating such an independent body would lead to witch hunts for quasi-slavery for the purpose of embarrassing them and challenging their cultural traditions unfairly (Meirs 2003, 366). Better, they argued, to shine a brighter light on Western governments' covert support for apartheid and Israeli oppression of Palestinians (Sawyer 1986, 233). Even the United States questioned the need for yet another U.N. body, especially because it risked giving voice to radicals.

By 1974, the Working Group of Experts on Slavery (renamed to cover "contemporary forms of slavery" in 1987) was formed to collect materials from countries in the form of annual reports on slavery within their boundaries. It would only meet every other year for a few days and would have a very limited staff, thereby preventing it from becoming pro-active (Meirs 2003, 385; Sawyer 1986, 226). Over time, the Working Group has managed to move beyond its initial institutional weaknesses and it now meets on an annual basis, selects the themes it will address, and initiates public hearings and even public criticisms of egregious cases of slavery (Meirs 2003, 393).

"Slavery" had acquired such a pejorative meaning that its use has proved a potent weapon against any activity one seeks to denigrate. Since the 1990s, U.N. agencies have gradually expanded the scope of "slavery" to include a wide range of practices, some of which never occurred to the drafters of the 1956 Convention: debt bondage, traffic in persons, sale of organs, the exploitation of prostitutes, the sale of children, child prostitution, child pornography, trafficking in children, exploitation of child labor, sexual mutilation of female children, and use of children in war (UNHCHR 2004). Attempts have also been made to apply the concept to religious brainwashing, pedophilia, incest, and cloning (Meirs 2003, 417). Although the Working Group and other U.N. bodies claim that these issues are regulated by the 1956 Convention, governments have been inclined to draft new instruments to cover issues that do not fall under the traditional definition.

The application of slavery to a broader range of activities seems to have done little to halt the expansion of the practice of traditional slavery itself. Most experts agree that close to thirty million individuals are held in involuntary servitude of one type or another (Bales 2004, 8; Re 2002, 33; Reinhardt 2001, 52), although some have suggested the figure could be closer to 200 million (Van der Anker 2004, 18). Estimates put the number of children in forced labor at roughly eight million (Hendricks 2003, 431). Half of the population of Mauritania may be enslaved, and nearly 100,000 have been forced into slavery in the Sudan (Jok 2001; Rassam 1999, 322; Re 2002, 33; Teyeb 2001, 52). As Bales pointed out, slavery today is not only more common than in the eighteenth century, it is also more pernicious. Table 7.3 presents some of the differences between "old" and "new" slavery. The conclusion is that current slaves are "disposable," meaning that they are likely to be worked to death and then discarded without hesitation (Bales 2004, 15). They are not considered an "investment" to be protected and passed on to one's children—rather they are like an inexpensive machine to be used up, thrown away, and replaced.

Table 7.3 Contrast between old and new slavery

Old Slavery	New Slavery
Ownership explicit and legal	Ownership denied due to its illegality
Price of slaves high ($5,000 equ.)	Price of slaves low (< $500)
Low profit from slave work	High profit from slave work
Shortage of potential slaves	Glut of potential slaves
Long-term relationship between master and slave	Short-term relationship between "master" and "slave"
Slaves cared for as an investment	Slaves are disposable as an expense
Ethnicity critical	Ethnicity almost irrelevant

Source: Adapted from Bales 2004, 15.

Reports of human trafficking increased during the 1990s. The International Organization for Migration estimated the number of trafficked persons to be in the hundreds of thousands in mid-1995 (Skrobabek et al. 1997, 99). In the same year, the Dutch government sponsored a study of the Southeast Asian sex tourism industry (viii). Another Dutch report entitled "The Sex Sector" insinuated that the country's system of legalized prostitution encouraged trafficking (Leuchtag 2003, 15). In 1997, the Clinton administration commissioned a study of laws against trafficking to discover that penalties for drug possession were often far greater than for human trafficking (Feve and Finzel 2001, 28). And in 1998, the International Human Rights Group—a conference of international legal scholars—met at Harvard to draft a proposal for a new trafficking instrument (Miller & Stewart 1998, 11).

As we will see, defining contemporary slavery and trafficking has required states to call upon previously established norms, although the results have been somewhat unpredictable. Because legalized chattel slavery has been abolished and norms governing slave-like conditions have been unevenly implemented, there seems to be an unwillingness simply to invoke the 1956 Convention to address contemporary slavery. Note that it was not the Working Group that sponsored the key debates of the 1990s and 2000s but rather other agencies in the U.N. system. Slavery and trafficking have been defined as a violation of labor norms, a threat to immigration law, a matter of child and women's rights, and even a trade law issue. It is as yet uncertain which analogies and referents will prevail.

The 1998 G-8 Summit included trafficking as a specific policy priority, as did the U.N. General Assembly in 1999 (Koslowski 2001, 337, 346). As early as 1997, Argentina proposed a new agenda item for the Crime Commission annual meetings to address trafficking. Some believed that enforcement would be stronger in this framework rather than as part of the Commission on the Rights of the Child or the Convention on the Elimination of Discrimination against Women, even though both instruments including articles against trafficking. Since the European Union and the United States were both moving forward on strengthening their own antitrafficking laws, the proposal was warmly received (Defeis 2004, 489; Ryf 2002, 53). Austria ultimately submitted the formal proposal for a legal instrument to be linked to the upcoming Convention against Organized Crime (Gallagher 2001, 981).

Although there was little disagreement over the need for a strengthened trafficking protocol, the negotiations were anything but smooth. In particular, a lively debate emerged over the question of choice: could a woman choose to be trafficked into prostitution? The NGO community found itself split on the issue. The International Human Rights Caucus, made up of women's advocacy groups from around the world, argued that the traditional view was the correct one: women could not reasonably be expected to choose to be trafficked and were therefore invariably "innocent" of any crime (Gallagher 2001, 983; Leuchtag 2003, 13). They were joined by Argentina, the Philippines, China, Colombia, France, Pakistan, and others. The opposing viewpoint, advocated by the Human Rights Caucus and such governments the United States, Australia, Canada, the Netherlands, and Japan, and a coalition of U.N. agencies (the Inter-Agency Group), was that there could be situations in which the trafficked woman was a consenting adult who understood the risks and decided to take them anyway (Abramson 2003, 483; Gallagher 2001, 983). The key question was whether the woman was a fully informed free agent. Ultimately, the issue was resolved with careful wordsmithing. As explained by Gallagher:

> After protracted debate, the Ad-Hoc Committee decided against including the phrase 'irrespective of the consent of the person.' The final definition now includes an unwieldy note to the effect that consent to the intended exploitation is to be irrelevant where any of the stated elements which actually define trafficking (coercion, fraud, abuse of power, etc.) have been used (2001, 985)

The final text of the 2000 UN Protocol to Prevent, Suppress, and Punish Trafficking in Persons also hedged on the question of deportation, urging states to consider providing protection for victims of trafficking and making repatriation voluntary (Abramson 2003, 477; Gallagher 2001, 983). The US Trafficking Victims Protection Act of 2000 was presented as a model, in that the United States now issues special visas to victims of trafficking that allow them to stay in the country legally (Defeis 2004, 489). Such arrangements were not made mandatory due to opposition from several European governments that feared this might end up encouraging trafficking (Fitzpatrick 2003, 1157). Likewise, the treaty encouraged but did not require provision of public services to victims of trafficking, out of deference to poorer states that lacked resources.

It is too early to assess the implementation of the Protocol, but because it lacks multilateral enforcement provisions or a forum for victims, enforcement will depend entirely on the willingness of states, many of which have already shown a lack of capacity or will to act. In many cases, state agents are complicitous or at least choose to ignore large-scale violations (Bales 2004, 29; Toepfer and Wells 1994, 84).

This said, numerous penalties for slavery and trafficking have been instituted and are enforced with considerable energy (Corrigan 2001, 179; Koslowski 2001, 343; Toepfer and Wells 1994, 112). Many European countries have laws barring the importation of slave-made goods, although they enforce the laws sporadically for fear of antagonizing major trading states (including China, India, and Pakistan, e.g.). Some states, among them Austria and Australia, have even enacted penalties for their citizens who travel overseas to use child prostitutes (Smith and Mattar 2004, 164).

From a historical point of view, it is useful to recall that slavery has been a constant in human existence. Slaves may have numbered more than half of the populations of ancient Greek and Roman cities, and indentured servitude was pervasive in the Middle Ages. Roughly four-fifths of all Russians were still in bondage in the mid-eighteenth century (Mavor 1965, 418). It is estimated that between twelve and fifteen million blacks were transported to the Americas, although there were likely less than half that number residing in the hemisphere at any given point in time. In 1850, the slave population of the United States numbered 3.2 million out of a total population of just over 23 million—or nearly 14 percent. It is estimated that today between twenty-five and thirty million people worldwide are still held in indentured servitude or other slave-like conditions, which translates to 1 in 250 people on the planet (roughly 0.4%).

But the persistence of slavery in the modern world serves as a stinging challenge to the sincerity of the international community's "zero tolerance" policy (Smith and Mattar 2004, 169). And although the United States as hegemon is making moves in the direction of tougher enforcement of slavery and trafficking rules, its commitment to codifying free trade law seems to create a conflict. The demand for ever-cheaper manufactured goods and the inexpensive labor to produce them is a juggernaut capable of rolling over any barriers intended to protect the weakest. Unless this inherent conflict can be overcome, slavery will likely continue to be tolerated.

Conclusions

Returning to the interplay between legal structures, conflicts and legal discourse, the case of slavery illustrates the utility of our overarching model. Norm change occurred through cycles of dispute; antislavery rules contributed to the stream of liberal, human rights norms. Recall that until the mid-1700s, slavery and the slave trade were sanctioned by international law—both secular and canon law. The first challenge came not from governments but from philosophers and ministers of religion. The idea of basic human rights proved remarkably powerful in shaping state policy, beginning in Britain, the United States and France and ultimately spreading to Spain, Portugal, Brazil, and beyond. But the ideas were not enough on their own to alter international norms. From the first declarations of the illegality of slave trading in 1807, Britain embarked on a century-long crusade to persuade, bribe, and coerce other major actors to comply with its vision. It did so at tremendous cost and risk and with mixed results, due in part to the counterargument by other states that the principles of sovereignty, autonomy, and freedom of the seas outweighed Britain's demands. The issue was ultimately resolved at two levels: many countries agreed to a ban on the slave trade, however timidly enforced, as a result of inducements and coercion while the ban on slavery itself typically grew out of domestic reforms that brought liberal reformers to power. In a few cases, slavery was abolished through conquest.

Once slavery had been accepted as anathema, a new dialogue emerged: how many actions can be outlawed under this rubric? Debates on the 1926 and 1956 Conventions revolved around forced labor, which was limited to public works projects but not banned. During the 1960s and 1970s, the range of practices that could be placed under the rubric of forced labor gradually expanded—to the point of absurdity—as part of the ideological struggle of the Cold War. Effectiveness and meaning were sacrificed to scoring debating points. Even after the Cold War, the inclination to expand the scope of the norm to a variety of contemporary practices is strong, but the will to enforce prohibitions is weak. Not only has the expanded antislavery norm had little effect on limiting such new phenomena as child pornography or organ sales, as proposed, but it has done little to halt activities clearly linked to its core meaning, such as indentured servitude and trafficking in women. Governments today seem less committed to eradicating slavery than they were one hundred years ago. And though the prohibition on chattel slavery is a peremptory international norm, the status of rules against related modern abuses remains ambiguous.

Chapter 8

Genocide

Kendall Stiles[1]

Polish legal scholar Raphael Lemkin coined the term "genocide" in 1944 by combining the Greek term *genos*, which refers to any race or tribe, with the Latin *cide*—to kill. The new term was needed, he felt, to "denote an old practice in its modern development" as it applied to the new phenomenon of the Holocaust, wherein the Nazi regime exterminated six million European Jews, 2–3 million Soviet POWs, 500,000 gypsies, 250,000 mentally handicapped individuals, and unknown numbers of communists, social democrats, Jehovah's Witnesses, and homosexuals. Lemkin defined genocide as "the coordinated and planned annihilation of a national, religious, or racial group by a variety of actions aimed at undermining the foundations essential to the survival of the group as a group" (Chalk and Johnassohn 1990). Although the term applied to a wide range of groups (not just people of a common ethnicity or race), it was revolutionary in its conception and in its effect. Within five years of

---

[1] With contributions from John Bunkall, Taylor Nuttall, Heather Jacques, Jason Anderson, Mike Connelly, Noah Eyre, Sam Goble, and Elizabeth Torres.

the term coming into the lexicon, international tribunals employed it in convicting Nazis and Japanese war criminals, and an international convention bearing the term in its title had already entered into effect (Morris 2003, 206).

Prior to the beginning of the twentieth century, genocidal killing occurred with depressing regularity around the world. From Antiquity through the Middle Ages, victors in war considered such massacres a necessary element in suppressing conquered and rebellious peoples. These atrocities rarely elicited anything more than expressions of regret from the international community. Against this context, the international norm prohibiting genocide developed through two cycles of norm change, one triggered by the Armenian genocide of 1915 and a second following the Holocaust. Subsequent cycles clarified the application of the norm.

With the first cycle, which began in the early 1900s, it was becoming clear to those who perpetrated genocide that their actions would prompt hostile responses. Turkish perpetrators of the Armenian genocide were thus careful to conceal the nature of their actions and, after they were discovered, sought to explain them away as justifiable responses to Armenian treachery and rebellion (Morgenthau 1918, chap. 26). The Turks even went so far as to criticize foreign governments for sympathizing with the Armenians, arguing that sympathy only encouraged Armenian rebellion, which in turn required an ever-firmer responses. The international community, however, could not agree on a clear statement against genocide prior to 1939. The second cycle of norm change responded to the Holocaust, and it unfolded fairly quickly. Churchill, for example, called Nazi extermination programs the "crime without a name." Within a few years, the Genocide Convention and the Geneva Conventions spelled out in relatively precise language the nature of the crime and put all on notice that there could be serious consequences for perpetrators of genocide.

Subsequent cycles, beginning in the 1950s, have involved the specific application, interpretation and modification of these rules as instances of genocide occur. Ultimately, while international duties are still somewhat ambiguous, the parameters of the norm are becoming clearer, due in part to the work of the International War Crimes Tribunals for Yugoslavia and Rwanda and the International Criminal Court. The cycles assessed here (and summarized in Figure 8.1) follow the pattern proposed in the Introduction: specific actions triggered debates, the outcomes of which modified the international norms. The development of norms prohibiting genocide has been an important part of the broader stream of liberal norms.

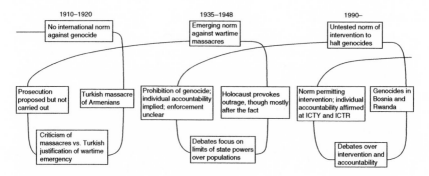

Figure 8.1 Cycles of the norm against genocide.

The Pre-World War II Period

Historically, the mass slaughter of groups of any type, whether it be for political, national, geographical, racial, or ethnic reasons, was condoned as a weapon of war. There is archeological evidence, supplemented by both folklore and historical documents, that genocide has taken place on all inhabited continents. The Athenians eliminated or enslaved peoples who would not submit to their rule. Thucydides documented the Athenian slaughter and enslavement of Melos in history's first written account of "genocide." Thucydides explains that the Melians were given the option to surrender rather than face the slaughter, but they chose to fight, apparently accepting slaughter as the cost of defeat.

Early Roman history is shaped by genocide against the people of Carthage. Like the Athenians before them, the Romans adopted a dispassionate attitude vis à vis the Carthaginians. As explained by Kuper, the "long drawn-out Roman conflict with Carthage was not premised on ethnic disdain" so much as it was rooted in "power, politics, and economics" (Kuper 1981, 11). Furthermore, the Third Punic War (149–146 BC) was undertaken to annihilate Carthage's resilient economic expansion (Hooker 1996). Despite Carthage's entreaties for peace, Rome "implemented a plan for Carthage's destruction—a decision, it should be noted, that was made by the Senate of democratic Rome, one hundred and fifty years prior to the rise of imperial Rome under the dictator-like Caesars" (Adcock 1932, 740). In the summer of 149 BC, the order for the final assault on Carthage was given.

The Roman legions "stormed the town and the army went from house to house slaughtering the inhabitants in what is perhaps the greatest systematic execution of noncombatants before World War II. Carthaginians who weren't killed were sold into slavery. The harbor and the city [were] demolished, and all the surrounding countryside was sown with salt to render it uninhabitable" (Adcock 1932, 740). Scipio's siege and final assault on the city was "truly one of the most brutal accounts of genocide in ancient recorded history." The Romans exterminated all forms of Carthaginian culture, religion and economic activity (Lloyd 1977). Even though great "orators such as Cato hated Carthage and persuaded the Roman Senate to crush it, the Senate did not act out of hate" (Scullard 1951). Rather, Rome destroyed Carthage as a preemptive strike against an economically powerful and resurgent Mediterranean city that had proven itself a potential military threat.

Other instances of genocide include: Genghis Khan and his hordes ravaging cities and towns across Central Asia; Europeans slaughtering Jews and Muslims in the Crusades and later the Inquisition; and countless conquerors killing indigenous peoples as they spread across the New World and beyond (Kuper 1981, 11–16). The fact that genocide was also perpetrated by the Hebrews in the Old Testament gave rise to a perception among Christian scholars in the Middle Ages that such practices were legitimate. Opposition to genocide began to emerge as some clerics and scholars questioned whether these Hebrew practices could be replicated without incurring God's disapproval. Aquinas refined the "Just War" theory and added that war should be waged "proportionally," limiting the number of unnecessary civilian casualties. He did not, however, specifically address the concept of genocide.

Hugo Grotius (1583–1685) argued that the Bible does not condone genocide unless God commands it. "There is no occasion to allege in this place, as an example, the conduct of the Hebrews, who slew the women and children of the Heshbonites, and who were commanded to execute vengeance upon the Canaanites, and upon all, who were involved in the same guilt. Those examples, where God *manifestly* interposes his commands, are not to be drawn into a precedent for authorizing actions of the *same* kind on *different* occasions, for the supreme and disposing power of God can never properly be compared with that, which men are allowed to exercise over each other" (Grotius 1901 [1625, Book III, chap. 4, § ix], 328).

Grotius cited the acts of "barbarians" to demonstrate the callousness of killing civilians, highlighting instances where prominent societies were involved in mass killings of innocents during warfare to show that it was not uncommon nor immoral for them, but reprehensible for a Christian society. "The Psalmist's expression of the Babylonian children being dashed against the stones is a much stronger proof of the custom commonly prevailing among nations, in the use of victory, to which the language of Homer bears a close resemblance, where the poet says, that 'in the cruel rage of war, even the bodies of infant-children were dashed against the ground'" (Grotius 1901 [1625, Book III, chap. 4, § ix], 328). Although Grotius deplored these acts, he did not deem them inconsistent with the common practices or norms of the time.

Some limited legal prohibitions against genocide arose in the Middle Ages through customary law in wartime (Kuper 1981, 12). The Knightly Code, recognized in the Middle Ages, denounced reckless violence against Christians and established a framework for accepted behavior among British nobility. A knight "had to swear to the knightly code which asked him to protect the weak, defenseless, and helpless, and fight for the general welfare of all" (Ross n.d.). History records at least one important early war crimes trial in which Peter von Hagenbach was convicted by a multinational tribunal in 1474 for atrocities committed against the civilian population under his authority (Schwarzenberger 1968, 462; Sunga 1992, 18).

As noted in the chapters on slavery and the slave trade and on the protection of cultural monuments, the major powers of Europe in the mid-nineteenth century were beginning to codify some basic laws of armed conflict. In 1863, for example, Abraham Lincoln arranged for the promulgation of a military code of conduct (the Lieber Code) that prohibited, among other things, "murder, maiming, assaults, highway robbery, theft, burglary, fraud, forgery and rape" (United States 1863). In 1864, the first Geneva Convention protected the sick and injured wartime casualties.

The Hague Regulations, approved in two treaties signed in 1899 and 1907, featured a unique approach that was unprecedented in international law regarding "crimes against humanity." We find in them the so-called Martens Clause:

> The inhabitants and the belligerents remain under the protection and the rule of the principles of the law of the nations, as they result from the usages established among civilized peoples, from the laws of humanity, and the dictates of the public conscience. (Kushalani 1982, 9)

It is expressed in "strong language, both rhetorically and ethically, which goes a long way toward explaining its resonance and influence on the formation and interpretation of the law of war and international humanitarian law" (Meron 2000, 79). These features have compensated for the somewhat vague and indeterminate legal content of the clause. Certain basic principles of humanity are acknowledged here and they have to be respected under any circumstance, even if they are not explicitly codified in treaty form. This principle, later to be known as humanitarian law, stands above national law. The clause highlights the legal and moral bases of humanitarian obligations by making reference not only to law, but "to pre-juridical principles [and] to the sentiments of humanity" (79). As such, the Martens Clause also provides a principle of interpretation. If "faced with two interpretations—one in keeping with the principles of humanity and moral standards, and one which is against these principles—then we should of course give priority to the former interpretation" (Schiessl 2002, 203).

These principles (of humanity and moral standards) would be put to test within just a few years of their drafting. The new Turkish government initiated the systematic deportation and extermination of the more than two million Armenians who had lived for centuries in the eastern provinces. However, this was not the first time governments in Istanbul attempted the extermination of Armenians. In 1895, roughly 200,000 people were slaughtered in government-sponsored campaigns. The 1915 program was more intensive and better organized. It began with the systematic disarmament of all Armenian men (many of whom had served in the military with distinction), followed by the execution of community leaders and the posting of deportation orders in villages throughout Armenian areas. Massive caravans of deportees were organized throughout the region with the announced aim of sending the people to the Syrian Desert. However, as explained by the American Ambassador to Turkey, Henry Morgenthau:

> As a matter of fact, the Turks never had the slightest idea of reestablishing the Armenians in this new country. They knew that the great majority would never reach their destination and that those who did would either die of thirst and starvation, or be murdered. . . . The real purpose of the deportation was robbery and destruction; it really represented a new method of massacre. (Morgenthau 1918, chap. 24)

Typical of the exodus was the story of the Harpoot caravan that started with 18,000 people but reached its destination of Aleppo with only 150. Where exposure and starvation were not enough to kill off the deportees, Turkish soldiers, local villagers, and others attacked them, leaving their bodies on the side of the road in heaps. It is generally estimated that one million Armenians were killed in 1915.

During the war, condemnation of Turkey was strong in Paris and London—two countries formally at war with the Porte. The term "crimes against humanity" appeared for the first time in a declaration issued by France, Great Britain, and Russia in May 1915. The Statement denounced the 1915 massacre as "crimes against humanity and civilization for which all members of the Turkish Government will be held responsible together with its agents implicated in the massacres" (Kushalani 1982, 14).

Germany refused to criticize its ally publicly; however, it issued a private note of protest to the Grand Vizier (a figurehead). While neutral, America's reaction was muted; nevertheless, after entering World War I, the United States condemned the actions of Turkey (even though the US was never formally at war with that country). Ambassador Morgenthau's pleas for a more forceful US response were rebuffed on the grounds that it would be inappropriate to intervene in the domestic affairs of a foreign state (Power 2002, 8).

After the War, however, the victors made attempts to exact justice against the Turkish government for genocide, and against the German High Command for having instigated the conflict. At the close of the war, a Preliminary Peace Conference in 1919 recommended prosecution of "all authorities, civil or military, belonging to enemy countries, however high their position may have been, without distinction of rank, including the heads of state who ordered, or with knowledge thereof and with power to intervene, abstained from preventing or taking measures to prevent, putting an end to, or repressing, violations of the laws or customs of war" (Cassese and Roling 1993, 71). The agreement required the German government "to hand over all persons accused," so that they could be brought before an allied military tribunal. It also provided for the possibility of setting up an international tribunal for persons "guilty of criminal acts against the nationals of more than one of the Allied and Associated Powers." Moreover, Article 227 stated that Kaiser Wilhelm II of Hohenzollern was responsible "for a supreme offence against international morality and the sanctity of treaties" and the Allied Powers agreed to establish "a special tribunal" composed of judges appointed by the United States, Great Britain, France, Italy, and Japan to try the accused (Greppi 1999, 537–8).

Now that the idea of international prosecution was opened, various initiatives emerged. The Council of the League of Nations appointed an Advisory Committee of Jurists in 1920, to draw up plans for international judicial institutions. The International Law Association and the International Association of Penal Law also studied the question of international criminal jurisdictions. Their efforts culminated in 1937 with the adoption of a treaty by the League of Nations contemplating the establishment of an international criminal court to try terrorist suspects, particularly those charged with regicide (see Chapter 5 on terrorism) (Schabas 2000, 22–3). The negotiations and treaties that came as a result of World War I paved the way for the future of international law and the enforcement of international rules. There was not, however, a codified statement specifically concerning the practice of mass murder.

Allied leaders set in motion plans to bring the Turkish leadership to trial for crimes committed against the Armenian minority. The proposed trial was the first acknowledgment that mass killings during wartime are a crime. In the Treaty of Sèvres, which was signed on August 10, 1920, Turkey recognized the right of trial "notwithstanding any proceedings of prosecution before a tribunal in Turkey" (Article 226) and was obliged to surrender all persons "accused of having committed an act in violation of the laws and customs of war, who are specified either by name or by rank, office or employment which they held under Turkish authority" (Martens 1924, 720). Though this formulation was similar to the war crimes clauses in the Treaty of Versailles, it contained a major innovation: prosecution of what we now define as "crimes against humanity" as well as war crimes (Schwelb 1946, 178). Article 230 reads:

> The Turkish Government undertakes to hand over to the Allied Powers the persons whose surrender may be required by the latter as being responsible for the massacres committed during the continuance of the state of war on territory which formed part of the Turkish Empire on August 1, 1914. The Allied Powers reserve to themselves the right to designate the tribunal which shall try the persons so accused, and the Turkish Government undertakes to recognize such tribunal. In the event of the League of Nations having created in sufficient time a tribunal competent to deal with the said massacres, the Allied Powers reserve to themselves the right to bring the accused persons mentioned above before such tribunal, and the Turkish Government undertakes equally to recognize such tribunal. (182)

However, the Treaty of Sèvres was never ratified and the trial never occurred. The treaty was later supplanted by the Treaty of Lausanne on 24 July 1923, which provided amnesty "for all offenses committed between August 1st, 1914 and November 20th, 1922" (Schabas 2000, 22).

With respect to our model, we have completed one "turn of the cycle," in that the norm that accepted genocide as part of war was challenged and then modified. Genocide, now considered a crime rather than an ordinary act of warfare, provoked outrage. International condemnation forced Turkey to respond, which it did by invoking sovereignty and national survival principles. Ultimately, the international community could not agree that international prosecution of genocide trumped sovereign prerogatives, and the Turkish government avoided criminal trials.

The Holocaust and the Genocide Convention

The Holocaust prompted universal condemnation, as could be expected from the pre-World War II consensus mentioned above, but serious questions arose with regard to appropriate consequences. In general, military planners in France, the United Kingdom, the United States and the U.S.S.R. were in agreement that the Nazi leadership should be held accountable for waging aggressive warfare and contributing directly to the deaths of nearly forty million in Europe and North Africa alone, including twelve million Jews and others exterminated in concentration camps. British and Soviet authorities preferred summary executions in the field or other more traditional military methods without resort to legal proceedings (Ball 1999, 45). Churchill told Roosevelt, "[His Majesty's Government is] deeply impressed with the dangers and difficulties of this course (judicial proceedings), and they think that the execution without trial is the preferable course. [A trial] would be exceedingly long and elaborate, [many of the Nazis' deeds] are not war crimes in the ordinary sense, nor is it at all clear that they can properly be described as crimes under international law" (Ball 1999, 45). Within the United States, the Treasury Department led by Henry Morgenthau, Jr. (son of the U.S. Ambassador to Turkey in 1915) sought an even more draconian approach: summary execution of the entire Nazi command structure and the deindustrialization of Germany (Bloxham 2001, 9).

It was the U.S. War Department that pressed for trials as part of a somewhat gentler peace plan. Secretary of War Henry Stimson, joined by Secretary of State Cordell Hull, argued that although

> executive action has the advantage of a sure and swift disposition, it would violate the most fundamental principles of justice,

> common to all United Nations. This would encourage the
> Germans to turn these criminals into martyrs . . . etc.
> Condemnation of these criminals after a trial, moreover,
> would command maximum public support in their own times
> and receive the respect of history. The use of the judicial
> method will, in addition, make available for all mankind to
> study in future years an authentic record of Nazi crimes and
> criminality. (Ball 1999, 45)

Roosevelt was persuaded by these arguments (Harry Truman would prove an even more ardent advocate of the tribunal). "It was the intention of all of the American proponents of trial, from Presidents Roosevelt and Truman downwards, to expand the concept of 'war crimes,' and this was realized in the formulation of 'crimes against humanity' " (Bloxham 2001, 19).

The case for a legal approach was helped by the fact that throughout the war the Allied leadership had repeatedly warned the Nazis of the possibility of severe consequences for atrocities, rumors of which began to leak as early as 1940. By 1940, Polish and Czech leaders in exile had begun receiving information from their occupied nations about the war crimes and crimes against humanity the Nazis committed, and in 1941, Churchill and Roosevelt issued warnings against Hitler about the "fearful retribution" he and his leaders would face at war's end because of the war crimes the Nazis committed. In 1942, leaders in exile of the nine occupied nations issued the St. James Palace Declaration, which announced that postwar criminal trials would take place because of Nazi war crimes and violations of The Hague and Geneva treaties (Paust et al. 2001, 20).

In 1942, Roosevelt and Churchill called for the creation of a United Nations War Crimes Commission to investigate the accusations, and in 1943, Stalin, Churchill, and Roosevelt announced that war criminals would be punished where the crimes had been committed. Crimes committed by Nazi leaders, including the military, that went beyond the territory of one nation would be punished by an international tribunal. The Declaration included the following warning:

> The United Kingdom, the United States, and the Soviet Union
> have received from many quarters evidence of atrocities, massa-
> cres and cold-blooded mass executions which are being perpe-
> trated by Hitlerite forces. . . . Those German officers and men and
> members of the Nazi Party who have been responsible for or have

taken a consenting part in the above atrocities, massacres and executions will be sent back to the countries in which their abominable deeds were done in order that they may be judged and punished. . . . Let those who have hitherto not imbrued their hands with the innocent blood beware lest they join the ranks of the guilty, for most assuredly the three Allied Powers will pursue them to the uttermost ends of the earth and will deliver them to their accusers in order that justice may be done. (Wilson 1999, 63)

To those who argued against trying defendants for acts that were not criminal at the time of their commission (ex post facto), Justice Robert H. Jackson, America's chief prosecutor responded: "Let's not be derailed by legal hair-splitters. Aren't murder, torture, and enslavement crimes recognized by all civilized people? What we propose is to punish acts which have been regarded as criminal since the time of Cain and have been so written in every civilized code" (Jackson 1945). At the Yalta Conference in February 1945, U.S. representatives put forward a proposal for the "Trial and Punishment of War Criminals" (Smith 1982, 117–22). Ultimately the United Kingdom removed its opposition and endorsed the plan. The Soviet Union had little choice but to go along with the plan since the vast majority of Nazi leaders were being held by the United States and United Kingdom. The Agreement for the Prosecution and Punishment of Major War Criminals of the European Axis, and Establishing the Charter of the International Military Tribunal (IMT) was formally adopted on August 8, 1945, and served as the framework for the trials at Nuremberg and subsequent lesser trials (under the authority of Control Council Law #10).

> Article 6 of the Agreement reads:
> The following acts or any of them are crimes coming within the jurisdiction of the Tribunal for which there shall be individual responsibility.
> (a) crimes against peace . . .
> (b) war crimes: namely, violations of the laws or the customs of war. Such violations include, but not be limited to, murder, ill treatment or deportation to slave labor or for any other purposes of civilian population of or in the occupied territory . . .
> (c) crimes against humanity: namely, murder, extermination, enslavement, deportation, and other inhumane acts

> committed against any civilian population, before or
> during the war, . . . whether or not in violation of the
> domestic law of the country where perpetrated. (UNGA,
> paras. 1–24)

Of central importance in the agreement was the stipulation that individuals could be held accountable for actions, regardless of whether they were merely obeying orders. That being said, the emphasis in the prosecution was to prove that a "conspiracy" existed among the Nazis to commit war crimes, aggression, and crimes against humanity.

While radical in their substance and scope, it is important to note that the agreements did not address the crime of "genocide" itself, and the term was almost never used during the proceedings or follow-on trials. Furthermore, the prosecution limited itself to crimes committed during the period of open military hostilities. As explained by Robert Jackson:

> [T]he way that Germany treats its inhabitants, or any other
> country treats its inhabitants is not our affair any more than it
> is the affair of some other government to interpose itself in
> our problems. The reason that this program of extermination
> of Jews and destruction of the rights of minorities becomes an
> international concern is this: *it is part of a plan for making an
> illegal war.* Unless we have a war connection as a basis for
> reaching them, I would think we have no basis for dealing
> with the atrocities. They were part of the preparation for war
> in so far as they occurred inside of Germany and that makes
> them our concern. (International Conference on Military
> Trials 1945)

Thus, the Tribunal never definitively answered the question whether genocide committed in peacetime could be prosecuted by an international tribunal (Franck and Yuhan 2003, 550–1; Paust et al. 2001, 10).

Immediately following WWII, the international community shared a consensus on the need to address the atrocities committed during the war, which quickly led to a proposal to enact legislation that would prevent the recurrence of genocide (Lippman 2002, 178). The United Nations General Assembly requested that the Economic and Social Council draw up a draft convention. At its forty-seventh meeting on November 9, 1946, the General Assembly referred to the Sixth, or Legal, Committee a draft resolution that was primarily written by Lemkin and was submitted by the representatives of Cuba, India, and Panama, inviting the study of a possibility of declaring genocide an international crime (UNGA 1946). At its twenty-fourth meeting on November 29, 1946, the Sixth Committee decided to entrust a Sub-Committee with the task of drafting a unanimously acceptable resolution on the basis of the various proposals submitted (Morton and Singh 2003, 53).

From the beginning, there were competing priorities at work in drafting the text of the treaty. Heavily exerting their influence were the ideas and situations created by the Cold War and the prevailing sentiment of the memory of the Holocaust. The Soviet Union and other Eastern Bloc countries wanted the preamble to include reference to the recent acts of genocide as a result of Fascist-Nazi ideologies. This met with opposition and was rejected on the grounds that reference to historical events might be interpreted as limiting the scope of the Convention. Sir Hartley Cross of Great Britain argued that the Nuremberg principles already encompassed genocide and furthermore a treaty that infringed on state sovereignty would face heavy opposition. Armed intervention was his solution to the prevention of genocide. The Norwegian representative noted on the other hand that an international convention was necessary because of the slim likelihood that states could be depended on to enforce the Nuremberg Principles against their own leadership.

The General Assembly resolution that emerged in December 1946, Resolution 96(I), gave considerable weight to Lemkin's new term.

Genocide is a denial of the right of existence of entire human groups, as homicide is the denial of the right to live of individual human beings; such denial of the right of existence shocks the conscience of mankind, results in great losses to humanity in the form of cultural and other contributions represented by these human groups, and is contrary to moral law and to the spirit and aims of the United Nations.

Many instances of such crimes of genocide have occurred when radical, religious, political and other groups have been destroyed, entirely or in part. The punishment of the crime of genocide is a matter of international concern.

The General assembly, therefore, affirms that genocide is a crime under international law which the civilized world condemns, and for the commission of which principals and accomplices—whether private individuals, public officials or statesman, and whether the crime is committed on religious, racial, political or any other grounds—are punishable;

Invites the Member States to enact the necessary legislation for the prevention and punishment of the crime. (UNGA 1946)

In 1948, the Economic and Social Council appointed an ad hoc committee consisting of seven members, including Raphael Lemkin, to revise the original draft (UNGA 1946, *Res. 96(I)*). Later that year, a draft treaty outlawing genocide was negotiated, drafted, redrafted, debated, and adopted. "Using Resolution 96(I) and two initial drafts as a springboard, the drafters of the Convention on the Prevention and Punishment of the Crime of Genocide criminalized the act itself" (Kelly 2002, 282–3).

The Ad Hoc committee wanted to make it clear that, unlike the Nuremberg Charter, the Genocide Convention did not limit the crime of genocide to acts committed in times of armed conflict. Article I of the convention declares that "genocide, whether committed in time of peace or in time of war, is a crime under international law which [the Contracting parties] undertake to prevent and punish."

Article II outlines what are to be considered as the five central components of genocide: "motive, intent, and extent of destruction, premeditation, and protected groups" (UN OHCHR 1948, Art. II). The overarching theme is the definition of genocide as the commission of any one of a series of acts with the "intent to destroy, in whole or in part, a national, ethnical, racial or religious group, as such." The following subparagraphs (a) through (e) then enumerate the acts which, when undertaken with the requisite mental state, constitute the international crime of genocide (UN OHCHR 1948, Art. II):

Any of the following acts committed with the intent to destroy, in whole or in part, a national, ethnical, racial or religious group, as such:
(a) Killing members of the group,
(b) Causing serious bodily or mental harm to members of the group,
(c) Deliberately inflicting on the group conditions of life calculated to bring about its physical destruction in whole or in part,

(d) Imposing measures intended to prevent births within the group,

(e) Forcibly transferring children of the group to another group. (UN OHCHR 1948, Art. II)

Political groups were dropped from the class of protected individuals, at the insistence of the USSR. The diplomatic exchange revolved around the fact that political groups are not like national, ethnic, racial, or religious groups into which people are generally born and which by their very nature are more enduring (Sahaydak 1976 [1974]). Some argued that the exclusion of political groups from the Genocide Convention implied that their deaths would be less serious, thus creating a legally indefensible "blind spot" (Van Schaack 1997, 2259–91). The only groups protected under the new treaty were national, ethnic, racial, and religious groups. Decades later, this provision became an obstacle to clearly designating the Cambodian holocaust as genocide (Power 2002, 127).

The Convention also expanded the crime of genocide beyond the immediate perpetrators. Article III assigns criminal liability to those who serve as an accomplice in any genocidal act or who conspire, attempt, or publicly incite others to commit any genocidal act (Kelly 2002, 284). Article III also included from the report from the Ad Hoc Committee the notion that "conspiracy to commit genocide would be punished based on the gravity of the crime of genocide, which was viewed as a collective offense" (Lippman 2002, 183). The U.S.S.R. and other Eastern Bloc satellites argued that preparatory acts should be punished as well, to prevent the development and deployment of techniques that were used against the Slavs and the Jews. Preparatory acts would also be considered a punishable crime under Article III (UN OHCHR 1948, Art. III).

Article IV eliminates any defense that could be raised on traditional sovereign immunity or head of state grounds. It states: "Persons committing genocide or any other acts enumerated in Article III shall be punished whether they are constitutionally responsible rulers, public officials or private individuals" (UN OHCHR 1948, Art. IV). Resolution 96(I) had named "heads of state" instead of "constitutionally responsible rulers." The differing language in the Convention may have come as a result of a "Swedish objection that a Monarch, as head of State, may not be brought before domestic or foreign courts" (Lippman 2002, 184). This was an important clarification necessary to Article IV as it imposed criminal liability on government ministers and officials, not just constitutional monarchs with immunity for criminal acts.

International legal scholars generally agree that the Genocide Convention codified a *jus cogens* norm. The International Court of Justice (ICJ) made this clear in 1951 when it considered the effect of reservations to the Genocide Convention and ruled that the prohibition of genocide is "binding on states, even without any contractual obligation." The Court stated:

> The Convention was manifestly adopted for a purely humanitarian and civilizing purpose. . . . [Its] object on the one hand is to safeguard the very existence of certain human groups and on the other to confirm and endorse the most elementary principles of morality. In such a convention the contracting States do not have any interests of their own; they merely have, one and all, a common interest, namely, the accomplishment of those high purposes which are the raison d'être of the convention. In other words, an *ius cogens* obligation is an obligation held *erga omnes*, or "among all." (ICJ 1951, 23)

Thus, though the Genocide Convention establishes the framework for a regime to prohibit genocide, it "does not represent the entirety of international law on the subject" (Bruun 1993, 193, 211–2). Rather, the *jus cogens* prohibition of genocide, "which predates the drafting of the Genocide Convention, provides something of a broader protection than the Convention itself. Political compromises, such as those that occurred during the drafting of the Genocide Convention that excluded the application of the treaty to political groups, cannot limit *jus cogens* norms" (Van Schaack 1997, 2272).

In addition to the Genocide Conventions, agreements on the nature of war crimes expanded and clarified states' obligations, which included protection against persecution by a citizen's own government. One of the most fundamental principles was stated in Article 3 of the fourth Geneva Convention in 1949:

> (1) Persons taking no part in the hostilities . . . shall in all circumstances be treated humanely, without any adverse distinction founded on race, color, religion or faith, sex, birth or wealth, or any other similar criteria. To this end the following acts are and shall remain prohibited . . .
>   (a) violence to life and person, in particular murder of all kinds, mutilation, cruel treatment and torture;

(b) outrages upon personal dignity, in particular humiliating and degrading treatment. . . . (UN OHCHR 1948, Art. III)

The Geneva Conventions also employ a version of the Martens clause in their denunciation clauses for a somewhat different, but parallel, goal: "to make clear that if they denounce the Conventions, the parties will remain bound by the principles of the law of nations, as they result from the usages established among civilized peoples, the laws of humanity, and the dictates of public conscience" (Meron 2000, 80). This provision thus guarantees that international customary law will still apply to states no longer bound by the Geneva Conventions (Alstotter 1948, 40, 58–9).

The ICJ confirmed the status of the Geneva Conventions and the Hague Regulations of 1907 as customary law in its advisory opinion on the Israeli Wall in 2004 (ICJ 2004, paras. 89–93), meaning that both are binding on nonsignatories. The 2004 decision, combined with the 1951 ruling on genocide, make clear that genocide and certain war crimes are prohibited by international custom and that the treaties, by and large, merely codify (however inaccurately) existing *jus cogens* obligations. This implies that reservations attached to signatures to these documents must be particularly narrow in scope so as to avoid violating international custom (Kelly 2002, 286).

Though the prohibition of genocide is widely considered a *jus cogens* norm, applicable to all without exception, the Genocide Convention itself has not been met with the enthusiastic welcome some anticipated. As Figure 8.2 shows, only 54 states had ratified the Convention in the first decade after its completion. Another forty-four ratified over the next thirty years, and thirty-nine more have ratified since the end of the Cold War. Even factoring in waves of independence in the Third World and Central Europe, this pace of ratification is hardly quick. In comparison, all but two states ratified the Convention on the Rights of the Child in its first decade.

The story of American ratification is instructive in that it demonstrates that delays in ratification may have little to do with approval of the norm against genocide. As the instigators of the Nuremberg Trials and co-inventors of the concept of "crimes against humanity," the United States has a clear record against genocide—at least in principle. Opposition to ratification of the Genocide Convention stemmed in part from perceived flaws in the language of the treaty itself. The American Bar Association expressed concern in a 1950 Senate hearing with regard to the vagueness of

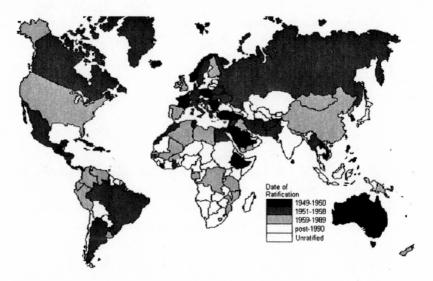

Figure 8.2 Genocide Convention ratifications as of September 2005.
Source: Compiled by the author from the U.N.'s Status of International Conventions (UN OHCHR 2006).

the definition of "genocide." Senator Brien McMahon (D-Conn.) wondered whether there was a critical threshold of deaths that must be achieved— or a certain proportion of a community that must die—before the term would apply (Power 2002, 66). Some argued that the treaty could be used to justify intervention in cases where only a few deaths had occurred, while still others argued that it could be used retroactively against the US government for its treatment of Native Americans in the nineteenth century.

Although the Senate was moving forward on ratification in the mid-1950s, the outbreak of the Korean War and the McCarthy hearings on Communist infiltration provoked a backlash against all human rights agreements then pending. In an effort to forestall passage of a constitutional amendment that would have limited the president's treaty-making powers, Dwight D. Eisenhower agreed to set aside all human rights treaties in 1953. It was only after decades of pressure by Senator William Proxmire (D-Wisc.), a misstep by Ronald Reagan (the visit to a German war cemetery that implied he was honoring former SS officers), and approval of a series of eviscerating reservations and understandings that the US finally ratified the Convention in 1986 (Power 2002, 155–67).

One could argue in the case of the United States that the Convention was a very low priority that offered few benefits other than the symbolic

(Reagan was eager to ratify the Convention to remove the stigma produced by the war cemetery incident and to prevent the Soviet Union from castigating the U.S. in public fora). On the other hand, it did present some risks—both real and perceived. For example, while many in the United States overstated the risks of Americans being arrested on genocide charges (a fear that would be repeated in the case of the Rome Statute creating the International Criminal Court), others noted that endorsing the Convention carried with it the obligation to take action against those committing genocide—perhaps by sending troops.

By 1960, the norm of genocide had developed through two cycles. The Nazi atrocities provoked a more vigorous effort than the Armenian genocide had to both define the nature of the crime and provide for its punishment on an individual basis. By the end of the period, the consensus was that genocide involved a systematic effort designed to eradicate in a significant way a community defined by language, ethnicity, race, or religion (although not the more ephemeral political identity) and that international bodies could prosecute such acts. Although the Genocide and Geneva Conventions spelled out the details, there was general agreement that these crimes were universally banned in international society, without exceptions or possible justification.However, the question of whether states had an obligation to stop or prevent genocide remained open.

Recent Norm Cycles: Bosnia to Darfur

The remainder of this chapter is essentially the story of the further specification of the rule against genocide through its application to specific events. The latest developments of the international rule against genocide focus on whether there is a duty to intervene to halt genocides and on how genocide should be defined in practice. As argued in Chapter 1, the application of general rules to specific events frequently compels actors to clarify and specify the meaning of the rules.

As we will see, enforcement of the prohibition on genocide has depended on a number of factors, many of them political rather than legal. The question of whether there is a responsibility to enforce the Convention has not been resolved definitively, although, as noted in the chapter on humanitarian intervention in this volume, there is a growing sense that acknowledging genocide carries with it a certain responsibility to intervene. Furthermore, the debate over the definition of genocide has yet to be resolved. It appears from state practice that much depends on the scale and speed of the acts. Put bluntly, the deaths of a few thousand over a decade is far less likely to prompt charges of genocide than the deaths of hundreds of thousands over a few months. Perhaps more problematic still is the fact that similar behavior by different states provokes different responses. The Rwanda genocide prompted far less international intervention than Serbia's, in part because it was distant from the center of geopolitical power in Europe. We explore these and other cases as a way to assess the ongoing development of international norms regarding genocide.

Between 1950 and 1990, the issue of genocide was largely ignored. Even when the Khmer Rouge slaughtered roughly two million Cambodians during the 1970s, the international response was decidedly mixed. The United States, for example, while deploring the violence, refused to use the term "genocide" and ultimately cooperated with the exiled Khmer Rouge regime after the invading Vietnamese army expelled it. Likewise, the gassing of Kurds by Saddam Hussein's regime in the 1980s brought little reaction. At the same time, states continued to proclaim the illegality of genocide. Several recent conflicts have provoked additional turns through the cycle of norm change.

Yugoslavia

The conflict in the former Yugoslavia forced the international community to apply the antigenocide norm to specific events. By 1993, Serb forces had killed more than 200,000 people under a policy of "ethnic cleansing" (Harvard Law Review Association 2001, 2012). In addition to ethnic cleansing and mass killings, other violations of international humanitarian law included torture, pillage and destruction of civilian property, destruction of cultural and religious property, and forced dislocation of nearly two million Bosnian refugees (Rubenstein 2004, 279–81).

In early 1993, Bosnia and Herzegovina filed an application to the International Court of Justice claiming that genocide was being committed in Yugoslavia (Schabas 2001, 24). In its petition, Bosnia and Herzegovina requested "that pursuant to the right of collective self-defense recognized by United Nations Charter Article 51, all other States parties to the Charter have the right to come to the immediate defense of Bosnia and Herzegovina—at its request—including by means of immediately providing it with weapons, military equipment and supplies, and armed forces (soldiers, sailors, air people, etc.)" (UN 1945).

The case of *Bosnia and Herzegovina v. Yugoslavia* marked a number of firsts. In response to Bosnia and Herzegovina's claim, the United Nations

Security Council used the word "genocide" for the first time in its history (Schabas 2001, 24). It was also the first time the International Court of Justice adjudicated claims under the Genocide Convention (Hurlock 1997, 319–20).

A norm implicit in the Genocide Convention was the responsibility to intervene to halt any declared and acknowledged instance of genocide. NATO filled this role by arranging a succession of unsuccessful cease-fires. Ultimately, the form of the Dayton Accords provided for the insertion of NATO peacekeepers. This represented the first time the international community took direct military measures with the primary purpose of stopping and preventing genocide (Rubenstein 2004, 279–81).

In May 1993, the United Nations Security Council unanimously passed Resolution 827, creating the International Tribunal for the Prosecution of Persons Responsible for Serious Violations of International Humanitarian Law committed in the Territory of the Former Republic of Yugoslavia (ICTY) (Hurlock 1997, 327–8; UNSC 1993a). The ICTY was the first judicial organ created by the U.N. Security Council (Harvard Law Review Association 2001, 2013). In the statute creating the tribunal, the Security Council gave the ICTY jurisdiction over the crime of genocide and other serious crimes (Schabas 2001, 25), granted it power to prosecute and sentence those who committed genocide, and defined the term "genocide" using the same language found in the Genocide Convention (Harvard Law Review Association 2001, 2012). The Secretary General of the United Nations indicated that the resolution—passed unanimously—confirmed that genocide was in fact an international crime (Lippman 2001, 497).

In addition to the traditional definition of genocide, the statute also clarified the nature of "crimes against humanity" in Article 5.

> The International Tribunal shall have the power to prosecute persons responsible for the following crimes when committed in armed conflict, whether international or internal in character, and directed against any civilian population:
> (a) murder;
> (b) extermination;
> (c) enslavement;
> (d) deportation;
> (e) imprisonment;
> (f) torture;
> (g) rape;

(h) persecutions on political, racial, and religious grounds;

(i) other inhumane acts (UNSC 1993, Art. 5).

Despite the tribunal's power to prosecute those who committed genocide, prosecutors have often chosen to issue indictments solely on charges of war crimes and crimes against humanity. This was due to the higher standards required to convict someone of genocide and the necessity to demonstrate the intent to eliminate, in part or whole, a distinct group. Consequently, as of 2007, only twenty three out of more than 150 indictments issued by the ICTY were for the crime of genocide (ICTY 2007). In the one case in which a verdict of guilty on genocide was rendered (Radislav Krstic), it was overturned on the grounds that intent could not be established beyond doubt.

The Tribunal also created a new crime—that of extermination—to deal with instances in which suspects were alleged to have directly participated in large-scale murders of members of a designated group, but where intent to destroy the group could not be established. As put by the Appeals Chamber in the Krstic case:

> The offense of extermination as a crime against humanity requires proof that the proscribed act formed a part of a widespread or systematic attack on the civilian population, and that the perpetrator knew of this relationship. These two requirements are not present in the legal elements of genocide. (ICTY 2004, para. 223)

In the indictment against Radovan Karadzic and Ratko Mladic, the ICTY made clear that intent is a specific requirement for genocide, developing an alternative offense, persecution, for discriminatory acts that are not intended to eliminate a group (Lippman 2001, 506). Additionally, "in part" was defined as "seeking to destroy a distinct part of the group as opposed to an accumulation of isolated individuals within it" (Hovani 2001, 1389).

The ICTY further clarified the meaning of genocide by ruling that any inference of genocidal intent requires that the accused's actions "affect a 'reasonably substantial number of the group relative to its total population'" (Hovani 2001, 1374). In 1996, the judges of the ICTY stressed that genocide was not ultimately determined by the number of people killed (Lippman 2001, 503).

Ultimately, the Bosnian experience, though it illustrated a lack of political will to act quickly to protect the Bosnian Muslims, nonetheless demonstrated a willingness on the part of the Security Council to link genocide with threats to international peace and security.

> Through the establishment of the International Tribunals for the former Yugoslavia and Rwanda, the Security Council has established a clear precedent for the extra-treaty enforcement of genocide, irrespective of whether it is considered as treaty law or a norm of international custom. Furthermore, it increasingly appears that the commission of genocide, even in the context of a purely internal armed conflict such as that of Rwanda, may constitute a threat to international peace and security. (Akhavan 1995)

Rwanda

The deaths of roughly 800,000 Tutsis and many Hutus in Rwanda in 1994 shocked the world (Mandlebaum 1999). But even as the scale of the violence became clear, Western powers were reluctant to use the term "genocide" to describe it. The reasons for the reluctance were clear in the wake of the Bosnia crisis and were spelled out by U.S. State Department spokesperson Christine Shelly: "there are obligations which arise in connection with the use of the term" (Fry 2004, 109).

Journalists and NGO representatives were not so hesitant. Even before the bloodletting in 1994, informed observers issued warnings. In March 1993, a group of international human rights experts from ten countries published a report that there had been 2,000 organized killings of Tutsis in Rwanda, but they did not use the word genocide (Melvern 2000, 56). However, the press release based on this report, published by William Schabas, was titled nonetheless "Genocide and war crimes in Rwanda." France dismissed the massacres as rumors, although the Belgian government began to express concerns (56).

On August 11, 1993, Bacre Waly Ndiaye, the Special Rapporteur for the Commission on Human Rights for Extrajudicial, Summary or Arbitrary Executions, published a report using the word "genocide" in relation to Rwanda. The report was set aside in order not to detract from the progress the warring parties were making in the Arusha Accord negotiations (Melvern 2000, 57). On April 24, Oxfam used the term publicly for the first time, prompting Lieutenant General Roméo Dallaire, commander of the U.N. force in Rwanda, to include the term in an internal report to the Secretary-General on the grounds that "calling it 'ethnic cleansing' just did not seem to be hitting the mark" (Dallaire 2003, 333).

In the Security Council, member-states were reluctant to employ the term "genocide" because it carried with it a responsibility to protect victims. They opted instead to describe the events as an instance of "civil war." By employing this language, Security Council members took solace in the legal structures against foreign intervention in civil wars and instead contented themselves with calling for a cease-fire and offering assistance to negotiate a settlement (Barnett 2002, 103). This tentativeness was echoed in the Secretary-General's statements on the topic, which have been described as "brief, vague and indecisive" (107). The fear was that because civilians always die in civil wars, it would be dangerous to set a precedent of declaring all such deaths instances of genocide (Garrett 1999, 68). It would not be until June that the United States would go so far as to acknowledge that there had been "acts of genocide" in Rwanda—although it noted that not all acts of murder there were necessarily acts of genocide (Fry 2004, 109).

By May, several states were on record condemning the killing in Rwanda as genocide. In particular, New Zealand representative Keating threatened to use his country's position as President of the Security Council in April formally to declare the situation a case of genocide, thereby creating a legal obligation on the part of the Council to act. He also threatened to make public the Council's deliberations on the subject (Melvern 2000, 179, 229). The Czech representative pressed his colleagues to act and the U.N. Commissioner for Human Rights José Ayala Lasso publicly acknowledged that genocide was occurring (193, 200). But most members of the Security Council were not willing to use the word "genocide," and that reticence was singled out as one of many of the Security Council's failures in the report of an inquiry commission in 1999.

> The reluctance by some states to use the term genocide was motivated by a lack of will to act, which is deplorable. If there is ever to be effective international action against genocide, states must be prepared to identify situations as such, and to assume the responsibility to act that accompanies that definition. (UNSC 1999a, 38)

In subsequent years, Security Council members would come to acknowledge that genocide had been committed in Rwanda. For example, in 1998,

President Bill Clinton visited Rwanda to issue what has been widely regarded as an apology for failure to intervene in 1994. The British government has yet to accept the use of the term (Melvern 2000, 230).

Seven months after the massacre, the Security Council, in direct response to a report it had commissioned, approved the creation of the International Criminal Tribunal for Rwanda. In Resolution 955, the members justified the action in part on the basis of the existence of acts of genocide in the country. Although it took several years for the Tribunal to begin functioning fully, in 1998 it handed down the first-ever genocide conviction in the case of Jean-Paul Akayesu, the mayor of Taba where roughly two thousand Tutsis were slaughtered. In rendering the judgment, the Tribunal began by arguing that even though the Tutsi were not a distinct racial, linguistic, or religious group, they had been clearly identified by years of government policy and social custom as a distinct group, meeting the requirement of the Genocide Convention (the language of which was incorporated in the Tribunal's Statute) (ICTR 1998, para. 171). In the case of Rwanda—unlike that of Yugoslavia—reaching the conclusion that the deaths of Tutsis were the result of a deliberate attempt to eradicate the group was relatively easy, given the numerous public statements of many Rwandan Hutu leaders at the time—including those of Akayesu himself (Amann 1999, 198).

Since then, the ICTR has handed down a total of eighteen convictions on charges of genocide (although one was reversed on appeal) and more than a dozen convictions on related charges of incitement, complicity, or conspiracy to commit genocide. The result has been ten life sentences (the maximum penalty) that have survived the appeal process. Of special interest are the guilty pleas to charges of genocide by a half-dozen indictees, including former Prime Minister Jean Kambanda who is now serving a life sentence. This represents the first time a former head of state was convicted of genocide. The ICTR has also convicted four Cabinet ministers and is trying several more (Table 8.1 presents the totality of ICTR actions through 15 June 2006).

One could make the argument, consistent with our theoretical model, that by the year 2000 the international community had reached considerable consensus on the nature of the rule on genocide. Not only was its character defined with considerable precision, the scope of international responsibility in its enforcement was becoming clear. While states denied a clear duty to intervene militarily to prevent genocide, they accepted the principle that those who perpetrate it should be held accountable, if only after the fact.

Table 8.1 Outcomes of cases at the ICTR, as of June 15, 2006

Name	Role	Verdicts					Date	Sentence
		1	2	3	4	5		
J-P Akayesu	Bourgmestre of Taba	C	A	C	C	C	Sep-98	Life
J Kambanda	Prime Minister	C	A	C	C	C	guilty plea - Sep-98	Life
O Serushago	Interhamwe Leader		A	C	C	C	guilty plea - Feb-99	15 years
B Ntuyahaga	Army Officer	A	A	A	A	A	charges dropped - Mar-99	
C Kayishema	Prefect of Kibuye		A	A	A	C	May-99	Life
O Ruzindana	Businessman		A	A	C	C	May-99	25 years
G Rutaganda	VP of Interhamwe		A	C	C	C	Dec-99	Life
A Musema	Businessman	A	A	A	A	A	Jan-00	Life
G Ruggiu	Belgian Journalist	C		C	A	A	guilty plea - Jun-00	12 years
I Bagilishema	Interhamwe Leader	A	A	A	A	A	Jun-01	
L Rusatira	Military Sch. Commander	A	A	A	A	A	charges dropped - Aug-02	
J Kamuhanda	Minister of Culture	Ca	A	A	C	C	Jan-03	Life
E. Ntakirutimana	Protestant Pastor	Ca	A	A	Ca	C	Feb-03	10 years
G Ntakirutimana	Doctor	Ca	A	C	A	C	Feb-03	25 years
J Kajelijeli	Bourgmestre of Rukingo	C	A	A	Aa	Aa	Feb-03	45a
E Niyitegeka	Minister of Information	C	A	C	C	C	May-03	Life
L Semanza	Bourgmestre of Bicumbi	A	A	C	A	A	May-03	35a
F Nahimana	Professor	C		C	C	C	Dec-03	Life
H Ngeze	Newspaper Editor	C		C	C	C	Dec-03	Life
J-B Barayagwiza	Politician and Radio Host	C		C	C	C	Dec-03	30 years (a.p.)
A Ntagerura	Minister of Transport	A	A	A	A	A	Feb-04	
E Bagambiki	Senior Army Officer	A	A	A	A	A	Feb-04	
S Imanishwe	Prefect of Cyangugu	A	C	C	C	A	Feb-04	27 years
S Gacumbitsi	Bourgmestre of Rusumo	A		C	C	C	Jun-04	30 years (a.p.)

		1	2	3	4	5		
E Ndindabahizi	Minister of Finance	A		C	C	C	Jul-04	Life
V Rutaganira	Prefect of Kibuye	A	A	A	C	A	guilty plea - Mar-05	6 years
M Muhimana	Counsellor for Gishyita	A		C		C	Apr-05	Life
M Simba	Counsellor for Butare	C	A	A	C	C	Dec-05	25 years (a.p.)
P Bisengimana	Bourgmestre of Gikoro	C		C	C	C	guilty plea - Apr-06	15 years
J Serugendo	Journalist	C		C		A	guilty plea - Jun-06	6 years

1 = conspiracy, incitement, complicity in genocide

2 = war crimes

3 = crimes against humanity

4 = extermination

5 = genocide

Compiled by Kendall Stiles from ICTR documents.

C = convicted

A = acquitted

a = reversed on appeal. Final verdict shown.

a.p. = appeal pending

The International Criminal Court

The ICTY and ICTR have narrowly defined mandates, limited to events that occurred during a specific period in a particular region. As a result, each suffered from several flaws, which could be remedied with the creation of a permanent war crimes tribunal. This in turn gave impetus to the incipient efforts to create the International Criminal Court (Barrett 1999, 90). According to UN Secretary-General Kofi Annan, the General Assembly of the United Nations had recognized since the 1950s the need to establish an international court where those accused of genocide could be prosecuted and punished for their crimes (UNSC 1999b, 123–4). The vision of a permanent international criminal tribunal became reality with the 1998 signature of the Rome Statute establishing the International Criminal Court (ICC). The Rome Statute entered into force in July 2002 following ratification by the sixtieth state party.

As put by the UN High Commissioner for Human Rights Mary Robinson, "The idea behind the Rome Statute is to establish a standing International Criminal Court capable of acting on a complementary basis to the domestic organs of a State party where the State may be unwilling or unable to prosecute crimes under international law" (Robinson 1999, 278). The Rome Statute provides the ICC with jurisdiction, in certain circumstances, over countries' officials and troops who engage in war crimes, crimes against humanity, genocide, and crimes of aggression when arrested in the country where the act occurred (Gray 2003, 652).[2] Under the Rome Statute and its subsidiary documents, rape, and forced pregnancy may also be prosecuted under Genocide.

Some members of the Ad Hoc Committee on the Establishment of an International Criminal Court had argued to expand the definition of genocide to include murder of certain social and political groups. However, the majority at the Rome Conference felt that the existing definition reflected customary international law and was already incorporated into the statutes of various states. As a result, the ICC conforms to the traditional definition of genocide as outlined by the Genocide Convention in order to avoid divergences in doctrine and conflicts in norms (Lippman 2001, 521).

Darfur Security Council Referral

Beginning in 2003, local militias, known as *janjaweed*, under the direction of the government in Khartoum, carried out attacks in the Darfur region

---

[2] The crime of aggression will be defined in future negotiations, and so does not yet fall under the ICC's operational jurisdiction.

of Sudan. The militias have been accused of killing tens and perhaps hundreds of thousands and destroying numerous villages. By 2005, the violence expanded as rebels and *janjaweed* both attacked international peacekeepers deployed by the African Union (AU) as well as humanitarian aid workers. As early as September 2004, Secretary of State Colin Powell declared that what was taking place in Darfur was genocide. The United States indicated that it felt no obligation to intervene militarily although it endorsed multilateral measures.

A U.N.-sponsored International Commission of Inquiry in January 2005 urged all the parties to join in a cease-fire and proposed that the Security Council strengthen the AU's force and take measures to hold perpetrators of genocide accountable. The Security Council acted on all three fronts with Resolutions 1590, 1591, and 1593 (UNSC 2005). The United States urged creation of a regional tribunal modeled on the Rwanda case, but a solid majority of the Security Council preferred to refer Sudan to the ICC under Articles 16 and 17 of the Rome Statute. Under threat of a veto, the members agreed to offer any American forces that might go to the Sudan as part of a multilateral force an exemption from ICC jurisdiction, thereby securing an abstention from the US and passage by a vote of 11–0–4 (Crook 2005b, 691).

The implications of the action on Sudan are mixed. Human rights organizations were pleased with the prospect of Sudanese *genocidaires* being brought before the ICC (the first indictments were issued in early 2007) (HRW 2005). At the same time, many fear that the repeated exemptions to nonsignatories would build a customary law that would severely limit the ICC's power and the principle of universal jurisdiction over the war crimes, crimes against humanity, and genocide (CICC 2005; Cash 2007).

Conclusions

The development of antigenocide rules has followed the cyclic pattern in which actions provoke debates, and arguments, in turn, modify the rules. Two major cycles produced a norm against genocide; subsequent events have led to further specification of the norm. The prohibition against genocide is a key part of the development of liberal norms. One could even argue today that condemnation of genocide is one of the defining characteristics of modern international law (Malanczuk 1997, 23).

This chapter complements the chapter on humanitarian intervention by arguing that although there is widespread agreement in principle on the nature and illegality of genocide, application of the term is far more contentious. The reticence of the Security Council to declare the events in Rwanda an instance of genocide—coupled with its current ambivalence over events in the Darfur region of Sudan—are clear indicators of this. Even though the United States has specifically declared that the atrocities being committed in Darfur can be described as genocide, it has accepted no responsibility for stopping them (although it agreed to allow the prosecution of suspects in the ICC). The fact that more than fifty states have yet to ratify the Genocide Convention, and the lack of consensus on the "responsibility to protect," are both indicators that the norm against genocide is still developing.

Nevertheless, each failed remedy for genocide produces pressure to clarify and strengthen international rules. The failure to intervene in Rwanda has left the West embarrassed and defensive and, in a few cases, penitent. The 1999 U.N. report drafted under the direction of Ingvar Carlsson further explains this failure:

> The failure by the United Nations to prevent, and subsequently, to stop the genocide in Rwanda was a failure by the United Nations system as a whole. The fundamental failure was the lack of resources and political commitment devoted to developments in Rwanda. . . . There was a persistent lack of political will by Member States to act, or act with enough assertiveness. The lack of political will affected the response by the Secretariat and decision-making by the Security Council. . . . (UNSC 1999a, 3).

Even the African Union has condemned the West's failure to intervene—an interesting twist on the customary resistance of former colonies to outside intervention. Though this has not necessarily given Western powers greater vigor with respect to thwarting genocide, it has made it clear that a failure to act where evidence of genocide is incontrovertible will result in international condemnation.

Once again, as in the case of slavery and piracy, even *jus cogens* rules are matters of dispute and contestation, making the model that governs this volume all the more relevant. One might conclude that nothing is entirely settled with respect to international norms, and the alert observer should always be on the lookout for disputes, reconsiderations, and reformulations. What is perhaps intriguing about the norm against genocide is how quickly, after the horrors of World War II, an international rule against it was agreed upon and formalized by treaty. Furthermore, though most international norms are qualified by exceptions or in potential conflict with other rules, states now find it impossible to reframe instances of genocide in terms of competing legal structures. The case of Rwanda shows how hollow the reference to "civil war" was in the context of massive killing. International law today offers no principles that could provide legal shelter for those committing genocide, and the failure to halt genocide triggers international condemnation. These observations are evidence that the normative cycles triggered by recent events have continued the development of international rules against genocide.

Chapter 9

Refugees and Asylum

William Chiu

International human rights norms now demarcate basic and universal rights of all persons. Under these rules, for instance, no state is justified in committing torture or subjecting any part of its population to genocide or apartheid. But a host of other rights and privileges have meaning and existence only within the context of a specific political system: who votes, who can hold office, who is entitled to public education or social payments. About these latter categories of rights, international norms have practically nothing to say. Each state has the exclusive authority to determine who may enter and reside in its territory and who possesses the rights and duties of citizenship. Indeed, the capacity of each state to regulate its own population has been one of the core elements of sovereignty.

The treatment of refugees and asylum seekers is a domain where international norms have begun to address the ways in which states regulate their populations. Historically, the exigencies of massive population flows have demanded that sovereign states deal with the unavoidable reality of stateless persons. In June 2005, the U.N. High Commissioner for Refugees (UNHCR 2005) conservatively estimated a global total of 9.2 million refugees, with an additional eight million persons considered at risk, a number that has held steady for the last ten years. Moreover, because people on the move in what are generally failed or failing states carry few possessions and no wealth, UNHCR believes that the numbers reported do not capture the full extent of this kind of human suffering. Humanitarian concerns have thus motivated the development of norms granting to impoverished, stateless persons permission to enter another country. International human rights principles thus imply protections and relief for refugees; that is, refugees should have refuges. But that norm is in tension with traditional conceptions of sovereignty as states defend their authority to regulate who may enter and reside in their territories and lay claim to rights and resources. States thus endorse the general norms of refugee rights, but at the same time they seek to minimize or avoid the practical problems that arise when they accept large refugee inflows. This chapter explores how, through various steps and missteps, international norms governing refugees and asylum-seekers have evolved in response to events and crises of the twentieth century. The two great wars of the twentieth century triggered crucial rounds of normative development. The debates over what to do with refugees created by World War I and the Russian Revolution led to ad hoc measures and an emerging norm of care for refugees. The Holocaust triggered a new cycle of norm change, out of which emerged international organizations (UNHCR) and treaties (the 1951 Convention and its 1967 Protocol) designed to ensure basic rights for refugees and asylum-seekers. In subsequent refugee crises, states have sought to limit their international responsibilities toward refugees. Figure 9.1 depicts the cycles of norm change.

Asylum and Refugees: Normative Context

As the introduction argues, international norms do not evolve out of abstract discussions of international rules. All international conduct takes place in a context of norms. Specific actions, events, or major changes in international society trigger disputes about norms. States and other actors argue about the content and application of the norms. The outcomes of those debates in turn change the rules. In the case of international refugee and asylum norms, events of global magnitude—the World Wars, decolonization, and the Cold War—provoked crises that led to norm changes.

Rules on refugee status and the treatment of refugees derive from two competing norms. On the one hand, states determine who, within their borders, qualifies for nationality and citizenship. Exclusive jurisdiction

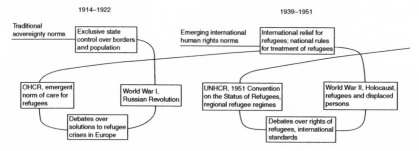

Figure 9.1 Cycles of Norms on the treatment of refugees.

over territory is thus closely linked to exclusive jurisdiction over population. On the other hand, universal human rights imply norms that protect individuals regardless of the nature or policies of national governments. The emergence of global norms to protect refugees and asylum seekers has created a lower bound on the policies that states can implement in this domain. Still, states retain considerable latitude and a study of actual state policy, as delimited by national law and court cases, shows that states continue to safeguard national prerogatives even as they acknowledge the ideal of refugee and asylum rights.

Historically, each state defined refugee status and granted asylum as a matter of entirely internal policy. People fled from one state to another for a variety of reasons: to flee from religious, social, and political persecution; to avoid criminal prosecution; to escape economic catastrophe. Beginning in Greek antiquity, sacred places offered the first refuges from political authorities under the assumption that divine ground was excluded from mere mortal intervention. Over time, refugee status and asylum developed increasingly complex rules, some of which began to distinguish between asylum for those in danger of politically motivated persecution and those who sought to escape the consequences of common criminality. Moreover, the inviolability of religious refuge came under pressure from secular sovereigns seeking to extend their power. To manage the flow of people and to establish order in the handling of claims for refuge, European states began to devise refugee policies.

In considering policies toward refugees, states were not motivated by general humanitarian concerns. Rather, they took an interest in the welfare of their own citizens and sometimes in that of religious compatriots outside their territories. The first recognizable state policy concerning a target group on the basis of what is now termed religious freedom occurred in 1598 when Henry IV ascended to the French throne after achieving victory in the wars of religion. He declared the first state policy of religious tolerance when he issued the Edict of Nantes. Though originally a Huguenot (Protestant), Henry had converted to Catholicism to maintain the peace. But he decreed that all his subjects would be allowed to worship freely. This policy of tolerance would not endure, however, and by 1685, Louis XIV revoked the Edict of Nantes (Robinson 1906). This led to renewed persecution of the Huguenots, who then sought to escape France. In retrospect, the Huguenots may be viewed as the first recognized group of refugees. Within days of the Revocation, Friedrich Wilhelm of Brandenburg, in response to Louix XIV's decree, issued the Edict of Potsdam, allowing the expelled French Huguenots to cross his borders and settle in his territories. This pair of edicts shows the intertwining of domestic lawmaking and international relations with respect to specific groups. As religious tension continued to fester, other governments enacted policies welcoming coreligionists who were subject to persecution in their homelands. Thus, in 1708, the English Parliament passed the Act of Naturalizing Foreign Protestants in order to allow religious refugees to enter England from continental Europe (Grahl-Madsen, Macalister-Smith, and Alfredsson 2001). By expelling or admitting categories of people on the basis of religious faith, states established foundational principles with respect to authority over the movement of people. In practice, however, until the early 1700s, states did not exercise effective immigration control because socioeconomic conditions and porous borders permitted essentially free movement among separate jurisdictions.

States subsequently began to define different categories of persecution, with corresponding policies of admission or rejection depending on the state's needs. Sinha notes that by the late seventeenth century, criminality had been excluded as grounds for asylum. In fact, the opposite of asylum—extradition—made its appearance, and "as a consequence, the notion of asylum as a right of the fugitive yielded to the notion that it was the right of a state to either grant him the privilege of residence within its territory or refuse to do so" (1971, 18). In this first stage, states agreed to a limited definition of the refugee, with severe restrictions based on the kind and origin of persecution, to limit the size of the potential refugee population.

Cycles of Norm Change

For a period of centuries, states managed their refugee policies independently, a pattern that would change in the twentieth century.

World War I and the Beginning of a New Era

World War I and the Bolshevik Revolution in Russia proved to be critical triggering events that forced states to abandon independent policies, thus producing the first rudimentary international norms on refugees and asylum. As Hathaway notes, the devastation wrought by the Great War created the world's first massive refugee movements at a time when political and economic nationalism was beginning to grip the Western world. Seeking to protect their economic security and maintain political stability, states began to erect barriers to the surges of humanity that had been displaced by war or were fleeing the aftermath of the October Revolution (1984, 348). From 1920 to 1950, the treatment of refugees would undergo what Hathaway terms three phases of development: juridical, social and individualist. This progression can also be seen as a move from rules that privileged state prerogatives to rules that acknowledged emerging human rights norms.

The first international agreements on the treatment of refugees were direct responses to events, specifically, displaced Russians outside of or leaving Russia. Between 1917 and 1922, approximately 1.5 million Russians fled their homeland due to devastation, political persecution, and famine. In 1922, the Soviet government, concerned with internal factions and the return of those who might lead a new civil war, exacerbated the problem of homeless, stateless Russians floating throughout Europe by revoking the citizenship of those who had either lived abroad for five years or who had left the country after November 7, 1917. Clearly, only international collective action could address the refugee crisis. Thus, through the proactive efforts of the International Committee of the Red Cross, in 1921, the League of Nations established the Office of the High Commissioner for Russian Refugees (OHCRR) and appointed its first High Commissioner, Dr. Fridtjof Nansen. Prior to becoming High Commissioner for Refugees Nansen had, in 1920, served as the League of Nations' High Commissioner for Prisoners of War and had managed the repatriation of 450,000 prisoners of war to twenty-six home countries. Driven by a powerful belief in human rights, Nansen worked tirelessly, and the breadth of the OHCRR's success was in large part a product of his leadership. In 1924, Nansen estimated that one million Russian refugees remained abroad, with half a million in Germany, 400,000 in France, and the remainder in Poland, Romania, and Yugoslavia (Marrus 1985). The OHCRR issued some 450,000 Certificates of Identity to stateless Russians (Hathaway 1984, 351); the Certificates became known as "Nansen passports."

Besides dealing with the enormous Russian problem, Nansen pushed for League recognition of the Greek and Armenian refugee crises. In response to these new problems, his organization was in 1923 renamed the Office of the High Commissioner for Refugees (OHCR). Nansen and the OHCR arranged the exchange of 1.2 million Greeks living on Turkish soil and 500,000 Turks living on Greek soil (Armenian Foreign Ministry). Indeed, for his pioneering work as High Commissioner for Refugees and for having resolved the prisoners of war issue, Dr. Nansen received the 1922 Nobel Peace Prize. Yet, although the aftermath of World War I saw the beginning of international cooperation, member states of the League of Nations were hesitant to articulate a general policy of refugee rights.

For example, criticizing High Commissioner Nansen in 1927, League of Nations Council member Nicolas Comnene of Romania averred that:

> The mere fact that certain classes of persons are without protection of any national Government is not sufficient to make them refugees; for on that theory all classes of persons without nationality would have to be included. (Hathaway 1984, 355)

Comnene implied that states feared creating an open door policy that would encourage refugee inflows and create domestic social and economic problems. Governments were therefore anxious to limit the scope of the Office of the High Commissioner for Refugees. Thus, from 1922 to 1935, the League of Nations enacted separate agreements specifically dealing with Armenians, Assyrians, Montenegrins, and Turks. The desire to limit the obligations of recipient states meant that in some cases, rules for handling refugees specified the precise number of persons in particular groups (Hathaway 1984, 355). The League's slow response to the Armenian refugee crisis was telling. The 1915–1922 genocide of Armenians on Turkish soil killed 0.6–1.5 million of 2.5 million Armenians (University of Michigan-Dearborn 1996, 1; see also Chapter 8). The remaining survivors were either deported to remote parts of the Ottoman Empire or escaped persecution to become refugees in neighboring states. Estimates of the numbers of Armenian refugees range from 0.4 to 0.8 million (Bryce and Toynbee 1916; Horton 1920).

In sum, World War I and the Russian Revolution created massive upheaval as empires collapsed and new states emerged. Displaced by interstate and civil wars, famine, and devastation, millions of Russians, Germans, Armenians, Turks, and others migrated across the Eurasian continent without documents, shelter, or food. The sheer size of these flows, and their material plight, triggered a pragmatic policy response by the international community. Unable to articulate a human rights norm that would bind the efforts of each country, the League of Nations pursued a piecemeal approach that was in many ways shepherded through to implementation by the leadership of Fridtjof Nansen. In this first phase, though the Office of the High Commissioner issued documentation to refugees and arranged for the resettlement of specific groups, it did not secure broad international agreement on underlying norms or principles.

World War II and the Emergence of International Human Rights

The first phase of norm change arising with World War I was predicated on practical responses to material concerns. The failure of the League and the collapse of international collective action offered important lessons for those who planned the recovery efforts following the Second World War. The atrocities of World War II, particularly those wrought by the Nazi regime, and the sheer magnitude of disaster created circumstances that led to a second cycle of development of norms for international refugees. The fighting, as well as the border adjustments following it, released a flood of some 14 million displaced persons and refugees, according to Allied and Soviet estimates. Of these, 7.2 million were Soviet citizens, 2 million French citizens, 1.6 million Polish citizens, 700,000 Italians, 350,000 Czech, 300,000 Dutch and 300,000 Belgians (Marrus 1985, 299). As Marrus observes, the Allies attempted to process individuals by first sorting them into the categories of refugees and displaced persons, with refugees defined as civilians who fled from their own country and displaced persons defined as people forcibly removed from their own country, due in large part to Nazi deportation policies (300).

To address this overwhelming problem, the United Nations Relief and Refugee Administration (UNRRA) was established in 1945 and managed to process the bulk of refugees and displaced persons in two years. Because the Allies had planned for refugee operations as part of their preparation for the liberation of Europe from Nazi Germany, the UNRRA benefited from British experience in operating the Middle East Refugee and Relief Administration when that region was liberated in 1944. Thus, the UNRRA proved astonishingly effective. From mid-1945 to late 1946, it managed to repatriate three quarters of the refugees and displaced persons (Marrus 1985).

However, approximately one million refugees remained, a significant share of whom did not want to return to their homelands. Many of
these were Russian émigrés who refused to return to the U.S.S.R. As
Marrus notes, the Soviet government did not acknowledge a refugee problem, preferring to characterize stateless people as traitors who had no
good reason not to return home after liberation (1985, 340). Meanwhile,
the Western powers, responding to Eleanor Roosevelt's campaign for
human rights, argued for a general solution to the humanitarian crisis.
In February 1946, the U.N. General Assembly adopted Resolution 8
Concerning the Question of Refugees, which pointed toward the creation
of an International Refugee Organization (IRO). A permanent organization, with capacity for action, would prove to be an important foundation
for the nascent human rights norm. Though they initially disagreed on
many points, the western and Soviet blocs negotiated the mission and
scope of the IRO. By the end of 1946, the two sides reached a compromise
wherein refugees would be treated as particular cases rather than as a class
of people with general rights. The IRO came into being in December 1946
as a specialized agency under Articles 57 and 63 of the United Nations
Charter. Forty-five countries signed the IRO's Constitution and agreed to
fund its operations. Of these, the United States contributed approximately
40 percent of its budget; the United Kingdom, 12 percent; and China,
France, and the U.S.S.R. about 6 percent each; India 4 percent; and Canada
3 percent; with the remaining 23 percent funded by the remaining signatories (IRO Constitution: Annex II).

The IRO's mission was to deal with World War II's last, most difficult
refugee cases. The IRO Constitution required the organization to be guided
by General Assembly Resolution 8 (12 February 1946), which distinguished
"between genuine refugees and displaced persons on the one hand, and the
war criminals, quislings and traitors . . . on the other" (UNGA *Resolution 8*).
Refugee status became a critical battle of ideology between the western
Allies and the Soviet Union, as the Soviets believed that all Soviet citizens
should be repatriated, irrespective of the person's preferences, and that the
process should be completed before the refugees could absorb Western-
inspired anti-Soviet beliefs (Marrus 1985). In other words, though the
West had begun to assert a general norm for the treatment of refugees, the
Soviets continued to press pragmatic, great-power interests. It was not
until the 1948 Universal Declaration of Human Rights (UDHR) and the
1951 Convention relating to the Status of Refugees (1951 Convention) that
an international human rights norm related to refugees clearly emerged.

The 1948 UDHR articulated global human rights principles. Prior to the UDHR, refugees had been a matter of national immigration policy and ad hoc international solutions to issues as they arose. Emerging human rights principles gave refugee advocates normative grounds to pressure states to change their policies. In particular, Articles 13–15 of the UDHR defined international norms that began to establish boundaries for acceptable state policies:

Article 13

1. Everyone has the right to freedom of movement and residence within the borders of each State.
2. Everyone has the right to leave any country, including his own, and to return to his country.

Article 14

1. Everyone has the right to seek and to enjoy in other countries asylum from persecution.
2. This right may not be invoked in the case of prosecutions genuinely arising from non-political crimes or from acts contrary to the purposes and principles of the United Nations.

Article 15

1. Everyone has a right to a nationality.
2. No one shall be deprived of his nationality nor denied the right to change his nationality.[1]

The language was a clear break with the past. The statements are not qualified by regime type or ethnicity. All people are guaranteed the same rights. Following the Universal Declaration, in 1950, the United Nations established an Office of the High Commissioner for Refugees (UNHCR) to coordinate the admission, assimilation, and settlement of refugees. Shortly thereafter, nineteen countries signed the landmark 1951 Convention Relating to the Status of Refugees. Among the signatories were France, West Germany, the United Kingdom, Greece, and Turkey, but not the United States or the Soviet Union. For the two Cold War adversaries, the Convention seemed an unnecessary constraint on superpower prerogatives. However, some forty

---

[1] Office of the High Commissioner for Human Rights, Universal Declaration on Human Rights, available at http://www.unhchr.ch/udhr/lang/eng.htm, last visited 29 September 2005.

years later, in 1993, the Russian Federation that succeeded the Soviet state signed the Convention. Meanwhile, though the United States did not accede to the Convention, it did, with the Refugee Act of 1980, harmonize its domestic statutes with Convention language.

The Preamble to the 1951 Convention declared that "all states recognizing the social and humanitarian nature of the problem of refugees will do everything within their power to prevent this problem from becoming a cause of tension between states," and that "the United Nations High Commissioner for Refugees is charged with the task of supervising international conventions providing for the protection of refugees" (UNHCR 1951). For the first time, international standards defined refugee status: a refugee is

> [a]ny person who, as a result of events occurring before 1 January 1951 and owing to a well-founded fear of being persecuted for reasons of race, religion, nationality, or political opinion, is outside the country of his nationality and is unable or, owing to such fear or for reasons other than personal convenience, is unwilling to avail himself of the protection of that country; or who, not having a nationality and being outside the country of his former habitual residence, is unable, or owing to such fear or for reasons other than personal convenience, is unwilling to return to it. (UNHCR 1951: Article 1(A)(2))

The critical development was that for the first time in international law, contracting states ceded some (albeit limited) authority over persons residing within their borders. The 1951 Convention provides for specific duties and responsibilities for the refugee and the state. The refugee must conform to the laws of the state to which he or she is applying for asylum. Restrictions on the state are more extensive. The state must not discriminate on the basis of race, religion, or country of origin. Furthermore, states shall treat refugees in a manner similar to how they treat their nationals. More importantly, the Convention, in Articles 32 and 33, articulates restrictions as to when a state may expel a refugee. In the absence of threats to national security or public order, a state may not expel a refugee except under due process of law. Article 33 defines the crucial principle of *non-refoulement*, under which a state may not expel anyone "in any manner whatsoever to the frontiers of territories where his life or freedom would be threatened on account of his race, religion, nationality, membership of a particular social group or political opinion."

States did, however, establish significant boundaries to their obligations under the 1950 UNHCR Statute and the 1951 Convention. Article 1(A)(2) of the 1951 Convention thus conferred refugee status only on people who left their country of residence before 1951. The Convention did not apply to persons who became refugees in the process of decolonization in the 1950s and later. In addition, under Art. 1(B)(1), countries could choose to confine the application of the Convention to refugees created by events in Europe. That is, states could limit their obligations under the treaty to exclude refugees created by events outside of Europe. For countries designating that option, the Convention was not universal because it would not apply, for example, to refugees from Asia or Africa.

The time restriction and the geographical clause were major points of contention between the Soviet bloc and the West. Western states advocated inclusive definitions of refugee status, whereas the Soviet bloc countries sought to prevent international refugee norms from becoming a lever by which western governments and human rights NGOs could agitate for refugee outflows from repressive communist regimes (Bem 2004). For example, there was considerable debate over how to treat Eastern European refugees, particularly East Germans and Hungarians.

However, decolonization and the continued flows of refugees soon revealed the deficiencies of the essentially ideological compromise over the scope of refugee status. As a result, the temporal and geographic restrictions were finally lifted with the adoption of the 1967 Protocol Relating to the Status of Refugees. With this agreement, the universal human rights norm was affirmed without limitation:

> (2). For the purpose of the present Protocol, the term "refugee" shall, except as regards the application of paragraph 3 of this article, mean any person within the definition of article I of the Convention as if the words "As a result of events occurring before 1 January 1951 and . . . " and the words " . . . as a result of such events", in article 1 A (2) were omitted.
>
> (3). The present Protocol shall be applied by the States Parties hereto without any geographic limitation, save that existing declarations made by States already Parties to the Convention in accordance with article I B (I) (a) of the Convention, shall, unless extended under article I B (2) thereof, apply also under

the present Protocol. (UN 1967, *Protocol Relating to the Status
of Refugees*: Article 1)

In other words, states could no longer limit the application of the Convention
to people who became refugees prior to 1951, nor could they opt to apply
the Convention's rules only to refugees created by events in Europe (World
War II).

A new paradigm had clearly emerged: the state did not have unlimited discretion as to the treatment of aliens at, or within, its borders. By
accepting human-rights-driven standards of treatment for refugees, states
have agreed that common international rules should trump certain
national practices. International society had completed a second turn
through the cycle of normative change. Yet a concern remained: without
U.S. and Soviet participation, the effect of the 1951 Convention on national
policies was limited. As shall be seen shortly, in the third phase of normative change, the domestic policies of these powerful actors began to
accommodate international norms.

Regional Diffusion of Norms

Regional subsets of states have also elaborated and reinforced the overarching international norms on refugees and asylum. For instance, twenty-
five states have ratified or acceded to the 1969 American Convention on
Human Rights (ACHR); as it did with the 1951 Convention, the United
States signed but has not ratified the ACHR. State parties to the American
Convention pledge to respect individual rights to life, personal liberty, a
fair trial, humane treatment, participation in government, and freedoms
of expression, conscience, and religion. The ACHR also mirrors the language of the 1967 Protocol Relating to the Status of Refugees. Article 22
details the individual's right to freedom of movement and residence:

> (2). Every person has the right lo leave any country freely,
> including his own....
> (7). Every person has the right to seek and be granted asylum
> in a foreign territory, in accordance with the legislation of the
> state and international conventions, in the event he is being
> pursued for political offenses or related common crimes.
> (8). In no case may an alien be deported or returned to a coun-
> try, regardless of whether or not it is his country of origin, if in
> that country his right to life or personal freedom is in danger

of being violated because of his race, nationality, religion, social status, or political opinions. (OAS 1969, *American Convention on Human Rights*: Article 22).

Though immigration policy remains a largely domestic matter, countries that are party to the American Convention have agreed to a supranational standard for the treatment of refugees.

In 1984, the Cartagena Declaration on Refugees, signed by various American countries, acknowledged that individuals needed greater protection from arbitrary state treatment. The Cartagena Declaration echoed many of the ideals of the 1948 Universal Declaration. One of its main thrusts was the recommendation to apply to Central America the 1951 Convention and 1967 Protocol norms for the treatment of refugees, thus diffusing an international norm to the regional level. Part II of the Declaration endorsed the commitments regarding refugees contained in the Contadora Act on Peace and Co-operation in Central America, quoting several of those provisions:

> (a) "To carry out, if they have not yet done so, the constitutional procedures for accession to the 1951 Convention and the 1967 Protocol relating to the Status of Refugees. . . ."
> (b) "To adopt the terminology established in the Convention and Protocol referred to in the foregoing paragraph with a view to distinguishing refugees from other categories of migrants."
> (d) "To ensure the establishment of machinery for consultation between the Central American countries and representatives of the Government offices responsible for dealing with the problem of refugees in each State." (Cartagena Declaration on Refugees 1984)

The Declaration adopted additional conclusions:

Article III
1. To promote within the countries of the region the adoption of national laws and regulations facilitating the application of the Convention and the Protocol and, if necessary, establishing internal procedures and mechanisms for the protection of refugees. In addition, to ensure that the national laws and regulations adopted

reflect the principles and criteria of the Convention and the Protocol, thus fostering the necessary process of *systematic harmonization of national legislation* on refugees. . . .

3. To reiterate that, in view of the experience gained from the massive flows of refugees in the Central American area, it is necessary to *consider enlarging the concept of a refugee*. . . . Hence the definition or concept of a refugee to be recommended for use in the region is one which, *in addition* to containing the elements of the 1951 Convention and the 1967 Protocol, includes among refugees persons who have fled their country because their lives, safety or freedom have been threatened by generalized violence, foreign aggression, internal conflicts, massive violation of human rights or other circumstances which have seriously disturbed public order.

4. To confirm the peaceful, non-political and exclusively humanitarian nature of grant of asylum or recognition of the status of refugee and to underline the importance of the *internationally accepted principle* that nothing in either shall be interpreted as an unfriendly act towards the country of origin of refugees. (Cartagena Declaration on Refugees 1984; emphasis added)

In Africa, the Organization of African Unity's 1969 Convention Governing the Specific Aspects of Refugee Problems in Africa constituted a regional attempt to meet the evolving international standard. Article 1(1) defines refugee status in language similar to the 1967 Protocol while Articles 1(2) and 1(7) emphasize the human right of freedom of movement. The OAU Convention included 35 initial signatories and was eventually ratified or acceded to by 44 countries. Noted apartheid countries South Africa and (then) Southern Rhodesia did not sign the treaty in 1969; however, each acceded to the Convention in 1985 (Southern Rhodesia as Zimbabwe).[2]

In Europe, the 1963 Protocol No. 4 to the 1950 European Convention on Human Rights (ECHR) explicitly provided protection for freedom of movement and residence:

Article 2

1. Everyone lawfully within the territory of a State shall, within that territory, have the right to liberty of movement and freedom to choose his residence.

---

[2] Organization of African Unity 2004.

2. Everyone shall be free to leave any country, including his own.

3. No restrictions shall be placed on the exercise of these rights other than such as are in accordance with law and are necessary in a democratic society in the interests of national security or public safety for the maintenance of 'ordre public', for the prevention of crime, for the protection of rights and freedoms of others.

Article 3

1. No one shall be expelled, by means either of an individual or of a collective measure, from the territory of the State of which he is a national.

2. No one shall be deprived of the right to enter the territory of the State of which he is a national.

Article 4

Collective expulsion of aliens is prohibited. (Protocol No. 4 to the Convention for the Protection of Human Rights and Fundamental Freedoms 1963)

An examination of the language used in these regional agreements reveals growing acceptance of the universal human rights norms expressed in 1948 and 1951. States had established an international structure of norms for dealing with refugees. This normative structure included treaties that defined refugee status and established baseline standards for the handling of refugees. The international community also created organizations, including the International Refugee Organization and the UNHCR, to oversee the humane treatment of refugees. From 1900 to 1938, states had created ad hoc, reactive policies for specific groups of displaced persons, identified by time and home country. Twenty-nine years later, with the 1967 Protocol, states had agreed to new refugee norms that encroached on state sovereignty. The catastrophic events of the World Wars and decolonization had affected all countries deeply, and governments responded to social and economic pressures to deal with population inflows.

International Norms and National Practices

Although international and regional agreements have established basic refugee rights, receiving states retain considerable latitude in responding to specific refugee flows. In particular, governments often claim leeway in defining "a well-founded fear of persecution" and interpreting non-refoulement. In principle, refugees who express fear should be admitted and must not be returned to places where they may be in jeopardy. But receiving states want to judge for themselves whether a refugee's fear of persecution is justified and whether, if refused, the refugee will then suffer for having attempted to leave. Governments also seek to skirt the non-refoulement rule. Non-refoulement does not require admittance, simply nonreturn to a place where the petitioner would be in danger. To shuttle asylum seekers away from their borders, governments reach agreements with so-called safe third countries. Under the terms of these bilateral accords, the "safe third country" (typically, an impoverished developing country) agrees to accept refugees. State refugee policies thus vary, reflecting a blend of international human rights norms and domestic political, economic and social interests. To show how states have melded humanitarian norms with state interests, the focus now shifts to the cases of the United States, the European Union, and Australia.

American Policy Developments

Though the United States is rightfully known as a land of immigrants, its immigration policies have often proven to be highly discriminatory. American policies have repeatedly barred specific national or ethnic groups: the 1882 Chinese Exclusion Act, 1917 Immigration Act excluding Japanese, 1924 Immigration Act excluding Asian Indians, 1934 Tydings-McDuffie Act that restricted Filipino admissions to fifty persons, and the restrictive, differential quota system of the 1952 McCarran-Walter Immigration and Nationality Act (Campi 2004). In fact, American policy toward foreign immigrants, whether regular or refugee, did not meet United Nations commitments until the domestic civil rights movement succeeded in changing the domestic political landscape in 1965. Moreover, the United States did not harmonize its immigration policy with United Nations norms until the passage of the 1980 Refugee Act (Center for Immigration Studies 1995).

During the Cold War, refugee policy became part of the rhetorical confrontation with the Soviet Union. The United States utilized refugee and asylum norms to pressure the Soviets on human rights. Michael Teitelbaum, for example, notes that from 1952 to 1980, American law defined a refugee as a person "fleeing from a Communist-dominated country or area, or from any country within the general area of the Middle East" (1984, 430). The United States "came to view the refugee situation as a means of weakening communist regimes" (McBride 1999, 4). Refugee policy, in short, was rooted partly in humanitarian concern and partly in Cold War interests.

Congressional debate on the Refugee Act, a bill first submitted in 1979 and passed in 1980, reveals American domestic concern for refugee inflows and acknowledges the need for internationalizing efforts to improve conditions in originating states. As Elizabeth Holtzman, Chair of the House Subcommittee on Immigration, Refugees and International Law, noted in her opening remarks, American law on refugees was tilted ideologically toward groups from the Middle East, Eastern Europe and the Soviet Union. That orientation was a Cold War relic that needed to be overhauled. House Resolution 2816 Title II thus defined refugees in accordance with the 1967 Protocol, applying protections to people regardless of nationality, ethnicity, race, or religion, and without time restrictions (U.S. Congress Hearings May 3, 1979).

Closer analysis of the hearings shows that American officials dealing with the aftermath of the Vietnam War lacked clear statutory guidelines for dealing with an influx of refugees. In the 1979–1980 discussions, Congress worked to clarify the terms of entry and what kinds of financial assistance would be given to individuals and to government agencies, at the federal, state and local levels. The Refugee Act also acknowledged human rights norms by giving special dispensation to the President to admit refugees beyond the nominal quota of 50,000 persons per year if it is "justified by grave humanitarian concern or is otherwise in the national interest" (U.S. HR 2816, Title II).

In his testimony, Ambassador Dick Clark, Coordinator for Refugee Affairs for the Carter Administration, acknowledged the widespread refugee problem, and spoke of the need for the United States to coordinate with international agencies such as UNHCR. An important first step was to "acknowledge the size and diversity of current refugee populations by extending the definition of refugees beyond narrow geographical and ideological criteria" (Clark 1979, 40). Similarly, Senator Edward Kennedy stated upon opening Senate hearings that American "immigration law is inadequate, discriminatory and totally out of touch with today's needs." Kennedy asserted that the proposed legislation (Refugee Act of 1979–1980) would "rationalize . . . how we treat all refugees and make our law conform to the United Nations Convention and Protocol Relating to the Status of Refugees" (U.S. Senate Report 1980, 2). At the same time, Senator Strom Thurmond, echoing the concerns of many Americans, noted that the Refugee Act provided the President carte blanche to admit an unlimited number of refugees. The refugee issue was politically sensitive given latent American prejudice toward the groups of people being admitted in the 1970s, of which 175,000 were from Southeast Asia (1979).

Ultimately, Congress passed the Refugee Act in 1980, bringing U.S. law more in line with international human rights norms. Today, the language of the U.N. Declaration of Human Rights is echoed in Department of Justice statements:

> The United States offers asylum and refugee protection based on an inherent belief in human rights and in ending or preventing the persecution of individuals. Asylum is a precious and important protection granted by federal law to qualified applications who are unable or unwilling to return to their country of nationality because of persecution or a well-founded fear of persecution. (U.S. Department of Justice 2006)

Though the law had changed, its effects in practice would depend crucially on the U.S. government's interpretation of the term "well-founded fear." An expansive view of refugee rights would tend to favor refugees while a narrow definition would tend to affirm state sovereignty. Under current U.S. law, the president consults with Congress to determine the annual quota for refugee admissions; the Attorney General has wide-ranging powers to determine the outcome of specific asylum cases by determining whether a person faces persecution at home. As a result, in practice, the United States determines "well-founded fear" not on the basis of the applicant's complaint but rather on the basis of its own assessment of conditions in the refugee's originating country.

The tension between refugee rights and state prerogatives is also evident in a pair of Supreme Court decisions. In *Immigration and Naturalization Service v. Stevic*, the Supreme Court held that "an alien must establish a clear probability of persecution" and that "a likelihood of persecution was required for the fear to be well-founded" (*INS v. Stevic*: Stevens). Three years later, the Supreme Court reinforced the context for ruling on refugee policy in *Immigration and Naturalization Service v. Cardozo-Fonseca*. In *Cardozo-Fonseca*, the Supreme Court acknowledged the importance of American accession to the 1967 Protocol, pointing out that the language of the 1980 Refugee Act mirrored the language of the Protocol. The Court also affirmed "likelihood of persecution" as a valid test for the approval of asylum. In fact, the Court ruled that the asylum applicant could not prevent deportation unless he could prove that he "would" be persecuted, rather than "could" or "might" be persecuted (*INS v. Cardozo-Fonseca*: Stevens).

The United States also imposes a quota on the total number of refugees from various regions, with disproportionate allocations for Europe: of 72,000 spaces in 1999, 48,000 were allocated to Europe, 12,000 to Africa, and 9,000 to East Asia (Center for Immigration Studies 1995). In examining the cases of asylum admissions from 1980 to 1985, Gibney (1988) created a five-level scale of states based on human rights violations and political persecution, as synthesized from Amnesty International and U.S. State Department reports. At the low end of the scale, Level 1, a country is deemed to have a secure rule of law, people are not imprisoned for their political views, and torture is rare or exceptional. Countries at Level 3 imprison large numbers of political dissidents, due process of law is denied, and torture and political murder occur. At Level 4, political murder, indefinite detention and disappearances are common and by Level 5, the state terrorizes the entire population (115). Given these categories, one would expect that a high proportion of admitted refugees would come from Level 3 to Level 5 countries.

What Gibney found was an unexpected combination, where grants of asylum were highest for refugees coming from Level 5 countries while refugees from Level 2 countries were being admitted at a rate higher than Levels 3 and 4 combined. Many of the Level 2 countries were Soviet Bloc countries; admission of refugees from that group could be construed as Cold War politicking. Meanwhile, the admission of Level 5 country refugees indicated that the United States was willing to address the suffering of those who were most at risk. In other words, though the United States frequently accepted refugee applicants in the most dire need, its refugee policy as a whole was not driven exclusively by international refugee norms but also by political considerations. A study commissioned by the UNHCR reveals the political bent of U.S. refugee policies for the period 1971 to 1990: approximately 95 percent of all refugees admitted to the United States came from Communist or Middle Eastern countries (McBride 1999). Whereas international norms do not discriminate among refugees on the basis of national origins, U.S. practice does tend to favor certain groups of refugees for domestic political reasons.

Finally, beginning in the mid-1980s, the number of asylum seekers from Cuba and Haiti began to rise and the United States adopted an active policy of interdiction on the high seas. U.S. authorities intercepted refugee vessels before they reached U.S. waters, and transferred the refugees to Guantanamo Bay or a military base in Panama. Pursuing a policy of deterrence, the U.S. hoped either to convince the Cuban government to stem the tide of "unsafe departures using mainly persuasive means" (McBride 1999, 6) or to deter Cubans and Haitians by imposing detention rather than granting asylum. By 2002, the UNHCR regional representative issued an Advisory Opinion on the U.S. policy, in which he held as follows:

> The practice or policy of using detention as a means of deterring asylum seekers from seeking protection in any given country or to penalize asylum seekers for their unlawful entry is contrary to the norms and principles of international refugee law. (UNHCR Advisory Opinion 2002)

Although the United States has been a major champion of human rights, it has pursued policies that conflict with broad international refugee norms. On the one hand, the U.S. is a major receiver of refugees. On the other hand, it places restrictions on who it accepts, contrary to international principles, and practices legally questionable policies such as interdiction and detention. Though the United States has adapted its laws to reflect international refugee norms, and although it declares support for human rights norms, actual behavior reveals mixed results.

European Union, Germany, and France

Europe has received more refugee applicants on a per capita basis than any other advanced industrialized region. Historical ex-colonial ties and geographic proximity explain much of Europe's importance as a destination for refugees, but a broad European commitment to international human rights norms in general, and refugee norms in particular, may also play a role. From 2000 to 2004, the European Union received 1,923,640 applications as compared with the United States' 411,700; on a per capita basis, Europe's application rate was nearly three times greater than that of the United States (4.2 vs. 1.5 per 1,000 inhabitants). In the same period, Germany and France received 324,200 and 279,200 applicants respectively (UNHCHR Report 2004). This significant number of applicants has created tension between European commitments to human rights norms and domestic social and economic challenges. Responding to those domestic demands, European countries have developed methods for reducing refugee inflows.

Because most asylum seekers come from the developing world and arrive in Europe looking for social and economic security, the receiving countries have been under strain both politically and economically. As a result, states have looked for ways to channel the inflows away from their shores without violating the principle of non-refoulement. Gil Loescher notes that policies of active prevention have led to increased bureaucracy, restrictive access to social and economic benefits such as housing and employment, and attempts to return refugees to countries through which they transited. Domestically, states have fined airlines and other transportation agents as a way of shifting the task of reducing refugee inflows from border control stations (such as airports and seaports) to the private carriers. Governments can threaten to revoke gate and air route access to those who fail to provide to port authorities advance notification of incoming refugees. National governments thus compel carriers to screen passengers before embarkation on Europe-bound flights (1989).

Another challenge for the European Union is that the removal of internal borders has led to coordination problems among countries. If refugees are unwanted, a state must be wary of its neighbor admitting them—one country's refugee can become another's immigrant.[3] In examining the recommendations from the 1990 Schengen Convention and the Dublin Asylum Convention, Marie-Claire Foblets argues that state interests have led to the articulation of restrictive policies of asylum, with barriers being erected that could meet the letter, if not the intent, of international commitments (1994, 801). In particular, economically strong states worried that they would be the ultimate destinations of refugees admitted by other EU states with lax entry controls.

Thus France, whose constitution accords respect for freedom from persecution, faced pressure from its neighbors. French policy is quite liberal, as the state offers three avenues for asylum: the Geneva Convention, conditional asylum, and UNHCR mandate status. Applicants must describe conditions in their origin country as a basis for asylum. Although France accepts about twenty-nine percent of asylum applicants, Foblets (1994) argues that restrictions that appeared in the 1990s were likely linked to pressure from other E.U. members. These included faster processing of asylum claims and a higher standard of evidence of persecution, including corroboration by embassies and consulates. Transporters would now face possible sanctions for carrying undocumented asylum seekers. The European-level policy for readmission was adopted, thereby enabling

---

[3] More recently, van Selm (2005) has argued that there is no real European Union policy; rather, UNHCR has been oriented toward Eurocentric policies while attempting to shepherd individual countries to comply with the 1951 Convention.

France to send denied asylum seekers home. Finally, a new "space" not covered by the Geneva Convention was created, the "transit zone," which attached to airports and allowed immigration authorities unilaterally to turn away unfounded requests for asylum. Meanwhile, for those who managed to enter the country, French authorities rescinded a 1975 policy that automatically granted work permits to asylees and instituted a restrictive work visa policy (Wihtol de Wenden 1994, 88).

The German response has been similar. With the fall of the Berlin Wall and subsequent reunification, the German government faced a mass of applicants at its new eastern frontier. In addition, the disintegration of Yugoslavia and civil war there caused a mass exodus of refugees, many of whom entered Germany. In 1992, Germany accepted refugees from Bosnia-Herzegovina and by 1996, over 345,000 had arrived, more than the total that entered all other EU states combined (German Federal Ministry of the Interior 2006). Although the German constitution provided for a right to asylum, the surge of asylum seekers led political parties to negotiate an amendment that would balance the asylum right with Germany's practical ability to absorb refugees. In principle, Germany has sought to acknowledge the horrors of a Nazi past by creating an open asylum policy "due to the painful experience during the Nazi regime, when many Germans faced persecution at home and were dependent on protection offered by other countries. This led to a strong desire for a free and democratic Germany to assume special responsibility for those seeking protection and refuge from political persecution" (50). To protect German interests, as Monika Bosche (2003) notes, German diplomats were instrumental in shaping the terms of the Schengen convention in ways favorable to Germany asylum policy. The German regions (Länder) had been largely ignored in negotiating the terms of the Maastricht Treaty and in its aftermath, moved to change the German Basic Law in favor of stronger federalism. As a result, in the approach to Schengen, the Länder shaped a new refugee policy that abandoned the liberal constitutional right of asylum. Germany's new policy allowed for deportation. The new framework also meant that asylum seekers who were allowed to enter Germany could receive a lower category of asylum—temporary residence—instead of permanent settlement.

In addition, Germany modified the Basic Law (Article 16(2)) to establish a safe third country policy. Under the German law, asylum seekers had to be from non-E.U. states, non-Convention states, or states that the German government had not specified as "safe." As Sam Blay and

Andreas Zimmerman have observed, political asylum is still held as an ideal but with significant restrictions: "Persons persecuted on political grounds shall enjoy the right of asylum. Persons who enter Germany from a state that maintains freedom from persecution will no longer be able to rely on [the right of political asylum]; the legislature is authorized to draw up a list of countries of origin for which there is a rebuttable presumption of freedom" (1994, 363).

The effect is that refugees, who typically originate in impoverished or war-torn developing countries, are forced to circulate. For example, in 1992, Italy returned Albanian refugees to their homeland; under the German amendment, had Albanians attempted to enter Germany from Italy, they would have been returned to Italy, a safe third country, which would then have deported them. Europe has also seen a growing number of "refugees in orbit," namely, persons denied entry at one port and shuttled about, with states unwilling to accept them but also unwilling to violate non-refoulement.

At the same time, the reality is that foreigners accounted for almost nine percent of the population in Germany in 2005, and the integration of such a large mass has proven challenging. In its 2001 report "Structuring Immigration, Fostering Integration," the Independent Commission on Migration to Germany noted that refugee and asylum policy must not only address the admission of applicants but be mindful of the ability to integrate and respect new members of society. For "effective refugee policy not only depends on general legal and procedural conditions, it must also foster and focus on the local population's acceptance of, and capability to take charge of refugees. In the long term, the protection of refugees cannot be implemented unless the host society is behind and not against this policy" (Germany 2001, 120). The integration of accepted refugees is, however, not the only problem. Germany has also faced challenges in dealing with those who abuse the asylum process and those who hide from the authorities after being denied entry.

In sum, E.U. governments do accept refugees and asylum seekers but also seek to limit their numbers and entitlements, thus acknowledging human rights norms but applying them restrictively.

Australia and the Pacific Solution

In Australia, refugee policy mirrors American and European practice by showing deference to general international norms but also attempting to limit Australian obligations. In addition, as Adrienne Millbank notes in an Australian Parliament Social Policy Group paper, "Australia is perhaps unique amongst Western countries in its capacity and willingness to remove failed asylum seekers" (2000, 3). Millbank articulates a concern of many receiving countries: the 1951 Convention creates state obligations toward refugees, but says little about the burdens that accepting refugees can place on the recipient society. The *Tampa* case and the recent Chen Yonglin case illustrate the tension between international principles and Australian practice.

Australia developed a policy of interdiction, the idea being that it would be easier to prevent would-be refugees from arriving than to remove them from Australian territory after denying them refugee status. A landmark case showed the harm that would-be refugees could suffer as a result of such preemptive action. In August 2001 the Australia Coast Watch intercepted the Norwegian freighter *Tampa* after it had picked up 433 "boat people" from Indonesia. An international human rights controversy erupted as the boat was moved from place to place without allowing the refugees to disembark. In the end, the Australian high court ruled against disembarkation, despite protests that confinement on the ship had amounted to illegal detention. The refugees eventually landed in Papua, New Guinea.

Australia has long been a popular destination for Asian refugees and asylum seekers and has sought ways to decrease the inflow. Much as the United States intercepted Cuban and Haitian refugees on the high seas, Australia began to interdict refugees en route rather than wait for them to reach its shores. The Pacific Solution of 2001 consists of three main prongs: border protection, including interdiction; denial of asylum to those transiting through landing zones near Australia, for example, the small chain of islands between Indonesia and Australia; and the statutory right to detain persons offshore or to take them to a "declared" country (a safe third country). The common destinations have been Nauru and Papua New Guinea, with which the Australian government has negotiated agreements. This policy does not run afoul of non-refoulement but as Mathew (2002) argues, the concept of "protection elsewhere" imposes a penalty on refugees by moving them against their will. When a refugee is diverted, there is no assurance that the third country will not in turn shuttle the refugee back to his or her original country, violating the norm of non-refoulement. Thus "protection elsewhere" and safe third country practices shift the burden of compliance but do not truly protect the refugee. Policies like Australia's Pacific Solution do not seem compatible with the 1979 UNHCR Executive Committee Conclusion No. 15 (XXX), Refugees Without an Asylum Country, which states that "asylum should not be refused solely on the ground that it could be sought from another State" (Mathew 2002, 669).

A second Australian case featured a higher profile applicant. In 2005, Chen Yonglin, a Chinese consulate official, petitioned the Australian government for political asylum. His case is unique in that he documented his duties as a coordinator for the espionage activities of approximately one thousand Chinese agents in Australia who were spying on Australian Chinese human rights activists. On the basis of an extraordinary change of heart, Chen promised to reveal his information and asked for refuge. The Howard government's treatment of his case received extensive news coverage, in part because the Australian government appeared to ignore his request for fear of disrupting delicate free trade negotiations with China. In the Australian House of Representatives, opposition members energetically questioned why the government rejected Mr. Chen's application given the human rights implications. For example, MP Brown of the Green Party, a staunch supporter of human rights, castigated the government for its timidity and its inability "to stand up to a police state" (2005). Meanwhile, MP Danby argued that Australia "must grant a protection visa to Mr. Chen Yonglin and it must not compromise Australia's foreign policy, its attitude to human rights" (2005).

Australia, like the United States and the European Union, seeks to restrict its obligations under international refugee norms. Indeed, as human rights advocate Klaus Neumann observes, "Australia does not have a well-established tradition of offering a place of refuge out of a sense of responsibility as a global citizen or for compassionate reasons" (2004, 1).

Conclusion

International norms governing refugee and asylum have changed significantly in the past one hundred years. At the start of last century, states were the sole subjects of international law; they retained exclusive authority over the treatment of refugees and asylum seekers. But massive international refugee crises in the twentieth century provoked debates about the rights of refugees and the duties of states toward them. In the first phase, following World War I and the Russian Revolution, states acknowledged refugees as a class and articulated a humanitarian concern. However, the international policies that emerged incorporated substantial territorial and time restrictions designed to minimize any entitlements that refugees might lay claim to under international norms. The system that emerged under Fridtjof Nansen and the OHCR allowed states to coordinate their responses to the refugee crises of the 1920s but created few genuine obligations for states or rights for refugees. In other words, states agreed to a common policy but did not create international rules.

A second cycle of normative change, responding to the massive atrocities of World War II, did begin to produce genuine international norms for the treatment of refugees. With the 1951 Convention Relating to the Status of Refugees and the 1967 Protocol, state policies for dealing with refugees and asylum seekers fell under international standards. Regional agreements further expanded the reach of international refugee norms from 1967 to 1984. Still, practice, even by the dominant supporters of the international liberal system, often departs from international ideals. In response to millions of refugees fleeing repressive, impoverished, or failed states, the United States, the European Union, and Australia have developed policies to suit their internal needs while circumventing some of the requirements of international norms, such as non-refoulement. Interdiction, detention, safe third countries, and refugees in orbit show that, although states subscribe to human rights norms, they are not always willing to comply fully, as indicated by the UNHCR opinions critical of the practices of detention and "protection elsewhere."

Still, outright repudiation has not been the problem, but rather restriction and inconsistent compliance. That is, international refugee norms continue to shape the context for policy making and for discourses about the rules. Even when states seek to reduce their obligations under international refugee norms, they justify their acts within the context of those norms. Thus the arguments are not about whether there should be international standards for the treatment of refugees, but rather about what specific norms, such as non-refoulement, should mean.

Clark has argued that refuge should be determined in view of the basket of human rights embodied in various international treaties including the International Covenant on Civil and Political Rights, the International Covenant on Economic, Social and Cultural Rights, the International Convention on the Elimination of All Forms of Racial Discrimination, the Convention on the Elimination of All Forms of Discrimination Against Women, the Convention on the Rights of the Child and optional protocols attached to these. In this view, international refugee law is becoming part of, and draws strength from, the broader body of international human rights law (2004, 607). International rules on refugees and asylum have thus emerged as part of the broader development of liberal norms.

Chapter 10

Humanitarian Intervention

Heather Jacques Wood, Taylor Nuttall, and Kendall Stiles

The disputes that generate international norm change frequently pit existing rules against each other. In the case of conquest (Chapter 3), for example, the right to self-determination was at odds with the traditional right to acquire territory through war. With refugees and asylum (Chapter 9), the tension pulled between the historically exclusive jurisdiction of states over their borders and populations and emerging international human rights standards.

With respect to humanitarian intervention, states face a clear conflict between two competing principles: noninterference versus human dignity (Crawford 2002, 400; Nadler 2002, 40). The tension between the two raises questions about the nature of statehood and sovereignty as well as the nature of humanity (Finnemore 2003, 52; Hui 2004, 83). As we will see, this collision of values and principles has produced an ambiguous and still evolving rule that cannot as yet be used to guide future action in predictable ways. As Crawford puts it, "the possibility and practice of humanitarian interventions raises the question of how to reconcile clashing normative beliefs. Humanitarian intervention thus pits powerful normative beliefs and international legal conventions against each other" (2002, 401–2). At most we now have a permissive rule that allows humanitarian intervention under very strict conditions—but does not require it (Sandholtz 2002, 202). Further, it is likely that this rule will continue to evolve as new crises provoke disputes about the meaning and application of international norms (Canada ICISS 2001).

Humanitarian intervention is "forcible transboundary action undertaken for the purpose of protecting the rights of individuals against violations by their own governments" (Téson 1997, 5). In fact, the definition of the term has undergone continuous change, going back to its original use in 1895 (Finnemore 2003, 20). In general, scholars agree that where the target state is willing to allow foreign troops voluntarily, what occurs is something other than humanitarian intervention. Humanitarian intervention therefore occurs when the target state does not consent to foreign military involvement. Of course, where no state is capable of exercising effective control of the territory, consent is immaterial. Moving beyond the abstract definition, it is important to note that interventions are almost never "purely" humanitarian (Walzer 1992, 101); humanitarian concerns nearly always mingle with other strategic considerations and political objectives. Examples of mixed motives include the 1990 intervention (led by the U.S. with U.N. Security Council approval) in Somalia, the Anglo-American intervention into Kurdistan following the end of major hostilities in Iraq in 1991, the French operation in Rwanda in 1994, and the deployment of NATO forces in Bosnia in the mid-1990s.

What follows is a review of the normative context (the state of the discourse and international practice regarding humanitarian intervention) circa 1945. We will then assess the extent to which the debates surrounding the UN Charter and ancillary postwar human rights treaties established principles relevant to humanitarian intervention. We next turn to the Cold War and the immediate post-Cold War period to chronicle how specific crises triggered the development of humanitarian intervention norms. Finally, we provide a more detailed examination of the debates surrounding intervention in Somalia, Rwanda, and Bosnia, with a brief discussion of the Darfur situation. Rules permitting humanitarian intervention have developed through four cycles since the end of the Cold War, and add a potential enforcement dimension to the expanding set of liberal norms. Figure 10.1 summarizes the developments discussed in this chapter, though it does not capture the temporal overlap among the cycles.

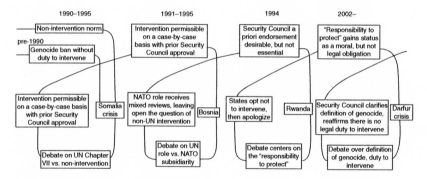

Figure 10.1 Humanitarian intervention norm cycles.

Normative Context

The conventional story of state sovereignty holds that since the Peace of Westphalia in 1648, states agreed to refrain from interference in each others' domestic affairs, based on the principle of national sovereignty (Abiew 1999, 29). Specifically, Westphalia allowed each prince in the Holy Roman Empire to make his own faith the religion of the realm without interference from the Emperor or the Pope. This prerogative provided a foundation for exclusive internal jurisdiction in all domains.

This story has been hotly contested, however, described by some as a "founding myth" (Hui 2004, 83; Krasner 1999). Sovereign authority was always circumscribed. Both the Peace of Westphalia, and the lesser known Treaty of Augsburg in 1555, enjoined states to respect the rights of minorities—at least to some extent (Abiew 1999, 45–6). Nevertheless, states continued to intervene to protect their own nationals overseas. This was especially true where their nationals were threatened by states which were led by what were perceived as "alien races." Kusani points out that Western Christian powers did not hesitate to intervene against the Ottomans in large part because they did not believe that the Turks deserved equal status and dignity (2004, 128). The same applies to East Asian kingdoms where Western powers imposed extraterritorial jurisdiction (see Chapter 6). For that matter, numerous multilateral treaties, from the Congress of Vienna to the UN Charter, provide for intervention in states that threaten the status quo and systemic stability.

But at least where relations between Western powers were concerned, sovereignty gave states considerable latitude with respect to the treatment of their own citizens. This was so in part because the major powers were capable of defending their borders and exercising control over their populations

(Hui 2004, 94). As a matter of reciprocity, major democratic states such as Britain, France, and the United States allowed nondemocratic states the same type of internal sovereignty they claimed for themselves. Such noninterference had roots in centuries of legal theory, beginning with Bodin and Vattel (Davis 2004, 8). Any intervention was suspect unless endorsed by a multilateral arrangement such as the Concert of Vienna or justified by the protection of nationals abroad. The War of 1812 between the US and Britain was fought in large part to reaffirm this principle.

Enlightenment ideals recognized limits on how governments could treat their populations. Liberal thinkers espoused universal rights, including the rights to life and conscience (Sandholtz 2002, 206), and argued that all people should be treated with dignity and respect (Finnemore 2003, 52). The broad stream of human rights values would, over time, produce wideranging shifts in international norms across diverse issue areas (see the chapters on slavery, genocide, refugees, and the right to democracy). Universal rights also implied limits to the authority of the state. Indeed, Kant went so far as to assert that human dignity and freedom superseded state sovereignty (Davis 2004, 9). Still, the conduct of states vis-à-vis their own citizens was seen as a purely internal matter. International enforcement of human rights norms was not yet part of the package. John Stuart Mill, for instance, opposed the dispatch of troops to support national liberation (8). Sovereignty precluded intervention, even in defense of basic rights.

The possibility of justifiable intervention began to emerge in the nineteenth century. States as different as France and Russia felt entitled to intervene in support of self-determination (Finnemore 2003, 59). Foreign intervention in Greece in 1827, for example, was justified largely by the desire to protect Christians from Ottoman oppression, on the premise that people (Christians, at any rate) should be free to practice their religion. Similar interventions occurred in Lebanon in the 1860s and Bulgaria in the 1870s (56). By the turn of the twentieth century, the notion that basic human rights circumscribed the powers of states was gaining international recognition. For example, the Martens Clause of the 1907 Hague Convention, like the Ninth Amendment to the U.S. Constitution,[1] presumes the existence of inherent rights that are beyond the reach of sovereign prerogatives.[2] International tribunals have invoked the Martens

---

[1] Ninth Amendment: "The enumeration in the Constitution, of certain rights, shall not be construed to deny or disparage others retained by the people."

[2] Martens Clause: "Until a more complete code of the laws of war is issued, the High Contracting Parties think it right to declare that in cases not included in the Regulations adopted by them,

Clause to affirm the primacy of individual rights as against government authority (Cassese 2000, 207).

Though a notion of justifiable intervention was emerging, the norm of nonintervention remained dominant. Intervention in China during the Boxer Rebellion, for example, aimed only to protect expatriates and those few Chinese who had converted to Christianity—not the oppressed in general. And the acute suffering of the Armenians did not trump the nonintervention norm in 1915 (Chapter 8).

The Postwar Period

World War II triggered broad, interconnected shifts in international rules, lending a particular impetus to the development of international human rights norms. As the centerpiece of international law after the war, the U.N. Charter embodies both liberal norms of human dignity and principles of sovereign privilege. This dual character was deliberate; it was in part a compromise that permitted broad approval of the document as a whole (Davis 2004, 9).

The U.N. Charter codifies both state sovereignty and nonintervention. Article 2(1) proclaims the sovereign equality of all Members. Article 2(4) exhorts member states to refrain from using force against other states. Article 2(7) explicitly states the U.N.'s intention to respect sovereignty: "Nothing contained in the present Charter shall authorize the United Nations to intervene in matters which are essentially within the domestic jurisdiction of any state." The 1950 Peace through Deeds Resolution (Res. 380 (V)) unequivocally condemned intervention (Sandholtz 2002, 206).

At the same time, under Chapter VII of the Charter, the Security Council has the authority to identify "threats to international peace and security" and to take measures to counter those threats—including the deployment of military forces. Of course, the Security Council cannot lightly exercise these powers. A resolution to use force can only pass if none of the five permanent members vetoes it. Furthermore, states must agree to provide troops, equipment, and logistical support for UN enforcement actions, and such participation is entirely voluntary (Voon 2002, 37–8; see also Wolfrum 2002, 98–100). Though the Charter allows the

---

populations and belligerents remain under the protection and empire of the principles of international law, as they result from the usages established between civilized nations, from the laws of humanity and the requirements of the public conscience" (Cassese 2000, fn. 1).

Security Council to authorize intervention to halt interstate violence, it does not explicitly contemplate UN intervention in cases of internal conflicts or large-scale human rights abuses. Davis argues that intervention in internal conflicts can only be justified with a very broad interpretation of the Charter (Davis 2004, 4).

Still, the Charter does call upon all Members to promote human rights. Articles 55 and 56 provide the following language:

> Art. 55. With a view to the creation of conditions of stability and well-being which are necessary for peaceful and friendly relations among nations based on respect for the principle of equal rights and self-determination of peoples, the United Nations shall promote:
> (c). universal respect for, and observance of, human rights and fundamental freedoms for all without distinction as to race, sex, language, or religion.
> Art. 56. All Members pledge themselves to take joint and separate action in co-operation with the Organization for the achievement of the purposes set forth in Article 55.

This language implies that U.N. member-states may take direct action under U.N. auspices to promote human rights, and these articles have served as a touchstone for advocates of humanitarian intervention (Abiew 1999, 131–2; ICISS 2001; Weiss and Collins 2000, 29). The Genocide Convention, drawn up at roughly the same time, opens similar possibilities, in Article 8:

> Any Contracting Party may call upon the competent organs of the United Nations to take such action under the Charter of the United Nations as they consider appropriate for the prevention and suppression of acts of genocide or any of the other acts enumerated in article III.

Note that the language is merely permissive, not obligatory. Few states in the immediate postwar period were willing to commit themselves in advance to armed intervention to halt a humanitarian calamity. Rather, in drafting the post-war conventions, states sought language that might permit them to intervene on a case-by-case basis—preferably with Security Council backing (Sandholtz 2002, 202).

Developments between 1948 and 1989

As further evidence that the international community was not committed to an obligation to intervene, we can look to the cases of intervention that occurred during the Cold War. To begin, it is worth noting that by any definition they were few in number: the 1971 Indian intervention in East Pakistan aimed at helping it achieve independence (and stem a refugee crisis), the 1978 intervention by Vietnam into Cambodia to depose the Khmer Rouge and curtail Chinese influence in Phnom Penh, and the 1979 Tanzanian intervention to overthrow Idi Amin in Uganda following a Ugandan incursion into Tanzanian territory. To this list one might add a number of measures adopted by the U.N. Security Council involving the imposition of sanctions against Rhodesia and South Africa during the 1960s and 1970s, which culminated in the end of apartheid and the independence of Namibia. But these did not involve the direct insertion of troops into a hostile environment and so would not qualify as humanitarian intervention.

In the case of India's intervention into East Pakistan, it is interesting to note that even though the action stopped the massacre of hundreds of thousands of Bangladeshis by Pakistani troops (going on since March 1971), the Indian government was reluctant to describe its actions as humanitarian. During Security Council and General Assembly debates on the event, India at one point said it was acting for humanitarian purposes, but quickly withdrew the comment and had it excised from record after numerous states condemned its unilateralism (Finnemore 2003, 73–6). Rather, India couched its justification in terms of self-defense under Article 51 of the Charter.

In the cases of Tanzania and Vietnam, neither country cited humanitarian justifications, relying instead on self-defense and national liberation, respectively. These countries were also challenged for their unilateral actions. The United States roundly condemned Vietnam's incursion as a violation of Cambodia's sovereignty, a position taken in part out of animus for the Hanoi regime (Power 2002, 145–55). Even though Julius Nyerere had described Amin as a "murderer," he learned from close observation that invoking humanitarianism would likely cause more problems than it would solve (Finnemore 2003, 77).

This is not to say that humanitarian justifications were never invoked during the Cold War. Both the United States and the Soviet Union routinely explained their insertion of troops in various satellite states as an effort to improve the lives and freedoms of the inhabitants. In his famous

"Tonkin Gulf" speech to Congress, Lyndon Johnson explained, "This is not just a jungle war, but a struggle for freedom on every front of human activity. Our military and economic assistance to South Vietnam and Laos in particular has the purpose of helping these countries to repel aggression and strengthen their independence" (VietnamWar.com 2006). Likewise, the Brezhnev Doctrine justified intervention by the Soviet Union. But these statements were political rhetoric and did not affect international rules on humanitarian intervention.

Cycles of Norm Change Post–1989

Between 1987 and 1990, the U.S.S.R. and United States signed a series of dramatic arms control agreements that reduced nuclear weapons stockpiles. Both superpowers withdrew troops and weapons from Afghanistan, Central America, and regions of Africa. Namibia achieved independence and apartheid was on its last legs. China, the Soviet Union, and other anti-Western states endorsed international human rights instruments at an impressive pace (Wolfrum 2002, 98). For some, it was a period of "UN-phoria."

In this context, the United States deployed troops in Panama (see Chapter 11) and Somalia at least partially on humanitarian grounds. In 1991, a U.S.-led international coalition—with Security Council endorsement—intervened militarily to expel Saddam Hussein's forces from Kuwait. Following that operation, Hussein's troops undertook to repress uprisings in the northern Kurdish and southern Shi'ite regions, with devastating effect. The Security Council approved the declaration of a "no-fly zone" over these areas and in Resolution 688 called upon the Iraqi government to allow humanitarian relief into the regions immediately. Furthermore, Resolution 688 referred to this case of serious domestic unrest as a "threat to international peace." By declaring a threat to international peace, the Council could exercise enforcement powers under Chapter VII of the Charter. Assertion of this authority freed the Council from the Charter's prohibition against intervening in purely domestic matters. Since 1991, the Security Council has described several domestic crises as "threats to international peace," as we will see below.

During this period of multilateralist enthusiasm, the Security Council commissioned the Secretary General to draft guidelines on intervention and peacekeeping that might allow the body to make full use of its powers. In *An Agenda for Peace*, which appeared in 1992, Boutros Boutros-Ghali identified new ways for the United Nations to engage in peacekeeping and peace-making after the end of the Cold War (1992). Boutros-Ghali defined peacekeeping as "action to bring hostile parties to agreement" and peacemaking as "the deployment of a United Nations presence in the field, hitherto with the consent of all the parties concerned, normally involving United Nations military and/or police personnel and frequently civilians as well" (1992, Art. 20). Both the Security Council and the General Assembly supported the Secretary-General's report, with both organizations recommending the implementation of reforms suggested in the *Agenda* (UN 1993, *Yearbook*, 37–41, 71–73). The expanded role Boutros-Ghali foresaw for the United Nations in both peacemaking and peacekeeping has materialized in, for example, Somalia, Haiti, Rwanda, and Yugoslavia.

The increased willingness of the Security Council to authorize the use of force in response to humanitarian crises has driven the development of humanitarian intervention norms (Falk 1996, 511–12; Levitt 1998, 340; Tesón 1996, 371). As Levitt argues:

> International law today recognizes, as a matter of practice, the legitimacy of collective forcible humanitarian intervention of military measures authorized by the Security Council for the purpose of remedying serious human rights violations. While traditionally the only ground for collective military action has been the need to respond to breaches of the peace, especially aggression, the international community now has accepted a norm that allows collective humanitarian intervention to respond to serious human rights abuses. (Levitt 1998, 340)

As the United Nations increasingly authorized humanitarian intervention as a peacekeeping measure, the norm became more accepted internationally and more clearly defined. However, between 1993 and 1994, dramatic setbacks and failures led to increased apprehension and reticence with respect to humanitarian intervention. The result today is profound ambivalence about the rights and duties of the international community with respect to stopping large-scale atrocities.

Somalia

Humanitarian intervention in Somalia was an unprecedented UN Security Council action. As one author explains, "Security Council decisions regarding Somalia are rightly regarded as a watershed for the doctrine of humanitarian intervention. Even if Resolution 794 [which authorized intervention] does not legalize or address the issue of unilateral humanitarian intervention, the Security Council expanded the scope of . . . the U.N. Charter with its course of action in Somalia" (Vessel 2003, 24–5). The key discursive move was to identify an essentially internal crisis as a threat to international peace and stability.

The grave humanitarian situation in Somalia that eventually motivated UN intervention began after warring factions ousted Somali President Mohammed Siad Barre in January 1991 (Chesterman 2001, 140). Barre's dictatorial rule had imposed order on Somalia, and with his ouster Somalia erupted into clan warfare and was divided into twelve zones of control. By November 1991 the country had erupted into full-scale civil war. The interim Prime Minister, Omer Arteh Qhalib, sent a letter to the U.N. Security Council in January 1992, requesting an immediate meeting to discuss the increasingly disastrous situation in Somalia (Tesón 1996, 348). The fighting in Somalia prevented the distribution of food, leading to widespread starvation that killed an estimated 300,000 people between November 1991 and the end of 1992 and immediately threatened at least another 1.5 million people (UN 1993, *Yearbook*, 199). Initially, the United Kingdom responded by passing several resolutions threatening future collective military action if the warfare continued. The Security Council did, in January 1992, unanimously approve Resolution 733, which imposed a comprehensive arms embargo on Somalia as a last measure before authorizing intervention.

On 24 April 1992, the United Nations initiated UNOSOM (United Nations Operation in Somalia), which involved 550 military and security personnel and seventy-nine civilians who were sent to Somalia to monitor a failing cease-fire among rival faction leaders and to oversee the delivery of humanitarian aid (UN 1993, *Yearbook*, 202). The resolution establishing UNOSOM was unanimously accepted by the Security Council, urging all parties concerned in Somalia, and the international community in general, to support United Nations efforts. In a report on 22 July 1992, the Secretary-General related the following:

> In the two months since the establishment of UNOSOM, significant developments had taken place which must be consolidated and built upon, as there was the risk of a renewal of hostilities. The desperate and complex situation in the country required energetic and sustained efforts on the part of the international community to break the cycle of violence and hunger. (UN 1993, *Yearbook*, 204)

In a public statement on 16 October 1992, the President of the Security Council also emphasized the importance of UNOSOM, proclaiming, "The members of the Council consider that persons hampering the deployment of UNOSOM would be responsible for aggravating an already unprecedented humanitarian disaster" (UN 1993, *Yearbook*, 208).

Though UNOSOM did have some successes in increasing the delivery of humanitarian aid and in helping the disputants work toward a cease-fire, the humanitarian situation in Somalia continued to degenerate. In a letter to the Security Council on 24 November 1992, the Secretary-General outlined the difficulties UNOSOM faced in Somalia: the absence of a government authority that could maintain law and order, the failure of the warring factions to cooperate with UNOSOM; the extortion of large sums of money from donor agencies and organizations (which was then used to support the warring factions instead of suffering Somalis); the hijacking of vehicles; the looting of relief supplies from convoys and warehouses; and the detention of expatriate personnel (UN 1993, *Yearbook*, 208). Though UNOSOM's efforts to curb starvation and maintain peace were substantial, often the humanitarian aid provided did not reach those it was intended to help: "it is estimated that upward of three-quarters of the United Nations food supplies were confiscated or stolen by the various factions for their own use or to sell for profit" (Tesón 1996, 349).

In response to the deteriorating situation in Somalia and the refusal of warring factions to cooperate with UN requests, the Security Council passed increasingly threatening resolutions. Resolution 767 (summer of 1992) labeled the conflict in Somalia a threat to international peace and security, and Resolution 775 (also passed in the summer of 1992) approved humanitarian aid airlifts and increased the number of UNOSOM forces in an effort to better facilitate the distribution of relief supplies (Hutchinson 1993, 628). Finally, in December 1992, the Security Council unanimously approved Resolution 794, which authorized the use of force "to restore peace, stability and law and order" to Somalia. Resolution 794 established the Unified Task Force (UNITAF), which would include 37,000 troops and increased the UNOSOM contingent by 3,500 personnel.

The unanimous vote for Resolution 794 was in itself surprising. No previous Chapter VII resolution had explicitly authorized collective intervention for solely humanitarian purposes. Because the disaster in Somalia did not directly threaten or destabilize neighboring countries, the Security Council action in Resolution 794 broke new ground by signaling that large-scale humanitarian catastrophes within a country could, in themselves, be deemed threats to international peace and thus justify intervention. As Loomis argues,

> The invoking of a Chapter VII peace enforcement operation for containing and controlling an internal domestic conflict was fundamentally different from previous applications of Chapter VII for the Korean War and the Gulf War. These previous applications were envisaged in the Chapter VII collective security measures to counter a state that was an aggressor against another and had broken the peace. In Somalia, the conflict was essentially within one state's boundary and UN intervention under these circumstances was never envisaged when the UN Charter was drafted and signed in 1945. In effect, the UN Security Council Resolution 794 called for the military invasion of Somalia to sort out its internal troubles. . . . (1996, 142)

Resolution 794 established the groundbreaking idea that the presence of extreme human suffering, in a failed state ravaged by civil war, can constitute a threat to the peace (Abiew 1999, 169).

Despite its unanimous passage, Resolution 794 triggered debates. A number of states were reluctant to establish a precedent of intervention in an internal conflict. In an effort to minimize the precedential value of Resolution 794, both Russia and China insisted that it include language characterizing the situation in Somalia as "unique," "exceptional," and "extraordinary." Russia stressed the uniqueness of the conflict, implying that it should not be seen as a precedent for future incursions by the Council into the internal affair of other countries (Endless 2003, 204). Still, neither Russia nor China vetoed the creation of UNITAF.

The UNITAF force, led by the United States with 24,000 troops and including contingents from twenty countries, entered Somalia in December 1992 (Malanczuk 1997, 404). According to reports on the operation, the distribution of supplies dramatically increased, saving several hundred thousand Somalis. In 1993, the Security Council expanded the role of the United Nations in Somalia to include nationbuilding operations (Tesón 1996, 350). In a unanimously approved resolution on 26 March 1993, the Security Council acted under Chapter VII to expand UNISOM forces, calling the new operation UNISOM II. UNITAF then transitioned to UNISOM II. In a March 1993 report, the Secretary-General related the reason for expanding UN operations in Somalia: "a secure environment had not yet been established and was a matter of grave concern" (UN 1995, *Yearbook*, 290). The Secretary-General also outlined some of the purposes of UNISOM II, including: using force to disarm rival factions and establish a stable environment; facilitating the return of refugees; and working to rebuild Somalia's economy and social, political, and educational structures (UN 1995, *Yearbook*, 289–90). UNISOM II was the first operation of its kind authorized by the United Nations (289). Somali militants severely resisted UNOSOM II nationbuilding efforts. Following the death of one hundred U.N. peacekeepers, and United States withdrawal from Somalia in 1994 (after the death of 18 U.S. soldiers in a failed raid) the United Nations scaled back its efforts to focus again solely on humanitarian aid distribution (Tesón 1996, 350).

Finally, the United Nations withdrew all forces from Somalia on 4 March 1995. This withdrawal date had been established on 4 November 1994, in the unanimously accepted Security Council resolution 954 (1994). The resolution emphasized that the lack of progress in the Somali peace process, due mostly to the lack of sufficient cooperation from the warring factions, had "fundamentally undermined the United Nations objective in Somalia, and, in these circumstances, continuation of UNISOM II beyond March 1995 cannot be justified" (UNSC 1994c, *Res. 954*).

Though the operations authorized by the Security Council had some significant successes in relieving the dire humanitarian situation in Somalia, the failure of U.N. intervention to restore lasting peace led to probing examinations of the intervention by the U.N. and the international community. The fact that Somalia was a precedent-setting intervention rendered an in-depth examination even more necessary, because U.N. action in this situation had serious implications for humanitarian crises to come (Hutchinson 1993, 625).

Beyond prompting the United Nations to evaluate its actions in Somalia, the failure of the intervention to establish order also led many states to question their national policies concerning intervention (Clarke and Herbst 1997, vii). Notably, the United States developed a new intervention policy, embodied in Presidential Decision Directive 25 (PDD 25), which was issued shortly after the United States pulled out of Somalia in April 1994 (239). One author summarizes the content and significance of PDD 25:

The policy enunciated in PDD 25 makes threats to vital U.S. interests the trigger for U.S. action or support in resolving complex humanitarian emergencies. This strict "vital national interests" test is a shift from the early 1990s interventionist "multilateralistic" attitude brought about as a result of several factors: emerging international norms of justifiable intervention, a post-Cold War reinvigorated UN, post-Gulf War euphoria and a new Democratic administration willing or even feeling compelled to seek UN authority to conduct unilateral intervention operations, among other things. A retreat to a strict "vital national interests" test and away from an expanded "just causes" test for intervention (*e.g.*, massive human rights abuses [)], has prevented and will continue to prevent the U.S. from acting in areas of the world where it does not have a vital national interest. . . . (Ware 1997, 2–3)

The U.S. experience in Somalia also led to bills in Congress aimed at drastically reducing U.S. contributions to U.N. peacekeeping operations (Clarke and Herbst 1997, 239). These responses had significant implications for U.N. peacekeeping, because the United Nations can neither conduct nor authorize intervention operations without U.S. diplomatic, financial, and military support (Ware 1997, 11). The reluctance of the United States to support intervention became critical in the next humanitarian situation requiring intervention, namely, Rwanda.

While Security Council authorized intervention in Somalia was groundbreaking, the aftermath of the intervention softened the effect—as seen in subsequent reluctance to pursue humanitarian intervention operations. Security Council approval of Chapter VII action for humanitarian purposes did indeed create an important precedent (Joyner and Arend 1999/2000, 38). After Somalia, it would be impossible to argue that humanitarian intervention was impermissible. However, the failure of the intervention to establish peace in Somalia raised practical (as opposed to normative or legal) questions regarding the effectiveness of intervention in rebuilding failed states or halting civil war.

Bosnia

The Balkan conflict began in 1991 with the breakup of Yugoslavia (DiPrizio 2002, 104). After the fall of the communist government, the various regions of the country experienced strong nationalist uprisings. The Serbian faction, led by Slobodan Milosevic, tried to exert more forceful control over the other republics (104), while those republics moved closer and closer to secession (Abiew 1999, 176). When Slovenia and Croatia proclaimed their independence on June 25, 1991, armed conflict erupted almost immediately. Milosevic attacked Slovenia with Serbian forces in an attempt to stifle the nationalist movement (Weiss 2005, 76). Serbian forces pulled out of the conflict after only two weeks, presumably to focus on areas with larger Serb populations (DiPrizio 2002, 104; Weiss 2005, 76).

Severe conflict thus began to spread into Croatia and then into Bosnia-Herzegovina, where the Serbs began what would be subsequently labeled ethnic cleansing and genocide. Although the international community and the Security Council quickly recognized the situation as a crisis and proposed action (Stiles 2005, 225), none was forthcoming. Indeed, the crisis in Bosnia created a difficult dilemma for the Western world and the United Nations in particular, one that would test developing norms of humanitarian intervention (Abiew 1999, 175). A key feature of the case was the complex ethnic mix in each republic. In 1991, Bosnia-Herzegovina was 43.7 percent Muslim, 17.3 percent Croat and 31.4 percent Serb (Weiss 2005, 78). The large Serb population virtually ensured that Bosnia would be a main target of interest to the Serbian republic and its leaders. Furthermore, large refugee flows and the possibility that the conflict could spill over into neighboring European countries further intensified the challenge facing the UNSC. By the same token, precisely because of the danger of conflict spreading in Europe, more states were willing to intervene more quickly than was the case in Rwanda.

Still, the international community was at first extremely hesitant to become involved militarily (Abiew 1999, 178). The debates regarding possible action from the international community began shortly after the initial Serbian attack upon Slovenia, as it became clear that the Serbs' intentions were to extend Serbian control over as much territory as possible (Abiew 1999, 177). The initial U.N. response, in late 1991, thus consisted of an arms embargo on all Yugoslav territories (DiPrizio 2002, 111). With a new conflict manifesting itself at its own doorstep, the European Community (EC) was eager to mediate the conflict in order to show that it was able to handle crises within its own region. Luxembourg's Foreign Minister Jacques Poos stated that "if anyone can do anything here (in Yugoslavia), it is the EC. It is not the US or the USSR or anyone else" (108).

The EC was able to arrange cease-fires and diplomatic talks, but these initiatives were short lived and ineffective (Abiew 1999, 178). With the failure of these measures, and with increasing reports of large-scale atrocities, media coverage and world attention became more intense. The United States was content to avoid a direct role, preferring that the Europeans take the lead (DiPrizio 2002, 108). However, the rest of the world, driven by the images being broadcast out of Bosnia, called for action. Security Council Representatives from Yugoslavia, Austria, Canada, and Hungary (to name a few) actively pushed to send in peacekeeping forces to alleviate the situation (Abiew 1999, 179).

In comparison with other conflicts requiring intervention, consensus to invoke Chapter VII and authorize the use of force in the case of Bosnia came relatively quickly (in Resolution 770 of August 1992), following a deliberate attack on civilians in Srebrenica in July of 1992. However, deployment of forces by member-states did not occur until much later. The Security Council debates over the use of force were not as intense as they had been in other conflicts, a fact that likely led Secretary General Boutros Boutros-Ghali to label the conflict a "rich man's war." The wealthy Western powers appeared much more willing to intervene in a European crisis than in similar conflicts in Africa or Asia.

Virtually all member-states stated their desire to settle the conflict peacefully without multilateral intervention, even after the use of force was authorized in resolution 770 (UNSC 1994, *Meeting 3475*). China, along with the US initially, urged respect for the principle of nonintervention, and argued that it was not appropriate to intervene in a civil war. Russia stressed the importance of a political settlement (though it argued that Bosnia was an intrastate conflict) to show the danger of separatist movements to the entire region (Abiew 1999, 179). The United Kingdom acknowledged the international dimension of the conflict and warned of the impact the conflict would have on the region, especially upon Yugoslavia's neighbors, with the issues of refugee flows and spillover fighting (179).

UNSC Resolution 752 condemned the mass killings and rape the Serbs perpetrated and called for an end to attempts to "change the ethnic composition of the population" (UNSC 1992, *Res. 752*). In resolution 771, the Security Council for the first time used the term "ethnic cleansing" and called for an investigation into breaches of the Geneva Conventions, though it made no mention of genocide (UNSC 1992, *Res. 771*). Although no one doubted the severity of the human rights violations occurring in the Balkans, the major international debate once again focused on the question of whether or not the atrocities constituted genocide (Power 2002, 288). U.S. officials, along with those of most other nations, were keen to refrain from the use of the word in order to avoid the obligations that came with it. Brent Scowcroft, National Security Adviser to President George H. W. Bush, stated:

> In Bosnia, I think, we all got ethnic cleansing mixed up with genocide. To me they are different terms. The horror of them is similar, but the purpose if not. Ethnic cleansing is not "I want to destroy an ethnic group, wipe it out." It's "They're not going to live with us. They can live where they like, but not with us." . . . There is a proscription on genocide, but there is not a proscription on killing people. . . . Therefore there is something of a national interest in preventing genocide because the United States needs to appear to be upholding international law. (Power 2002, 288)

The Security Council did not directly address genocide until 1994, when the representatives from Bosnia, the United States and Argentina invoked the term (UNSC 1994, *Meeting 3363*).

In the end, international pressure became too great and NATO forces carried out a bombing campaign that stopped the war; even though it did not halt the atrocities. NATO's role and the legitimacy of its intervention provided another interesting dimension to the Bosnia conflict. NATO offered to contribute troops (without Americans) to the conflict as early as August 1992 (after resolution 770), which troops were accepted and incorporated into the U.N. peacekeeping force UNPROFOR (DiPrizio 2002, 114). Until 1995, the Clinton administration policy was "hands-off" regarding NATO's presence in the former Yugoslavia (118–120). It was not until August 1995 that the United States convinced NATO to conduct bombings on Serb forces and installations. Resolution 770 in 1992 called upon states "to take nationally or through regional agencies or arrangements all measures necessary to facilitate in coordination with the United Nations the delivery . . . of humanitarian assistance . . . in . . . Bosnia-Herzegovina" (UNSC 1992, *Res. 770*). This language specifically authorizes the use of regional agreements such as NATO to intervene in the conflict.

The debates regarding the Bosnia crisis, coupled with those of Somalia and Rwanda, are evidence of an overall normative shift that justified international intervention in humanitarian crises. The Bosnia case solidified the legality of interventions authorized by the Security Council. The invocation of Chapter VII in this instance was a relatively easy process, when compared with other crises. As with other cases, however, there were significant delays, centering in part on the debates over the timing of intervention and on the problems associated with recognizing genocide.

In any case, in less than five years, the international community went from "UN-phoria" and optimism regarding the potential of humanitarian intervention to halt crises, to apprehension and reticence with respect to taking specific actions. The reticence to act continues to prevail, as will be apparent in our discussion of the current crisis in the Sudan.

Rwanda

By establishing that international intervention in internal humanitarian crises was permissible, the Somalia episode broke new normative ground. The disappointing conclusion to the intervention left many countries, notably the United States, reluctant to participate in such missions. But that hesitancy represented a practical or policy concern, not a normative shift. Any humanitarian crisis requires outside states to answer two key questions. First, is intervention justified under international norms? And second, would intervention in this case be, in political and policy terms, sound policy? Governments might well decide that intervention would be permissible (justified), but that it would not be wise policy (the costs might be too high, the chance of success might be too low, the domestic political environment would not support it, and so on). The Somalia intervention strengthened the norm that humanitarian intervention is permissible, but it also raised states' sensitivity to the political and practical costs of intervening. This ambivalence—normative justification but practical concerns—decisively affected international responses to the 1994 crisis in Rwanda.

The problems in the Rwandan state began long before the genocide in 1994. Colonial rule by the Belgians and Germans exacerbated already existing political and social divisions (particularly by preserving minority Tutsi rule). The Hutus rebelled in 1959, overthrowing the Tutsi monarchy. In 1973, Major General Juvenal Habyarimana, a Hutu, led a bloodless coup in which he overthrew the existing Hutu leader and established the "Second Republic," declaring himself President (O'Halloran 1995, 3).

The genocide began when President Habyarimana's plane was shot down on 6 April 1994 (DiPrizio 2002, 63). Immediately afterward, the Hutu-dominated military launched a preplanned slaughter of Tutsis and moderate Hutus in supposed retaliation for the president's assassination, which they blamed on the Rwandan Patriotic Front (RPF), the Tutsi revolutionary group.[3] The RPF then responded by breaking a cease-fire (established earlier by the Arusha Peace accords) with a new wave of violence (Tesón 1997, 258). Thousands were killed within hours of the assassination, and refugee flows to neighboring countries (Tanzania, Uganda, Congo) began within a few days. From Rwanda came reliable reports of a massive and systematic slaughter, with the number of victims rising to the tens and then hundreds of thousands.

The international community responded with denial, delay, and inaction. Prior to the assassination, 2,700 U.N. observers (the UNAMIR mission) were in Rwanda monitoring the Arusha Peace accords. However, when ten Belgians from the U.N. force were massacred, just days after the start of the genocide, Belgium began to evacuate all its military forces and nationals. By 10 April, Belgium had withdrawn all of its observers. As a direct result of the massacre of these U.N. observers, the Security Council voted on 21 April to reduce the number of observers to 270, so that further casualties of U.N. personnel would be averted (Tesón 1997, 259).

As the enormity of the horror became clearer, the delegation from Rwanda appealed to the Security Council in April 1994 to help reestablish peace in Rwanda: "The people of Rwanda continue to hope that the Council will realize that it has a duty to act resolutely to maintain peace in Rwanda and to guarantee stability in the region" (UNSC 1994, *Meeting 3368*). The Czech Republic, along with New Zealand, Argentina, and Spain, pressured the Council to restore and expand the UNAMIR force and increase the U.N. mandate. In an informal meeting of the Security Council on 28 and 29 April, the delegations from these states proposed to label the killing as genocide (Wheeler 2000, 225–6). China, the United Kingdom, and the United States opposed the proposal because, under the Genocide Convention, labeling the Rwandan catastrophe a genocide would obligate them to act to stop it. Using the term "genocide" would also swell international demands for decisive action. The president of the Security Council finally issued a statement that addressed the events in Rwanda, but it did not use the word genocide to describe the situation (UN 1995, *Yearbook*, 21).

---

[3] No one is completely sure who carried out the attack on the president's airplane. Many scholars agree that he was actually in danger from extremist Hutus, who were angry with the president for his role in bringing about the Arushu Peace accords. The extremists were totally unwilling to give up any kind of power to either Tutsis or even moderate Hutus. For an account, see Wheeler 2000, 211–4.

By mid-May, the International Committee of the Red Cross was estimating that 500,000 Rwandans had been killed. Finally, on 17 May, the Security Council adopted Resolution 916 (1994), which increased the size of the UNAMIR forces to 5,500 (DiPrizio 2002, 67). But, again, the international response was sluggish and inadequate. A few African countries volunteered troops, but they were unequipped and other member states failed to provide funding, equipment, or transport for such a mission. As then Secretary-General Boutros Boutros-Ghali stated during the crisis:

> The international community appears paralysed in reacting . . . even to the revised mandate established by the Security Council. We all must recognize that, in this respect, we have failed in our response to the agony of Rwanda, and thus have acquiesced in the continued loss of human lives. Our readiness and capacity for action has been demonstrated to be inadequate at best, and deplorable at worst, owing to the absence of the collective political will. (UN 1995, *Yearbook*, 640)

Boutros-Ghali asked the Security Council to take "forceful action to restore law and order" (UN 1995, *Yearbook*, 518).

Forceful action never came from the Security Council. In fact, the genocide ended not by international intervention but by the military success of the Tutsi Rwanda Patriotic Front (RPF). The RPF had been building its strength at camps in Uganda. When the massacres began in early April 1994, the RPF immediately launched an offensive. By late May, the RPF had gained control of the northern and eastern parts of the country, as well as the Kigali airport. The capital and parts of southern Rwanda fell to the RPF in early July. On 18 July, the RPF declared victory and installed a government in Kigali.

The revived UNAMIR was still mired in argument and inaction. The United States, as the only country that could have provided immediate logistical support for equipping a multilateral force and flying it to Rwanda, played a central role. The loss of eighteen American soldiers in Somalia was fresh in the minds of U.S. government officials, and President Clinton decided to oppose any sort of humanitarian mission that would put U.S. personnel in danger (Wheeler 2000, 224). Of course, PDD-25 had declared that the United States would not participate in intervention missions that did not serve U.S. interests. As U.S. Secretary of State Warren Christopher stated:

> Realism must guide US policies toward these conflicts. Some touch our interest—or will, if they are not checked. But we must accept that other conflicts may not. . . . Our own role and involvement will need to be informed by a strict assessment of our interests and the interests of other. We must examine every case—asking rigorous questions, and giving measured answers—to find the course commensurate with our interests. (Christopher 1994)

In any case, neither the public nor Congress supported U.S. intervention (Diprizio 2002, 75). Consequently, Clinton refused to act, citing public opinion and PDD 25 as justification. He stated that U.S. forces could not be deployed to remedy every conflict where people were "offended by human misery" (Klinghoffer 1998, 97).

In addition, although many members of the international community had labeled the Rwanda situation a genocide, the United States (and other governments) still refused to use the term, as doing so would have triggered a duty to act. In fact, a directive reportedly circulated among government officials to the effect that they were not permitted to use the term genocide to describe the situation in Rwanda (Wheeler 2000, 225). Thus the United States (along with Russia and China) labeled the situation in Rwanda a civil war, in which intervention was not required (Chesterman 2001, 146). The United States' attitude toward the conflict was that "whatever effort the United Nations may undertake, the true key to the problems in Rwanda is in the hands of the Rwandese people. . . . The killing—by all parties—must stop" (UNSC 1994, *Meeting 3377*, U.S. Delegation). The United States and other sates did not want to get involved in Rwanda for fear of "another Somalia" and because the country offered no strategic interest.

In the meantime, France proposed a unilateral intervention. French Foreign Minister Alain Juppé stated in June 1994 that France had "a real duty to intervene in Rwanda . . . to put an end to the massacres and protect the populations threatened with extermination" (Wheeler 2000, 231). Juppé indicated that France was ready to send in an intervention force (Prunier 1997, 280). Security Council Resolution 929 (22 June 1994) authorized French intervention, but the French plan was controversial.

Many believed that the French had an ulterior motive in undertaking the operation (Abiew 1999, 195), whether it be the historic French support for the Hutu government, or even "French neoimperialism in Africa" (Weiss 1999, 150). Some states would have preferred a strengthened UNAMIR II to a unilateral French intervention (Wheeler 2000, 232). The New Zealand ambassador, for example, asserted the following:

> We have strongly urged that France redirect the energy, enthu-siasm and resources which it is employing in this initiative to support the one operation that we believe would be effectively able to curtail the genocide—and that is UNAMIR. If that energy, enthusiasm and money were put at the disposal of the United Nations, we have no doubt that the delays that UNAMIR is currently facing would disappear overnight. (UNSC 1994, *Meeting 3392*)

In the vote on Resolution 929, China, Brazil, New Zealand, Pakistan, and Nigeria abstained; they were uncomfortable with French motives but unwilling to criticize the mission in light of the desperate circumstances (Wheeler 2000, 232). The resolution invoked Chapter VII of the U.N. Charter and authorized the French to use military force to bring order and halt the killing. The resolution also instructed the French to direct a mis-sion that was "strictly humanitarian . . . impartial and neutral" (UNSC, *Res. 929*, 1994a). In any case, the French force arrived in Rwanda in late June, after the RPF had already gained control of large parts of the country and was closing in on Kigali.

In retrospect, the refusal of leading powers, including the United States, to halt the Rwandan genocide represents a catastrophic failure of political will and leadership. A study conducted by the Carnegie Commission on Preventing Deadly Conflict, the U.S. Army, and the Institute for the Study of Diplomacy at Georgetown University concluded that timely intervention by a force of only five thousand would have saved more than half a million lives (Wheeler 2000, 225). In March of 1998, President Clinton gave a speech in Kigali, Rwanda, in which he offered an apology for the failure of the United States and the rest of the international community to stop the massacres: "The international community . . . must bear its share of responsibility for this tragedy as well. We did not act quickly enough after the killings began . . . We did not immediately call these crimes by their rightful name: genocide" (CNN 1998).

The refusal to intervene was based not on international norms but, as Kofi Annan put it, on a reluctance "to pay the human and other costs of intervention" (Welsh 2004, 36). The norm of justified humanitarian intervention was in place, and those who opposed intervention did not claim that it would violate international rules. Rather, the opponents of intervention cited practical or policy concerns: the disaster in Rwanda was a civil war; Rwanda was of no direct strategic or national interest; the public would not support a mission that might entail peacekeeper casualties. Intervention was not impermissible *per se*; it was simply unpalatable.

Darfur

Analysis of the precedents set by post-Cold War humanitarian crises provides the setting for the current crisis in the Sudan. This large African nation is no stranger to conflict—colonialism and the carving up of the "big African pie" by the British had produced an unstable ethnic mixture. The country has been in a state of civil war since the 1970s, pitting the Arab-controlled government in the north against the black African population in the south.

The current conflict began in 2003 when two rebel groups accused the government of oppressing non-Arabs in favor of Arabs. The primary rebel groups, Justice and Equality Movement (JEM) and Sudan Liberation Movement (SLM), consist of non-Arabs. In February 2003, JEM and SLM rebels attacked government installations. Following this attack, the government organized aerial bombing along with ground attacks from Arab militia, known as the *janjaweed*. Since then, *janjaweed* attacks have multiplied. The militias have killed up to 200,000 in Darfur, razed hundreds of villages, and driven over two million people into refugee camps in western Darfur and in Chad (Human Rights Watch 2006).

The Security Council has been reticent to do anything more than condemn the attacks and send investigative teams to the area. Resolution 1547 in June of 2004 was the first to hint at international action. It "declares readiness to consider establishing a United Nations peace support operation to support the implementation of a comprehensive peace agreement" (UNSC 2004a, *Res. 1547*). This resolution also reiterates the importance of maintaining the sovereignty and independence of Sudan. Resolution 1556 in July 2004 addressed the situation in stronger language, but did not recommend or authorize any military intervention by U.N. forces. It stated that the situation was "a threat to international peace and security and to stability in the region" (UNSC 2004b, *Res. 1556*), and approved of African Union initiatives to solve the conflict regionally. Further, it established an arms embargo on the *janjaweed* militia and implored member nations to send humanitarian aid.

Over the past several years, many national delegations and human rights groups have visited Sudan in order to gauge the extent of the atrocities. US Secretary of State Colin Powell visited Darfur in the summer of 2004, and in September of that same year reported to the Senate that the crisis in Darfur was genocide (Crook 2005a). President George W. Bush then addressed the Security Council on September 21, stressing the urgency of resolving the crisis. However, despite the US declaration of genocide, the United Nations has not officially applied the term to the Darfur crisis.

The U.S. declaration of genocide is interesting because of the legal responsibility it implies. Throughout the crises in Somalia, Rwanda, and Bosnia, the United States and the international community as a whole actively sought to avoid the word, due to the obligations that came with it. It would seem that US recognition of genocide in Darfur would be followed by a push for either multilateral or unilateral intervention in order to alleviate the growing crisis.

Nevertheless, the United Nations has been slow to take action under Chapter VII of the U.N. Charter. In fact, in January 2005, a UN report declared that the Darfur crisis could not be appropriately labeled as genocide arguing, "The crucial element of genocidal intent appears to be missing, at least as far as the central government authorities are concerned" (CNN 2005). Despite these findings, the report still recommended that Sudanese authorities be tried by the International Criminal Court (ICC). U.S. officials, who have opposed the ICC, proposed the creation of an ad hoc tribunal similar to the ICTR and the ICTY that would prosecute those guilty of serious breaches of human rights (Crook 2005c). The Security Council referred the Darfur situation to the Prosecutor of the ICC in Resolution 1593 in March 2005 (UNSC 2005, *Res. 1593*). Interestingly, the U.S. did not veto this referral to the ICC, the first time the United States had refrained from actively opposing the Court. Subsequent UNSC resolutions regarding Darfur have generally been weak, though in February 2006 the UNSC approved a force of 20,000 peacekeepers with a mandate of protecting civilians. However, the Sudanese government refused entry to preliminary U.N. tactical teams and declined to issue the necessary visas (CNN 2006a).

Much of the work in terms of negotiating a cease-fire has been left in the hands of the African Union. A small African Union peacekeeping force entered Sudan in 2004 and gradually grew to more than six thousand personnel (troops and police) (African Union Mission in the Sudan—AMIS, 2008). The AMIS force was too small and poorly equipped to protect the vulnerable population of Darfur. In a May 2006 breakthrough, the African Union brokered a peace deal between the government and the rebel groups. The highlight of the agreement is a cease-fire, along with steps towards power and wealth sharing among the government and rebel groups. The May 2006 agreement was originally signed only by the government and the SLM faction, and as of late 2007 the recalcitrant rebel groups had still not signed the accord (UN 2008).

In late 2006, the African Union, the Security Council, and the government of Sudan agreed on a plan by which a United Nations peacekeeping force would replace the African Union mission. Acting under Chapter VII, the Security Council in June 2007 (Resolution 1769) authorized the final stage of that plan, the creation of a U.N. mission for Darfur, UNAMID. At the end of 2007, the African Union force merged into UNAMID, which aims to reach a total deployment of some twenty thousand soldiers plus six thousand police officers and a civilian component (UN 2008).

The long inaction of the international community once again meant that humanitarian intervention came too late for hundreds of thousands of victims in Darfur. It would seem that the memory of failed peacemaking missions has had lasting effects. States were not willing to authorize U.N. intervention until the government of Sudan had agreed to a peace plan and explicitly accepted an international presence in Darfur. As in previous cycles, the debate played sovereignty norms against intervention on behalf of human rights.

Conclusion

Events in Somalia, Rwanda, Bosnia, and Darfur triggered cycles of norm development regarding humanitarian intervention, contributing to the evolution of liberal norms. Cumulatively, these cycles of change have clearly weakened, if not removed, the presumption against intervention in cases of large-scale human rights abuses. It is simply no longer possible to argue that humanitarian intervention is prohibited by international law. Where a serious crisis exists, the Security Council has been willing to expand the concept of a "threat to the peace" to encompass purely domestic human rights catastrophes. The Security Council has approved intervention by individual states (like France in Rwanda) and by multilateral organizations (including NATO in Bosnia and the African Union in Darfur).

The African Union has perhaps gone farther than any other body in claiming the right of intervention:

> The Union [claims the] right . . . to intervene in a Member State pursuant to a decision of the Assembly in respect of grave circumstances, namely war crimes, genocide and crimes against humanity. (The African Union 2000, Article 4(h))

When a willing and capable state or organization offers to lead an operation, the Security Council appears disposed to approve it. Thus, humanitarian intervention will be an option whenever mass atrocities occur.

Of course, the Security Council does not always take up the intervention option, even though it is now available. The use of force to halt gross human rights violations or genocide is still a collective action problem: states must supply the troops, the equipment, and the logistics. And states are frequently wary of taking on the risks and costs of such military action. As a result, the Security Council—as it did most obviously in Rwanda and Darfur—may stall and prevaricate until the moment for intervention has passed. The move to prosecute the perpetrators, like the ICTR for Rwanda and the referral of the Darfur situation to the ICC, may be, in part, an attempt to assuage the guilt of having failed to stop their crimes.

In addition, though humanitarian intervention is now permissible, it is not required. There is as yet no obligation on the part of the international community to intervene in humanitarian crises. The Genocide Convention and U.N. Charter have not yet been widely construed as implying such a duty. The International Commission on Intervention and State Sovereignty (ICISS) has proposed that governments recognize a "responsibility to protect," which would entail an obligation to intervene. The ICISS agenda may influence the debate in years to come to the extent that it gains support from legal scholars and "like-minded" states (Canada, the Netherlands, and others).

In future humanitarian crises, the question will no longer be whether international norms permit intervention. The question will be the practical one that has hindered international responses to atrocities in Rwanda, Bosnia, and Darfur: Are states willing to pay the costs and risk the casualties in order save the lives of people in distant lands? Declining to act may be shameful, but states have shown that where their direct interests are not at stake, they have ample capacity for accepting shame. The international right to intervene may yet develop into a duty to intervene, but that will clearly require numerous further turns through the cycle of normative change.

Chapter 11

The Emerging Right to Democracy

Alix van Sickle, with Wayne Sandholtz

Over the past fifteen years, democracy has consolidated its position as "the best form of government" (Inglehart 2003; Norris 1999). International lawyers and intergovernmental organizations (IGOs) now argue that there is an emerging right to democracy in international law (Fox and Roth 2000; Franck 1992; Reisman 2000). Indeed, in 1997 the U.N. Secretary General asserted that it is an "established norm" that "military coups against democratically elected governments by self-appointed juntas are not acceptable" (UN 1997, 7). This chapter examines how the "right to democracy" gained normative force in the 1990s.

The changes in international politics surrounding the "Third Wave of Democracy" (Huntington 1991) triggered a reexamination of such fundamental principles as sovereignty, nonintervention, and self-determination. Democratic transitions in Africa, Latin America, and Eastern and Central Europe in the 1980s and 1990s produced shifts in global public attitudes toward democracy and fueled the development of international prodemocracy norms (Inglehart 1997; Norris 1999). Whereas a country's form of government had traditionally been a purely internal matter, the international community has increasingly recognized a "right to democracy" or "democratic entitlement" (Franck 1992). Such a right challenges traditional understandings of sovereignty and related norms (nonintervention, self-determination).

International prodemocracy norms are emerging, but are far from being fully defined. As argued in Chapter 1, actors engage in disputes as they attempt to apply a general norm to a specific circumstance. The dispute cycles that we examine in this chapter demonstrate that contestation in this issue area has tended to focus on enforcement. International attempts to enforce pro-democracy norms range from diplomatic persuasion, to "democratic assistance" such as election monitoring, to economic sanctions, and finally to military intervention. Each mode of enforcement has triggered disputes about the legitimacy of international intervention into the domestic political affairs of sovereign states. The outcomes of these disputes have begun to define what the international community views as legitimate enforcement of the norm.

We begin by discussing the normative context that prevailed in the international system prior to the Third Wave of Democracy. We then turn to a discussion of the key events and disputes that drove the idea a "right to democracy" to the forefront of international normative debates. We focus on three cycles of norm change, arising out of the 1991 coup in Haiti, the 1992 "self-coup" in Peru, and the 1997 West African intervention in Sierra Leone.[1] Figure 11.1 provides a schematic view of these cycles. We explore the arguments offered in these disputes. Finally, we examine the extent to which the outcomes of these disputes have shaped how the international community responds to situations in which a democratic government is overthrown or threatened.

Normative Context

Prior to the 1990s, the idea of a "right to democracy" did not figure prominently in international discourse (Fox and Roth 2000). Although there

---

[1] Recent disputes over the right to democracy indicate that the development of this norm may have reached a plateau or declined since 2001. Recent US foreign policy has clearly exacerbated the concern that the idea of a universal "right to democracy" can be abused by states to justify self-interested and illegal violations of the principle of sovereignty (see Hawkins and Shaw 2005).

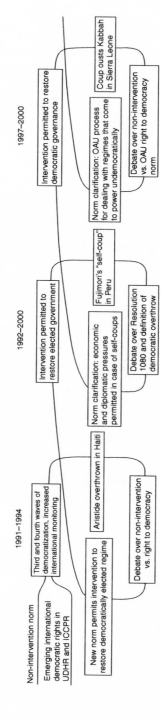

Figure 11.1 Right to democracy norm cycles.

were some critical developments in the evolution of this norm before the 1990s—particularly the 1948 Universal Declaration of Human Rights (UDHR) and the 1966 International Covenant on Civil and Political Rights (ICCPR)—pro-democracy international norms really only emerged after the Cold War (Hawkins and Shaw 2005). We review the period before the 1948 Universal Declaration of Human Rights and then examine the introduction of universal participatory rights in the post-WWII period. Though they remained, for many years, mainly hortatory in nature, the declarations and treaties immediately following WWII require particular attention as they provide the foundation and legal framework for the disputes over the right to democracy that were to come in the 1990s (Crawford 2000).

The modern (post-Westphalia) idea of sovereignty holds that "the final authority over most if not all social, economic, and political matters should rest with those in effective control of the territorial units that make up the system" (Murphy 1996, 82). That is, sovereignty implied that each state possessed exclusive internal jurisdiction. Henry Wheaton, writing in the mid-1800s, expressed the dominant view of that period: "Every state, as a distinct moral being, independent of every other, may freely exercise all its sovereign rights in any manner not inconsistent with the equal rights of other states. Among these is that of establishing, altering, or abolishing its own municipal constitution of government" (1863, 132). Wheaton further asserted that "the perfect independence of every sovereign State in respect to its political institutions, extends to the choice of the supreme magistrate and other rulers, as well as the form of government itself" (135). That is, no matter how selected, the government in power was to be recognized as the embodiment of the sovereign rights of the state (Fox 2000, 51). Modern international law has, generally affirmed the rule that domestic political institutions are not within the reach of international law (Taft 1924).

The Post WWII Framework: A Changing Conception of Sovereignty?

The 1948 Universal Declaration of Human Rights (UDHR) began to modify the traditional formulation of state sovereignty (Sohn 1982). The widespread acceptance of a set of universal human rights, in the UDHR and subsequent conventions, was a necessary precursor to the principle that a state's external legitimacy could be predicated in part on how its government interacted with its own citizens. International lawyers have argued that Article 21 of the UDHR, which states that "the will of the people shall be the basis of authority of government," reflects a shift in the location of sovereignty, replacing the "sovereignty of the sovereign [with] the sovereignty of the people" (Reisman 1990). The international recognition of citizens as the basis for government authority represents an important marker for the development of democracy norms.

In addition to challenging the traditional understanding of State sovereignty, the rights promulgated in the UDHR and later reinforced by International Covenant on Civil and Political Rights (ICCPR) indicate that a set of liberal democratic principles—namely, freedom of association, freedom of opinion and expression, the right to participate in government, equal protection under the law, and protection against arbitrary arrest—were widely shared values across the globe. The UDHR and the ICCPR thus signaled that, for a large number of states, the domestic political arrangements of states were matters of legitimate international concern.[2]

The UDHR, the ICCPR, and their regional counterparts (like the European Convention on Human Rights and the American Convention on Human Rights) laid the foundations for the later development of a right to democracy. One key principle was the definition of democracy in terms of free and fair elections. Article 25 of the ICCPR[3] states that all citizens have the right to "take part in the conduct of public affairs, directly or through freely chosen representatives" and "to vote and be elected at genuine periodic elections which shall be by universal and equal suffrage and shall be held by secret ballot, guaranteeing the free expression of the will of the electors." The 1952 First Protocol to the Convention for the Protection of Human Rights and Fundamental Freedoms (also known as the European Convention on Human Rights) also affirmed the right to participate in free elections, declaring in Article 3, "The High Contracting Parties undertake to hold free elections at reasonable intervals by secret ballot, under conditions that ensure the free expression of opinion of the people in the choice of the legislature" (*Protocol to the Convention for the Protection of Human Rights and Fundamental Freedoms* 1952). The language

---

[2] There were 48 signatories to the ICCPR in 1976. As of April 2008, there are 70 signatories and 161 parties to the ICCPR (Office of the United Nations High Commissioner for Human Rights 2008).

[3] "Every citizen shall have the right and the opportunity, without any of the distinctions mentioned in article 2 and without unreasonable restrictions: (a) To take part in the conduct of public affairs, directly or through freely chosen representatives; (b) To vote and to be elected at genuine periodic elections which shall be by universal and equal suffrage and shall be held by secret ballot, guaranteeing the free expression of the will of the electors; (c) To have access, on general terms of equality, to public service in his country" (United Nations General Assembly 1966).

of the 1969 American Convention on Human Rights (ACHR) is almost identical to that of the ICCPR in its affirmation of participatory rights. Article 23 of the ACHR states that "every citizen shall enjoy" the right "to vote and to be elected in genuine periodic elections, which shall be by universal and equal suffrage and by secret ballot that guarantees the free expression of the will of the voters" (OAS 1969, Article 13).

The focus on free and fair elections for ascertaining the "will of the people" was further enshrined by treaties and resolutions concerning decolonization. Decolonization spurred an international debate on how to ascertain the will of the people living in the many new states entering the international system in the post-War period (Franck 1992). In 1953 a General Assembly resolution specified what was required for new states to lay claim to self-determination. The resolution stated that new states must have "informed and democratic processes" and make provisions for "universal and equal suffrage, and free periodic elections, characterized by an absence of undue influence and coercion of the voter or of the imposition of disabilities on particular political parties" (UNGA 1953). The clear trend was to define democracy primarily by the presence of elections.

The post-WWII framework also provided a set of principles with which the international community could justify its concern with the internal domestic political affairs and institutions of sovereign states. The early justifications for international involvement in internal political questions depicted democracy as necessary to the attainment of some other, well established, international goal. In particular, the key justification was that the spread of democratic government was necessary for the promotion and maintenance of international peace and security.

The "democratic peace" justification also appears in a number of post-War inter-governmental regional treaties and conventions. The Preamble to the 1950 Charter for the Organization of American States (OAS) states, for example, that "representative democracy is an indispensable condition of the stability, peace and development of the region" (*Charter of the Organization of American States* 1950). The European Convention on Human Rights refers to "Fundamental Freedoms which are the foundation of justice and peace in the world and are best maintained on the one hand by an effective political democracy" (Council of Europe 1950, Preamble). Thus, in addition to establishing a procedural definition of democracy, the post-War treaties also introduced one of the central justifications for an international "right to democracy," namely, that it secures international peace.

Another common justification for international involvement in the domestic political affairs of states was that democracy and human rights are intricately connected. States and international organizations argued, and continue to argue, that democratic governance is necessary for the full realization of human rights. The human rights justification for international attention to spreading democracy would become widely referenced in international resolutions and declarations after the Cold War.

The post-WWII framework, though clearly setting important precedents for the later development of a right to democracy, did not fully specify what a "free and fair election" required. Nor did this early framework specify what the international response would be toward states whose democratic institutions were either absent, significantly compromised, or entirely dissolved. It was not until the 1990s that international agreements and state practices began to establish more clearly the requirement for a free and fair election as well as a set of mechanisms for implementing democracy norms and for sanctioning a failure to comply with those norms.

Normative Tensions

The idea that the domestic political arrangements of states could be a proper subject of international concern clashed with the traditional conception of sovereignty, as discussed above. But the emerging right to democracy was also in tension with related international norms. For instance, sovereignty has traditionally been connected to a nonintervention norm. Indeed, the nonintervention rule has long been seen as essential to international order (Vincent 1984, chap. 9). The United Nations Charter prohibits that organization (and, by extension, states) from intervening "in matters which are essentially within the domestic jurisdiction of any state" (Article 2(7)).[4] A series of General Assembly resolutions expressed the international community's consensus on nonintervention.[5] Foreign concern with a state's political system could be condemned as intervention.

---

[4] Regional counterparts to the U.N. Charter also reaffirm the principle of nonintervention in internal domestic affairs. The OAS Charter states, "[n]o State or group of states has the right to intervene, directly or indirectly, for any reason whatever, in the internal or external affairs of any other State" (OAS 1948, Article 19).

[5] These included the 1950 Peace Through Deeds Resolution, the 1957 Declaration Concerning the Peaceful Coexistence of States, the 1965 Declaration on the Inadmissibility of Intervention in Domestic Affairs of States and Protection of their Independence and Sovereignty, and the 1970 Declaration on Principles of International Law Concerning Friendly Relations.

In addition to pushing the boundaries of sovereignty and noninter-vention, "the right to democracy" also has important implications for the principle of self-determination. Article 1 of the ICCPR states that "all peo-ples have the right to self-determination. By virtue of that right they freely determine their political status and freely pursue economic, social, and cultural development" (UNGA 1966, Art. 1). A sovereignty-oriented inter-pretation of the right to self-determination would enshrine the right of a population to choose nondemocratic forms of government. In contrast, the norm of democratic governance suggests that self-determination can only be exercised via democratic institutions that give citizens effec-tive political voice. Indeed, Thomas Franck has argued that the right to democracy stems from the principle of self-determination (1992).

Finally, the notion that international actors can, in some circum-stances, intervene militarily in support of democratic governance also challenges historic international rules on the use of force. The United Nations Charter requires states to "refrain in their international relations from the threat or use of force" (Art. 2(4)). The Charter permits the use of force only for self-defense (Art. 51) or when authorized by the Security Council to maintain international peace and security (Art. 39). To the extent that the Security Council is prepared to authorize pro-democracy interventions, in the absence of a genuine threat to international peace and security, it is further modifying traditional rules.

The Emergence of Pro-democracy Norms

The end of the Cold War, and the accompanying fall of numerous dicta-torships across Latin America, Eastern Europe, and Africa, witnessed a mounting interest in establishing international norms for the promotion and maintenance of democratic government. Moreover, the push toward greater international cooperation aimed at supporting democratic gover-nance came not only from elites, but also from civil society groups that had endured years of repressive government and were anxious to establish mechanisms for ensuring the consolidation of their new democracies. Chapter 1 argues that many major developments in international rules come after a triggering event, sometimes an international catastrophe or global conflict.[6] Contested actions provoke debates about what international rules

---

[6] See also Bederman (2001), who declares that "defining moments for international law of the last three and a half centuries have come only after periods of intense global conflict" (2–3).

require, or how they should be modified to prevent subsequent disasters. The toppling of Cold War dictatorships was such a triggering event. The Chilean delegate to the signing of the 1992 Washington Protocol to the OAS Charter stated, "Look, I am a part of an entire generation that came into adulthood under a military regime. . . . We have established democracies out of our own traumatic experiences. We are tired of internal war. So you've got to try to set up some kind of mechanism to protect these democracies" (NYT June 9, 1991, quoted in Hawkins and Joachim 2003). This statement expressed a feeling shared by many people living in both older and newer democracies who, with the end of the Cold War, felt that international institutions were needed to help new democracies consolidate and avoid reversions to authoritarianism.

Election Monitoring

During the wave of post-Cold War democratization, professional election monitoring emerged as a key mechanism for diffusing pro-democracy norms. In addition, international validation, or rejection, of election outcomes offers a tool for promoting compliance with emerging international norms regarding electoral rights. At its forty-fifth session in 1990, the U.N. General Assembly adopted a nonbinding resolution aimed at "Enhancing the Effectiveness of the Principle of Periodic and Genuine Elections." This resolution states that "determining the will of the people requires an electoral process that provides equal opportunity for all citizens to become candidates and put forward their political views" (UNGA 1990). The following General Assembly meeting gave electoral assistance greater international legal stature when it adopted Resolution 46/137. This resolution "established a procedure for authorizing the monitoring of national elections and endorsed the Secretary General's decision to create an office, headed by a senior official to 'act as focal point . . . in order to ensure consistency in the handling of requests of member states organizing elections'" (Franck 1992, 65).

Election monitoring has become an increasingly important method for spreading democracy norms. Not only the UN but states and international nongovernmental organizations and domestic monitoring organizations have increasingly devoted resources to monitoring elections (Carothers 1999; Lean 2004). Nongovernmental organizations aimed at promoting free and fair electoral process have proliferated in recent years. The Carter Center, the National Endowment for Democracy, the National Democratic Institute, the International Republican Institute, the

International Institute for Democracy and Electoral Assistance, are just a few of the many U.S.-based nongovernmental organizations that are involved in monitoring elections. Similar groups exist in other countries.

The experience of Latin America over the past two decades illustrates the spread of election monitoring:

> In the mid-1980s (1982–1988), when the contemporary prac-
> tice of democracy assistance was just beginning to develop,
> just 25% of elections in the region were monitored. By the
> end of the following decade (1996–2002) fully 90% of all elec-
> tions held in the region were monitored. With the single
> exception of Cuba, every country in the region had at least
> one national election monitored over the twenty year period
> between 1982–2002. The vast majority of countries have had
> monitors present during three of more national elections.
> (Lean 2004, 230)

This tremendous increase in the use of election monitoring is a signal that states in this region have come to accept that internal legitimacy is at least partially dependent on external validation and that external legitimacy depends in part on electoral processes that meet international standards.

The proliferation of election monitoring is not unique to Latin America. The Organization for Security and Cooperation in Europe (OSCE) has monitored numerous elections across Europe, including recent elections in Albania, Kyrgyzstan, the Yugoslav Republic of Macedonia, and Moldova. The OSCE also monitored the US 2004 presidential election (de Sola 2004; Murphy 2004). The European Union also has a division devoted to election observation and in 2006 it monitored elections in the West Bank and the Gaza Strip, Afghanistan, Lebanon, Ethiopia, and Guinea Bissau.

The widespread willingness of states to accept, or even seek out, external election monitoring is additional evidence of the spread of pro-democracy norms in the international community. A number of studies have found that democratic values are shared by people in all parts of the globe (Inglehart 2003; Norris 1999). Welcoming foreign observers is a way for governments to gain validation and legitimacy from both the international community and their own citizens. It is also evidence of widespread recognition that the international community has a legitimate role in promoting democracy norms.

International Institutions

In addition to election monitoring organizations, there are other types of international democracy assistance programs and resolutions that have sought to further "legalize" and spread democracy norms. For example, actions taken by U.N. Credentials Committee have arguably contributed to the development of international democracy norms. In the 1990s, the U.N. Credentials Committee chose, in a number of cases, to accredit the democratically elected representatives of governments that did not exercise effective control over their territory. In the cases of Haiti, Sierra Leone, Cambodia, Liberia, and Afghanistan, the United Nations accredited the representatives that had been democratically elected rather than the *de facto* governments. This practice departed from the long held international norm that the United Nations would accredit those having effective control over a territory. Matthew Griffin argues that although the General Assembly is far from adopting a rule that would bar non-democracies from United Nations participation, the Credentials Committee has, at least selectively, begun to take democracy into account when it considers who it will accredit (2000).

International declarations and resolutions in the 1990s also affirmed the international recognition of democracy norms. The 1993 Vienna Declaration is an important development. The Vienna Declaration held human rights and democracy to be inseparable (UNGA 1993). The linking of democracy and human rights has become a common approach to justifying international democracy promotion and intervention. Democracy is seen as the institutional arrangement that best allows for the full realization of human rights. UNESCO has also adopted resolutions that affirm international democracy norms and, in particular, cite a connection between democracy and the promotion of human rights (UNESCO 1990).

In 1999, the UN Commission on Human Rights adopted a resolution called the "Promotion of the Right to Democracy." The resolution passed with 51 in favor and none against, with Cuba and China abstaining (Dennis 2001).

In 2000, the Commission adopted another resolution on promoting and consolidating democracy. The 2000 resolution passed with 45 in favor, none against, and 8 abstentions (Bhutan, China, Congo, Cuba, Pakistan, Qatar, Rwanda, and Sudan). The misgiving of the abstaining states was that the resolution promoted a single model of democracy that may not fit all states (2001). Clearly, however, there is a broad consensus among states on a specific set of institutions that define democracy.

International democracy norms have been further enshrined with the establishment of the "Council of the Community of Democracies." In 2000, representatives from more than one hundred countries met in Warsaw, Poland, to establish the Community of Democracies, whose mission would be to "work together to promote and strengthen democracy, recognizing that we are at differing stages in our democratic development." The participating states declared, "We will cooperate to consolidate and strengthen democratic institutions, with due respect for sovereignty and the principle of noninterference in internal affairs. Our goal is to support adherence to common democratic values and standards." The Warsaw Resolution, which was adopted at this meeting, recognizes the "universality of democratic values" and pledges to "uphold core democratic principles and practices" including:

> regular, free and fair elections with universal and equal suffrage, open to multiple parties, conducted by secret ballot, monitored by independent electoral authorities, and free of fraud and intimidation. The right of every person to equal access to public service and to take part in the conduct of public affairs, directly or through freely chosen representatives. . . . (Community of Democracies 2000)

Adherence to these rights is required for membership in the Community of Democracies. The Council for the Community of Democracies has met twice since Warsaw. It met in 2002 in Seoul and in 2005 in Santiago. One of the key objectives of the Community of Democracies has been to establish a UN Democracy Caucus. The first meeting of the UN Democracy Caucus occurred in September 2004. The idea of the caucus is to better communicate and coordinate democracy promotion efforts among the participating governments and also with NGOs (Council for a Community of Democracies 2004).

The U.N. Millennium Declaration also recognizes democracy as an international goal and states that democracy best allows for the realization of other internationally recognized universal human rights. The Millennium Declaration states, "Men and women have the right to live their lives and raise their children in dignity, free from hunger and from the fear of violence, oppression or injustice. Democratic and participatory governance based on the will of the people best assures these rights" (UN 2000).

Regional Democracy Norms

Within the broad framework of international democracy norms, regions vary. In Europe and the Americas, the right to democracy is arguably more developed than it is at the level of the United Nations. In the following sections, we examine the regional democracy norms.

Europe

Europe has perhaps the strongest regional democracy norms (Hawkins and Joachim 2003). The main tool for promoting and solidifying democratic governance in Europe has been the adherence to political criteria for membership in the region's important organizations, in particular, the Council of Europe and the European Union. The Council of Europe (COE), founded in 1949, has as its primary purpose the strengthening and safeguarding of Europe's shared values of "individual freedom, political liberty and the rule of law, principles which form the basis of all genuine democracy" (Council of Europe 1949, Preamble). Countries that are "able and willing" to "accept the principles of the rule of law and of the enjoyment by all persons within [their] jurisdiction of human rights and fundamental freedoms" may be invited to join the organization (Council of Europe 1949, Articles 3, 4). The COE is home to the world's best developed supranational human rights system, based on the European Convention for the Protection of Human Rights and Fundamental Freedoms (often referred to as the European Convention for Human Rights). Individuals residing within states that are party to the Convention may file complaints at the European Court of Human Rights (ECHR) for violation of their Convention rights. The Court's decisions are binding, and it routinely rules against national governments.

With the wave of democratization that swept through Central and Eastern Europe after 1989, the Council of Europe assumed a central role in assisting the transition countries to establish and consolidate democratic institutions and human rights. During the 1990s, seventeen countries from Central and Eastern Europe joined the Council. At the COE summit in May 2005, the heads of state agreed on a declaration laying out the organization's principal tasks for the future. First among these was "promoting the common fundamental values of human rights, the rule of law and democracy" (Council of Europe 2005).

The European Union (EU) also actively reinforces democracy norms. From the outset, the presence of functioning democratic institutions has been a prerequisite for membership in the EU. Indeed, the "southern expansion" of the EU could not take place until authoritarian regimes in Greece, Portugal, and Spain had left the scene and democratic institutions had taken their place.[7] The recent round of EU enlargement, which concluded in 2004 and added ten new members to the existing fifteen, made democracy an explicit condition for accession. The 1993 Copenhagen criteria, which established the conditions that applicant states would have to meet before they could be considered as members, included requirements for democratic governance. The European Commission in 1997 published its *Agenda 2000* report—a more detailed plan for accession—which included a section on "Political Criteria." The Political Criteria set out numerous specific standards for democratic institutions, laws, and practices. Furthermore, the Commission provided an assessment of conditions in each of the ten applicant countries, which amounted to customized lists of requirements for reforms. The EU heads of state endorsed the Commission plan, and negotiations with the applicant states began in 1998. As part of the negotiation process, the Commission issued annual reports on the progress of each applicant. The Political Criteria section of each report had two subsections, one on "Democracy and the rule of law" and another on "Human rights and the protection of minorities."[8] The ten countries that joined the EU in 2004 were judged to have met the EU's democracy standards.

In addition, the EU in 2000 adopted a Charter of Fundamental Rights. The Charter declares that "the Union is founded on the indivisible, universal values of human dignity, freedom, equality and solidarity; it is based on the principles of democracy and the rule of law" (European Union 2000, Preamble). The Charter guarantees to every EU citizen freedom of expression, association, and assembly, and the right to vote and stand for election (Articles 11, 12, 39, 40). The Charter is not legally binding. The EU Constitution, agreed by the heads of state at Rome in June 2004, incorporates the Charter on Fundamental Rights. However, the future of the EU Constitution is in doubt, having failed in ratification referenda in France and the Netherlands.

The EU has also made efforts to establish a common approach to aiding new and developing democracies. The "Resolution of the council and of the member states meeting in the council on human rights, democracy

---

[7] Greece joined the EU in 1981, Spain and Portugal in 1986.
[8] See, e.g., Commission of the European Communities 2002a, 2002b, 2002c.

and development" represents one of these efforts. The Resolution states, "The Council shares the analysis contained in the Commission's communication of 25 March 1991 and acknowledges that human rights have a universal nature and it is the duty of all States to promote them. At the same time, human rights and democracy form part of a larger set of requirements in order to achieve balanced and sustainable development" (European Union 1991). A subsequent Council Regulation specifies the kinds of democratic activities that the EU will support and finance in "third countries" (European Union 1999).

Latin America

The idea of liberal democracy has been a central part of the political ideology of the Americas since the French and American Revolutions and the Wars for Independence in Latin America in the 1800s. Though North America has experienced more continuous, stable democratic rule over the years, all Latin American countries have, throughout their history, written democratic constitutions and constructed some form of democratic institutions. For a number of reasons, including legacies of colonial exploitation, corrupt governments, civil wars, and U.S. intervention in the region, it has been more difficult to consolidate and deepen democratic institutions in Latin America. Nevertheless, the idea and the promise of democracy have proven to be an enduring force that have now saturated the rhetoric of civil society groups, political parties across the spectrum, and governments throughout the Hemisphere.

One of the first declarations of an inter-American commitment to democracy emerged out of the 1907 Conference of Washington. The conference produced the General Treaty of Peace and Friendship, which "agreed to withhold recognition of any Central American government that was the product of rebellion rather than free elections" (Munoz 1995, 3). In 1936, the Inter-American Conference on the Consolidation of Peace announced the "existence of democracy as a common cause in America," indicating that a principled commitment to the idea of democracy was not only broadly shared throughout the Americas, but also that all countries in the Americas had an interest, or "common cause," in the spread and development of democracy across the region. The norm was beginning to be seen as an international obligation of states, rather than simply a moral ideal.

In 1945, the idea that countries should engage in collective action to "defend democracy" was introduced by Uruguay's foreign minister in a note to the American governments. The note "proposed multilateral action to defend democracy and human rights" (Munoz 1995). The notion that states had an interest in the democratic development of the region as a whole was affirmed in a resolution on "Preservation and Defense of Democracy" (1995). At the 1948 Bogota Conference (at which the OAS Charter was created along with the American Declaration of Human Rights) the norm of democratic governance began to take on greater specificity and legal weight. In particular, the Charter states that one of the primary goals of the OAS is to "promote and consolidate representative democracy, with due respect for the principle of non-intervention" (Organization of American States 1948).

The military dictatorships in Latin America in the 1960s, 1970s, and 1980s stunted the development of a right to democracy in the Americas. U.S. interventions in the region also undermined the development of democracy in the region (Smith 2003). U.S. interventions in Latin America in fact helped to overthrow democratically elected leaders and/or maintain the power of the military regimes (Guatemala, 1954; Chile, 1973; Nicaragua, 1984). However, with the end of the Cold War, the interest in establishing a stronger international legal framework for upholding democracies became a truly regional interest.

Two important regional agreements were products of the "Third Wave" of democracy: OAS Resolution 1080 and the Washington Protocol. Resolution 1080, adopted in 1991 in Santiago, states that "the solidarity of the American states and the high aims which are sought through it require the political organization of those states on the basis of the effective exercise of representative democracy." More importantly, the resolution specifies that if there has been a disruption to democracy in a member state, the OAS is to convene immediately to decide what action should be taken. Action can range from suspension from the OAS to the imposition of economic sanctions to the use of force (which has to be authorized by the U.N. Security Council) (Organization of American States 1991). The United Nations itself has no such automatic response to a "disruption to democracy" (Donoho 1996). The "Washington Protocol" (1992) approved an amendment to the OAS Charter, which allows for the suspension of a member state whose government has seized power by force. The suspension requires a two-thirds vote of OAS member states (Organization of American States 1992).

Africa

The 1990s also brought attempts to define and defend democracy norms in Africa. Sovereignty and nonintervention have been core principles of the Organization of African Unity (OAU) since its inception, and these two norms continue to play a dominant role in the discussion over regional democracy norms. The normative weight of sovereignty and nonintervention are evident in the 1963 OAU Charter. Claphan (1996) says of the 1963 OAU Charter that it is "the most clear-cut possible victory of juridical sovereignty, over any pretensions of supranational continental union." Unlike in the Inter-American system, the constituting charter of the OAU does not mention democracy nor does it guarantee participatory rights to individuals within states. The OAU was reconstituted as the African Union in 2002; sovereignty and nonintervention clearly remain its core principles. However, these principles are undergoing some reassessment in the context of global democracy norms.

The 1981 African Charter on Human and Peoples' Rights declared certain participatory rights. Article 13 does not mention democracy specifically, but it does state that "every citizen shall have the right to participate freely in the government of his country" (African Charter on Human and Peoples' Rights 1981). State practice, of course, has frequently been at odds with this principle. The 1989 OAU Declaration on South Africa also pronounced a regional commitment to participatory rights. The Declaration states, "We believe that all men and women have the right and duty to participate in the government of their countries, as equal members of society. No individual or group of individuals has the right to rule without the public consent of the rest of society" (Organization of African Unity 1989). Thus the 1981 Charter and the 1989 Declaration professed a regionwide value in free and equal political participation. Still, these two regional agreements are neither highly specific nor obligatory. And unlike the Inter-American system and the European system, the African Union does not require countries to be democratic in order to join.

Norm Dispute Cycles

Over the last fifteen years, various events have triggered disputes, which have in turn modified international pro-democracy norms. In the following sections we examine key disputes and their effects on the implementation of democracy norms. Each episode displays the cycle pattern proposed in Chapter 1.

Intervention in Haiti

Action

Reverend Jean-Bertrand Aristide won election as president of Haiti in 1990; international observers deemed the election free and fair. It was the first democratic election in Haiti after many years of rule under the repressive Duvalier family dynasty. Unfortunately, the celebration was short lived. A military coup ousted Aristide from office in 1991 and launched a repressive campaign to root out Aristide supporters. The coup, occurring shortly after the signing of OAS Resolution 1080, provided a crucial test case for the organization's mechanism for responding to an interruption of democracy.

Dispute

The OAS recognized the coup as a critical test and members promptly convened to address the Haitian crisis. The OAS foreign ministers met and adopted "Support for the Democratic Government of Haiti," a resolution that condemned the coup and recognized "the representatives designated by the constitutional Government of President Jean-Bertrand Aristide as the only legitimate representatives of the Government of Haiti to the organs, agencies, and entities of the Inter-American system" (Inter-American Commission on Human Rights 1991). The resolution called for the immediate restoration of Aristide's government and asked that countries suspend trade and diplomatic relations with the military regime in Haiti until such restoration occurred.

The coup in Haiti also went immediately before the UN Security Council. However, a number of countries, including China, Romania, and India, argued that there should be no formal meeting on the situation in Haiti, as it was a domestic matter. Shortly thereafter, Aristide addressed the Security Council and formally asked for assistance. Nevertheless, a majority of the Council opposed action for what they saw as an internal political question. Instead, the Security Council issued a statement condemning the coup and supporting OAS activities (Donoho 1996).

The OAS economic sanctions and diplomatic isolation had very little impact on the military regime. One of the reasons the sanctions failed to generate any kind of response was that the United States bowed to domestic business lobbies and selectively lifted sanctions for certain goods

(Swindells 1997). Nevertheless, the OAS continued to lobby the United Nations to take action on the situation. In 1992, OAS requests for U.N. action led to the appointment of Dante Caputo as the U.N. special envoy to Haiti. This began a series of negotiations between the UN and the de facto Haitian government.

Caputo was able to negotiate a human rights mission to monitor the situation in Haiti. The Haitian military government, however, reneged on its end of the bargain and placed a number of restrictions on the human rights observers, significantly limiting their freedom of movement. This breach of the agreement led the United States, France, and Venezuela to propose that the U.N. impose mandatory economic sanctions on Haiti, which became the next major step in the Haitian intervention (UNSC 1993b). The sanctions were ultimately justified by citing the Haitian situation as a "threat to international peace and security" (Resolution 841). The Security Council cited the following as reasons for its action: the dislocation of Haitians due to economic and political persecution, which was a source of instability for neighboring countries (understood as the U.S.); an escalating humanitarian crisis; and the continued intransigence of the military government with regard to the restoration of constitutional government (Res. 841). Resolution 841 determined that "in these exceptional and unique circumstances, the continuation threatens international peace and security in the region." The resolution also, under Chapter VII authority, accepted the recommendations of the OAS to impose an extensive and mandatory trade embargo on Haiti. The embargo brought the Haitian military to the bargaining table almost immediately (Morrell 1995).

The ensuing negotiations produced the "Governor's Island Agreement." The agreement included the following compromise:

> Aristide would appoint a prime minister; that trade sanctions would be lifted after the Prime Minister's appointment, but *before* President Aristide returned to Haiti; that multinational forces would train the Haitian army and create new political force; that the coup leader would take early retirement; and that the military leaders would be granted amnesty for crimes committed while in office. (Koh 1994)

The agreement was signed by the Haitian military at Governor's Island, but was unfortunately later ignored. In October of 1993, the Council reimposed sanctions on Haiti. In addition, the Security Council ordered a full naval blockade and the United States imposed travel sanctions and froze assets (Donoho 1996).

Arguments

When the economic embargo failed to restore the constitutional government of Haiti, the Security Council in July 1994 adopted Resolution 940, authorizing military force to restore Aristide to power. Resolution 940 affirmed that the goal of the international community was the restoration of democracy in Haiti and "the prompt return of the legitimately elected president . . . within the framework of the Governors Island Agreement" (UNSC 1994b). The justifications offered in the resolution reveal the normative basis for intervention, within the limits set by the need for consensus within the Security Council. There were three main justifications for intervention: (1) maintaining international peace and security, (2) halting a humanitarian crisis, and (3) restoring a constitutional government.

With regard to the first justification, one possible implication was that democracy itself promotes peace and stability. Indeed, the Preamble to the OAS Charter declares that "representative democracy is an indispensable condition for the stability, peace and development of the region" (Organization of American States 1948). A similar notion had been expressed at the United Nations. Secretary General Boutros-Ghali asserted in 1993, "Democratization is the thread which runs through all the work of the Organization. Within nations as much as within the family of nations, democracy should underpin the structures of international peace and security. . . . Governments which are responsive and accountable are likely to be stable and to promote peace" (UN Chronicle 1993). Still, Resolution 940 does not rely explicitly on this argument.

An alternative interpretation would view the Haitian refugee crisis as the main danger to international peace and security. Refugee crises can sometimes lead to international or regional instability (as they did in Uganda and the Democratic Republic of the Congo following the 1994 genocide in Rwanda). But the flow of refugees from Haiti, though troubling, did not trigger instability in surrounding countries. The Haitian refugee crisis was a thorny political issue for the George H. W. Bush and Clinton administrations, but it was not a threat to regional stability (Koh 1994). As Tesón concludes, "No one can seriously argue that the Haitian situation posed a threat to international peace and security in the region" (1996, 359).

A second justification suggested by Resolution 940 was that the grave humanitarian situation in Haiti made external intervention legitimate.

Humanitarian crisis is increasingly becoming an accepted justification for international interventions (see Chapter 10 in this volume; Murphy 1996; Sandholtz 2002; Tesón 1997). Substantial human rights violations committed by the military government in Haiti were documented by a human rights observation mission. Still, the scale of human rights abuses certainly did not approach those occurring in Somalia or Bosnia. Indeed, the human rights abuses themselves probably did not trigger intervention. However, the proximity of the human rights abuses to the United States, and the resulting refugee flows, may explain the strong support of the United States for intervention. The United States had an interest in regional order and in halting the refugee influx that was becoming a domestic political problem.

Finally, in addition to these justifications for intervention, Resolution 940 made explicit reference to the restoration of a democratically elected government. The preamble to the resolution takes note of a July 1994 letter "from the legitimately elected President of Haiti." It then directly reaffirms "that the goal of the international community remains the restoration of democracy in Haiti and the return of the democratically elected President, Jean-Bertrand Aristide" (UNSC 1994). Haiti was the first case in which the Security Council asserted the restoration of a democratically elected government as a basis for military intervention.

Norm change

The Haiti intervention may therefore signal a fundamental shift in the understanding of sovereignty. Michael Reisman notes that "sovereignty can be violated as effectively and ruthlessly by an indigenous as by an outside force, in much the same way that the wealth and natural resources of a country can be spoiled as thoroughly and efficiently by a native as by a foreigner" (2000, 250). An intervention to restore democracy, in this perspective, does not violate but rather upholds (popular) sovereignty. In addition, the Haiti case may indicate a continuing shift in criteria for recognition. International law in recent decades has held that international recognition of a state depends on "objective" criteria, specifically, the presence of a government with effective control over a territory and population. Resolution 940 implies that it may not be enough for a government to be in effective control. The Haiti case may portend an emergent norm by which the international community can withhold recognition from a government that gains power through antidemocratic means. Even then, Resolution 940 does not provide a precedent for intervention in countries where no previously established democratic government existed. In other words, the Security Council was prepared to authorize intervention to restore a democratic government, but that by no means implies that the Council would authorize intervention to create a democratic government where it did not previously exist. Furthermore, the Haiti precedent does not obligate the Security Council to intervene in similar cases. It does make it impossible to argue, in future instances, that pro-democracy interventions are absolutely impermissible.[9]

Though recent events suggest a tempering of the initial enthusiasm that characterized the early right to democracy literature (Franck 1992), we should nevertheless recognize that the widespread sense within the international community that the 1994 intervention in Haiti was legitimate indicated that a norm of democratic governance did carry weight.

Responses to Fujimori's Autogolpe

Action

The Washington Protocol had established that the OAS membership of a State "whose democratically constituted government has been overthrown by force may be suspended" (Organization of American States 1992). In the case of Peru, however, the military did not overthrow the president. Rather, in April 1992, President Alberto Fujimori, with the backing of the military, dissolved the Peruvian congress, purged the courts, and suspended constitutional protections of civil liberties. The government censored the news media and some journalists and opposition leaders were arrested (Schnably 1994). Although there was some protest by the opposition, there are reports that 80 percent of the public was in favor of the "self-coup" (Cameron 1994).[10]

Fujimori's *autogolpe* therefore gave rise to a regional discussion about how to interpret the phrase in OAS Resolution 1080 that refers to a "sudden or irregular interruption of the democratic political institutional process" (Organization of American States 1991). The international response to Fujimori's coup further clarified the boundaries of international norms on the "right to democracy."

---

[9] The 2004 departure of Aristide from Haiti, with at least tacit U.S. approval, demonstrates the difficulty of postintervention consolidation of democracy. In fact, Aristide himself was widely thought to have compromised human rights and undermined democracy in Haiti.

[10] There was widespread belief that the courts and the congress were corrupt. In addition, Sendero Luminoso and drug trafficking were increasing threats to public safety. Fujimori argued that his self-coup was aimed at cleaning up the courts and congress and combating Sendero Luminoso (Schnably 2000).

Arguments

The international response to the *autogolpe* demonstrated that the OAS was prepared to take some action, albeit limited, against a leader whose self-coup was perceived as a setback for democratic development in the region. Invoking Resolution 1080, the OAS Foreign Ministers convened a week after the coup and condemned Fujimori's actions. The ministers demanded that Peru show progress by the next month toward the restoration of democracy (Schnably 2000). The meeting sent a signal to Fujimori that his actions had overstepped regional democracy norms. And although the OAS did not adopt economic sanctions against Peru, the United States did halt aid to Peru and opposed further lending by the IMF until Fujimori took steps to restore democracy (Lean 2004; Palmer 1996; Schnably 2000).

The combination of the economic sanctions imposed by the United States and the IMF and the regional disapproval by the OAS forced Fujimori to promise to hold new elections for a new Constituent Congress that would serve until the next scheduled election, in 1995. Although democracy was far from restored, this pledge by Fujimori satisfied the OAS and the US and sanctions were lifted (Lean 2004). Fujimori decided to hold the elections early and on November 22, 1992, Peruvians voted for a new Democratic Constituent Congress. The OAS monitored the election of the new congress and found it to be "generally satisfactory." The fact that Fujimori responded to international pressure to restore democracy is cited by some as an example of the strengthening of democratic norms in the Americas (Franck 1992). However, others find serious flaws with the OAS handling of the self-coup. Given that Fujimori shut down congress and the courts and single-handedly called for the rewriting of the constitution, many viewed the OAS response as weak (Cooper and Legler 2001; Palmer 1996). Fujimori held elections for a new congress but maintained dominating authority over the writing of the new constitution, which conveniently expanded the powers of the president.

Though the OAS's response to Fujimori has been criticized as weak, one of the more promising aspects of the international response to the self-coup was that international election monitoring organizations devoted attention and resources to Peru. Sharon Lean argues that international election monitoring organizations played an important role in helping domestic election monitoring organizations develop and gain legitimacy within Peru (2004). The proliferation and development of these groups is one mechanism through which democracy norms diffuse. Lean finds evidence that the assistance given to domestic monitoring groups has helped spread the norm and expectation of free and fair elections in Peruvian civil society.

The presence of increasingly strong democracy norms in Peruvian civil society became evident in 2000 when protests erupted in response Fujimori's announcement that he would run for an unprecedented third term in office. The 2000 election quickly became another opportunity for the OAS to define how it would respond to irregularities in the democratic process. International observers and Peruvian opposition leaders noted considerable irregularities in the 2000 elections (Cooper and Legler 2001; Lean 2004). Two of the major parties boycotted the election and eventually international monitoring organizations left the country so as not to provide credibility to the marred elections (Lean 2005). Despite domestic protests and international disapproval of the election process, Fujimori took office in 2000.

The OAS responded to the flawed electoral process by sending a mission to Peru to help "strengthen democracy." It also adopted Resolution 1753, which authorized a multilateral effort to help build democracy in Peru. At the meeting, Mexico, Venezuela, Brazil, and of course Peru expressed opposition to collective efforts to restore democracy in Peru and argued for sovereignty and nonintervention to trump international involvement in the restoration of democracy (Cooper and Legler 2001). These countries did not believe that election irregularities justified the invocation of Resolution 1080. The US, along with Canada and Argentina, argued in favor of collective action to restore democracy in Peru. Resolution 1753 eventually passed as a compromise between the sovereignty/nonintervention position and collective enforcement of democracy position. The 2000 election results were not overturned, but an OAS mission arrived in Peru with the aim of establishing a dialogue among civil society, the opposition parties, and the government. There is debate over whether this compromise was a satisfactory response by the OAS (Cooper and Legler 2001; McClintock 2001).

Norm change

The dispute that arose as a result of Fujimori's self-coup forced the international community into a discussion about what constitutes a "disruption to democracy." Whereas a military coup is relatively easy to identify, it is harder for the international community to determine when a president has exceeded his or her constitutional authority, to the detriment of democracy. Nevertheless, the Peru case demonstrated that the international community was prepared to make judgments and take action where a democratically elected president overstepped his constitutional powers. Moreover, the Peruvian case indicates that the OAS is seeking to develop a more nuanced approach to collectively building and enforcing democracy norms. The case also demonstrates that civil society and international nongovernmental organizations can play an important role in spreading and consolidating democracy norms at the grassroots level.

The OAS involvement in Peru clearly differs from its involvement in Haiti. For a number of reasons, the response to the Fujimori self-coup was more muted. First, in Peru there was no humanitarian crisis, nor was there a threat to international peace and security. Second, the United States did not have an immediate or significant security interest in Peru. Third, identifying an interruption in democratic processes beyond an overthrow of a democratically elected leader requires increased international scrutiny of internal domestic political processes. A number of large states within the OAS, as evidenced by the debate over Resolution 1753, were concerned that this increased scrutiny and monitoring encroached on national sovereignty.

Sierra Leone

Action

A May 1997 military coup in Sierra Leone sparked a regional discussion about the specificity and obligation of democratic norms. The military coup that ousted President Kabbah came only six months after Sierra Leone held its first democratic election after many years of military rule. The coup received immediate condemnation from the international community, including the OAU, the European Union, the Commonwealth, the Economic Community of West African States (ECOWAS), and a number of NGOs. The United Nations was less prompt, but it did condemn the coup five months later.

Neighboring Nigeria was especially attuned to events unfolding in Sierra Leone. As the largest and strongest of the West African states, Nigeria had a particular interest in maintaining regional order. Nigeria thus took a leading role within ECOWAS in pressuring the coup leaders to step down and eventually in deploying military force against them. The dominant role of Nigeria in deposing the military regime in Sierra Leone spawned a regional and international discussion over the legitimacy of a subregional organization using force to restore a democratically elected leader.

Arguments

At the June 1997 Summit of the Organization of African Unity, the question of how to deal with the coup in Sierra Leone dominated the agenda. At the opening of the summit, U.N. Secretary General Kofi Annan declared, "Where democracy has been usurped, let us do all in our power to restore it to the people . . . . Neighboring states, regional groups and international organizations must all play their parts to restore Sierra Leone's constitutional and democratic government" (Meldrum 2007). The Zimbabwean President, who was then chair of the OAU, also expressed concern for the restoration of democracy. President Mugabe stated, "Democracy must be restored in Sierra Leone as a matter of urgency." He added, "We are getting tougher and tougher on coups . . . Coup-plotters and those who overthrow democratic governments will find it more difficult to get recognition from us. Democracy is getting stronger in Africa and we now have a definite attitude against coups" (Meldrum 2007). At this summit the OAU authorized ECOWAS to initiate a military campaign against the coup leaders in Sierra Leone.

ECOWAS convened shortly thereafter (in August 1997) and declared the coup in Sierra Leone a "threat to international peace and security." The ECOWAS decision also cited the rising number of refugees as threatening international peace and security. As further justification of economic sanctions, the ECOWAS decision also cited the Secretary General's statement that the overthrow of a democratically elected president was "unacceptable" (ECOWAS 1997). The decision called for an embargo on petroleum, arms, and military equipment. It also required all members to freeze funds held by the military regime in Sierra Leone and forbade the delivery of humanitarian aid to the military regime. The U.N. Security Council met in October to discuss the situation in Sierra Leone. The result was Resolution 1132, which authorized sanctions against Sierra Leone and also authorized ECOWAS to ensure that sanctions were implemented according to the resolution (UNSC 1997).

Peace talks between the junta and the deposed government began in October of 1997 and culminated in the Conakry Agreement, which laid out a six-month plan for the restoration of democracy and the reinstatement of President Kabbah. But the peace agreement quickly disintegrated as fighting among the junta and opposition groups escalated. Before the six-month deadline had passed, Nigerian troops, under the banner of ECOWAS, took over Freetown and ousted the military junta. Although the military intervention was not authorized by the United Nations, the

United Nations never condemned the ECOWAS intervention. In fact both the United Nations and the OAU expressed satisfaction with the outcome of the intervention.

The Nigerian-led intervention was justified in multiple ways, including self-defense (see Nowrot and Schabaker 1998). In a press conference after the ECOMOG[11] intervention, the Permanent Ambassador from Sierra Leone, James Jonah, argued that the United Nations' lack of action in Sierra Leone permitted, under Article 51, the use of force. Ambassador Jonah stated:

> When member states are asked by the Charter to refrain from the use of force, it was on the expectation that the Security Council will come to their aid in time of need. What we are seeing now is the Security Council tittering, and hesitating in dealing with African problems. When we came to the Security Council eight months ago when Sierra Leone was going through its anguish, what were we told? We were told in almost cynical terms that we had to go and deal with the boys [the junta] on the ground; meaning that the junta were in control. Therefore, for small vulnerable states like ours, we cannot just sit back. We had to look around for those who can come to our assistance. So we are grateful that ECOMOG, led by Nigeria, were able to come to our assistance. So, we do not believe that there was any need for us to seek permission from the Security Council. There is nothing in the Charter which says that a country in distress must first seek permission of the Security Council when the Council is not even willing to act. If this were allowed to happen, it would lead us to a very dark age in international politics. (UN 1998)

The Ambassador thus argued that the United Nations' failure to act had justified ECOMOG's use of force. Whether or not ECOMOG's action was actually self-defense is debatable (Nowrot and Schabaker 1998), though Sierra Leonean officials claimed that ECOMOG forces had come under attack. However, the lack of any significant international criticism of ECOMOG's intervention indicated that many states were willing to condone it.

---

[11] ECOMOG was the military force of ECOWAS.

In addition, the United Nations as well as ECOWAS justified economic sanctions in terms of international peace and security. As in the Haitian intervention, the increased flow of refugees was cited as a primary threat to international peace and security. However, unlike in the U.N. Resolution that authorized the use of force in Haiti, the economic sanctions on Sierra Leone were not couched in terms of "unique circumstances." The Security Council seemed more ready to say that coups, and the refugee crises they produce, in themselves represent a threat to international peace and security (UNSC 1997).

Another element of the United Nations' justification for economic sanctions in Resolution 1132 was a concern with the "continued violence and loss of life in Sierra Leone . . . the deteriorating humanitarian conditions in that country" (UNSC 1997). Human Rights organizations such as Amnesty International and Human Rights Watch documented widespread atrocities. However, as in the Haitian case, a humanitarian crisis on its own might not be enough to generate an international response. In the case of Haiti, the United States was a powerful regional actor with an interest in regional stability. In the case of Sierra Leone, Nigeria was the powerful regional actor concerned with maintaining stability. These two cases suggest that the presence of a dominant state with an interest in maintaining regional order significantly increases the chances that a humanitarian intervention will occur.

The restoration of democracy also appears as a central justification for the military intervention as well as the UN sanctions. In Resolution 1132 the U.N. Security Council cited a letter that the U.N. Secretary General had written to the Security Council, which stated that "at stake is a great issue of principle, namely, that the efforts of the international community for democratic governance . . . shall not be thwarted through illegal coups" (UN 1997). ECOWAS also made reference to the Secretary General's statements that coups are no longer acceptable. The fact that the purpose of the sanctions was to restore a democratically elected leader seems to have boosted the legitimacy of U.N. and ECOWAS actions.

Moreover, the fact that the exiled democratically elected president of Sierra Leone effectively appealed both to ECOWAS and to the United Nations for assistance in restoring democracy strengthens the democratic norms. As we saw in the Haitian intervention, the international community enabled an exiled but elected leader to ask for foreign military assistance. The international community seems increasingly willing to recognize a democratically elected leader without effective control of his or her country over governments that come to power through military coups.

Norm change

The intervention in Sierra Leone launched a regional discussion of democracy norms, which in turn led to a set of treaties and resolutions. In 2000 the OAU specified how it would handle unconstitutional changes in the Lomé Declaration. The resolution expresses concern for recent coups d'etat in Africa and labels them a setback to "ongoing processes of democratization on the Continent." The resolution identifies criteria of democratic governance[12] and defines "unconstitutional change in government"[13] (Organization of African Unity 2000). The resolution gives the perpetrators of the unconstitutional change in power six months to restore constitutional order. If constitutional order has not been restored in six months, sanctions and suspension from participation in the OAU may follow (similar to OAS rules).

A year after the Lomé Declaration, the "New Partnership for Africa's Development" (NEPAD) acknowledged a link between development and democracy. The NEPAD states:

> It is now generally acknowledged that development is impossible in the absence of true democracy, respect for human rights, peace and good governance. With the New Partnership

---

[12] The criteria are: "i) adoption of a democratic Constitution: its preparation, content and method of revision should be in conformity with generally acceptable principles of democracy; ii) respect for the Constitution and adherence to the provisions of the law and other legislative enactments adopted by Parliament; iii) separation of powers and independence of the judiciary; iv) promotion of political pluralism or any other form of participatory democracy and the role of the African civil society, including enhancing and ensuring gender balance in the political process; v) the principle of democratic change and recognition of a role for the opposition; vi) organization of free and regular elections, in conformity with existing texts; vii) guarantee of freedom of expression and freedom of the press, including guaranteeing access to the media for all political stake-holders; viii) constitutional recognition of fundamental rights and freedoms in conformity with the Universal Declaration of Human Rights of 1948 and the African Charter on Human and Peoples' Rights of 1981; ix) guarantee and promotion of human rights" (Organization of African Unity 2000).

[13] Unconstitutional change in government includes: "i) military coup d'etat against a democratically elected Government; ii) intervention by mercenaries to replace a democratically elected Government; iii) replacement of democratically elected Governments by armed dissident groups and rebel movements; iv) the refusal by an incumbent government to relinquish power to the winning party after free, fair and regular elections" (Organization of African Unity 2000).

for Africa's Development, Africa undertakes to respect the
global standards of democracy, which core components
include political pluralism, allowing for the existence of
several political parties and workers' unions, fair, open, free
and democratic elections periodically organized to enable the
populace choose their leaders freely. (NEPAD 2001)

The NEPAD goes on to declare a commitment to improving governance
through such measures and judicial reforms and parliamentary oversight.
The NEPAD thus represents a regional attempt to define democratic
norms.

In 2001 the OAU became the African Union. The Constitutive Act of
the African Union reiterates the importance of respect for sovereignty and
nonintervention, but it also states that one of the objectives of the Union is
to "promote democratic principles and institutions" (African Union 2002,
Art. 3). The AU in 2002 adopted the "African Union Declaration on the
Principles Governing Democratic Elections in Africa," affirming that
democratic elections are the basis of representative government and a
crucial element of conflict prevention. The declaration specifies necessary
elements of a free and fair election, including "impartial, all-inclusive
competent accountable electoral institutions staffed by well-trained personnel and equipped with adequate logistics" (Art. 2). The declaration
further states that election monitoring is an important aspect of "strengthening the democratization process" (Art. 5). The Declaration thus specifies
the role of election monitoring by the OAU and specifies the rights and
responsibilities of election observers. Finally, the 2003 "Protocol to the
African Charter on Human and People's Rights on the Rights of Women
in Africa" further specified democracy norms in the region. Article 9 of
the Protocol states that women should have equal participatory rights and
requires states to ensure that women have access to political participation
and representation.[14]

---

[14] Parties shall take specific positive action to promote participative governance and the equal
participation of women in the political life of their countries through affirmative action,
enabling national legislation and other measures to ensure that: (a) women participate without
any discrimination in all elections, (b) women are represented equally at all levels with men in
all electoral processes, (c) women are equal partners with men at all levels of development and
implementation of State policies and development programmes. (African Commission on
Human Rights and Peoples Rights 2003, Article 9).

Conclusion

The landmark human rights conventions that emerged after World War II—the Universal Declaration of Human Rights and the International Convention on Civil and Political Rights—enunciated the principle that every human being was entitled to basic democratic rights. The norm of democratic governance, however, remained largely declaratory. Regional organizations—the European Union, the Organization of American States, and the African Union—began to establish more formalized and specific standards for democracy. In fact, the regional bodies were the first to translate democracy norms from declarations of shared ideals into practical norms that could even, under certain circumstances, justify international intervention.

As Chapter 1 argues, international norms do not evolve as a result of abstract reflection. Rather, rules change through the course of arguments that arise out of concrete events and disputes. The third wave of democratization was a transformative era in world politics. The democratic transitions in Africa, Latin America, and Central and Eastern Europe provided a crucial impetus to the development of international norms regarding a right to democracy. International election monitoring was one important mechanism for giving practical content to international norms, as the legitimacy of regimes was tied to international validation of elections that met basic standards of fairness. Regional institutions further developed democracy norms, in two modes.

First, Europe's major regional bodies capitalized on the incentive of membership to promote and consolidate democracies in Eastern and Central Europe. The Council of Europe helped the transition countries to design and implement democratic procedures. In addition, through its highly developed European Court of Human Rights, the Council offered a means for states to subject themselves to enforceable European standards—a way of enhancing the credibility of their democratic reforms. The European Union offered immense and concrete benefits to the newly independent states of Eastern and Central Europe, namely, membership in the world's largest common market. All of the transition states made European Union accession a top priority. That commitment gave the European Union considerable leverage, which it exercised in the form of political criteria that required functioning democratic institutions and the rule of law.

Democracy norms developed via a different mode in Africa and Latin America, where international intervention emerged as a response to events that undercut democracy. In Africa, ECOWAS organized a military intervention—condoned after the fact by the Security Council—in Sierra Leone; among its principle justifications were the need to halt gross human rights violations and the need to restore democracy. The landmark event in Latin America was the coup in Haiti and the response of, first, the OAS and, later, the United Nations. The OAS immediately imposed a series of penalties on the military junta in Haiti and pressed the United Nations for a broader international response. That came in the form of binding economic sanctions and a military intervention authorized by the Security Council. For the first time, international democracy norms were backed by U.N.-authorized armed force.

The emergence of international norms enshrining a right to democracy thus fits the pattern of cyclical development. Existing norms provide the context, but specific actions and events trigger debates about how the rules should be applied or modified. The wave of democratization in the 1980s and 1990s gave rise to events and arguments that produced more robust international democracy norms.

The disputes we have examined also demonstrate that winning arguments tend to use and incorporate existing and recognized international norms to make a case for a new norm. In the cases of Haiti and Sierra Leone, actors argued that in addition to being a disruption to democracy the crises also represented "threats to international peace and security" and humanitarian disasters. By attaching the new norm of a right to democracy to these more well established norms, actors were in a better position to win the argument. In addition to improving our understanding of the process of norm development in general, this analysis also allows us to draw some conclusions about the development of democracy norms in particular. First, the dominant international definition of democracy has been a procedural one, mainly in terms of free and fair elections. Though we would not want to ignore the importance of elections for establishing and protecting individual rights, this procedural definition does exclude important attributes of democracy. For example, access to resources such as education, which enable citizens to effectively exercise their political rights, has not been a central part of the discussion on a right to democracy. Poverty and income inequality can also undermine or severely constrain democratic equality. Although recent evidence suggests that some regional discussions are turning toward analyzing the "quality" or "depth" of democracy (UNDP 2004), international democracy norms have largely been minimalist and procedural.

Second, the question of how the international community can enforce a right to democracy is far from being resolved. The cases of Haiti and Sierra Leone suggest that the international community is developing an enforcement norm which allows the international community to intervene in cases where a democratically elected leader is overthrown. However, these cases do not establish a precedent for imposing a democracy in a country that has not yet had a democratically government. The negative international response to US action in Iraq suggests that the imposition of democracy by force is not deemed legitimate by the broader international community.

Thomas Franck is perhaps the most widely cited proponent of an emerging right to democracy. His vision for the future of this international legal norm is unwaveringly optimistic. He states, "Increasingly, governments recognize that their legitimacy depends on meeting a normative expectation of the community of states. This recognition has led to the emergence of a community expectation: that those who seek the validation of their empowerment patently govern with the consent of the governed. Democracy, thus, is on the way to becoming a global entitlement, one that increasingly will be promoted and protected by collective international processes" (1992, 46). In light of Haiti and Sierra Leone, however, it may be that the right to democracy is most likely to be enforced internationally when a regional power perceives an interest in enforcing it.

This chapter has traced the development of what seems to be an increasingly recognized international right to democratic governance. We have seen a particular concern with establishing legal mechanisms capable of confronting "interruptions" in democratic governance. Domestic political arrangements, under certain conditions, are no longer an exclusively internal matter. Disruptions of democracy in Haiti, Sierra Leone, and Peru generated international arguments, which in turn produced normative innovations allowing international intervention on behalf of democracy. The ongoing emergence of pro-democracy norms has contributed to the expansion of liberal norms in international society.

Chapter 12

Cycles of International Norm Change

Kendall Stiles and Wayne Sandholtz

International norms change through a dispute-driven, cyclic process. Events or actions trigger disputes over the meaning and application of norms. Actors argue, seeking to challenge or expand existing norms or to invoke competing norms. These arguments inevitably modify the rules. Cycles of disputes and argumentation can thus alter the content of norms, as in the case of conquest. Whereas conquest was once a sovereign prerogative, a contrary norm emerged through cycles of change. Similarly, cycles of norm change triggered by the two World Wars of the twentieth century introduced international rules on the status of refugees and asylum seekers, where no such norms existed before. But disputes and arguments also modify norms without altering their substantive content, by making them more specific or more formal or by establishing exceptions and qualifications. The point is that rules cannot stand still, that norm systems are inherently dynamic. The cycle of norm change, we have claimed, is ubiquitous.

We also suggested that norm cycles are not discrete episodes but rather are linked forward and backward in time. The long historical view adopted in this book thus offers an additional advantage. Any given cycle takes place in a normative context shaped by previous disputes. Every cycle also shapes the normative context for subsequent disputes. The arguments in one cycle draw on rules and precedents developed in earlier cycles, and add to the stock of rules and precedents that disputants will invoke in later controversies. The historical perspective is indispensable for understanding these chains of normative development. Studying one cycle or episode in isolation would provide a truncated and misleading view. The piracy chapter thus spans some five hundred years. The accounts of norms against slavery and plundering both cover more than two hundred years, and the chapters on conquest and extraterritoriality evaluate developments lasting a century. All of the cases we examine confirm the importance of analyzing cycles of norm change as they are connected across time.

In addition, we offered several propositions regarding the nature of cycles of norm change. For instance, we suggested that gaps and tensions within normative systems are fertile grounds for disputes and that certain kinds of international contexts and events are likely to trigger such disputes. We also proposed that international norm change has occurred along two main streams—sovereignty norms and liberal norms—and that tensions between the two have been a rich source of norm-changing cycles. We can now review those claims in light of the case analyses.

Our empirical cases include variation on multiple dimensions that could affect the nature of normative disputes and their outcomes. First, some cases assess developments along the stream of sovereignty rules, others assess cycles along the stream of liberal (human rights) rules, and others highlight collisions (and tensions) between the two main currents. Second, the cases cover broad variation in substantive domains, ranging from the monopoly of states on the use of force (piracy, terrorism), to the use of force in interstate conflict (conquest, plunder), to personal rights and freedoms (slavery, genocide, refugees), to the rights of populations vis-à-vis their own governments (humanitarian intervention, the right to democracy). Third, we draw from a broad spectrum of temporal contexts, from the sixteenth century to the twenty-first. Moreover, within most of the chapters, we analyze norm cycles that are linked across centuries (piracy, slavery, plunder). Yet despite the many axes of variation in the cases, we consistently observe cycles of norm change as the model would predict.

Triggering Cycles of Norm Change

The cycle of norm change, we proposed, begins with an event or action that challenges some set of international norms, provoking a dispute. One implication is that norm development is inescapably path dependent: the nature and direction of norm change depend crucially on the specific dispute that triggered the cycle and on the outcomes of previous disputes. In its general form, the process of international norm change resembles the case-driven development of common law. Previous cases establish broad parameters within which the judge decides a new dispute. Law develops through the accretion of such decisions. But the course of that development depends on the cases that present themselves as different fact patterns give rise to different claims and different legal arguments. Once decided, each case pushes the law toward one set of possible paths and away from others (Stone Sweet 2002b).

Norm change in the international system is analogous, though it generally occurs in the absence of an authoritative third-party dispute resolver, or judge. Actions trigger a dispute, which generates normative arguments, which states (not judges) decide. But the nature of the dispute, the content of the arguments offered, and the collective decision all grow out of—as in the common law legal system—the facts of the events in question and the heritage of previously resolved disputes. Past cases frame the normative questions and establish lines of argumentation; the facts of a new dispute determine what normative questions need to be resolved. Triggering events therefore push the course of norm development toward certain paths out of the multiple paths that would, in principle, be available.

Our cases demonstrate the centrality of triggering events or actions. In almost every instance, we found that specific actions provoked arguments among states and other actors. In Chapter 3, specific conquests launched cycles of argumentation and norm development, beginning with Prussian annexation of Alsace and Lorraine and ending with the Iraqi seizure of Kuwait. Antiplunder norms evolved in response to dramatic acts of plunder, especially the massive looting the French carried out in the Napoleonic Wars and Nazi Germany in World War II. Norms condemning terrorism arose in the wake of specific waves of terrorist action, first in the 1950s and 1960s, then in the 1980s, and finally after the attacks of September 11, 2001. Norms regarding extraterritoriality, genocide, refugees, humanitarian intervention, and enforcement of the right to democracy all evolved through identifiable cycles triggered by specific events.

In the remaining cases (piracy, slavery), norms evolved through cycles of dispute and argument, but not in response to specific triggering events. Antipiracy norms developed as a result of longer-term trends in shipbuilding (steel-hulled ships) and in the expansion of national navies. States at one time relied on privateers to harass and plunder enemy vessels. Steel-hulled ships were expensive to produce; states could build them, but pirates could not. The emergence of larger and better equipped navies meant that powerful maritime states could do without the services of privateers, who then became mere pirates, a nuisance to be eliminated. Similarly, antislavery norms gained ground not in response to specific, dramatic events, but as a result of longer-term social and political movements. Abolitionists won the domestic battle against the slave trade and slavery first in Great Britain, and then the antislavery movement became transnational. But the abolitionists could not have suppressed the slave trade without the might of the British navy to exert pressure and enforce the rules. In short, the cases of piracy and slavery suggest that the disputes and arguments that produce cycles of norm change need not arise out of triggering events; underlying shifts in technology, society, and politics can also generate these debates. Still, it is striking that in eight of our ten cases, specific actions or events were responsible for launching processes of norm development. Table 12.1 summarizes the principal cycles of norm change and what triggered them.

We also argued that certain kinds of international contexts are especially likely to generate normative disputes. Indeed, one hallmark of unsettled international environments is that multiple states engage in actions that challenge existing norms. And once the international order appears to be destabilized, additional states capitalize on the moment by taking dramatic or controversial steps. Such unsettled international contexts include major wars, sweeping technological innovations, and large-scale political upheavals (such as revolutions and the collapse of empires). In such settings, actors perceive an opportunity to challenge existing norms, through breech or contestation or both.

Major wars disrupt existing systems of rules and patterns of behavior and shift the distribution of power. Thus, in our cases, the two World Wars of the twentieth century provoked cycles of norm change in multiple domains. World War I prompted norm development with respect to conquest, extraterritoriality, genocide, and refugees. World War II was even more cataclysmic, and it produced more far-reaching cycles of norm change.

Table 12.1 Cycles of norm change and principal triggers

Case	Number of Cycles	Cycles of Change Initiated by	
		Specific Action or Event	Contextual Shift or Movement
Piracy	2	2nd cycle: - 20th-century terrorism	1st cycle: - Technology (steel hulled ships) - Growth of national navies
Conquest	6	- Germany and Alsace-Lorraine - World War I - Japan and Manchuria - Nazi invasions of Czechoslovakia and Poland - North Korean invasion of South Korea - Iraqi invasion of Kuwait	
Plunder	2 +	- French plundering in the Napoleonic Wars - Nazi art looting in World War II	
Terrorism	3	- 1950s-60s hijackings & attacks on diplomats - 1980s-90s: bombings - 9/11 attacks	
Extraterritoriality	3	- Turkey: World War I - China: World War II	- Japan: internal reforms
Slavery	3	- 20th century human trafficking	- Domestic abolitionist movements - Expansion of British naval power
Genocide	3	- Armenian genocide - Holocaust - Bosnia, Rwanda, Darfur	
Refugees & asylum	2	- World War I and Russian Revolution - World War II	
Humanitarian intervention	4	- Somalia - Rwanda - Bosnia - Darfur	
Right to democracy	3	- Haiti - Peru - Sierra Leone	

The Allied response to Germany's expansionist aggression in World War II consolidated the previously emerging norm against conquest, and at the end of the war Article 2(4) of the United Nations Charter embodied the rule against the use of force. World War II also initiated a cycle of change that finally abolished extraterritorial courts. With the end of the war and the rise of American and Soviet influence—both of which adopted an anticolonial position—it became impossible for France, Britain and others to justify their intrusion on foreign legal systems. The masses of refugees and displaced persons produced by the Second World War triggered a norm cycle that resulted in more formal and more specific norms governing the treatment of refugees. With respect to genocide, the atrocities the Nazis committed in World War II shocked international sensibilities and triggered the discussions that led to the Genocide Convention. Finally, massive Nazi art looting in World War II led to efforts to consolidate and codify antiplunder norms that had been developing for over a century, since the Napoleonic Wars.

Technology has also at times generated challenges to existing norms and thus cycles of norm change. The introduction of steel-hulled ships was such a dramatic innovation that it essentially priced privateers out of the market for naval power. This was part of the ongoing construction of a monopoly by sovereign states on the use of force. Under developing sovereignty rules, it was natural to prohibit private sources of military power.

Technology has also facilitated the development of norms against genocide and permitting humanitarian intervention. Because of television and the Internet, news and images flash almost instantaneously to most of the globe. Mass atrocities in places such as Bosnia, Somalia, and Rwanda have been impossible to ignore—unlike the Armenian genocide. Modern communications technologies have made humanitarian crises and genocide more visible, increasing the pressure on governments to act and fueling the arguments that have pushed the development of norms allowing for international intervention.

Political upheaval has frequently triggered cycles of norm change. This is true, for example, with each of the several waves of democratization. The 1789 French Revolution, for example, resulted in the temporary emancipation of slaves in French territories and contributed directly to Toussaint L'Ouverture's successful revolt in Haiti. The period of political upheaval which began in 1789 and lasted until at least 1848 contributed indirectly to the delegitimization of slavery and the slave trade. The so-called third and fourth waves of democratization, in Spain and Portugal in the 1970s then subsequently in Latin America and Central and Eastern Europe, have contributed directly to the notion that new democratic regimes have special claims on the international community. Specifically, there is now considerable global support for the notion that the overthrow of a democratic regime should trigger international responses, possibly even including forcible intervention, as in Haiti.

In earlier eras, other forms of political upheaval have similarly triggered cycles of norm change. The consolidation of nation-states, such as Germany and Italy in the late 1800s, and the dismemberment of multinational states such as the Ottoman and Austro-Hungarian empires after World War I, coincided with the emergence of a norm of self-determination. As the right to self-determination gained strength, both conquest and extraterritoriality lost legitimacy.

We also argued that *transnational networks* complement the cycle theory of norm change. The abolition of the slave trade is a case in which the mobilizing efforts of activist groups triggered cycles of norm change. The analysis of transnational activists can also benefit from an appreciation of the broader normative context, namely, cycles of norm development linked forward and backward in time. Norm entrepreneurs and activist networks do not begin from scratch. They frequently draw on previous norm developments to construct persuasive arguments; they can also capitalize on the dramatic events that trigger cycles of norm change to garner publicity for their causes and reinforce the need for international action. For instance, transnational legal activists in the late 1800s pushed for the codification of rules of war, including the prohibition of wartime plundering of cultural treasures. The plunder case illustrates the importance of viewing the work of transnational activists in the longer historical context of cycles of norm change. The law activists of the late 1800s invoked the restitution of artworks at the conclusion of the Napoleonic Wars, and were motivated in the immediate term by acts of plunder that had occurred in the 1870 Franco-Prussian War. The efforts of the international law activists would be unintelligible without connecting them to earlier cycles of norm change (the Napoleonic Wars) and tracing their effects on later cycles (World War I and World War II).

Likewise, the developing norm of democratic governance did not emerge as a response to specific events (wars, political changes), though the norm permitting international intervention to support elected governments against usurpation clearly did. More broadly, the right to democracy emerges out of the stream of liberal norms: popular sovereignty, political and civil rights, and self-determination. The cycles of norm change examined in Chapter 11 contributed to defining a norm of democratic governance, but the prior broad acceptance of basic liberal norms was a necessary precondition for those arguments and normative shifts.

Tensions among Norms

Tensions between existing norms are a regular feature of the disputes that lead to norm change (see Chapter 1). Every normative system includes rules that, in some situations, conflict with each other. In the domestic setting, for example, laws that guarantee freedom of expression sometimes collide with laws designed to sanction hate speech or incitements to violence. In many disputes, actors seek to resolve such conflicts between norms. Even the case of slavery and the slave trade involved contradictory norms. The disputes were not just about human dignity. Opponents of abolition invoked a right to property, one protected in both in liberal theory and in national constitutions. Thus slavery counted many advocates in democratic regimes, as witnessed by the speeches of Senator James Calhoun or the Liverpool MPs. But even after societies declared that no human being could be owned as property, the question remained as to the point at which control and exploitation amounted to something like ownership. Thus, though slavery is prohibited, slave-like practices have persisted or even expanded.

Terrorism, as implied earlier, has also involved a contest between two norms: self-determination, which justifies the use of force against occupiers, and the basic right to life and personal security, especially on the part of civilians. Because almost every established state has gone through a period of revolution or a war of independence, it has been difficult to deny in absolute terms that violence may be justified under some circumstances. Thus the Palestinians, East Timorese, Chechens, Kashmiris, Irish, and Basques, among others, have sought to justify their violence in terms of the right of self-determination. On the other hand, the right of innocents to life and personal security is a central tenet of modern human rights norms. Debates center on whether specific actions are instances of the use of force for self-determination or simply terrorist crimes.

Disputes that poise one norm against another are engines of significant normative change, but the arguments underlying them can endure.

When the rules in tension are both part of the international norm structure, repeated disputes are almost a certainty. It was a rather simple matter to criminalize piracy and abandon privateering as there were no competing norms that underpinned those practices. But where existing norms conflict, there are generally arguments on both sides, guaranteeing additional disputes in the future and leaving all actors with ammunition for subsequent debates. This observation explains why several of the liberal norms we have examined—refugees, humanitarian intervention, the right to democracy—are best described as emerging, continually being defined in response to specific events or crises. In these domains, liberal, rights-based norms are bound to be in ongoing tension with norms that undergird sovereignty and national jurisdiction.

Arguments

In Chapter 1 we offered a number of propositions regarding the nature of normative arguments. We argued that actors rely on precedents and "metanorms" in their efforts to persuade other actors of the merits of their claims. We repeatedly observed such arguments.

Consider the case of conquest. Actors were quick to rely on precedents—often taken from accounts in Antiquity or the Bible—to persuade others of the correctness of their position. The implicit condemnation of conquest in the account of the Peloponnesian War and in early Christian writings gave confidence to those opposing the traditional norm permitting conquest. In the arguments over slavery and war plunder, actors similarly invoked prior instances. They strove to present their arguments as historical givens, consistent with previous outcomes. Abolitionists pointed to restrictions on slavery in the Bible and Ancient Greek and Roman practice as evidence that masters never had unlimited power over their slaves. In the arguments over Nazi art plundering, actors cited not just the experience of World War I and the Hague Conventions but also reached back to the Napoleonic Wars. With humanitarian intervention, advocates of intervention used historical precedent to show both the virtue of interventions in Bangladesh and Uganda as well as the shame of nonintervention on behalf of the Armenians and Rwanda. Thus both sides of a dispute employ precedents.

We also find instances in which actors seek to establish analogies between a current problem and a practice already covered by international rules. Such analogies have worked best when the position being advocated appeared consistent with a firmly established norm. In the case of terrorism, for example, proponents of a hard line routinely compared terrorists to pirates, who were an enemy of all humanity under international law. The clearest prohibitions, however, are often narrowly defined, limiting their usefulness as an analogy. For example, though the analogy between terrorists and pirates was effective with respect to terrorist attacks on neutral shipping or aircraft in international space, the analogy did not hold so well with respect to attacks on military targets in occupied territories.

In a different domain, the definition of genocide excluded political groups. That exclusion has created an opening for those opposed to international action to halt mass killings. Mass killers in Rwanda or Somalia, for example, argued that they were not committing genocide but rather combating insurrectionists, which could not equate to a Holocaust. States that did not favor international intervention could seize upon that argument to characterize the slaughters as something other than genocide, as a civil war, for instance.

In other words, norms that narrowly define prohibited acts tend to be less useful as analogies to new categories of behavior. Consequently, actions that are apparently similar to the proscribed behavior are not covered by the rule. Thus the international community struggles with conditions that may not constitute slavery but are clearly "slave like." Chattel slavery has been outlawed for close to a century, but the international community has yet to vigorously prosecute the abduction of innocents and their trafficking into the sex trade. Likewise, the prohibition against piracy does not cover piratical acts carried out for political motives, which meant that the *Aquille Lauro* attackers fell into a legal no-man's land.

Power

Power is crucial to norm change, but not because hegemons can dictate rules to the rest of international society. Indeed, not even superpowers, acting alone, can create international norms. Powerful states can often impose outcomes on other states, but that does not necessarily mean that they are at the same time modifying international norms or making new ones. The difference is that whereas specific actions are individual, rules are social. Because norms are social, they evolve through collective processes of argumentation and persuasion. For instance, in 2003, the United States was able to force regime change upon Iraq in the face of broad international disapprobation. The United States claimed that prior Security Council resolutions authorized individual states to use force against Iraq if it failed to comply with obligations imposed on it after the 1991 Persian Gulf War. Some U.S. leaders also suggested that the United States was exercising its right under international law to preemptive self-defense.

The United States obtained the outcome it sought—forcible regime change in Iraq. But it did not thereby modify international rules on the use of force. The vast majority of states rejected both the U.S. interpretation of Security Council resolutions and its argument in favor of preventive self-defense (Sandholtz, forthcoming). In other words, the United States achieved its desired outcome, but it did not by any means impose on the rest of the world new norms regarding the use of force.[1]

Power is important for the creation of norms, but it is power in the form of consensus among the leading states that matters. Normative claims are more likely to prevail when multiple major powers support them. The conventional wisdom regarding "tipping points" seems relevant (Finnemore and Sikkink 1998). But when tallying the roster of countries that support a new norm, the tallies should be weighted. The adherence of major powers to an emergent norm is most critical. The upshot is that even great powers must think normatively and argue persuasively in order to gain the assent of other leading states to modifications in international rules. The set of major powers is a crucial subset of international society, and it is a group that no one state can dominate or direct. Even superpowers must be able to win support from other major powers for shifts in international norms.

The only case in this volume that comes close to the imposition of a new norm by a dominant state is the prohibition of the slave trade. It was only when the British Empire adopted an aggressive policy against slave trading that the debate and the norm began to shift decisively. British patrols in the Atlantic, combined with its extraordinary pressure on slaving states to join it in sundry agreements, turned the tide. And there were limits to what the British could accomplish until the United States abolished slavery in the 1860s. Still, it was not British naval power alone

---

[1] Even the notion that the United States "got away with" violating international law by invading Iraq is mistaken. Because most of the world considered the invasion illegal, the United States had to bear almost the entire burden of the war and the occupation. That burden has cost the United States, so far, over 4,000 lives and about $500 billion. In this instance, even the world's lone superpower suffered costs for violating international law.

that induced the normative shift. British enforcement worked, in part at least, because Britain had relentlessly sought and obtained agreements with the other major European powers.

In every other case we examined, norm change emerged out of agreement among the leading powers of the time. Extraterritoriality died out as the major western countries, in a more or less ad hoc and decentralized fashion, gave it up. With respect to piracy, all of the chief naval powers eventually abandoned privateering and suppressed piracy. In each cycle of the development of norms against conquest, opposition to acts of conquest came from coalitions of major states. In the last two cycles (Korea and Kuwait), the international consensus emerged among the leading powers and other states in the United Nations. Norms against plunder developed among the major states allied, first, against Napoleon and, later, against Hitler. With terrorism, genocide, refugees, humanitarian intervention, and the right to democracy, the key international rules emerged out of multilateral institutions (the United Nations and some regional bodies), in which the major powers could exercise leadership and influence but could not impose norms.

Recent history supports our conclusion regarding power and norms. With the end of the Cold War, the United States remained the sole superpower, with immense advantages over any other state in virtually every dimension of power—economic, technological, military. During its "unipolar moment," American priorities have influenced the development of international norms, especially with respect to terrorism (a domain in which, after 9/11, the United States was the country that was both the most motivated and the most capable of taking the lead against terrorists). In other areas—refugees, humanitarian intervention, the right to democracy—the United States has worked with other leading states to develop common norms. And even at its (already passed) unipolar apogee, the United States frequently had to work hard to persuade other major powers and it did not always succeed. The United States utterly failed to persuade the international community to endorse the invasion of Iraq in 2003. And in yet other instances, when the United States withdrew from multilateral norm-building efforts (the International Criminal Court, climate change) or did not participate fully (landmines), other states pressed ahead anyway (Brem and Stiles, forthcoming). In short, our cases show that major powers have been crucial to the development or modification of international norms, not via hegemonic imposition but through the forging of consensus among leading states.

The Architecture of International Norms

We argued that the development of international rules over the last several centuries has included two major norm streams, one for sovereignty norms (the rights and duties of sovereign states) and one for liberal norms (human rights for individual people). Having examined ten substantive domains, we remain persuaded that our conception of two primary lines of norm development captures both an important feature of the international norm structure and a vital motor of its development over time. The international system that emerged after Westphalia was a society of sovereign states. It should not be surprising that states would test, debate, and elaborate the rules that defined sovereign statehood and its rights and prerogatives.

The cases examined in the first part of the book deal with the ongoing elaboration of sovereignty rules. A crucial set of those rules concern states' exclusive hold on armed power. Rules against piracy sought to eliminate a source of naval power that was not under state control. Antiterrorism norms similarly aimed at suppressing the use of force by nonstate actors. Rules prohibiting conquest served to codify one of the most essential rights of sovereign states: their right to exist. Antiplunder norms affirmed states' rights to their cultural patrimony. The demise of extraterritorial courts extended sovereignty rights (exclusive internal jurisdiction) to nonwestern states.

The second major stream of international norm development emerged out of the Enlightenment commitment to inherent individual rights. The irreducible value and dignity of each person informed the earliest development of liberal (human-rights-based) international norms: the abolition of the slave trade. Liberal norms inevitably collided with sovereignty rules. Sovereignty rules had developed to define and protect the rights and prerogatives of states. Indeed, how a state treated its own people was a purely internal matter, not a subject for international law (see Chapters 10 and 11). Liberal norms developed (first in national constitutions and law) to delineate and defend the rights of people, even against their own governments.

By the latter half of the nineteenth century, sovereignty norms and liberal norms were already rubbing against each other. The humanitarian law movement of the late 1800s—to protect sick and wounded soldiers, to shield civilians, to immunize private and cultural property—was, in part, an assertion of liberal ideals on the dignity and rights of individuals as against a broad sovereign right to conduct war. World War I provided an impetus to efforts to bound sovereign rights and to enhance individual rights. The League of Nations system and the Kellogg-Briand Pact sought, for instance, to regulate states' resort to force. Heightened awareness of human rights found expression in the (ultimately ineffectual) movement to prosecute those responsible for the Armenian genocide and in ad hoc international efforts to care for refugees. Still, it was the cataclysm of World War II and the Holocaust that propelled liberal, human rights norms into more direct collision with sovereignty. The postwar proliferation of international human rights treaties and declarations thus opened a new era of international human rights norms. Sovereignty was no longer a hard shell. How states treated those within their borders, both their own citizens and refugees, became a subject of international law (Chapter 8 on genocide; Chapter 9 on refugees) and even international intervention (Chapter 10 on humanitarian intervention; Chapter 11 on the right to democracy).

Our conception of the two main streams of international norm development thus helps to make sense of the broad architecture of international norms and illuminates important patterns of change. One of the most dramatic movements of the past century has been the emergence of universal human rights under international law. International human rights standards conflicted with, and implied boundaries to, state sovereignty. The tension between sovereignty norms and liberal norms has thus been at the heart of many of the most significant developments in international norms. We examined that tension and evaluated the related cycles of norm change regarding terrorism, slavery, genocide, refugees, humanitarian intervention, and democracy.

Final Thoughts

We argued that dispute-driven norm change is a feature of every system of rules. The cyclic dynamic may not be the only mode of norm change, but it is an important and ubiquitous one. It is ubiquitous because it derives its motive force from inherent features of norm systems: the inevitable disputes over the application of rules to specific acts or events; the norm- and precedent-based arguments that actors offer in those disputes; the way in which the outcomes of those arguments inevitably modify the rules. In ten diverse cases, we find confirming instances of the cycle of norm change. The case studies also demonstrate the validity of our claim that cycles of norm change link forward and backward in time. Previous cycles establish the context of norms and precedents in which new disputes arise; the outcome of those new disputes alters the context of norms and precedents for subsequent controversies. Our cases establish the value of the long historical view, in which episodes are not discrete events but are, instead, links in a chain of norm cycles.

Though the analyses presented in this volume confirm our main propositions, we view this as a beginning, not an end. Additional theoretical development and empirical research could further illuminate specific phases of the cycle of norm change. For instance, though disputed actions and events clearly generate arguments about international norms, we would like to develop a better understanding of normative argumentation in such disputes.[2] We offered broad propositions on which kinds of arguments are more likely to prevail, but we would like to know more about how actors frame normative claims and select precedents. Over time, through linked cycles of norm change, do actors in decentralized international relations develop "argumentation frames" similar to those that build up in judicialized contexts (Stone Sweet 2002b)? We would expect that such frames do emerge as they appear to have in the case of conquest: basic lines of argumentation against conquest appear consistently in the later cycles.

Furthermore, though our ten cases cover a broad array of substantive rules, we certainly have not examined every important domain of international norms. We did not, for instance, investigate the complex of norms governing international economic relations. Laws regulating international trade and investment constitute an immense domain, one that could fill an additional volume (or two). We would, nevertheless, expect the cycle model to explain much of the development of international economic rules. In its broad contours, for example, the evolution of modern trade law appears to have occurred through event-driven cycles of argumentation and change. The collapse of free trade and the prevalence of "beggar-thy-neighbor" exchange rate policies prior to World War II were events that triggered intense disputes, which in turn generated arguments and negotiations both during and after the war. Those arguments produced the normative framework of the General Agreement on Tariffs and Trade (GATT), with its rules to liberalize trade. A crisis in GATT launched a second major cycle of norm change. The crisis was the product of surging protectionism following the global recessions of 1973–74 and 1979–80. The Uruguay Round of negotiations (1986–94) aired all of the arguments among 123 participating countries (World Trade Organization 2008). The debates created a new institution, the World Trade Organization (WTO) and produced new rules to eliminate barriers to trade and extend the free-trade regime to new areas (services, agriculture).

---

[2] Building on the work, for instance, of Crawford (2002), Hawkins (2004), and Risse (2000).

Since the Uruguay Round, controversies over the application of WTO rules go before the WTO's dispute resolution mechanism, a highly judicialized, court-like arrangement. Under the WTO dispute resolution procedure, trade disputes are subject to an institutionalized cycle of norm change (Stone Sweet 2002a). Indeed, judicial bodies simply formalize our cycle of norm change and transfer the decision phase from the set of concerned states (decentralized international relations) to a third-party dispute resolver.[3] As in our cycle model, actions generate disputes, which the parties then argue before a dispute resolver (in this case, a WTO panel), which in turn decides the issue. Each resolved case modifies and (presumably) strengthens WTO rules by clarifying their meaning and application. The rules of trade, then, have evolved through two major cycles—the founding of the GATT and the creation of the WTO; they continue to develop in formalized cycles under the WTO dispute resolution procedure.

Our cases have also revealed various linkages across norm domains. Debates over combating terrorism, for example, have drawn analogies to the earlier effort to outlaw and eliminate piracy. The development of norms against wartime plundering overlapped with the movement to codify limits on warfare. The demise of extraterritoriality both drew on and reinforced the parallel development of norms of self-determination and decolonization. Mapping such connections and theorizing the nature of norm "borrowing" or norm synergies would be a major contribution.

International norms have developed through cycles of change, linked forward and backward in historical processes. Students of national legal systems constantly work with cycles of norm change, though the terminology may differ. Lines of jurisprudence in the United States Supreme Court, for example, are linked cycles as we have defined them: each case arises out of a specific act, which triggers a dispute, which the parties argue, and the Court decides. The Court's decisions generally build on a line of precedents and shape the legal context for subsequent disputes. Linked cycles of norm change in Supreme Court jurisprudence are relatively easy to identify and assess; each case is a cycle and the cycles are clearly linked through chains of citations. It may not be so obvious that rules evolve through a similar cyclic dynamic in the decentralized realm of international relations, where states themselves decide the outcome of disputes among them and power is ever present. Yet that is precisely what our model proposes and what our case analyses show.

---

[3] On the shift from decentralized to third-party dispute resolution, see Stone Sweet (1999). For an application of these concepts to international relations, see Sandholtz and Stone Sweet (2004).

References

Cases

Immigration and Naturalization Service v. Cardozo-Fonseca. (1987). 480 U.S. 481.

Immigration and Naturalization Service v. Stevic. (1984). 467 U.S. 407.

International Conference on Military Trials. (1945). *Minutes of Conference Session of July 23, 1945, in Report of Robert H. Jackson, United States Representative to the International Conference on Military Trials.* London.

International Court of Justice. (1951). *Reservations to the Convention on the Prevention and Punishment of the Crime of Genocide, Advisory Opinion: I.C.J. Reports 1951,* 15. 28 May 1951. Available at http://www.icj-cij.org/docket/files/12/4283.pdf. Accessed 30 May 2008.

International Court of Justice. (1986). *Military and Paramilitary Activities in and Against Nicaragua (Nicaragua v. United States of America), Judgment of 27 June 1986– Merits.* 27 June 1986. Available at http://www.icj-cij.org/docket/index.php?p1=3&p2=3. Accessed 21 May 2008.

International Court of Justice. (2004). *Legal Consequences of the Construction of a Wall in the Occupied Palestinian Territory, Advisory Opinion: I.C.J. Reports 2004,* 136. 9 July 2004. Available at http://www.icj-cij.org/docket/files/131/1671.pdf. Accessed 30 May 2008.

International Criminal Tribunal for the Former Yugoslavia. (2007). *Indictments and Proceedings.* Available at http://www.un.org/icty/cases-e/index-e.htm. Accessed 6 July 2007.

International Criminal Tribunal for Rwanda. (1998). *The Prosecutor v. Jean-Paul Akayesu—Judgement.* Case No. ICTR-96-4-T. 2 September 1998. Available at http://69.94.11.53/default.htm. Accessed 30 May 2008.

International Criminal Tribunal for the Former Yugoslavia. Appeals Chamber. (2004). *Prosecutor v. Radislav Krstic— Judgement.* Case No. IT-98-33-A. 19 April 2004. http://www.un.org/icty/krstic/Appeal/judgement/krs-aj040419e.pdf. Accessed 30 May 2008.

United Nations War Crimes Commission. (1947). "Alstotter Case." *Law Reports of Trials of War Criminals*. Vol. 6, 58–59. London: Published for the United Nations War Crimes Commission by H.M.S.O.

Government and IGO Documents

African Union. (2002). *African Union Declaration on the Principles Governing Democratic Elections in Africa*. 10 July 2002. Durban, South Africa. 38th Ordinary Session of the Assembly of the OAU. Available at http://www2.ohchr.org/english/law/compilation_democracy/ahg.htm. Accessed 28 April 2008.

African Union Mission in the Sudan. (2008). "*African Union Mission in the Sudan*." Available at: http://www.amis-sudan.org/. Accessed 22 April 2008.

American Commission for the Protection and Salvage of Artistic and Historic Monuments in War Areas. (1946). *Report of the American Commission for the Protection and Salvage of Artistic and Historic Monuments in War Areas*. Washington, DC: United States Government.

Armenia. Ministry of Foreign Affairs. (2004). "Ministry of Foreign Affairs Launches Nansen Exhibit at Council of Europe." 24 June 2004. http://www.armeniaforeignministry.com/pr_04/040624_nansen.html. Accessed 26 September 2005.

Boutros-Ghali, Boutros. (1992). *Agenda for Peace: Preventative Diplomacy, Peacemaking and Peacekeeping*. New York: United Nations.

Brown Letter. (1945). *Letter from John N. Brown, Adviser on Cultural Matters, to General Lucius Clay, Deputy Military Governor*. 9 August 1945. National Gallery Archives. Record Group 28, Collections of Donated Papers—Monuments, Fine Arts and Archives.

Bush, George. (1990). "Toward a New World Order," Address to Joint Session of Congress. Washington, DC, 11 September 1990. National Archives, Washington, DC.

Canada. International Commission on Intervention and State Sovereignty. (2001). *The Responsibility to Protect: Report of the International Commission on Intervention and State Sovereignty*. Available at http://www.iciss.ca/report-en.asp. Accessed 5 May 2008.

Canova, Antonio. (1815). *Note from Canova to the Allied Plenipotentiaries*. Paris. 11 September 1815. Public Record Office (United Kingdom). F.O. 139/39, p. 162 (PRO pagination).

Carlshausen letter. (1815). *Letter from Baron Carlshausen to the Allied Plenipotentiaries*. 5 September 1815. Public Record Office (United Kingdom). F.O. 139/39, p. 139 (PRO pagination).

Castlereagh letter. (1815). *Letter from Lord Castlereagh to the Prince Regent*. Paris. 11 September 1815. Public Record Office (United Kingdom). F.O. 92/26, p. 111 (PRO pagination).

Castlereagh Memoir. (1815). *Memoir of Lord Castlereagh.* Paris. September 1815. Public Record Office (United Kingdom). F.O. 92/26, no. 50, p. 117 (PRO pagination).

Center for Immigration Studies. (1995). "Three Decades of Mass Immigration: The Legacy of the 1965 Immigration Act." Available at http://www.cis.org/articles/1995/back395.html. Accessed 20 February 2007.

Clay Note. (1945). *Note initialed L.D.C. (Lucius D. Clay) to Ambassador Edwin Pauley.* 18 August 1945. National Archives, Washington, DC. Record Group 59, Box 19.

Commission of the European Communities. (2002a). *Enlargement of the European Union: Guide to the Negotiations, Chapter by Chapter.* Available at http://europa.eu.int/comm/enlargement/negotiations/chapters/negotiationsguide.pdf. Accessed 17 March 2003.

Commission of the European Communities. (2002b). *Regular Reports on Progress Toward Accession.* Country reports available at http://europa.eu.int/comm/enlargement/report2002/index.htm. Accessed 19 March 2003.

Commission of the European Communities. (2002c). *Towards the Enlarged Union: Strategy Paper and Report of the European Commission on the Progress Towards Accession by Each of the Candidate Countries.* COM (2002) 700 final and SEC (2002) 1400–1412. Available at http://www.fifoost.org/EU/strategy_en_2002/index.php. Accessed 31 May 2008.

Community of Democracies. (2000). *Toward a Community of Democracies Ministerial Conference Final Warsaw Declaration.* 27 June 2000. Warsaw, Poland. Available at http://www.ccd21.org/articles/warsaw_declaration.htm. Accessed 28 April 2008.

Council for a Community of Democracies. (2004). "Democracy Caucus." Available at http://www.ccd21.org/Initiatives/undc.htm. Accessed 24 April 2008.

Council of Europe. (1949). *Statute of the Council of Europe.* European Treaty Series No. 1. Available at http://conventions.coe.int/Treaty/EN/Treaties/Html/001.htm. Accessed 24 April 2008.

Council of Europe. (1950). *Convention for the Protection of Human Rights and Fundamental Freedoms.* 4 November 1950. "European Convention on Human Rights." Available at http://conventions.coe.int/Treaty/Commun/QueVoulezVous.asp?NT=005&CL=ENG. Accessed 28 April 2008.

Council of Europe. (2005). "About the Council of Europe." Available at http://www.coe.int/T/e/Com/about_coe/. Accessed September 29, 2005.

Danby, Michael. (2005). "Speech: Asylum Seekers." House of Representatives. 16 June 2005. Available at http://parlinfoweb.aph.gov.au/piweb/view_document.aspx?ID=2445569&TABLE=HANSARD. Accessed August 31, 2005.

ECOWAS. (1997). *Decision on the Sanctions against the Junta in Sierra Leone.* 29 August 1997. Twentieth Session of the Authority of Heads of State and Government. Available at http://www.sierra-leone.org/ecowas082999.html. Accessed 28 April 2008.

Eisenhower Order. (1944). *Order of 26 May 1944, Preservation of Historical Monuments.* AG (SHAEF/G-5/751). Public Record Office (United Kingdom). W.O. 202/798.

European Union. (1991). "Resolution of the council and of the member states meeting in the council on human rights, democracy and development." 28 November 1991. Available at http://ec.europa.eu/external_relations/human_rights/doc/cr28_11_91_en.htm. Accessed 24 April 2008.

European Union. (1999). *Council Regulation (EC) No 976/1999 of 29 April 1999.* Available at http://www2.ohchr.org/english/law/compilation_democracy/councilregulation.htm. Accessed 24 April 2008.

European Union. (2000). *Charter of Fundamental Rights of the European Union.* 18 December 2000. *Official Journal of the European Communities.* C 364/1. Available at http://ue.eu.int/uedocs/cms_data/docs/2004/4/29/Charter%20of%20fundemental%20rights%20of%20the%20European%20Union.pdf. Accessed 24 April 2008.

France. Ministère de l'Intérieur. (2003). "La lutte contre le financement du terrorisme." Feburary 2003. Available at http://www.interieur.gouv.fr/rubriques/c/c3_police_nationale/c332_dcpj/La_lutte_contre_le_financement_du_terrorisme. Accessed 21 May 2008.

France. Ministère de l'Intérieur. (2005). "Guide for Asylum Seekers 2005: Information and Orientation." Available at http://www.interieur.gouv.fr/misill/sections/a_la_une/publications/etrangers/guide-du-demandeur-d-asile-2005/view. Accessed 10 August 2006.

G7/P8. (1996). "Ministerial Conference on Terrorism." Paris. 30 July 1996.

German Federal Ministry of the Interior. (2001). *Structuring immigration, Fostering Integration.* Report by the Independent Commission on Migration to Germany. Available at http://www.bmi.bund.de/nn_148138/Internet/Content/Broschueren/2001/Structuring__Immigation__-__Fostering__Id__66078__en. html. Accessed 18 March 2006.

German Federal Ministry of the Interior. (2006). "Immigration Today: Refugee." http://www.zuwanderung.de/english/2_neues-gesetz-a-z/fluechtlinge.html. Accessed 1 July 2006.

Hardenberg Note. (1815). *Confidential Note from Prince Hardenberg to Lord Castlereagh.* Paris. September 1815. Public Record Office (United Kingdom). F.O. 139/33, p. 78 (PRO pagination).

Inter-American Commission on Human Rights. (1991). *MRE/RES.1/91, Support for the Democratic Government of Haiti.* 2 October 1991. Meeting of Foreign Ministers. Washington, DC. Available at http://www.cidh.org/annualrep/91eng/chap.4c.htm#_ftn5. Accessed 28 April 2008.

Jackson, Robert H. (1945). "Report to the President." *Department of State Bulletin.* 10 June 1945, 1071–74.

Johnson, Lyndon B. (1964). *Tonkin Gulf Incident Address.* 5 August 1964. Vietnam War.Com. Available at http://www.vietnamwar.com/tonkingulfpresaddress. htm. Accessed 15 May 2006.

Joint Commission on Human Rights. (2001). *Anti-Terrorism, Crime and Security Bill: Report, Together with the Proceedings of the Committee Relating to the Report and Minutes of Evidence,* 5th Report. London: The Stationery Office.

Lee Letter. (1946). *Letter from Rensselaer W. Lee, President of the College Art Association of America, to Secretary of State James F. Byrnes.* 15 January 1946. National Gallery Archives. Record Group 17a, Records of the Chief Curator WWII. Box 9, Folder 7.

Metternich Note. (1815). *Note from Prince Metternich.* Paris. 31 August 1815. Public Record Office (United Kingdom). F.O. 139/30, p. 17 (PRO pagination).

Minutes of the Conference of Allied Plenipotentiaries. (1815). Meeting of 6 September 1815. Annex 104. Public Record Office (United Kingdom). F.O. 139/39, p. 135 (PRO pagination).

Murphy Letter. (1945). *Letter from Robert Murphy, Political Advisor, U.S. Military Government in Germany, to General Lucius Clay and others.* 31 August 1945. National Gallery Archives. Record Group 28, Collections of Donated Papers— Monuments, Fine Arts and Archives Officers, Walter I. Farmer Papers, Box 1, Folder 2.

National Gallery Press Release. (1945). *Statement marked for "Immediate Release."* 26 September 1945. National Gallery Archives. Record Group 17a, Records of the Chief Curator WWII. Box 1, Folder 4.

NEPAD. (2001). *The New Partnership for Africa's Development (NEPAD).* 23 October 2001. Abuja , Nigeria. Available at http://www2.ohchr.org/english/ law/compilation_democracy/nepad.htm. Accessed 28 April 2008.

Netherlands Letter. (1815). *Letter to Prince Talleyrand.* 26 August 1815. Public Record Office (United Kingdom). F.O. 139/39, p. 137 (PRO pagination).

Office of the United Nations High Commissioner for Human Rights. (2008). *Status of Ratification of the International Covenant on Civil and Political Rights.* Available at http://www2.ohchr.org/english/law/ccpr.htm. Accessed 28 April 2008.

Organization of African Unity. (1969). *Convention Governing the Specific Aspects of Refugee Problems in Africa.* 10 September 1969. Available at http://www. africa-union.org/root/au/Documents/Treaties/Text/Refugee_Convention.pdf. Accessed 10 March 2007.

Organization of African Unity. (1989). "Declaration of the OAU Ad-hoc Committee on Southern Africa on the Question of South Africa." Harare, Zimbabwe. 21 August 1989. Available at http://www.anc.org.za/ancdocs/ history/oau/harare.html. Accessed 24 April 2008.

Organization of African Unity. (2000). *Lome Declaration of 2000, On the Framework for an OAU Response to Unconstitutional Changes of Government.* 12 July 2000.

Lome, Togo. Assembly of Heads of State and Government Thirty-sixth Ordinary Session/ Fourth Ordinary Session AEC. Available at http://www2.ohchr.org/english/law/compilation_democracy/lomedec.htm. Accessed 28 April 2008.

Organization of American States. (1948). *Charter of the Organization of American States.* Organization of American States. Department of International Law. Available at http://www.oas.org/juridico/English/charter.html. Accessed 24 April 2008.

Organization of American States. (1969). *American Convention on Human Rights.* 22 November 1969. San Jose, Costa Rica. Available at http://www.oas.org/juridico/English/treaties/b-32.html. Accessed 28 April 2008.

Organization of American States. (1991). *"Resolution 1080."* AG/RES. 1080 (XXI-O/91). Organization of American States. Department of International Legal Affairs. Available at http://www.oas.org/juridico/english/agres1080.htm. Accessed 24 April 2008.

Organization of American States. (1992). *Protocol of Amendments to the Charter of the Organization of American States "Protocol of Washington."* A-56. 14 December 1992. Organization of American States. Department of International Law. Available at http://www.oas.org/juridico/english/Sigs/a-56.html. Accessed 24 April 2008.

Pauley Cable. (1945). *Cable from Edwin Pauley to the Secretary of State.* 18 August 1945. National Archives. Record Group 59, Box 19. Pauley Reparations Mission.

Protocol of the Conference. (1815). *Meeting of 6 September 1815.* Public Record Office (United Kingdom). F.O. 139/39, p. 131 (PRO pagination).

Royal Navy. (2005). "The Rise of the Royal Navy 1660–1815." Royal Navy History. Available at http://www.royal-navy.mod.uk/static/pages/3539.html. Accessed 31 May 2008.

Russian Memoir Relative to the Statues, etc. (1815). Included with a memoir of Lord Castlereagh, Paris, September 1815. Public Record Office (United Kingdom), CAB 154/1&2, p. 263 (PRO pagination).

Smith, Bradley. (1982). "Memorandum for the President, Subject: Trial and Punishment of Nazi War Criminals." *The American Road to Nuremberg: The Documentary Record, 1944–1945.* Stanford: Hoover Institution Press.

Smyth Letter. (1945). *Letter from Craig H. Smyth to L. B. La Farge.* National Gallery Archives. Record Group 28, Collections of Donated Papers—Monuments, Fine Arts and Archives Officers, Craig Hugh Smyth Papers. Box 1, Folder 1.

Standen, Edith A. (n.d.). "Monuments, Fine Arts and Archives: May 1945–July 1947." National Gallery of Art Archives. Record Group 28, Collections of Donated Papers—Monuments, Fine Arts and Archives Officers, Edith A. Standen Papers. Box 1, Folder 11.

Standen Letter. (1945). *Letter from Edith A. Standen to Walter Farmer, enclosing copies of the MFA&A statement (the Wiesbaden Manifesto).* 1 December 1945.

National Gallery Archives. Record Group 28, Collections of Donated Papers—Monuments, Fine Arts.

Sutton, Denys. (1945). "The Commission for the Protection and Restitution of Cultural Material." AME/A/148. 15 December. National Gallery Archives. Record Group 17a, Records of the Chief Curator WWII, Box 1, Folder 5.

Talleyrand Note. (1815). *Note from Talleyrand to Castlereagh.* 19 September 1815. République Française. Ministère des Affaires Étrangers. Archives. France et divers états de l'Europe. 20 Novembre 1815. No. 692, Négociations, traités et conventions.

U.S. Chief Counsel for Prosecution of Axis Criminality. (1946). *Nazi Conspiracy and Aggression.* Washington, DC: United States Government Printing Office.

UNESCO. (1990). *Declaration of Montevideo: Democratic Culture and Governance.* 30 November 1990. Montevideo, Uruguay. Available at http://www.unesco.org/webworld/peace_library/UNESCO/HRIGHTS/320-326.HTM#one. Accessed 28 April 2008.

United Nations Development Program. (2004). *Democracy in Latin America: Toward a Citizen's Democracy.* New York: United Nations Development Programme.

UNHCHR. (2004). *Report of the Working Group on Contemporary Forms of Slavery.* E/CN.4/Sub.2/2004/L.11. 12 August 2004. New York: United Nations.

UNHCR. (1946). *Constitution of the International Refugee Organization.* December 15. http://www.yale.edu/lawweb/avalon/decade/decad053.htm. Accessed 25 September 2005.

United Nations. (1984). *Slavery—Report prepared by Benjamin Whitaker to the Sub-Commission on Prevention of Discrimination and Protection of Minorities.* E/CN.4/Sub.2/1982/20/Rev.1. New York: United Nations.

United Nations. (1993). *Yearbook of the United Nations 1992.* Dordrecht, The Netherlands: Martinus Nijhoff Publishers.

United Nations. (1995). *Yearbook of the United Nations 1994.* Dordrecht, The Netherlands: Martinus Nijhoff Publishers.

United Nations. (1997). *Daily Press Briefing for Office of Spokesman for Secretary General.* 7 October 1997. Available at http://www.un.org/News/briefings/docs/1997/19971008.db100897.html. Accessed 28 April 2008.

United Nations. (1998). *Press Briefing by UN Ambassador James O.C. Jonah.* 17 February 1998. UN Press Conference by the Permanent Representative of Sierra Leone. Available at http://www.un.org/News/briefings/docs/1998/19980218.jonah.html. Accessed 1 May 2008.

United Nations. (2000). *United Nations Millennium Declaration.* General Assembly Resolution 55/2 of 8 September 2000. Available at http://www.ohchr.org/english/law/millennium.htm. Accessed 15 January 2007.

United Nations. (2008). "Darfur—UNAMID—Background." Available at http://www.un.org/Depts/dpko/missions/unamid/background.html. Accessed 22 April 2008.

United Nations Chronicle. (1993). "The 38th floor: Challenges and Opportunities in the 21st Century." *United Nations Publications.* Available at http://www.findarticles.com/p/articles/mi_m1309/is_n2_v30/ai_13214071/pg_2. Accessed 28 April 2008.

United Nations Commission of Experts. (1994). *Final Report, Annex XI: Destruction of Cultural Property Report.* S/1994/674/Add.2 (Vol. V). 28 December 1994.

United Nations Counter-Terrorism Committee. (2002a). *Note by the Chairman, February 8.*

United Nations Counter-Terrorism Committee. (2002b). *Minutes of Meeting, March 21.*

United Nations Counter-Terrorism Committee. (2004). *Minutes of 4688th Meeting: High Level Meeting of the Security Council: Combating Terrorism* [S/PV.4688].

United Nations General Assembly. *Resolution 8(I).* 12 February 1946. Available at http://daccessdds.un.org/doc/RESOLUTION/GEN/NR0/032/59/IMG/NR003259.pdf?OpenElement. Accessed 3 August 2008.

United Nations General Assembly. (1946). *"Resolution 96(I)."* UN Document A/64/Add. 1.

United Nations General Assembly. (1950a). *Formulation of the Nuremberg Principles*—Reported by J. Spiropoulos, Special Rapporteur. A/CN.4/22.

United Nations General Assembly. (1950b). *"Resolution 376."* The Problem of the Independence of Korea. 7 October 1950. 294th Plenary Meeting. Available at http://daccessdds.un.org/doc/RESOLUTION/GEN/NR0/059/74/IMG/NR005974.pdf?OpenElement. Accessed 5 July 2006.

United Nations General Assembly. (1950c). *"Resolution 377."* Uniting for Peace. 3 November 1950. 302nd Plenary Meeting. Available at http://daccessdds.un.org/doc/RESOLUTION/GEN/NR0/059/75/IMG/NR005975.pdf?OpenElement. Accessed 5 July 2006.

United Nations General Assembly. (1951). *"Resolution 500."* Additional Measures to be Employed to Meet the Aggression in Korea. 18 May 1951. 330th Plenary Meeting. Available at http://daccessdds.un.org/doc/RESOLUTION/GEN/NR0/744/47/IMG/NR074447.pdf? OpenElement. Accessed 26 June 2006.

United Nations General Assembly. (1953). *"Resolution 742 (VIII)."* Factors which should be included in deciding whether a territory is or is not a territory whose people not yet attained a full measure of self-government. 27 November 1953. Resolutions adopted by the General Assembly during its Eighth Session. Available at http://www.un.org/documents/ga/res/8/ares8.htm. Accessed 28 April 2008.

United Nations General Assembly. (1966). "*Resolution 2200A (XXI)*." International Covenant on Civil and Political Rights. 16 December 1966. Available at http://www2.ohchr.org/english/law/ccpr.htm. Accessed 28 April 2008.

United Nations General Assembly. (1993). *The Vienna Declaration and Programme of Action*. 25 June 1993. Vienna, Austria. World Conference on Human Rights. Available at http://www.unhchr.ch/huridocda/huridoca.nsf/(Symbol)/A.CONF.157.23.En. Accessed 28 April 2008.

United Nations General Assembly. (2001a). *Measures to Eliminate International Terrorism: Report of the Secretary-General*. 3 July 2001. A/56/160.

United Nations General Assembly. (2001b). *Sixth Committee: Measures to Eliminate International Terrorism: Report of the Working Group*. 20 October 2001. A/C.6/56/L.9.

United Nations Office at Geneva. (2005). "Refugees Mixed Archival Group 1919–1947 (Nansen Fonds)." Available at http://biblio-archive.unog.ch/Detail.aspx?ID=256. Accessed 26 September 2005.

United Nations Office of the High Commissioner for Human Rights. (2004). *Status of Ratifications of the Principal International Human Rights Treaties*. Geneva: UNHCHR. Available at http://www.unhchr.ch/pdf/report.pdf. Accessed 10 March 2007.

United Nations Office of the High Commissioner for Human Rights. (2006). *Status of Genocide Convention*. Available at http://ww2.ohchr.org/english/bodies/ratification/1.htm. Accessed 14 January 2006.

United Nations Office of the High Commissioner for Refugees. (1984). *Cartagena Declaration on Refugees*. 22 November 1984. http://www.unhcr.org/basics/BASICS/45dc19084.pdf. Accessed 12 March 2006.

United Nations. *Press Release*. (2004). "*Negotiations Continue at Headquarters on Two Anti-Terrorism Treaties*." 1 January 2004. L/3073.

United Nations Security Council. (1950). *Resolution 82*. Complaint of Aggression Upon the Republic of Korea. 25 June 1950. *473rd Meeting*. S/1501. Available at http://daccessdds.un.org/doc/RESOLUTION/GEN/NR0/064/95/IMG/NR006495.pdf?OpenElement. Accessed 1 May 2008.

United Nations Security Council. (1982). *Provisional Rules of Procedure of the Security Council*. Available at http://www.un.org/Docs/sc/scrules.htm. Accessed 6 July 2004.

United Nations Security Council. (1990a). *Resolution 660*. The Situation Between Iraq and Kuwait. S/RES/660. 2 August 1990. *2932nd Meeting*. Available at http://daccessdds.un.org/doc/RESOLUTION/GEN/NR0/575/10/IMG/NR057510.pdf?OpenElement. Accessed June 26, 2006.

United Nations Security Council. (1990b). *Resolution 661*. 6 August 1990. Available at http://daccessdds.un.org/doc/RESOLUTION/GEN/NR0/575/11/IMG/NR057511.pdf?OpenElement. Accessed 3 August 2008.

United Nations Security Council. (1990c). *Resolution 662*. Demanding Iraq's Removal From Kuwait. S/RES/662. 9 August 1990. *2934th Meeting*. Available at http://daccessdds.un.org/doc/RESOLUTION/GEN/NR0/575/12/IMG/NR057512.pdf?OpenElement. Accessed 28 June 2006.

United Nations Security Council. (1992a). *Resolution 752*. 15 May 1992. S/RES/752. Available at http://daccessdds.un.org/doc/RESOLUTION/GEN/NR0/011/11/IMG/NR001111.pdf?OpenElement. Accessed 6 April 2005.

United Nations Security Council. (1992b). *Resolution 770*. 13 August 1992. S/RES/770. Available at http://daccessdds.un.org/doc/UNDOC/GEN/N92/379/66/ IMG/N9237966.pdf?OpenElement. Accessed 6 April 2005.

United Nations Security Council. (1992c). *Resolution 771*. 13 August 1992. S/RES/771. Available at http://daccessdds.un.org/doc/UNDOC/GEN/N92/379/72/IMG/ N9237972.pdf?OpenElement. Accessed 6 April 2005.

United Nations Security Council. (1993a). *Resolution 827*. 25 May 1993. S/RES/827. Available at http://daccessdds.un.org/doc/UNDOC/GEN/N93/306/28/IMG/N9330628.pdf?OpenElement. Accessed 1 May 2008.

United Nations Security Council. (1993b). *Resolution 841*. 16 June 1993. S/RES/841. Available at http://daccessdds.un.org/doc/UNDOC/GEN/N93/354/58/IMG/N9335458.pdf?OpenElement. Accessed 24 April 2008.

United Nations Security Council. (1994a). *Resolution 929*. 22 June 1994. S/RES/929. Available at http://daccessdds.un.org/doc/UNDOC/GEN/N94/260/27/PDF/N9426027.pdf?OpenElement. Accessed 6 April 2005.

United Nations Security Council. (1994b). *Resolution 940*. 31 July 1994. S/RES/940. Available at http://daccessdds.un.org/doc/UNDOC/GEN/N94/312/22/PDF/N9431222.pdf?OpenElement. Accessed 24 April 2008.

United Nations Security Council. (1994c). *Resolution 954*. 4 November 1994. S/RES/954. Available at http://daccessdds.un.org/doc/UNDOC/GEN/N94/431/95/PDF/N9443195.pdf?OpenElement. Accessed 6 April 2005.

United Nations Security Council. (1994d). *Statement by the President of the Security Council S/PRST/1994/21*. 30 April 1994. Available at http://daccessdds.un.org/doc/UNDOC/GEN/N94/199/86/PDF/N9419986.pdf?OpenElement. Accessed 28 December 2006.

United Nations Security Council. (1994a). *3363rd Meeting*. 14 April 1994. S/PV.3363. Available at http://daccessdds.un.org/doc/UNDOC/PRO/N94/854/08/PDF/N9485408.pdf?OpenElement. Accessed 28 December 2006.

United Nations Security Council. (1994b). *3368th Meeting*. 21 April 1994. S/PV.3368. Available at http://daccessdds.un.org/doc/UNDOC/PRO/N94/855/62/PDF/N9485562.pdf?OpenElement. Accessed 28 December 2006.

United Nations Security Council. (1994c). *3377th Meeting*. 16 May 1994. S/PV.3377. Available at http://daccessdds.un.org/doc/UNDOC/PRO/N94/856/51/PDF/N9485651.pdf?OpenElement. Accessed 28 December 2006.

United Nations Security Council. (1994d). *3392nd Meeting*. 22 June 1994. S/PV.3392. Available at http://daccessdds.un.org/doc/UNDOC/PRO/N94/857/93/PDF/N9485793.pdf?OpenElement. Accessed 28 December 2006.

United Nations Security Council. (1994e). *3475th Meeting*. 2 December 1994. S/PV.3475. Available at http://daccessdds.un.org/doc/UNDOC/PRO/N94/873/30/PDF/N9487330.pdf?OpenElement. Accessed 28 December 2006.

United Nations Security Council. (1997). *Resolution 1132*. 8 October 1997. S/RES/1132. Available at http://daccessdds.un.org/doc/UNDOC/GEN/N97/267/ 13/PDF/N9726713.pdf?OpenElement. Accessed 24 April 2008.

United Nations Security Council. (1999a). *Report of the Independent Inquiry into the Actions of the United Nations During the 1994 Genocide in Rwanda*. 16 December 1999. SC/1999/1257.

United Nations Security Council. (2004b). *Resolution 1556*. 30 July 2004. S/RES/1556. Available at http://daccessdds.un.org/doc/UNDOC/GEN/N04/446/02/PDF/N0444602.pdf?OpenElement. Accessed 6 April 2005.

United Nations Security Council. (2005a). *Resolution 1593*. 31 March 2005. S/RES/1593. Available at http://daccessdds.un.org/doc/UNDOC/GEN/N05/292/ 73/PDF/N0529273.pdf?OpenElement. Accessed 6 April 2005.

United Nations Security Council. (2005b). "Security Council Refers Situation in Darfur, Sudan, to Prosecutor of International Criminal Court." Press Release. SC/8351.

United States. Adjutant General's Office. (1863). *Instructions for the Government of Armies of the United States in the Field, General Orders No. 100*. 24 April 1863. Washington, DC: Government Printing Office, 1898.

U.S. Department of State. (1943). *Press Release No. 348*. 20 August 1943. National Archives. Record Group 239.

U.S. Department of State. (2005). "The Proliferation Security Initiative." Bureau of Nonproliferation. May 26. Available at http://www.state.gov/t/np/rls/other/46858.htm.

U.S. Group Control Council (n.d.). "Subject: Art Objects in US Zone." National Archives. Record Group 59, Box 19.

United States Senate. (1980). *Report on the Refugee Act of 1980*. Senate Report no. 256. 96th Cong., 2d session.

Wiesbaden Manifesto. (1945). *Statement signed by MFA&A officers*. 7 November 1945. Copy enclosed with Edith Standen letter to Walter Farmer of 1 December 1945. National Gallery Archives. Record Group 28, Collections of Donated Papers—Monuments, Fine Arts and Archives Officers, Walter I. Farmer Papers. Box 1, Folder 10.

Woolley, Leonard. (1947). *A Record of Work Done by the Military Authorities for the Protection of the Treasures of Art and History in the War Areas*. London: His Majesty's Stationery Office.

World Trade Organization. (2008). "The Uruguay Round." *Understanding the WTO*. Available at http://www.wto.org/english/thewto_e/whatis_e/tif_e/fact5_e.htm. Accessed 30 April 2008.

Treaties and Charters

African Charter on Human and Peoples' Rights. (1981). African Commission on Human and Peoples' Rights. June 1981. Available at http://www.achpr.org/english/_info/charter_en.html. Accessed 24 April 2008.

American Convention on Human Rights "Pact of San Jose, Costa Rica." (1969). Organization of American States. 22 November 1969. http://www.oas.org/juridico/english/Treaties/b-32.htm. Accessed 21 May 2008.

Charter of Fundamental Rights of the European Union. (2000). 18 December 2000. *Official Journal of the European Communities*. C 364/1. Available at http://eur-lex.europa.eu/LexUriServ/LexUriServ.do?uri=OJ:C:2000:364:0001:0022:EN:PDF. Accessed 21 May 2008. Accessed 24 April 2008.

Constitutive Act of the African Union. (2000). African Union. 11 July 2000. Available at http://www.africa-union.org/About_AU/Constitutive_Act.htm#Article2. Accessed 24 April 2008.

Convention Governing the Specific Aspects of Refugee Problems in Africa. (1969). African Union. 10 September 1969. Available at http://www.africa-union.org/Official_documents/Treaties_%20Conventions_%20Protocols/Refugee_Convention.pdf. Accessed 21 May 2008.

Convention for the Protection of Human Rights and Fundamental Freedoms as Amended by Protocol 11. Rome. 4 November 1950. http://conventions.coe.int/Treaty/en/Treaties/Html/005.htm. Accessed 26 September 2005.

Convention on the Prevention and Punishment of the Crime of Genocide. (1948). 9 December 1948. Office of the High Commissioner for Human Rights. Available at http://www.unhchr.ch/html/menu3/b/p_genoci.htm. Accessed 21 May 2008.

Convention Relating to the Status of Refugees. 28 July 1951. Available at http://www.unhchr.ch/html/menu3/b/o_c_ref.htm. Accessed 10 March 2006.

Covenant of the League of Nations. (1924). The Avalon Project at Yale Law School. Available at http://www.yale.edu/lawweb/avalon/leagcov.htm. Accessed 21 May 2008.

Geneva Convention Relative to the Treatment of Prisoners of War. (1949). 12 August 1949. Available at http://www.unhchr.ch/html/menu3/b/91.htm. Accessed 21 May 2008.

Protocol to the African Charter on Human and Peoples' Rights on the Rights of Women in Africa. (2003). African Commission on Human Rights and Peoples Rights. 11 July 2003. 2nd Ordinary Session of the Assembly of the Union. Available at http://www.achpr.org/english/_info/women_en.html. Accessed 28 April 2008.

Treaty between the United States and other Powers Providing for the Renunciation of War as an Instrument of National Policy ("Kellogg-Briand Pact"). (1928). *United States Statutes at Large, vol.* 26, part 2, 2343. 27 August 1928. Available at http://www.yale.edu/lawweb/avalon/imt/kbpact.htm. Accessed 4 July 2006.

Treaty Between the United of States of America, Belgium, the British Empire, China, France, Italy, Japan, the Netherlands, and Portugal. (1922). 6 February 1922. The Avalon Project at Yale Law School. Available at http://www.yale.edu/lawweb/avalon/diplomacy/forrel/1922v1/tr22-01.htm. Accessed 22 July 2005.

United Nations. (1945). *Charter of the United Nations.* 26 June 1945. Available at http://www.un.org/aboutun/charter/. Accessed 1 May 2008.

United Nations. (1967). *Protocol Relating to the Status of Refugees.* 4 October 1967. 606 U.N.T.S. 267.

United Nations. (1999). *Rome Statute of the International Criminal Court.* 17 July 1998. Available at http://www.un.org/law/icc/general/overview.htm. Accessed 23 March 2006.

Books and Articles

Abiew, Francis Kofi. (1999). *The Evolution of the Doctrine and Practice of Humanitarian Intervention.* The Hague: Kluwer Law International.

Abramson, Kara. (2003). "Beyond Consent: Toward safeguarding human rights— Implementing the United Nations Trafficking Protocol." *Harvard International Law Journal* 44: 473–502.

Adams, Jane Elizabeth. (1925). "The Abolition of the Brazilian Slave Trade." *The Journal of Negro History* 10(4): 607–37.

Adcock, F. E. (1932). "Caesar's Dictatorship." In *The Roman Republic 133–144 BC,* ed. S.A. Cook, F. E. Adcock, and M. P. Charlesworth, 736–49. Cambridge Ancient History, vol. 9. London: Cambridge University Press.

Akhavan, Payam. (1995). "Recent Development: Enforcement of the Genocide Convention: A Challenge to Civilization." *Harvard Human Rights Journal* 8: 229–36.

Akinsha, Konstantin, and Girgorii Kozlov. (1995). *Beautiful Loot: The Soviet Plunder of Europe's Art Treasures.* New York: Random House.

Aktan, Gunduz S., and Ali M. Koknar. (2002). "Turkey." In *Combating Terrorism: Strategies of Ten Countries,* ed. Yonah Alexander, 260–99, Ann Arbor: University of Michigan Press.

Al Baharna, Husain M. (1998). *British Extra-Territorial Jurisdiction in the Gulf 1913–1971.* Slough, UK: Archive Editions Ltd.

Alexander, Yonah. (2002). *Combating Terrorism: Strategies of Ten Countries.* Ann Arbor: University of Michigan Press.

Alvarez, José. (2003). "Hegemonic International Law Revisited." *American Journal of International Law* 97: 873–88.

Amann, Diane Marie. (1999). "Prosecutor v. Akayesu. Case ICTR-96–4–T." *The American Journal of International Law* 93(1): 195–9.

American Civil Liberties Union. (2005). "Summary of the USA Patriot Act." Accessible at http://www.aclu.org/SafeandFree/SafeandFree.cfm?ID=11813& c=207#FileAttach.

Amnesty International. (2005). "Who Are the Guantànamo Detainees?" Accessible at http://web.amnesty.org/library/Index/ENGAMR511152004?open&of= ENG-EGY.

Anderson, Malcolm. (2000). "Counterterrorism as an Objective of European Police Cooperation." *In European Democracies Against Terrorism: Governmental Policies and Intergovernmental Cooperation*, ed. Fernanco Reinares, 227–43. Aldershot, UK: Ashgate.

Anstey, Roger. (1975). *The Atlantic Slave Trade and British Abolition, 1760–1810*. London: Macmillan.

Aristotle. (1988). *Politics*. Trans. Benjamin Jowett. Cambridge Texts in the History of Political Thought. Cambridge: Cambridge University Press.

Bales, Kevin. (2004). *Disposable People: New Slavery in the Global Economy*. Rev. ed. Berkeley: University of California Press.

Ball, Howard. (1999). *Prosecuting War Crimes and Genocide*. Lawrence: University of Kansas Press.

Bankwitz, Philip Charles Farwell. (1978). *Alsatian Autonomist Leaders: 1919–1947*. Lawrence, KS: The Regents Press of Kansas.

Bantekas, Ilias. (2003). "The International Law of Terrorist Financing." *American Journal of International Law* 97: 315–31.

Barnett, Michael. (2002). *Eyewitness to a Genocide: The United Nations and Rwanda*. Ithaca: Cornell University Press.

Barnett, Michael, and Martha Finnemore. (2004). *Rules for the World: International Organizations in World Politics*. Ithaca, NY: Cornell University Press.

Barrett, Matthew A. (1999). "Ratify or Reject: Examining the United States' Opposition to the International Criminal Court." *Georgia Journal of International and Comparative Law* 28(3): 83–110.

Barrios, Erik. (2005). "Casting a Wider Net: Addressing the maritime piracy problem in Southeast Asia." *Boston College International and Comparative Law Review* 28: 149–63.

Barry, Ian Patrick. (2004). "The Right of Visit, Search and Seizure of Foreign Flagged Vessels on the High Seas Pursuant to Customary International Law: A Defense of the Proliferation Security Initiative." *Hofstra Law Review* 33: 299–330.

Bazyler, Michael J. (2003). *Holocaust Justice: The Battle for Restitution in America's Courts*. New York: New York University Press.

BBC World Service. (1991). *Gulf Crisis Chronology*. Essex, U.K.: Longman Current Affairs.

Becker, Michael A. (2005). "The Shifting Public Order of the Oceans: Freedom of navigation and the interdiction of ships at sea." *Harvard International Law Journal* 46: 131–229.

Bederman, David J. (2001). *International Law Frameworks*. New York: Foundation Press.

Bem, Kazimierz. (2004). "The Coming of a 'Blank Cheque'—Europe, the 1951 Convention, and the 1967 Protocol." *International Journal of Refugee Law* 16(4): 609–27.

Bendix, Reinhard. (1978). *Kings or People: Power and the Mandate to Rule*. Berkeley: University of California Press.

Beneš, Zdeněk, et al. (2002). *Facing History: The Evolution of Czech-German Relations in the Czech provinces, 1848–1948*. Prague: Galery.

Bennett, Andrew, Joseph Lepgold, Danny Unger eds. (1997). *Friends in Need: Burden Sharing in the Persian Gulf War*. New York: St Martin's Press.

Bernhardi, Friedrich von. (1914). *Germany and the Next War*. New York: Longman, Greens & Co.

Bernstein, Barton. (1966). "Southern Politics and the Attempt to Reopen the African Slave Trade." *Journal of Negro History* 51(1): 16–35.

Bethell, Leslie. (1966). "The Mixed Commissions for the Suppression of the Transatlantic Slave Trade in the Nineteenth Century." *Journal of African History* 7(1): 79–93.

Bevan, Bryan. (1971). *The Great Seamen of Elizabeth I*. London: Robert Hale.

Bhoumik, Arunabha. (2005). "Democratic Responses to Terrorism: A Comparative Study of the United States, Israel, and India." *Denver Journal of International Law and Policy* 33: 285–345.

Blakesley, Christopher L. (1982). "Criminal Law: United States Jurisdiction over Extraterritorial Crime." *Criminal Law and Criminology* 73: 1109–64.

Blakesley, Christopher L. (1992). *Terrorism, Drugs, International Law, and the Protection of Human Liberty*. Ardsley-on-Hudson, NY: Transnational Pubs.

Blay, Sam, and Andreas Zimmerman. (1994). "Recent Changes in German Refugee Law: A Critical Assessment." *American Journal of International Law* 88(2): 361–78.

Bloxham, Donald. (2001). *Genocide on Trial: War Crimes Trials and the Formation of Holocaust History and Memory*. New York: Oxford University Press.

Boli, John, and George Thomas. (1998). "INGOs and the Organization of World Culture." In *Constructing World Culture: International Nongovernmental Organizations Since 1875*, ed. John Boli and George Thomas, 13–49. Stanford, CA: Stanford University Press.

Bosche, Monika. (2003). "Trapped inside the European fortress? Germany and the European Union asylum and refugee policy." Paper presented at the Annual Meeting of the International Studies Association, Portland, Oregon,

25 February–1 March 2003. Available at http://isanet.ccit.arizona.edu/portlandarchive.html#B. Accessed 20 June 2005.

Bowles, Thomas Gibson. (1910). *Sea Law and Sea Power as They Would be Affected by Recent Proposals; With Reasons Against Those Proposals*. London: John Murray.

Brem, Stefan, and Kendall Stiles, (forthcoming). *Cooperating without America: Theories and Case-Studies of Non-hegemonic Regimes*. London: Routledge.

Brown, Bob. (2005). "Government Criticized over Treatment of Defector's Plea for Asylum." *The World Today*. 9 June 2005. Available at http://www.abc.net.au/worldtoday/content/2005/s1388421.htm. Accessed 30 May 2008.

Brownlie, Ian. (1963). *International Law and the Use of Force by States*. Oxford: Clarendon Press.

Bruun, Lori Lyman. (1993). "Beyond the 1948 Convention—Emerging Principles of Genocide in Customary International Law." *Maryland Journal of International Law and Trade* 17: 193–212.

Bryce, James and Arnold Toynbee. (1916). *The Treatment of Armenians in the Ottoman Empire, 1915–16*. Available at http://armenianhouse.org/bryce/treatment/index.html. Accessed 15 March 2006.

Brysk, Alison. (1993). "From Above and Below: Social Movements, the International System and Human Rights in Argentina." *Comparative Political Studies* 26(3): 259–85.

Brysk, Alison. (2000). *From Tribal Village to Global Village: International Relations and Indian Rights in Latin America*. Stanford, CA: Stanford University Press.

Buhler, Phillip A. (1999). "New Struggle with an Old Menace: Towards a revised definition of maritime policy." *Currents: International Trade Law Journal* 8: 61–70.

Bull, Hedley. (1995) [1977]. *The Anarchical Society: A Study of Order in World Politics*. 2nd ed. New York: Columbia University Press.

Bulloch, John, and Harvey Morris. (1991). *Saddam's War: The Origins of the Kuwait Conflict and the International Response*. London: Faber and Faber.

Buzan, Barry. (1993). "From International System to International Society: Structural Realism and Regime Theory Meet the English School." *International Organization* 47(3): 327–52.

Byers, Michael. (1999). *Custom, Power, and the Power of Rules*. Cambridge: Cambridge University Press.

Bynkershoek, Cornelius van. (1930) [1737]. *Quaestionum Juris Publici Libri Duo*. Trans., Tenney Frank. Oxford: Clarendon Press.

Cameron, Maxwell. (1994). *Democracy and Authoritarianism in Peru: Political Coalitions and Social Change*. New York: St. Martin's Press.

Campi, Alicia. (2004). "The McCarran-Walter Act: A Contradictory Legacy on Race, Quotas, and Ideology." American Immigrant Law Foundation.

http://www.immigrationpolicy.org/index.php?content=pr0604. Accessed 31 July 2008.

Caputi, Robert J. (2000). *Neville Chamberlain and Appeasement: Fifty Years of Conflict*. Selinsgrove, PA: Susquehanna University Press.

Carothers, Thomas. (1999). *Aiding Democracy Abroad: The Learning Curve*. Washington, DC: Carnegie Endowment for International Peace.

Cash, Heather. (2007). "Security Council Resolution 1593 and Conflicting Principles of International Law: How the Future of the International Criminal Court is at Stake." *Brandeis Law Journal* 45(1): 573–95.

Cassese, Antonio, and B.V.A. Roling. (1993). *The Tokyo Trial and Beyond*. Cambridge: Polity Press.

Cassese, Antonio. (1996). "The International Community's 'Legal' Response to Terrorism." In *Terrorism*, ed. Conor Gearty, 73–92. Aldershot, England: Dartmouth Pub.

Cassese, Antonio. (2000). "The Martens Clause: Half a Loaf or Simply Pie in the Sky?" *European Journal of International Law* 11(1): 187–216.

Center for Immigration Studies. (1995). "Three Decades of Mass Immigration: The Legacy of the 1965 Immigration Act." Available at http://www.cis.org/articles/1995/back395.html. Accessed 20 February 2007.

Chalk, Frank, and Kurt Johnassohn. (1990). *The History and Sociology of Genocide*. New Haven: Yale University Press.

Chalk, Peter. (1998). "Low-Intensity Conflict in Southeast Asia: Piracy, Drug Trafficking and Political Terrorism." *Conflict Studies* 305/306: 1–38.

Chalk, Peter. (2000). "The Third Pillar on Judicial and Home Affairs Cooperation, Anti-terrorist Collaboration and Liberal Democratic Acceptability." In *European Democracies Against Terrorism: Governmental policies and intergovernmental cooperation*, ed. Fernando Reinares, 175–210. Burlington: Ashgate.

Chang, Richard T. (1984). *The Justice of the Western Consular Courts in Nineteenth-Century Japan*. Westport, CO: Greenwood Press.

Chatelain, Jean. (1973). *Dominique Vivant Denon et le Louvre de Napoléon*. Paris: Librairie Académique Perrin.

Chayes, Abram, Thomas Ehrlich, and Andreas F. Lowenfeld. (1968). *International Legal Process*. 3 vols. Boston, MA: Little, Brown.

Chayes, Abram and Antonia Handler Chayes. (1995). *The New Sovereignty: Compliance with International Regulatory Agreements*. Cambridge, MA: Harvard University Press.

Chesterman, Simon. (2001). *Just War or Just Peace? Humanitarian Intervention and International Law*. New York: Oxford University Press.

Christopher, Warren. (1994). "American Foreign Policy: The Strategic Priorities." Speech delivered before the Senate Foreign Relations Committee, 4 November 1993. *Vital Speeches of the Day* 60(6): 162–67.

Clapham, Christopher. (1996). *Africa and the International System. The Politics of State Survival.* Cambridge: Cambridge University Press.

Clark, Richard. (1979). *Statement to the Subcommittee on Immigration, Refugees, and International Law of the House Committee on the Judiciary.* 96th Congress, 1st Session.

Clark, Roger S. (1999). "Steven Spielberg's *Amistad* and Other Things I Have Thought About in the Past Forty Years: International (Criminal) Law, Conflict of Laws, Insurance and Slavery." *Rutgers Law Journal* 30: 371–440.

Clarke, Walter, and Jeffrey Herbst. (1997). *Learning From Somalia: The Lessons of Armed Humanitarian Intervention.* Boulder, CO: Westview Press.

Clyde, Paul H. (1948). "The diplomacy of 'playing no favorites': Secretary Stimson and Manchuria, 1931." *The Mississippi Valley Historical Review* 35(2): 187–202.

CNN. (1998). "Clinton meets Rwanda genocide survivors." 25 March 1998. Available at http://www.cnn.com/WORLD/9803/25/clinton.africa/index.html? eref=sitesearch. Accessed 28 December 2006.

CNN. (2005). "U.N. report: Darfur not genocide." 31 January 2005. Available at http://www.cnn.com/2005/WORLD/africa/01/31/sudan.report/index.html. Accessed 28 December 2006.

CNN. (2006a). *Sudan balks at step toward U.N. troops in Darfur.* 24 May 2006.

CNN. (2006b). *Rebel Groups Holding Out on Darfur Deal.* 1 June 2006.

Cooper, Andrew F., and Thomas Legler. (2001). "A Model for the Future?" *Journal of Democracy* 12(4): 123–136.

Cornell, Savante E. (2003). "The War Against Terrorism and the Conflict in Chechnya: A Case for Distinction." *The Fletcher Forum of World Affairs Journal* 27: 167–82.

Corrigan, Katrin. (2001). "Putting the Brakes on the Global Trafficking of Women for the Sex Trade: An Analysis of Existing Regulatory Schemes to Stop the Flow of Traffic." *Fordham International Law Journal* 25: 151–213.

Cortell, Andrew, and James Davis. (1996). "How Do International Institutions Matter? The Domestic Impact of International Rules and Norms." *International Studies Quarterly* 40: 451–78.

Cortell, Andrew P., and James W. Davis, Jr. (2000). "Understanding the Domestic Impact of International Norms: A Research Agenda." *International Studies Review* 2(1): 65–87.

Cowling, Maurice. (1975). *The Impact of Hitler: British Politics and British Policy 1933–1939.* Cambridge University Press.

Crawford, James. (2000). "Democracy and the Body of International Law." In *Democratic Governance and International Law,* ed. Gregory Fox and Brad Roth, 91–122. Cambridge: Cambridge University Press.

Crawford, Neta. (2002). *Argument and Change in World Politics.* Cambridge: Cambridge University Press.

Crook, John R. (2005a). "Contemporary Practice of the United States Relating to International Law: President and Secretary of State Characterize Events in Darfur as Genocide." *The American Journal of International Law* 99: 266–67.

Crook, John R. (2005b). "Contemporary Practice of the United States Relating to International Law: United States Abstains on Security Council Resolution Authorizing Referral of Darfur Atrocities to International Criminal Court." *American Journal of International Law* 99: 691–93.

Crook, John R. (2005c). "Contemporary Practice of the United States Relating to International Law: U.S. Proposes New Regional Court to Hear Charges Involving Darfur, Others Urge ICC." *American Journal of International Law* 99: 501–02.

Crozier, Andrew J. (1997). *The Causes of the Second World War*. Malden, MA: Blackwell Publishers.

Current, Richard N. (1954). "The Stimson Doctrine and the Hoover Doctrine." *The American Historical Review* 59: 513–42.

D'Amato, Anthony A. (1971). *The Concept of Custom in International Law*. Ithaca, NY: Cornell University Press.

D'Anjou, Leo. (1996). *Social Movements and Cultural Change: The First Abolition Campaign Revisited*. New York: Aldine de Gruyter.

Dallaire, Romeo. (2003). *Shake Hands with the Devil: The Failure of Humanity in Rwanda*. Toronto: Random House Canada.

Daudet, Yves. (1997). "International Action against State Terrorism." In *Terrorism and International Law*, ed. Rosalyn Higgins and Maurice Flory, 207–23. New York: Routledge.

Davis, Michael. (2004). "The Emerging World Order: State Sovereignty and Humanitarian Intervention." In *International Intervention in the Post-Cold War World: Moral Responsibility and Power Politics*, ed. Michael Davis, Wolfgang Dietrich, Bettina Scholdan, and Dieter Sepp, 3–22. Armonk, NY: M.E. Sharpe.

De Sola, David. (2004). "International Team to Monitor Presidential Election." CNN.com. 9 August 2004. Available at http://www.cnn.com/2004/ALLPOLITICS/08/08/international.observers/. Accessed 20 September 2006.

De Souza, Philip. (1999). *Piracy in the Graeco-Roman World*. New York: Cambridge University Press.

Defeis, Elizabeth F. (2004). "Protocol to Prevent, Suppress and Punish Trafficking in Persons: A New approach." *ILSA Journal of International and Comparative Law* 10: 485–491.

Dennis, Michael. (2000). "The Fifty-Fifth Session of the UN Commission on Human Rights." *American Journal of International Law* 94(1): 189–97.

Detling, Karen J. (1993). "Eternal Silence: The Destruction of Cultural Property in Yugoslavia." *Maryland Journal of International Law and Trade* 17(1): 41–75.

DiPrizio, Robert C. (2002). *Armed Humanitarians: U.S. Interventions from Northern Iraq to Kosovo*. Baltimore, MD: Johns Hopkins University Press.

Donoho, Douglass Lee. (1996). "Evolution or Expediency: The United Nations Response to the Disruption of Democracy." *Cornell International Law Journal* 29: 329–82.

Downs, George, David Rocke, and Peter Barsoom.(1996). "Is the Good News About Compliance Good News About Cooperation?" *International Organization* 50: 379–406.

Drescher, Seymour. (1986). *Capitalism and Antislavery: British Popular Mobilization in Comparative Perspective*. New York: Oxford University Press.

Dubner, Barry Hart. (1997). "Human Rights and Environmental Disaster – Two Problems that Defy the 'Norms' of the International Law of Sea Piracy." *Syracuse Journal of International Law and Commerce* 23: 1–42.

DuBois, W.E.B. (1970/1896). *The Suppression of the African Slave-Trade to the United States of America: 1638-1870*. New York: Dover Pubs.

Dunne, Timothy. (1998). *Inventing International Society: A History of the English School*. New York: St Martin's.

Eagleton, Clyde. (1932). *International Government*. New York: Ronald Press.

Earle, Jonathan H. (2004). *Jacksonian Antislavery and the Politics of Free Soil, 1824-1854*. Chapel Hill: University of North Carolina Press.

Endless, Brian. (2003). *International Legitimacy and the United Nations Security Council*. PhD Dissertation, Loyola University Chicago.

Erdem, Y. Hakan. (1996). *Slavery in the Ottoman Empire and its Demise, 1800-1909*. London: Macmillan.

Ericson, David F. (2000). *The Debate over Slavery: Antislavery and Proslavery Liberalism in Antebellum America*. New York: New York University Press.

Evans, Alona. (1978). "Aircraft and Aviation Facilities." In *Legal Aspects of International Terrorism*, ed. Alona Evans and John F. Murphy, 3–147. Lexington, MA: Lexington Books.

Falk, Richard. (1996). "The Complexities of Humanitarian Intervention: A New World Order Challenge." *Michigan Journal of International Law* 17: 491–512.

Feliciano, Hector. (1997). *The Lost Museum: The Nazi Conspiracy to Steal the World's Greatest Works of Art*. New York: Basic Books.

Fenwick, Helen. (2000). *New Labour, Freedom and the Human Rights Act*. Harlow, UK: Pearson Education.

Feuchtwanger, Edgar. (2002). *Bismarck*. London: Routledge, Taylor and Francis Group.

Feve, Sabrina, and Christina Finzel. (2001). "Trafficking in People." *Harvard Journal on Legislation* 38: 279–90.

Finnemore, Martha. (1996). *National Interests in International Society*. Ithaca, NY: Cornell University Press.

Finnemore, Martha. (2003). *The Purpose of Intervention: Changing Beliefs About the Use of Force*. Ithaca, NY: Cornell University Press.

Finnemore, Martha. (2004). *The Purpose of Intervention: Changing Beliefs about the Use of Force*. Ithaca, NY: Cornell University Press.

Finnemore, Martha, and Kathryn Sikkink. (1998). "International Norm Dynamics and Political Change." *International Organization* 52(4): 887–917.

Fishel, Wesley R. (1952). *The End of Extraterritoriality in China*. Berkeley, CA: University of California Press.

Fitzpatrick, Joan. (2003). "Trafficking as a Human Rights Violation: The Complex Intersection of Legal Frameworks for Conceptualizing and Combating Trafficking." *Michigan Journal of International Law* 24: 1143–1167.

Flanner, Janet. (1947). *Men and Monuments*. New York: Harper & Brothers.

Flint, George Lee Jr., and Marie Juliet Alfaro. (2003). "Secured Transactions History: The Impact of English Smuggling on the Chattel Mortgage Acts in the Spanish Borderlands." *Valparaiso University Law Review* 37: 703–791.

Foblets, Marie-Claire. (1994). "Europe and Its Aliens after Maastricht. The Painful Move to Substantive Harmonization of Member-States' Policies Towards Third-Country Nationals." *American Journal of Comparative Law* 42(4): 783–805.

Fowler, Elaine W. (1965). *English Sea Power in the Early Tudor Period, 1485–1558*. Amherst, MA: Folger Books.

Fox, Gregory. (2000). The Right to Political Participation. In *Democratic Governance and International Law,* ed. Gregory Fox and Brad Roth, 48–90. United Kingdom: Cambridge University Press.

Fox, Gregory, and Brad Roth eds. (2000). *Democratic Governance and International Law*. United Kingdom: Cambridge University Press.

Franck, Thomas. (1992). "The Emerging Right to Democratic Governance." *American Journal of International Law* 86(1): 46–91.

Franck, Thomas M., and Bert B. Lockwood, Jr. (1974). "Preliminary Thoughts Towards an International Convention on Terrorism." *American Journal of International Law* 68(1): 69–90.

Franck, Thomas M., and Stephen H. Yuhan. (2003). "The United States and the International Criminal Court: Unilateralism Rampant." *New York University Journal of International Law and Politics* 35(1): 519–58.

Frank, Jonathan A. (2002). "A Return to Lockerbie and the Montreal Convention in the Wake of the September 11th Terrorist Attacks: Ramifications of Past Security Council and International Court of Justice Action." *Denver Journal of International Law and Policy* 30: 532–46.

Freamon, Bernard K. (1998). "Slavery, Freedom, and the Doctrine of Consensus in Islamic Jurisprudence." *Harvard Human Rights Journal* 11: 1–48.

Freestone, David. (1997). "International Cooperation against Terrorism and the Development of International Law Principles of Jurisdiction." *In Terrorism and International Law,* ed. Rosalyn Higgins and Maurice Flory, 43–67. New York: Routledge.

Fry, Robert., ed. (2004). *The Genocidal Temptation: Auschwitz, Hiroshima, Rwanda, and Beyond.* Lanham, MD: University Press of America.

Fujii, Shin'ichi. (1925). *View of League of Nations and Japan.* Tokyo: The Mangetsudo Press.

Gallagher, Anne. (2001). "Human Rights and the New UN Protocols on Trafficking and Migrant Smuggling: A Preliminary Analysis." *Human Rights Quarterly* 23(4): 975–1004.

Gao, Wang. (2003). *Wan Qing Zhong Guo De Zheng Zhi Zhuang Xing.* Beijing: Zhong Guo She Hui Ke Xue Chu Ban She.

Garitee, Jerome R. (1977). *The Republic's Private Navy.* Middletown, CT: Wesleyan University Press.

Garmon, Tina. (2002). "International Law of the Sea: Reconciling the Law of Piracy and Terrorism in the Wake of September 11th." *The Maritime Lawyer* 27: 257–75.

Garrett, Stephen A. (1999). *Doing Good and Doing Well—An Examination of Humanitarian Intervention.* Westport: Praeger.

Gattini, Andrea. (1996). "Restitution by Russia of Works of Art Removed from German Territory at the End of the Second World War." *European Journal of International Law* 7(1): 67–88.

George, David Lloyd. (1918). "British War Aims." 5 January 1918. The World War I Document Archive. Available at http://wwi.lib.byu.edu/index.php/Prime_Minister_Lloyd_George_on_the_British_War_Aims. Accessed 22 May 2008.

Gibney, Mark. (1988). "A 'Well-Founded Fear' of Persecution." *Human Rights Quarterly* 10(1): 109–121.

Goertz, Gary, and Paul Diehl. (1992). "Toward a Theory of International Norms: Some Conceptual and Measurement Issues." *Journal of Conflict Resolution* 36(4): 634–64.

Goldstein, Judith, et al. (2000). "Legalization and World Politics." *International Organization* 54(3): 385–99.

Gong, Gerrit W. (1984). *The Standard of 'Civilization' in International Society.* Oxford: Clarendon Press.

Goodman, Timothy H. (1999). "'Leaving the Corsair's Name to Other Times:' How to Enforce the Law of Sea Piracy in the 21st Century through Regional International Agreements." *Case Western Reserve Journal of International Law* 31: 139–168.

Goodrich, Leland M. (1956). *Korea: A Study of US Policy in the United Nations.* New York: Council on Foreign Relations.

Gottschalk, Jack A., and Brian Flanagan. (2000). *Jolly Roger with an Uzi: The Rise and Threat of Modern Piracy.* Annapolis, MD: Naval Institute Press.

Gould, Cecil. (1965). *Trophy of Conquest: The Musée Napoléon and the Creation of the Louvre*. London: Faber and Faber.

Gow, James. (1993). *Iraq, the Gulf Conflict and the World Community*. London: Brassey's.

Grahl-Madsen, Atle, Peter Macalister-Smith, and Gudmundur Alfredsson eds. (2001). *The Land Beyond: Collected Essays on Refugee Law and Policy*. Hague: Martinus Nijhoff Publishers.

Grant, Kevin. (2005). *A Civilised Savagery: Britain and the New Slaveries in Africa, 1884–1926*. London: Routledge.

Gray, Talitha. (2003). "Securing Justice through the International Criminal Court." *Arizona Journal of International and Comparative Law* 20(3): 645–88.

Greppi, Edoardo. (1999). "The evolution of individual criminal responsibility under international law." *International Review of the Red Cross* 835: 537–8.

Grey, Wilfrid. (2000). *U.N. Jigsaw*. New York: Vantage.

Griffin, Mathhew. (2000). "Accrediting Democracies: Does the Credentials Committee of the United Nations Promote Democracy Through Its Accreditation Process, and Should It?" *New York University Journal of International Law and Politics* 32: 725–85.

Grotius, Hugo. (1901). *The Rights of War and Peace*. Universal Classics Library. Washington, DC: M. Walter Dunne.

Grotius, Hugo (1901) [1625]. *The Rights of War and Peace*. Trans. A. C. Campbell. Washington, DC: M. Walter Dunne.

Hafner, Gerhard. (2003). "Certain Issues of the Work of the Sixth Committee at the 56th General Assembly." *American Journal of International Law* 97: 147–62.

Halberstam, Malvina. (1988). "Terrorism on the High Seas: The *Aquille Lauro*, piracy and the IMO Convention on Maritime Safety." *American Journal of International Law* 82: 269–310.

Haraksingh, Kusha. (1995). "The Worker and the Wage In a Plantation Economy: Trinidad in the late-Nineteenth Century." In *From Chattel Slaves to Wage Slaves: The Dynamics of Labour Bargaining in the Americas*, ed. Mary Turner, 224–39. Kingston: Ian Rand.

Hart, H. L. A. (1994). *The Concept of Law*. 2nd ed. Oxford: Oxford University Press.

Harvard Draft. (1932). "The Supplement: Research in International Law—Part IV—Piracy." *American Journal of International Law* 26: 739–885.

Harvard Law Review Association. (2001). "Developments in the Law—International Criminal Law: IV. Defining Protected Groups Under the Genocide Convention." *Harvard Law Review* 114: 2007–24.

Hathaway, James. (1984). "The Evolution of Refugee Status in International Law: 1920–1950." *International and Comparative Law Quarterly* 33(2): 348–80.

Hattendorf, John B., R.J.B. Knight, A.W.H. Pearsall, N.A.M. Rodger, and Geoffrey Till eds. (1993). *British Naval Documents, 1204–1960*. Aldershot: Scolar Press.

Hawkins, Darren. (2004). "Explaining Costly International Institutions: Persuasion and Enforceable Human Rights Norms." *International Studies Quarterly* 48(4): 779–804.

Hawkins, Darren, and Jutta Joachim. (2003). "Legalizing Human Rights and Democracy: Comparing the EU, OAS, and CE." Paper presented at the joint conference of the Central and Eastern European International Studies Association and the International Studies Association, Budapest, Hungary, 26–28 June 2003.

Hawkins, Darren, and Carolyn Shaw. (2005). "Legalizing Norms of Democracy in the OAS." Paper presented at the "Democratization in the Americas" workshop at Mount Allison University, Sackville, New Brunswick, 24–26 June 2005.

Hendriks, Mary Ross. (2003). "Modern Slavery and the Production of Consumer Goods in a Global Economy: Consumer Choice – Not Law – Will Trigger the Next Diaspora." *Thomas M. Cooley Law Review* 20: 431–51.

Herman, Arthur. (2004). *To Rule the Waves: How the British Navy shaped the modern world*. New York: Harper Collins.

Hermann, Wilfried A. (2004). "Piracy: Increasing Challenge with New Dimensions." *Naval Forces* 25(2): 18–24.

Herzfeld, Beth. (2000). "Campaigning Against Bonded Labour." *IFWEA Journal*. Available at http://www.ifwea.org/journal/1200/campaigning_against_bonded_labour.html. Accessed 30 May 2008.

Hevia, James L. (2003). *English Lessons: The Pedagogy of Imperialism in Nineteenth-Century China*. Durham, NC: Duke University Press.

Hinsliff, Gaby and Martin Bright. (2005). "Chaos: How the War on Terror Became a Political Dogfight." *The Observer*. 13 March 2005. Available at LexisNexis Academic. Accessed 18 April 2008.

Hochfield, Sylvia. (2000). "A German-Russian Breakthrough." *ARTnews* (March 2000): 68–70.

Hollis, Duncan B. (1995). "Accountability in Chechnya: Addressing Internal Matters with Legal and Political International Norms." *Boston College Law Review* 36: 793–846.

Honoré, Tony. (1996). "The Right to Rebel." *In Terrorism*, ed. Conor Gearty, 131–52. Aldershot: Dartmouth Pub.

Hooker, Richard. (1996). "Rome: The Punic Wars." 6 June 1999. Washington State University World Civilizations: An Internet Classroom and Anthology. Available at http://www.wsu.edu/~dee/ROME/ROME.HTM. Accessed 30 May 2008.

Horowitz, Richard S. (2004). "International Law and State Transformation in China, Siam, and the Ottoman Empire during the Nineteenth Century." *Journal of World History* 15(4): 445–486.

Horton, George. (1926). *The Blight of Asia– An Account of the Systematic Extermination of Christian Populations by Mohammedans and of the Culpability of*

Certain Great Powers; with the True Story of the Burning of Smyrna. Available at http://www.hri.org/docs/Horton/HortonBook.htm. Accessed 20 March 2006.

Hovani, Erica. (2001). "Book Annotation: Genocide in International Law: The Crime of Crimes by William A. Schabas." *Journal of International Law and Politics* 33(2): 1258–60.

Hsu, Ming-Chen. (1949). *The Rise and Fall of Extraterritoriality in China.* M.A. Thesis. University of California, Los Angeles.

Hui, Victoria Tin-bor. (2004). "Problematizing Sovereignty: Relative Sovereignty in the Historical Transformation of Interstate and State-society Relations." In *International Intervention in the Post-Cold War World: Moral Responsibility and Power Politics*, ed. Michael Davis, Wolfgang Dietrich, Bettina Scholdan and Dieter Sepp, 83–103. Armonk, NY: M.E. Sharpe.

Hulton, Susan. (2004). "Council Working Methods and Procedure." In *The UN Security Council: From the Cold War to the 21st Century*, ed. David Malone, 237–51. Boulder, CO: Lynne Rienner.

Human Rights Watch. (2005). "UN Security Council Refers Darfur to the ICC." 31 March 2005. Available at http://hrw.org/english/docs/2005/03/31/sudan10408. htm. Accessed 30 May 2008.

Human Rights Watch. (2006). "Q&A: Crisis in Darfur." 25 April 2008. Available at http://www.hrw.org/english/docs/2004/05/05/darfur8536.htm. Accessed 30 May 2008.

Hunter, Thomas. (1999). "The Growing Threat of Modern Piracy." *U.S. Naval Institute Proceedings.* 125(7): 72–76.

Hurlock, William L. (1997). "The International Court of Justice: Effectively Providing a Long Overdue Remedy for ending State-Sponsored Genocide (Bosnia-Herzegovina v. Yugoslavia)." *American University Journal of International Law and Policy* 12: 299–328.

Hurrell, Andrew. (2000). "International Law and the Changing Constitution of International Society." *In The Role of Law in International Politics*, ed. Michael Byers, 327–47. Oxford: Oxford University Press.

Hurrell, Andrew. (2002). "Norms and Ethics in International Relations." In *Handbook of International Relations*, ed. Walter Carlsnaes, Thomas Risse, and Beth A. Simmons, 137–54. London: Sage.

Hutchinson, Mark R. (1993). "Recent Development: Restoring Hope: U.N. Security Council Resolutions for Somalia and An Expanded Doctrine of Humanitarian Intervention." *Harvard International Law Journal* 34: 624–640.

Hyde, Charles Cheney. (1922). *International Law Chiefly as Interpreted and Applied by the United States.* Boston: Little, Brown and Company.

Ikenberry, G. John, and Charles A. Kupchan. (1990). "Socialization and Hegemonic Power." *International Organization* 44(3): 283–315.

Imlay, Talbot C. (2003). *Facing the Second World War: Strategy, Politics, and Economics in Britain and France 1938–1940.* New York: Oxford University Press.

Inglehart, Ronald. (1997). *Modernization and Postmodernization*. Princeton, NJ: Princeton University Press.

Inglehart, Ronald. (2003). "How Solid is Mass Support for Democracy—And How Can We Measure It?" *PS: Political Science and Politics* 36: 51–57.

Irwin, Ray W. (1970). *The Diplomatic Relations of the United States with the Barbary Powers, 1776–1816*. New York: Russell & Russell.

Itabashi, Isao, and Masamichi Ogawara, with David Leheny. (2002). "Japan." In *Combating Terrorism: Strategies of Ten Countries*, ed. Yonah Alexander, 337–74. Ann Arbor: University of Michigan Press.

Jackson, L. P. (1924). "Elizabethan Seamen and the African Slave Trade," *The Journal of Negro History* 9 (1): 1–17.

Jackson, Robert. (1993). "The Weight of Ideas in Decolonization: Normative Change in International Relations." In *Ideas and Foreign Policy: Beliefs, Institutions and Political Change*, ed. Judith Goldstein and Robert O. Keohane, 111–38. Ithaca, NY: Cornell University Press.

Jackson, Robert H. (1945). "Report to the President." *Department of State Bulletin*. 10 June 1945: 1071–4.

Jennings, Judith. (1997). *The Business of Abolishing the British Slave Trade, 1783–1807*. London: Frank Cass.

Jennings, Lawrence C. (2000). *French Anti-Slavery: The Movement for the abolition of slavery in France, 1802–1848*. New York: Cambridge University Press.

Jok, Jok Madut. (2001). *War and Slavery in Sudan*. Philadelphia: University of Pennsylvania University Press.

Jones, F. C. (1931). *Extraterritoriality in Japan and the Diplomatic Relations Resulting in Its Abolition, 1853–1899s*. New Haven, CT: Yale University Press.

Joyner, Christopher C., and Anthony Clark Arend. (1999/2000). "Anticipatory Humanitarian Intervention: An Emerging Legal Norm?" *United States Air Force Academy Journal of Legal Studies* 10: 27–51.

Julius, Kevin. (2004). *The Abolitionist Decade, 1829–1838: A Year-by-Year History of Early Events in the Antislavery Movement*. Jefferson, NC: McFarland & Co.

Kahn, Lawrence J. (1996). "Pirates, Rovers, and Thieves: New Problems with an Old Enemy." *Maritime Lawyer* 20: 293–323.

Kash, Douglas. (1993). "Abduction of Terrorists in International Airspace and on the High Seas." *Florida Journal of International Law* 8: 65–96.

Kastenberg, Major Joshua E. (2004). "The Use of Conventional International Law in combating Terrorism." *The Air Force Law Review* 55: 87–125.

Katzenstein, Peter J. (1996). "Introduction: Alternative Perspectives on National Security." In *The Culture of National Security: Norms and Identity in World Politics*, ed. Peter J. Katzenstein, 1–32. New York: Columbia University Press.

Kaufman, Chaim D., and Robert A. Pape. (1999). "Explaining Costly International Moral Action: Britain's Sixty-year Campaign against the Atlantic Slave Trade." *International Organization* 53(4): 631–68.

Keck, Margaret E., and Kathryn Sikkink. (1998). *Activists Beyond Borders: Advocacy Networks in International Politics*. Ithaca, NY: Cornell University Press.

Keeton, G. W. (1928). *The Development of Extraterritoriality in China*. New York: Howard Fertig.

Kelley, P.X., and Robert F. Turner. (2007). "War Crimes and the White House." *Washington Post*. 26 July 2007. A21.

Kelly, Michael J. (2002). "Can Sovereigns Be Brought to Justice? The Crime of Genocide's Evolution and the Meaning of the Milosevic Trial." *St John's Law Review* 76(1): 257–332.

Kelsey, Harry. (1998). *Sir Francis Drake: The Queen's Pirate*. New Haven: Yale University Press.

Kelsey, Harry. (2003). *Sir John Hawkins: Queen Elizabeth's Slave Trade*. New Haven: Yale University Press.

Kennedy, John F. (1940). *Why England Slept*. New York: W. Funk and Company.

Kerstetter, Wayne A. (1978). "Practical Problems of Law Enforcement." *In Legal Aspects of International Terrorism*, ed. Alona Evans and John F. Murphy, 535–51. Lexington, MA: Lexington Books.

Keyuan, Zou. (2000). "Enforcing the Law of Piracy in the South China Sea." *Journal of Law and Commerce* 31: 107–17.

Khalilieh, Hassan S. (1998). *Islamic Maritime Law: An Introduction*. Leiden: Brill.

Kim, Gye-Dong. (1993). *Foreign Intervention in Korea*. Aldershot, England: Dartmouth Publishing Company Limited.

Kirby, Michael. (2005). "The Institute for Advanced Study Branigin Lecture: Terrorism: The International Response of the Courts." *Indiana Journal of Global Legal Studies* 12: 313–44.

Klinghoffer, Arthur Jay. (1998). *The International Dimension of Genocide in Rwanda*. New York University Press: New York, NY.

Klotz, Audie. (1995). *Norms in International Relations: The Struggle Against Apartheid*. Ithaca, NY: Cornell University Press.

Koh, Harold Hongju. (1994). "The 'Haiti Paradigm' in United States Human Rights Policy." *Yale Law Journal* 103: 2391–2435.

Koh, Harold Hongju. (1996). "Transnational Legal Process." *Nebraska Law Review* 75: 181–207.

Koh, Harold Hongju. (1997). "Why Do Nations Obey International Law?" *Yale Law Journal* 106: 2599–2659.

Koh, Harold Hongju. (1998). "The 1998 Frankel Lecture: Bringing International Law Home." *Houston Law Review* 35: 623–81.

Kontorovich, Eugene. (2004a). "Implementing Sosa v. Alvarez-Machain: What Piracy Reveals about the Limits of the Alien Tort Statute." *Notre Dame Law Review* 80: 111–61.

Kontorovich, Eugene. (2004b). "The Piracy Analogy: Modern universal jurisdiction's hollow foundation." *Harvard International Law Journal* 45: 183–237.

Korman, Sharon. (1996). *The Right of Conquest: The Acquisition of Territory by Force in International Law and Practice*. Oxford: Clarendon Press.

Koslowski, Rey. (2001). "Economic Globalization, Human Smuggling, and Global Governance." In *Global Human Smuggling: Comparative Perspectives*, ed. David Kyle and Rey Koslowski, 257–93. Baltimore: John Hopkins University Press.

Kowalski, Wojciech. (1994). *Liquidation of the Effects of World War II in the Area of Culture*. Warsaw: Institute of Culture.

Kowalski, Wojciech. (1998). *Art Treasures and War: A Study on the Restitution of Looted Cultural Property, Pursuant to Public International Law*. Leicester, UK: Institute of Art and Law.

Krasner, Stephen D. (1999). *Sovereignty: Organized Hypocrisy*. Princeton, NJ: Princeton University Press.

Kratochwil, Friedrich V. (1989). *Rules, Norms and Decisions: On the Conditions of Practical and Legal Reasoning in International Relations and Domestic Affairs*. Cambridge: Cambridge University Press.

Kratochwil, Friedrich V. (2000). "How Do Norms Matter?" In *The Role of Law in International Politics*, ed. Michael Byers, 35–68. Oxford: Oxford University Press.

Kronenwetter, Michael. (2004). *Terrorism: A Guide to Events and Documents*. Westport, CT: Greenwood.

Kuhn, Arthur K. (1933). "The Lytton Report on the Manchurian Crisis." *The American Journal of International Law* 27(1): 96–100.

Kuper, Leo. (1981). *Genocide: Its Political Use in the Twentieth Century*. New Haven: Yale University Press.

Kurtz, Michael J. (1985). *Nazi Contraband: American Policy on the Return of European Cultural Treasures, 1945–1955*. New York: Garland.

Kusani, Hiroki. (2004). "Humanitarian Intervention: The Interplay of Norms and Politics." In *International Intervention in the Post-Cold War World: Moral Responsibility and Power Politics*, ed. Michael Davis, Wolfgang Dietrich, Bettina Scholdan and Dieter Sepp, 123–41. Armonk, NY: M.E. Sharpe.

Kushalani, Yougindra. (1982). *Dignity and Honour of Women as Basic and Fundamental Human Rights*. The Hague: Martinus Nijhoff Publishers.

Kyle, David, and Rey Koslowski eds. (2001). *Global Human Smuggling: Comparative Perspectives*. Baltimore: John Hopkins University Press.

Lafontant, Julien J. (1979). *Montesquieu et le problème de l'esclavage dans L'Esprit des Lois*. Sherbrooke, Canada: Éditions Naaman.

Lamounier, Lucia. (1995). "Between Slavery and Free Labour: Early Experiments with Free Labour and Patterns of Slave Emancipation in Brazil and Cuba." In

From Chattel Slaves to Wage Slaves: The Dynamics of Labour Bargaining in the Americas, ed. Mary Turner, 185–200. Kingston: Ian Rand.

Lane, Kris E. (1998). *Pillaging the Empire: Piracy in the Americas, 1500–1750*. Armonk, NY: M.E. Sharpe.

Langer, Robert. (1947). *Seizure of Territory: The Stimson Doctrine and Related Principles in Legal Theory and Diplomatic Practice*. Princeton, NJ: Princeton University Press.

Lanzac de Laborie, L. de. (1913). *Paris sous Napoléon: Spectacles et Musées*. Paris: Librairie Plon.

Lean, Sharon. (2004). *The Transnational Politics of Democracy Promotion: Election Monitoring in Latin America*. Thesis (Ph. D., Political Science) University of California, Irvine.

Leang-Li, T'ang ed. (1935). *The Puppet State of "Manchukuo."* Shanghai: China United Press.

Legro, Jeffrey W. (1995). *Cooperation Under Fire: Anglo-American Restraint During World War II*. Ithaca, NY: Cornell University Press.

Leich, Marian Nash. (1984). "Four Bills Proposed by President Reagan to Counter Terrorism." *American Journal International Law* 78: 915–28.

Lenczowski, George. (1987). *The Middle East in World Affairs*. Ithaca and London: Cornell University Press.

Lenin, V. I. (1964). *Collected Works*. 4th ed. vol. 24. Moscow: Progress Publishers.

Leuchtag, Alice. (2003). "Human Rights, Sex Trafficking, and Prostitution." *The Humanist* 63: 10–16.

Levitt, Jeremy. (1998). "Humanitarian Intervention by Regional Actors in Internal Conflicts: And the Cases of ECOWAS in Liberia and Sierra Leone." *Temple International and Comparative Law Journal* 12: 333–75.

Lillich, Richard B., ed., (1982). *Transnational Terrorism: Conventions and Commentary*. New York: The Mitchie Company.

Lippman, Matthew. (2002). "A Road Map to the 1948 Convention on the Prevention and Punishment of the Crime of Genocide." *The Journal of Genocide Research* 4(2): 177–95.

Litfin, Karen T., ed., (1998). *The Greening of Sovereignty in World Politics*. Cambridge, MA: MIT Press.

Liu, Shih Shun. (1965 [1925]). *Extraterritoriality: Its Rise and Its Fall*. New York: AMS Press.

Lloyd, Alan. (1977). *Destroy Carthage! The Death Throes of an Ancient Culture*. London: Souvernir Press.

Lloyd, Christopher. (1968). *The Navy and the Slave Trade: The Suppression of the African Slave Trade in the Nineteenth Century*. London: Frank Cass.

Lloyd, Christopher. (1974). *The Nation and the Navy: A History of Naval Life and Policy*. Westport, CT: Greenwood Press.

Loades, David. (1992). *The Tudor Navy: An Administrative, Political and Military History*. Aldershot: Scolar Press.

Loescher, Gil. (1989). "The European Community and Refugees." *International Affairs* 65(4): 617–636.

Loomis, Dan. (1996). *The Somalia Affair: Reflections in Peacemaking and Peacekeeping*. Ottawa: DGL Publications.

Lord, Robert Howard. (1966). *The Origins of the War of 1870: New Documents from the German Archives*. New York: Russell & Russell.

Lowe, Vaughan. (2000). "The Politics of Law-Making: Are the Method and Character of Norm Creation Changing?" In *The Role of Law in International Politics*, ed. Michael Byers, 207–226. Oxford: Oxford University Press.

Lowenheim, Oded. (2003). "'Do Ourselves Credit and Render a Lasting Service to Mankind': British Moral Prestige, Humanitarian Intervention, and the Barbary Pirates." *International Studies Quarterly* 47(1): 23–48.

Luck, Edward. (2004). "Tackling Terrorism." In *The UN Security Council: From the Cold War to the 21st Century*, ed. David Malone, 85–100. Boulder, CO: Lynne Rienner.

Lydon, James G. (1970). *Pirates, Privateers, and Profits*. Upper Saddle River, NJ: Gregg Press.

Lyons, F.S.L. (1963). *Internationalism in Europe, 1815–1914*. Leyden, Germany: A.W. Sythoff.

MacCormick, Neil. (1978). *Legal Reasoning and Legal Theory*. Oxford: Clarendon Press.

Mackenzie-Grieve. (1968). *The Last Years of the English Slave Trade: Liverpool 1750–1807*. New York: Augustus Kelley.

Mahbubani, Kishore. (2004). "The Permanent and Elected Council Members." In *The UN Security Council: From the Cold War to the 21st Century*, ed. David Malone, 253–266. Boulder, CO: Lynne Rienner.

Malamani, Vittorio. (1914). *Canova*. Milan: Ulrico Hoepli.

Malanczuk, Peter. (1997). *Akehurst's Modern Introduction to International Law*. 7th rev. ed. New York: Routledge.

Mandlebaum, Michael. (1999). "A Perfect Failure: NATO's War Against Yugoslavia." *Foreign Affairs*. 78(5): 2–8.

Maogoto, Jackson Nyamuya. (2005). "Countering Terrorism: From Wigged Judges to Helmeted Soldiers—Legal Perspectives on America's Counter-Terrorism Responses." *San Diego International Law Journal*. 6: 243–94.

Marcus, G.J. (1961). *A Naval History of England, vol. 1: The Formative Years*. Boston: Little, Brown & co.

Marques, João Pedro. (1995). "Resistance or Support for the 'Cause of Humanity'? The Septembrists and the Abolition of the Slave Trade, 1836–42." Trans. from "Resistencia ou Adeseão a 'Causa da Humanidade"? Os Setembristas e a supressão do traifico de traifico de escravos (1836–42)." *Análise Social* 30: 375–402.

Marrus, Michael Robert. 1985. *The Unwanted: European Refugees in the Twentieth Century*. New York: Oxford University Press.

Martens, G.F. (1924). Recueil Général des Traités. 3rd ed. Vol. 99, 12. In William Schabas, *Genocide in International Law*. New York: Cambridge University Press, 2000, 22.

Marx, Jenifer. (1992). *Pirates and Privateers of the Caribbean*. Malabar, FL: Krieger Publishing.

Masterson, William E. (1929). *Jurisdiction in Marginal Seas with Special Reference to Smuggling*. NY: MacMillan.

Mathew, Penelope. (2002). "Australian Refugee Protection in the Wake of the Tampa." *American Journal of International Law* 96(3): 661–676.

Mathieson, William Law. (1967). *British Slave Emancipation, 1838–1849*. New York: Octagan Books.

Matthews, Ken. (1993). *The Gulf Conflict and International Relations*. New York: Routledge.

Mavor, James. (1965). *An Economic History of Russia*. New York: Russell & Russell.

Maxwell, John Francis. (1975). *Slavery and the Catholic Church: The History of Catholic Teaching Concerning the Moral Legitimacy of the Institution of Slavery*. Ringwood: Brown & Son.

Mazzetti, Mark. "Military at Risk, Congress Warned." *Los Angeles Times* (3 May 2005), A1. Available at Lexis-Nexis Academic.

McBride, Michael. (1999). "The Evolution of U.S. Immigration and Refugee Policy: Public Opinion, Domestic Politics, and UNHCR." United Nations High Commissioner for Refugees, Centre for Documentation and Research, Working Paper No. 3. Available at http://www.jha.ac/articles/u003.pdf. Accessed 22 May 2008.

McClintock, Cynthia. (2001). "Room for Improvement." *Journal of Democracy* 12(4): 137–140.

McDougal, Myres S., Harold D. Lasswell, and Lung-chu Chen. (1980). *Human Rights and World Public Order*. New Haven, CT: Yale University Press.

McDougal, Myres S., and W. Michael Reisman. (1981). *International Law Essays*. Mineola, NY: Foundation Press.

McDougal, Myres S., (1987). *Studies in World Public Order*. New Haven, CT: New Haven Press.

McGinley, Gerald P. (1985). "The Achille Lauro Affair: Implications for International Law." *Tennessee Law Review* 52: 691–738.

McKeown, Timothy J. (1986). "The Limitations of 'Structural' Theories of Commercial Policy." *International Organization* 40(1): 43–64.

McNair, A. D. (1956). *International Law Opinions: Selected and Annotated*. Cambridge: Cambridge University Press.

McWhinney, Edward. (1987). *Aerial Piracy and International Terrorism: The Illegal Diversion of Aircraft and International Law*. Dordrecht, NE: Martinus Nijhoff Pubs.

Meirs, Suzanne. (2003). *Slavery in the Twentieth Century: The Evolution of a Global Problem*. Lanham, MD: Alta Mira Press.

Meldrum, Andrew. (2007). "Coups No Longer Acceptable." *Africa Recovery*. United Nations. Available at http://www.un.org/ecosocdev/geninfo/afrec/vol11no1/coups.htm. Accessed 30 January 2007 Accessed 28 April 2008.

Mellor, Justin S.C. (2002). "Missing the Boat: The Legal and Practical Problems of the Prevention of Maritime Terrorism." *American University International Law Review* 18: 341–97.

Meltzer, Milton. (1993). *Slavery: A World History*. Updated ed. New York: Da Capo Press.

Melvern, Linda R. (2000). *A People Betrayed: The Role of the West in Rwanda's Genocide*. New York: Zed Books.

Meron, Theodor. (2000). "The Martens Clause, Principles of Humanity, and Dictates of Public Conscience." *American Journal of International Law* 94(1): 78–89.

Merrill, Louis Taylor. (1945). "The English Campaign for Abolition of the Slave Trade." *The Journal of Negro History* 30(4): 382–99.

Meyer, John W., John Boli, and George M. Thomas. (1987). "Ontology and Rationalization in the Western Cultural Account." In *Institutional Structure: Constituting State, Society, and Individual*, ed. George M. Thomas, John W. Meyer, Francisco Ramirez, and John Boli, 12–37. Newbury Park, CA: Sage Publications.

Middleton, Harry J. (1965). *The Compact History of the Korean War*. New York: Hawthorn Books, Inc.

Millbank, Adrienne. (2000). *The Problem with the 1951 Refugee Convention*. Research Paper 5-2000-01. Social Policy Group, Parliament of Australia. http://www.aph.gov.au/library/Pubs/rp/2000-01/01rp05.htm. Accessed 2 June 2006.

Miller, Ali, and Alison N. Stewart. (1998). "Report from the Roundtable on the Meaning of 'Trafficking in Persons': A Human Rights Perspective." *Women's Rights Law Reporter* 20(1): 11–19.

Miller, Ronnie. (1994). *Following the Americans to the Persian Gulf: Canada, Australia, and the Development of the New World Order*. London: Associated University Presses.

Millman, Richard. (1965). *British Foreign Policy and the Coming of the Franco-Prussian War*. Oxford: Clarendon Press.

Mitter, Rana. (2000). *The Manchurian Myth: Nationalism, Resistance, and Collaboration in Modern China*. Berkeley: University of California Press.

Monod, Gabriel. (n.d.). *Allemands et Francais: Souvenirs de Campagne*. Metz: Sedan, la Loire. Paris.

Morgenthau, Henry. (1918). *Ambassador Morgenthau's Story*. Garden City, NY: Doubleday, Page & Co.

Morrell, Jim. (1995). "Haiti: Success Under Fire, a Commentary on U.S. policy toward Haiti Following President Aristride's Reinstatement." Center of International Policy Research. Available at http://americas.irc-online.org/articles/2004/0403haiti-int_body.html. Accessed 27 January 2007.

Morris, Madeline. (2001). "The Role of Justice in Building Peace: Genocide Politics and Policy." *Case Western Reserve Journal of International Law* 205(1): 205–11.

Morton, Jeffrey, and Neil Vijay Singh. (2003). "The International Legal Regime on Genocide." *The Journal of Genocide Research* 5(1): 47–69.

Mueller, John. (1989). *Retreat from Doomsday: The Obsolescence of Major War.* New York: Basic Books.

Mueller, John. (1991). "Changing Attitudes Towards War: The Impact of the First World War." *British Journal of Political Science* 21: 1–28.

Müffling, Carl von. (1997). *The Memoirs of Baron von Müffling, A Prussian Officer in the Napoleonic Wars.* London: Greenhill Books.

Muhammad, Patricia M. (2004). "The Trans-Atlantic Slave Trade: A Forgotten Crime against Humanity as Defined by International Law." *American University International Law Review* 19: 883–947.

Munoz, Heraldo. (1995). *The Right to Democracy in the Americas.* Estudios Internacionales.

Müntz, E. (1895). "Les annexions de collections d'art ou de bibliothèques et leur role dans les relations internationales, principalement pendant la Révolution Française (Suite)." *Revue d'Histoire Diplomatique* 9: 375–93.

Müntz, E. (1896). "Les annexions de collections d'art ou de bibliothèques et leur role dan les relations internationales, principalement pendant la Révolution Française (Fin)." *Revue d'Histoire Diplomatique* 10: 481–508.

Murphy, Alexander. (1996). "The Sovereign State System as Political-Territorial Ideal: Historical and Contemporary Considerations." In *State Sovereignty as Social Construct*, ed. Thomas J. Biersteker and Cynthia Weber, 81–120. Cambridge: Cambridge University Press.

Murphy, Craig N. (1994). *International Organization and Industrial Change: Global Governance since 1850.* New York: Oxford University Press.

Murphy, John. (1978). "Protected Persons and Diplomatic Facilities." In *Legal Aspects of International Terrorism*, ed. Alona Evans and John F. Murphy, 277–339. Lexington, MA: Lexington Books.

Murphy, John F. (2004). *The United States and the Rule of Law in International Affairs.* New York: Cambridge University Press.

Nadelmann, Ethan. (1990). "Global Prohibition Regimes: The Evolution of Norms in International Society." *International Organization* 44(4): 479–526.

Nadler, Arie. (2002). "When Is Intervention Likely?" In *International Intervention: Sovereignty versus Responsibility,* ed. Michael Keren and Donald Sylvan, 40–55. London: Frank Cass.

Neumann, Klaus. (2004). "Australia's Refugee Policy Has Always Been Calculating." *Australia's e-journal of Social and Political Debate* (24 June 2004). Available at http://onlineopinion.com.au/print.asp?article=2284. Accessed 22 May 2008.

Newton, Michael A. (1996). "Continuum Crimes: Military Jurisdiction over Foreign Nationals Who Commit International Crimes." *Military Law Review* 153: 1–93.

Nicholas, Lynn H. (1994). *The Rape of Europa: The Fate of Europe's Treasures in the Third Reich and the Second World War*. New York: Vintage Books.

Norris, Pippa. (1999). *Critical Citizens: Global Support for Democratic Governance*. Oxford University Press.

Nowrot, Karsten, and Emily Schabacker. (1998). "The Use of Force to Restore Democracy: International Legal Implications of the ECOWAS Intervention in Sierra Leone." *The American University International Law Review* 14(2): 321–412.

O'Connell, Mary Ellen. (2005). "Enhancing the Status of Non-State Actors Through a Global War on Terror?" *Columbia Journal of Transnational Law* 43: 435–58.

O'Halloran, Patrick J. (1995). *Humanitarian Intervention and the Genocide in Rwanda*. Conflict Studies No. 277. London: Institute for the Study of Conflict.

Oldfield, J. R. (1992). "The London Committee and Mobilization of Public Opinion against the Slave Trade." *The Historical Journal* 35(2): 331–43.

Oldfield, J. R. (1995). *Popular Politics and British Anti-Slavery: The Mobilization of Public Opinion against the Slave Trade, 1787–1807*. Manchester: Manchester University Press.

Onuf, Nicholas. (1998). "Everyday Ethics in International Relations." *Millenium: Journal of International Studies* 27: 669–93.

Onuf, Nicholas and Peter Onuf. (2006). *Nations, Markets, and War: Modern History and the American Civil War*. Charlottesville, VA: University of Virginia Press.

Oppenheim, Lassa. (1952–1955). *International Law: A Treatise*. 8th ed. 2 vols. Ed. Hersch Lauterpacht. New York: D. McKay.

Paladini, Jon M. (2004). "Terrorism: War or Piracy?" *Arizona Attorney* 40: 38–43.

Palmer, David Scott. (1996). "Peru: Collectively Defending Democracy in the Western Hemisphere." In Tom Farer, ed., *Beyond Sovereignty: Collectively Defending Democracy in the Americas*, 257–76. Baltimore: The Johns Hopkins University Press.

Palmer, Norman. (2000). *Museums and the Holocaust: Law, Principles and Practice*. Leicester, UK: Institute of Art and Law.

Paroff, Sasha P. (2004). "Another Victim of the War in Iraq: The Looting of the National Museum in Baghdad and the Inadequacies of International Protection of Cultural Property." *Emory Law Journal* 43: 2021–54.

Paust, Jordan J., et al. (2006). *Human Rights Module: On Crimes Against Humanity, Genocide, Other Crimes Against Human Rights, and War Crimes*. 2nd ed. Durham, NC: Carolina Academic Press.

Paust, Jordan J., M. Cherif Bassiouni, Michael P. Scharf, Jimmy Gurule, Leila Sadat, B. Williams, and Sharon A. Williams eds. (2001). *Human Rights Module: On Crimes Against Humanity, Genocide, Other Crimes Against Human Rights: War Crimes.* Durham, North Carolina: Carolina Academic Press.

Pennell, C.R., ed. (1989). *Piracy and Diplomacy in Seventeenth-Century North Africa: The Journal of Thomas Baker, English Consul in Tripoli, 1677–1685.* Rutherford, NJ: Farleigh Dickinson University Press.

Pérotin-Dumon, Anne. (2001). "The Pirate and the Emperor: Power and the Law of the Seas, 1450–1850." In *Bandits at Sea: A Pirates Reader,* ed. C. R. Pennell, 25–54. New York: New York University Press.

Petropolous, Jonathan. (2000). "Art Historians and Nazi Plunder." *New England Review* 21(1): 5–30.

Phillipson, Coleman. (1916). *The Termination of War and Treaties of Peace.* London: T. Fischer Unwin.

Plaut, James S. (October 1946). "Hitler's Capital: Loot for the Master Race." *The Atlantic* 178: 73–78.

Porter, Dale H. (1970). *The Abolition of the Slave Trade in England, 1784–1807.* New York: Archon Books.

Potter, Pitman B. (1950). "Legal Aspects of the Situation in Korea." *The American Journal of International Law* 44: 709–712.

Power, Samantha. (2002). *A Problem from Hell: America and the Age of Genocide.* New York: Perennial Publishing.

Price, Richard M. (1997). *The Chemical Weapons Taboo.* Ithaca, NY: Cornell University Press.

"Primacy of International Law." *The New Straits Times* (Malaysia). 18 September 2004. 10. Available at Lexis-Nexis Academic.

Prunier, Gerard. (1997). *The Rwanda Crisis: History of a Genocide.* New York: Columbia University Press.

Randall, Kenneth C. (1988). "Universal Jurisdiction Under International Law." *Texas Law Review* 66: 785–841.

Rassam, A. Yasmine. (1999). "Contemporary Forms of Slavery and the Evolution of the Prohibition of Slavery and the Slave Trade Under Customary International Law." *Virginia Journal of International Law* 39: 303–52.

Ray, James Lee. (1989). "The Abolition of Slavery and the End of International War." *International Organization* 43(3): 405–39.

Re, Richard. (2002). "A Persistent Evil: The Global Problem of Slavery." *Harvard International Review* 23: 32–36.

Redman, Renee Colette. (1994). "Beyond the United States: The League of Nations and the Right to be Free from Enslavement—The First Human Right to Be Recognized as Customary International Law." *Chicago-Kent Law Review* 70: 759–800.

Reinhardt, Emma Dorothy. (2001). "Modern-day Slavery in America." *World & I* 16: 52.

Reisman, W. Michael. (2000). "Sovereignty and Human Rights in Contemporary International Law." In *Democratic Governance and International Law*, ed. Gregory Fox and Brad Roth, 239–58. United Kingdom: Cambridge University Press.

Reynolds, Douglas R. (1993). *China, 1898–1912: The Xinzheng Revolution and Japan*. Cambridge, MA: Harvard University Press.

Rice, Willy E. (2003). "'Commercial Terrorism' from the Transatlantic Slave Trade to the World Trade Center Disaster: Are Insurance Companies and Judges 'Aiders and Abettors' of Terror? A Critical analysis of American and equitable actions, 1654–2002." *The Scholar* 6: 1–119.

Richardson, Kristin M.J. (1990). *International Law and Privateering: Philip II's Waging of the Channel War*. History MA Thesis, Brigham Young University.

Rifaat, Ahmad M. (1979). *International Aggression*. Atlantic Highlands, N.J.: Humanities Press.

Risse, Thomas, and Kathryn Sikkink. (1999). "The Socialization of Human Rights into Domestic Practices: Introduction." In *The Power of Principles: International Human Rights Norms and Domestic Change*, ed. Thomas Risse, Stephen C. Ropp and Kathryn Sikkink, 1–38. Cambridge: Cambridge University Press.

Risse, Thomas. (2000). ""Let's Argue!" Communicative Action in World Politics." *International Organization* 54(1): 1–39.

Risso, Patricia. (2001). "Cross-Cultural Perceptions of Piracy: Maritime Violence in the Western Indian Ocean and Persian Gulf Region during a Long Eighteenth Century." *Journal of World History* 12(2): 293–320.

Robinson, James Henry, ed. (1906). "The Edict of Nantes (1598)." *Readings in European History*. Vol. 2, 287–291. Boston: Ginn. Available at http://www.historyguide.org/earlymod/nantes.html. Accessed 24 September 2005.

Robinson, Mary. (1999). "Dedicated to the United Nations High Commission for Human Rights Introduction: Genocide, War Crimes, Crimes Against Humanity." *Fordham International Law Journal* 23(6): 275–85.

Romero, Jessica. (2003). "Prevention of Maritime Terrorism: The Container Security Initiative." *Chicago Journal of International Law* 4: 597–605.

Rosand, Eric. (2003). "Security Council Resolution 1373, the Counter-Terrorism Committee, and the Fight against Terrorism." *American Journal of International Law* 97: 333–41.

Rosenstock, Robert. (1971). "Declaration of Principles of International Law Concerning Friendly Relations: A Survey." *American Journal of International Law* 65: 713–35.

Ross, David. (n.d.). "Medieval Knights and Warfare." Britain Express. At http://www.britainexpress.com/History/Knights_and_Fights.htm. Accessed 23 March 2006.

Rothwell, Victor. (2001). *The Origins of the Second World War*. New York: Manchester University Press.

Roxan, David, and Ken Wanstall. (1964). *The Rape of Art: The Story of Hitler's Plunder of the Great Masterpieces of Europe*. New York: Coward-McCann, Inc.

Rubenstien, William D. (2004). *Genocide: A History*. London: Pearson Education Limited.

Rubin, Alfred P. (1988). *The Law of Piracy*. Newport, RI: Naval War College Press.

Ruggie, John Gerard. (1982). "International Regimes, Transactions, and Change: Embedded Liberalism in the Postwar Economic Order." *International Organization* 36(2): 379–415.

Ryf, Kara C. (2002). "The First Modern Anti-Slavery Law: The Trafficking Victims Protection Act of 2000." *Case Western Reserve Journal of International Law* 34: 45–71.

Sahaydak, Maksym ed., (1976) [1974]. *Ethnocide of the Ukrainians in the USSR*. Baltimore, MD: Smoloskyp Publishers.

Said, Edward W. (1979). *Orientalism*. New York: Vintage Books.

Said, Edward W. (1993). *Culture and Imperialism*. New York: Knopf.

Sandholtz, Wayne. (1999). "Globalization and the Evolution of Rules." In *Globalization and Governance*, ed. Aseem Prakash and Jeffrey Hart, 77–102. London: Routledge.

Sandholtz, Wayne. (2002). "Humanitarian Intervention: Global Enforcement of Human Rights?" In *Globalization and Human Rights*, ed. Alison Brysk, 201–25. Berkeley: University of California Press.

Sandholtz, Wayne. (2005). "The Iraqi National Museum and International Law: A Duty to Protect." *Columbia Journal of Transnational Law* 44(1): 185–240.

Sandholtz, Wayne. (2007). *Prohibiting Plunder: How Norms Change*. New York: Oxford University Press.

Sandholtz, Wayne. (2008). "Dynamics of International Norm Change: Rules against Wartime Plunder." *European Journal of International Relations* 14: 101–131.

Sandholtz, Wayne and Alec Stone Sweet. (2004). "Law, Politics, and International Governance." In *The Politics of International Law*, ed. Christian Reus-Smit, 238–71. Cambridge: Cambridge University Press.

Sandholtz, Wayne. (forthcoming). "The Iraq War and International Law." In *Handbook of International Law*, ed. David Armstrong. London: Routledge.

Saunier, Charles. (1902). *Les Conquêtes Artistiques de la Revolution et de L'Empire*. Paris: Librairie Renouard.

Sawyer, Roger. (1986). *Slavery in the Twentieth Century*. London: Routledge & Kegan Paul.

Schabas, William A. (2000). *Genocide in International Law*. New York: Cambridge University Press.

Schabas, William A. (2001). "Essay: Twelfth Annual Philip D. Reed Memorial Issue the Balkans Regional Legal Perspectives and Analyses was Genocide Committed in Bosnia and Herzegovina? First Judgments of the International Criminal Tribunal for the Former Yugoslavia." *Fordham International Law Journal* 25: 23–53.

Schachter, Oscar. (1991). *International Law in Theory and Practice: Developments in International Law*. Dordrecht: Martinus Nijhoff Publishers.

Scharf, Michael P., and Thomas C. Fisher. (2001). "Universal Jurisdiction: Myths, Realites, and Prospects – Foreward." *New England Law Review* 35: 227–32.

Schiessl, Christoph. (2002). "An Element of Genocide: Rape, Total War, and International Law in the Twentieth Century." *Journal of Genocide Research* 4(2): 197–210.

Schindler, Dietrich, and Jiří Toman eds. (1973). *The Laws of Armed Conflicts: A Collection of Conventions, Resolutions and Other Documents*. Leiden: A. W. Sijthoff.

Schindler, Dietrich, and Jiří Toman eds. (1988). *The Laws of Armed Conflicts*. Geneva: Henry Dunant Institute.

Schmidt-Nowara, Christopher. (1999). *Empire and Antislavery: Spain, Cuba, and Puerto Rico, 1833–1874*. Pittsburgh: University of Pittsburgh Press.

Schnably, Stephen J. (1994). "The Santiago Commitment as a Call to Democracy in the United States: Evaluating the OAS Role in Haiti, Peru, and Guatemala." *University of Miami Inter-American Law Review* 253: 393–587.

Schnably, Stephen. (2000). "Constitutionalism and Democratic Government in the Inter-American System." In *Democratic Governance and International Law*, ed. Gregory Fox and Brad Roth, 155–198. Cambridge: Cambridge University Press.

Schultz, Karen. (2005). "The Crisis of Empire and the Problem of Slavery: Portugal and Brazil c. 1700–c.1820." *Common Knowledge* 11(2): 264–82.

Schwarzenberger, G. (1968). *International Law as Applied by International Courts and Tribunals, vol. II: The Law of Armed Conflict*. Stevens: London.

Schwelb, Egon. (1946). "Crimes Against Humanity." *British Yearbook of International Law* 23: 178–226.

Scullard, H.H. (1951). *Roman Politics 200–150 BC*. Oxford: Clarendon Press.

Sebenius, James K. (1984). *Negotiating the Law of the Sea*. Cambridge: Harvard University Press.

Silverman, Dan P. (1972). *Reluctant Union: Alsace-Lorraine and Imperial Germany 1871–1918*. London: The Pennsylvania State University Press.

Silverstein, Paul A. (2005). "The New Barbarians: Piracy and Terrorism on the North African Frontier." *The New Centennial Review* 5(1): 179–214.

Simon, Matila. (1971). *The Battle of the Louvre: The Struggle to Save French Art in World War II*. New York: Hawthorn Books.

Sinha, Prakash. (1971). *Asylum and International Law*. Hague: Martinus Nijhoff Publishers.

Skrobanek, Siriporn, Nattaya Boonpakdi and Chutima Janthakeero. (1997). *The Traffic in Women: Human realities of the international sex trade*. London: Zed Books.

Slaughter, Anne-Marie. (2004). *A New World Order*. Princeton, NJ: Princeton University Press.

Smith, Linda, and Mohamed Mattar. (2004). "Global Challenges: Trafficking in Persons, Humanitarian Intervention, and Energy Policy—Creating International Consensus on Combating Trafficking in Persons: U.S. Policy, the Role of the UN, and Global Responses and Challenges." *The Fletcher Forum of World Affairs Journal* 28: 155–174.

Smith, Sara R. (1948). *The Manchurian Crisis: 1931-1932. A Tragedy in International Relations*. New York: Columbia University Press.

Smith, W.H.C. (1969). "Anglo-Portuguese Relations 1851–1861." *Studia* 27–28: 107–279.

Sorek, Patrick. (1983). "Jurisdiction Over Drug Smuggling on the High Seas: It's a Small World after All." *University of Pittsburgh Law Review* 44: 1095–1114.

Spruyt, Hendrik. (1994). *The Sovereign State and Its Competitors: An Analysis of Systems Change*. Princeton, NJ: Princeton University Press.

Stark, Francis. (1967/1898). *The Abolition of Privateering and the Declaration of Paris*. New York: AMS Press.

Starkey, David J. (1990). *British Privateering Enterprise in the Eighteenth Century*. Exeter: University of Exeter Press.

Starkey, David J. (2001). "The Origins and Regulation of Eighteenth-Century British Privateering." In *Bandits at Sea: A Pirates Reader*, ed. Pennell, C.R., 69–81. New York: New York University Press.

Stephens, Thomas B. (1992). *Order and Discipline in China: The Shanghai Mixed Court, 1911–27*. Seattle, WA: University of Washington Press.

Stiles, Ethan C. (2004). "Reforming Current International Law to Combat Modern Sea Piracy." *Suffolk Transnational Law Review* 27: 299–326.

Stiles, Kendall W. (2005). *Case Histories in International Politics*. 4th ed. New York: Pearson Longman Publishers.

Stiles, Kendall, and Deborah Wells. (2007). "On the Crossing of Rubicons: Norm Dissemination and Policy Idiosyncrasy in the UK." *Political Science Quarterly* 122(3): 461–80.

Stone Sweet, Alec. (1999). "Judicialization and the Construction of Governance." *Comparative Political Studies* 32(2): 147–84.

Stone Sweet, Alec. (2002a). "Islands of Transnational Governance." In *On Law, Politics, and Judicialization*, ed. Martin Shapiro and Alec Stone Sweet, 323–42. Oxford: Oxford University Press.

Stone Sweet, Alec. (2002b). "Path Dependence, Precedent, and Judicial Power." In *On Law, Politics, and Judicialization,* ed. Martin Shapiro and Alec Stone Sweet, 112–35. Oxford: Oxford University Press.

Stone Sweet, Alec, and Wayne Sandholtz. (1998). "Integration, Supranational Governance, and the Institutionalization of the European Polity." In *European Integration and Supranational Governance,* ed. Wayne Sandholtz and Alec Stone Sweet, 1–26. Oxford: Oxford University Press.

Strang, David. (1992). "The Inner Incompatibility of Empire and Nation: Popular Sovereignty and Decolonization." *Sociological Perspectives* 35(2): 367–84.

Strang, David. (1996). "Contested Sovereignty: The Social Construction of Colonial Imperialism." In *State Sovereignty as Social Construct,* ed. Thomas J. Biersteker and Cynthia Weber, 22–49. Cambridge: Cambridge University Press.

Strang, G. Bruce. (1996). "Once More Into the Breach: Britain's Guarantee to Poland." *Journal of Contemporary History* 31: 721–752.

Sugden, Robert. (1989). "Spontaneous Order." *Journal of Economic Perspectives* 3(4): 85–97.

Sunga, Lyal S. (1992). *Individual Responsibility in International Law for Serious Human Rights Violations.* Martinus Nijhoff: The Hague.

Swindells, Felicia. (1997). "Note U.N. Sanctions in Haiti: A Contradiction under Articles 41 and 55 of the U.N. Charter." *Fordham International Law Journal* 20: 1878–1960.

Sword, Keith. (1991). "British Reactions to the Soviet Occupation of Eastern Poland in September 1939." *Slavonic and Eastern European Review* 69: 81–101.

Szasz, Paul. (2002). "The Security Council Starts Legislating." *American Journal of International Law* 96: 901–05.

Taft, William. (1924). "Arbitration Between Great Britain and Costa Rica." *The American Journal of International Law* 18(1): 147–174.

Talleyrand-Périgord. (1957) [1807–1815]. *Mémoires II, 1807–1815. 2.* Paris: Librairie Plon.

Talwar, Namrita. (2004). "Consensus, Not Confrontation Sought Over Controversial Issues in International Law." *UN Chronicle.* Available at http://www.un.org/Pubs/chronicle/2004/issue1/0104p.30.asp. Accessed 28 July 2006.

Teece, David R. (1997). "Global Overfishing and the Spanish-Canadian Turbot War: Can International Law Protect the High-seas Environment?" *Colorado Journal of International Law and Policy* 8: 89–125.

Teitelbaum, Michael. (1984). "Immigration, Refugees, and Foreign Policy." *International Organization* 38(3): 429–450.

Temperley, Howard. (2000). "Introduction." In *After Slavery: Emancipation and Its Discontents,* ed. Howard Temperley,1–10. London: Frank Cass.

Teneti, Alberto.(1967). *Piracy and the Decline of Venice, 1580–1615.* Trans. Janet and Brian Pullam. New York: Longmans.

Tesón, Fernando. (1996). "Collective Humanitarian Intervention." *Michigan Journal of International Law* 17: 323–71.

Tesón, Fernando R. (1997). *Humanitarian Intervention: An Inquiry into Law and Morality*. 2nd ed. Irvington-on-Hudson, NY: Transnational Publishers.

Teyeb, Moctar. (2000). "Slavery in Mauritania is a Serious Problem." *Tikkum* 15: 10.

Thomas, Martin.(1996). *Britain, France and Appeasement: Anglo-French Relations in the Popular Front Era*. New York: Berg.

Thomson, Janice E. (1990). "State Practices, International Norms, and the Decline of Mercenarism." *International Studies Quarterly* 34(1): 23–47.

Thornton, Richard C. (2000). *Odd Man Out: Truman, Stalin, Mao, and the Origin of the Korean War*. Washington, DC: Brassey's.

Toepfer, Susan Jeanne, and Bryan Stuart Wells. (1994). "The Worldwide Market for Sex: A Review of International and Regional Legal Prohibitions Regarding Trafficking in Women." *Michigan Journal of Gender & Law* 2: 83–128.

Tohmatsu, Haruo, and H.P. Willmott. (2004). *A Gathering Darkness: The Coming of War to the Far East and the Pacific, 1921–1942*. New York: SR Books.

Tomczak, Martiin. (2002). "Treaty of Frankfurt." In *The Franco-Prussian War: 1870–71*. Available at http://uk.geocities.com/fpw1870/frankfurt.html. Accessed 21 July 2005.

Toope, Stephen J. (2000). "Emerging Patterns of Governance and International Law." *In The Role of Law in International Politics*, ed. Michael Byers, 91–108. Oxford: Oxford University Press.

Treue, Wilhelm. (1961). *Art Plunder: The Fate of Works of Art in War and Unrest*. New York: The John Day Company.

Trevor-Roper, Hugh. (1970). *The Plunder of the Arts in the Seventeenth Century*. London: Thames and Hudson.

Tyler, Patrick E. "U.N. Chief Ignited Firestorm by Calling Iraq War Illegal." *New York Times* (17 September 2004), 11. Available at Lexis-Nexis Academic.

Ubah, C.N. (1991). "Suppression of the Slave Trade in the Nigerian Emirates." *Journal of African History* 32(3): 447–70.

Van Bueren, Geraldine. (2004). "Slavery as Piracy: The Legal Case for Reparations for the Slave Trade." In *The Political Economy of New Slavery*, ed. Christien Van der Anker, 235–247. London: Palgrave.

Van der Anker, Christien. (2004). "Contemporary Slavery, Global Justice and Globalization." *In The Political Economy of New Slavery*, ed. Christien Van der Anker, 15–36. London: Palgrave.

Van Schaack, Beth. (1997). "The Crime of Political Genocide: Repairing the Genocide Convention's Blind Spot." *The Yale Law Journal* 106(7): 2259–91.

Vattel, Emmerich de. (1916). *The Law of Nations, or the Principles of Natural Law [1758]*. Washington, DC: The Carnegie Institution of Washington.

Verwey, Wil. (1981). "The International Hostages Convention and National Liberation Movements." *American Journal of International Law* 75: 70–84.

Vessel, David. (2003). "The Lonely Pragmatist: Humanitarian Intervention in an Imperfect World." *BYU Journal of Public Law* 18: 1–58.

Vincent, R. J. (1984). "Racial Equality." In *The Expansion of International Society*, ed. Hedley Bull and Adam Watson, 239–54. Oxford: Clarendon Press.

Voon, Tania. (2002). "Closing the Gap Between Legitimacy and Legality of Humanitarian Intervention: Lessons From East Timor and Kosovo." *UCLA Journal of International Law and Foreign Affairs* 7: 32–97.

Wallensteen, Peter, and Patrick Johansson. (2004). "Security Council Decisions in Perspective." In *The UN Security Council: From the Cold War to the 21st Century*, ed. David Malone, 17–33. Boulder, CO: Lynne Rienner.

Waltz, Kenneth N. (1979). *Theory of International Politics*. Boston, MA: Addison-Wesley.

Walvin, James. (1986). *England, Slaves and Freedom, 1776–1838*. London: Macmillan.

Walzer, Michael. (1992). *Just and Unjust Wars: A Moral Argument with Historical Illustrations*. New York: Basic Books.

Wanquet, Claude. (1998). *La France et al. Première Abolition de l'Esclavage, 1794–1802*. Paris: Karthala.

Ward, W.E.F. (1969). *The Royal Navy and the Slavers: The Suppression of the Atlantic slave trade*. New York: Pantheon Books.

Ware, Glenn T. (1997). "The Emerging Norm of Humanitarian Intervention and Presidential Decision Directive 25." *Naval Law Review*: 1–58.

Watson, Adam. (1992). *The Evolution of International Society: A Comparative Historical Analysis*. London: Routledge.

Weiss, Thomas G. (1999). *Military-civilian Interactions: Intervening in Humanitarian Crises*. Lanham, MD: Rowman & Littlefield.

Weiss, Thomas G. and Cindy Collins. (2000). *Humanitarian Challenges and Intervention*. 2nd ed. Boulder: Westview Press.

Welsh, Jennifer M. ed. (2004). *Humanitarian Intervention and International Relations*. Oxford: Oxford University Press.

Wendt, Alexander. (1999). *Social Theory of International Politics*. Cambridge: Cambridge University Press.

Wetzel, David. (2001). *A Duel of Giants: Bismarck, Napoleon III, and the Origins of the Franco-Prussia War*. Madison, WI: The University of Wisconsin Press.

Wheaton, Henry. (1863). *Elements of International Law*. 2nd annotated ed. Boston: Little Brown.

Wheeler, Nicholas J. (2000). *Saving Strangers: Humanitarian Intervention in International Society*. New York: Oxford University Press.

White, G. Edwards. (1989). "The United States Constitution in the Third Century: Foreign affairs history: The Marshall Court and international law: The Piracy cases." *American Journal of International Law* 83: 727–735.

Wihtol de Wenden, Catherine. (1994). "The French Response to the Asylum Seeker Influx, 1980–93." *Annals of the American Academy of Political and Social Science* 534: 81–90.

Wilkinson, Paul. (2000). *Terrorism Versus Democracy: The Liberal State Response.* London: Frank Cass.

Williams, Eric. (1970). *The British West Indies at Westminster, 1789–1823: Extracts from the Debates in Parliament.* Westport, CT: Negro University Press.

Williams, Sharon A. (1978). *The International and National Protection of Movable Cultural Property: A Comparative Study.* Dobbs Ferry, NY: Oceana Publishers.

Willoughby, Westel W. (1935). *The Sino-Japanese Controversy and the League of Nations.* Baltimore: The Johns Hopkins Press.

Willoughby, Westel L. (1966). *Foreign Rights and Interests in China.* Taipei, Taiwan: Ch'eng-Wen Publishing Co.

Wilson, David L. (1999). *International Law and Genocide: An Evolutionary Process.* MA Thesis, Brigham Young University.

Wilson, George Grafton. (1910). *Handbook of International Law.* St Paul, MN: West Publishing.

Wilson, George Grafton. (1935). *International Law.* New York: Silver, Burdett, and Company.

Wilson, Woodrow. (1917). *Speech to Congress, 2 April 1917.* FirstWorldWar.com. Primary Documents: U.S. Declaration of War with Germany, 2 April 1917. Available at http://www.firstworldwar.com/source/usawardeclaration.htm. Accessed 4 August 2008.

Winslow, Peter E. (1988).'*Wealth and Honour': Portsmouth During the Golden Age of Privateering, 1775–1815.* Portsmouth, ME: Peter Randall.

Witten, Samuel. (1998). "The International Convention for the Suppression of Terrorist Bombings." *American Journal of International Law* 92: 769–789.

Wolfrum, Rüdiger. (2002). "The UN Experience in Modern Intervention." In *International Intervention: Sovereignty versus Responsibility,* ed. Michael Keren and Donald Sylvan, 95–113. London: Frank Cass.

Woodrooffe, Thomas. (1958). *Vantage at Sea: England's Emergence as an Oceanic Power.* New York: St. Martin's.

Wright, Quincy. (1935). "The legal foundation of the Stimson Doctrine." *Pacific Affairs* 8(4): 439–446.

Young, C. Walter. (1928). "Sino-Japanese interests in Manchuria." *Pacific Affairs* 8(7): 1–20.

Zhang, Yongjin. (1991). *China in the International System, 1918–20: The Middle Kingdom at the Periphery.* New York: St. Martin Press.

Index

INTERNATIONAL NORMS AND CYCLES OF CHANGE